T0185539

Oracle on Docker

Running Oracle Databases in Linux Containers

Sean Scott

Apress®

Oracle on Docker: Running Oracle Databases in Linux Containers

Sean Scott
Boise, ID, USA

ISBN-13 (pbk): 978-1-4842-9032-3   ISBN-13 (electronic): 978-1-4842-9033-0
https://doi.org/10.1007/978-1-4842-9033-0

Managing Director, Apress Media LLC: Welmoed Spahr
Acquisitions Editor: Jonathan Gennick
Development Editor: Laura Berendson
Coordinating Editor: Jill Balzano

Cover designed by eStudioCalamar

Cover image designed by Freepik (www.freepik.com)

Distributed to the book trade worldwide by Springer Science+Business Media New York, 1 New York Plaza, Suite 4600, New York, NY 10004-1562, USA. Phone 1-800-SPRINGER, fax (201) 348-4505, e-mail orders-ny@ springer-sbm.com, or visit www.springeronline.com. Apress Media, LLC is a California LLC and the sole member (owner) is Springer Science + Business Media Finance Inc (SSBM Finance Inc). SSBM Finance Inc is a **Delaware** corporation.

For information on translations, please e-mail booktranslations@springernature.com; for reprint, paperback, or audio rights, please e-mail bookpermissions@springernature.com.

Apress titles may be purchased in bulk for academic, corporate, or promotional use. eBook versions and licenses are also available for most titles. For more information, reference our Print and eBook Bulk Sales web page at http://www.apress.com/bulk-sales.

Any source code or other supplementary material referenced by the author in this book is available to readers on GitHub (https://github.com/Apress). For more detailed information, please visit http://www.apress.com/source-code.

Printed on acid-free paper

Table of Contents

About the Author

 **Sean Scott** is an Oracle ACE Pro and Oracle Certified Professional. His Oracle career spans over 25 years as an application developer, database administrator, systems and database architect, and database reliability engineer. He specializes in Oracle's Engineered Systems; migrations, upgrades, and database consolidations; cloud implementations; database reliability and resilience; automation; virtualization; and containers. Sean is active in the user community as a volunteer and has presented at Oracle OpenWorld, Collaborate, IOUG, and as a featured speaker at regional user groups worldwide.

About the Technical Reviewer

Byron Pearce has a long history working in the technology industry, with most of his career serving as a professional services consultant. He has served a wide range of clients from startups to Fortune 100 organizations in the areas of systems administration, database administration, infrastructure, cloud computing, and information security. He currently works as a security and compliance engineer for a medical technology services company.

Acknowledgments

This book is incomplete without extending my gratitude to those who made it possible:

To my friends Reece and the Ligernaut team for introducing me to the beauty of DevOps and shepherding me through my beginnings with Docker.

To Maggie, for the love and support over the years and your endless patience and understanding during this project.

Introduction

In 2013, Docker took a Linux construct that had existed for years—*containerization*—and wrapped it into a convenient interface, making it accessible to a broad audience. Since then, container adoption has blossomed. Much of the Web runs on containers. Everything at Google, from Search, through Gmail, to YouTube, runs in containers. Containers are inescapable!

Inescapable, that is, except by one corner of the enterprise—the database.

Databases are special. Data is the most valuable commodity in an organization, and for many, they entrust the most precious data—the Crown Jewels of the enterprise—to Oracle databases. A failed web server is quickly rebuilt or exchanged. Reconstructing data isn't so easy, and the prized status of data is often projected onto the database, mistakenly asserting that the vault is as priceless as its contents.

Objectively, database hosts are little more than compute and storage. As Laine Campbell and Charity Majors write in *Database Reliability Engineering* (O'Reilly, 2017), "Databases are not special snowflakes." As enterprises move toward a consolidated, containerized platform, the pressure falls on databases to follow. Still, databases (particularly Oracle) are *different*. They can't (or, more correctly, *shouldn't*) run like other containers!

That's where this book comes in. It's a guide for running Oracle databases on Docker with the same confidence, reliability, and security as traditional platforms. It's not a book on Oracle database administration, nor Docker and containers. Instead, it covers the remarkable marriage of the two technologies. Whether you're an Oracle database administrator investigating Docker solutions, a systems engineer exploring infrastructure consolidation, or a user searching for a reliable way to host Oracle databases for a development team, I've attempted to pour the things I wish I'd known when beginning my Docker journey in 2014 into this book.

PART I

Introduction to Containers

I've divided this book into two parts. This first part covers the basics of containers. You'll create (or download) an Oracle database as a package, then run it on your system. These packages are portable across all popular operating systems—Windows, Mac, and Linux—and are the cornerstone behind the speed and simplicity Docker introduces to development.

PART I

Introduction to Containers

## CHAPTER 1

Introducing Docker and Oracle

Over the past decade, we've witnessed a fundamental shift in how infrastructure is built, deployed, and run. The rise of reliability engineering is a response to systems' increasing complexity and scale. Without its tools and methods, managing and monitoring the environments of hundreds or thousands of hosts and services is an unimaginable, impossible task.

In traditional organizations, deploying infrastructure is a slow, manual process that relies on operations teams and their specialized skills. When consumers, like development teams, need new environments, they depend on operations teams to do the work. Administrators are the bottlenecks in the pipeline.

DevOps is a set of practices, tools, and organizational philosophies that drive cooperation and collaboration between *Development* and *Operations* teams. The key to successful DevOps organizations is automation. Automated processes can be delegated to users, empowering them to provision infrastructure on demand and removing dependencies on operations teams.

DevOps emphasizes quality and performance through observation and measurement. Responding to performance metrics is only possible when test environments accurately represent the observed systems. It's far easier to reliably reproduce systems backed by automation than those built and managed manually.

DevOps is much more than an organizational approach. It's a business model affecting the bottom line. DevOps' cooperative framework allows teams to deliver new features faster and with greater confidence, leading to competitive advantages in the marketplace. Monitoring application performance keeps customers happy. Tracking user behavior offers insight into improvements to the user experience and potentially exposes methods attackers use against the organization!

Yet as *DevOps* practices are accepted and adopted in organizations, databases (and database administrators) remain largely unaffected. The data tier seems resistant to automation, configuration management, Infrastructure as Code, and version control. The argument I often hear is that data is too valuable to trust to these processes—and by association, databases. Databases are stable, persistent, and unique. They make up a small fraction of the enterprise, and wasting time on concepts invented for mass-producing dynamic components with short lifetimes doesn't make sense.

Yes, data is priceless. Databases are special. But databases are vessels for data. Bank safes are valued by how well they work. Their value doesn't change according to their contents, and whether they hold the Hope Diamond or family documents isn't relevant. Safes protect things, and controlled processes allow manufacturers to guarantee every safe resists threats and secures what's inside, precisely as those tested by certifying agencies and independent labs. Adding custom or manual steps introduces variability and the potential for mistakes or inconsistency.

Databases are no different. The value of data makes consistent, repeatable processes crucial, perhaps more so than "less important" infrastructure. Database hosts built and governed under configuration management can be rebuilt precisely and rapidly. Changes applied and tracked through version control can be reverted in response to performance problems and promoted from lower environments into production. Reliability engineering is all about *confidence*—confidence that changes made in test behave the same in production; issues in one environment are reproducible elsewhere; we can recreate any or every component in the stack at will.

Docker (or, more generally, *Linux containers*[1]) is a piece of the reliability engineering puzzle. Docker allows us to confidently build, deploy, and run multiple identical containers for services—applications, web hosts, monitoring, and even databases!

---

[1] The mechanisms behind containers have been a part of the Linux kernel for years. Docker's API lowered the technical threshold for using containers. Making containers more accessible and easier to use revolutionized the way enterprises develop and deploy code and infrastructure. The Docker name became synonymous with containers. When someone says, "We'll put it in Docker," they're really talking about Linux containers. The terms *Docker* and *containers* refer to the same thing and are often used interchangeably.

Why Docker?

One of the first questions people ask about running Oracle databases in Docker is "Why?" Answering this requires an objective look at how we do things now and asking if there are better tools or ways to accomplish the job. Then, determine if the new methods are compelling. How will it improve things? Is it worth the effort and risk to change? What is the return on investment?

When running Oracle on Docker, we can distill these motivations into a handful of opportunities: simplicity, speed, portability, reliability, and cost.

Simplicity

Docker is *Infrastructure as Code*.[2] Docker automates operating system preparation, installing and patching Oracle software, and configuring databases. Users don't need to understand or remember detailed steps. Calling Docker and supplying optional parameters to customize the environment is all that's required. Users who aren't familiar with or comfortable installing a database no longer rely on a DBA to create new working environments.

Docker presents an even broader set of possibilities for database administrators beyond just automating database installations. Consider the effort to set up a primary and standby database in Data Guard. At a high level:

- Provision the hosts

- Install software

- Configure networking

- Create and configure a primary database

- Prepare and recover the standby database

- Set up the broker

- Test and validate

---

[2] Infrastructure as Code is a model for defining infrastructure as a set of rules or instructions that automation tools, like Docker, follow when building platforms to support software and applications. Code can be saved to source control, shared among teams, and subject to review and inspection. It leads to repeatable, reliable results, and allows teams to confidently provision hosts, storage, and networks without specialized knowledge or skills.

It's a very linear and time-consuming process: set up the environments before building the primary; wait for the primary database to be created before restoring the standby; wait for the standby to come online before setting up the broker. The number of steps creates opportunities for missed commands and mistakes. One wrong or overlooked parameter early on may leave things in a questionable state further on.

The expense and complexity of setting up Data Guard makes it something many DBAs do infrequently, making it challenging to get familiar with the technology. It's unusual for most companies to have a Data Guard environment dedicated to testing—where operations teams can break, fix, and explore how it works.[3] In my experience, most shops that run Data Guard treat the systems with kid gloves. They're reluctant to test it to extremes because of the effort needed to rebuild. That's especially true when Data Guard only exists in production!

If database teams are uncomfortable building and fixing Data Guard, how effective can they be if it breaks? Do they have practice diagnosing and addressing problems? Will they recognize and react to situations appropriately?

With Docker, the effort of building test environments drops significantly and, with it, concerns of recreating (previously) fragile systems. Suppose staff can create (and rebuild) full Data Guard Data Guard environments that mimic production topology in just minutes on a laptop. In that case, they have the opportunity to practice and perfect their skills and respond confidently in a crisis.

Limited or inadequate testbeds aren't limited to Data Guard—it applies to any complex environment or feature. Patch, upgrade, secure, restore—any change potentially tricky or time-consuming to recover from.

It's an odd contradiction: we're often reluctant to practice and test activities, some critical to business continuity and security, for fear of breaking lower environments. Yet failing to do so increases risk. Procedures earn less scrutiny and practice. Teams are less familiar and comfortable with the process when they reach production.

---

[3] It's unusual to see environments *dedicated to infrastructure testing*. Test systems are typically shared by end users, limiting their usefulness for any effort that might jeopardize their availability. They're effectively production systems for internal users.

Self-Contained

To appreciate Docker, it may help to reframe the way we think of enterprise applications. Application software are the rules for executing specific tasks installed on a host. Microsoft Word, for instance, manages and edits documents.

There's a distinction between *having* Word and *running* Word. Installing it means I *have* Word, as a static collection of files that define its behavior. *Running* Word puts the software *into action*. It starts a process that executes rules prescribed by the software and allocates resources like memory and CPU. An active Word process can use existing files or create new ones and captures configurations and metadata as it's running, but the installed software—the rules—don't change.

It's easy to lose sight of this when thinking of an Oracle database. We think of databases as collections of hardware, software, data, and configurations rather than recognizing individual components, but they're still *just applications*. Figure 1-1 illustrates the similarities between Word and an Oracle database. The software in the ORACLE_HOME specifies the rules for working with data. Starting a database instance creates processes, allocates resources, and reads and writes data and configurations to files on disk.

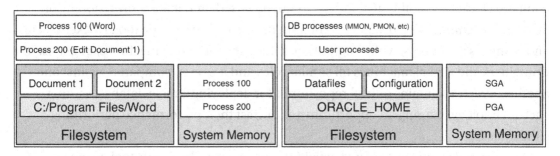

Figure 1-1. *An Oracle database is an application with components like those found in other applications, including Microsoft Word*

Applications are all the rules and dependencies needed to do something, compiled into a package. "Starting" the package runs the application and performs work.

In Docker, *images* are the packages containing all the software and dependencies necessary to support a given application. Images are the software installation—the files and metadata that prescribe a function. *Running* an image creates a *container* for delivering services.

The most significant difference between databases running natively on physical or virtual hosts and those running in containers are the locations of files. In traditional systems, prerequisite libraries and packages are installed directly into the operating system. Updating the OS risks changes to these dependencies, and many shops delay or limit their patching rather than jeopardize database stability and performance.

Systems running in containers, however, are far more forgiving. Dependencies are built into the image, and changes to the underlying host OS aren't a concern.[4] The flexibility to manage the host operating system, with less regard for database compatibility, affords greater freedom to stay current with the latest security updates.

Patching and upgrading databases is different, too. Container images are complete, self-contained collections of database software, entirely separate from data and configuration. In Docker, rather than updating the active Oracle Home, stop the container running the old version, then start a new container using a new, updated image!

Speed

Docker's speed benefits go beyond its ability to build infrastructure quickly. Let's compare Docker to another technology frequently used for database provisioning on desktops: *Vagrant*. Like Docker, Vagrant is an Infrastructure as Code tool. Docker creates and manages containers, while Vagrant does the same for virtual machines, or *guests*. Containers and virtual machines fill similar roles and are often compared against one another. Oracle maintains official repositories for deploying Oracle databases under each technology, offering an opportunity to contrast their performance performing similar tasks.

I performed simple tests of two activities. The first was the time it took to create a database, including configuring the environment, installing prerequisites and database software, then creating a new database. The second was starting (or restarting) the system.

I used Oracle's Vagrant project (`https://github.com/oracle/vagrant-projects`) for my VM and Oracle's Docker image builds (`https://github.com/oracle/docker-images`) for my image. I used the same archive file to install Oracle 19c Enterprise Edition and create a 19.3 container database and single pluggable database. All assets

---

[4] Provided changes on the OS are compatible with the container engine, of course.

were already available locally to eliminate dependencies on downloads. Both tests were performed on the same machine, a MacBook Pro running the latest Vagrant and Docker Desktop versions. I ran each operation five times, captured timings, and computed their averages. Docker was just over 25% faster than Vagrant for building a new database and 37% faster to start than resuming a VM.

Why is Docker so much faster? It boils down to differences in the way virtual machines and containers work. Virtual machines rely on a *hypervisor* to emulate hardware, then start an operating system. There's a level of abstraction that translates calls from the guest operating system to the host and back.

Docker containers are processes running natively on the host. There's no operating system to initialize and nothing to boot. Containers (usually) include only the dependencies—executables, libraries, and other files—necessary to run the service they're meant for, making them smaller than a comparable VM.

Figure 1-2 illustrates the differences between virtual machines and containers. Both systems have host operating systems and an interpretive layer that supports virtualization. And in both environments, there are software dependencies—binaries, libraries, and application code. But virtual machines include a guest operating system that isn't present in containers. Why not? Containers leverage files and resources already present in the host operating system!

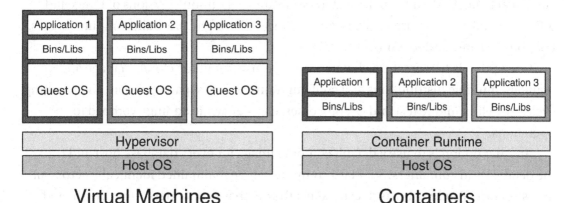

Figure 1-2. *Running the same applications in a virtual machine and a container requires the same application code and dependencies. The difference lies in where the operating system needed to support the application exists. In virtual machines, each guest has its own OS. Containers share the host's OS*

In Figure 1-2, the virtual machines are isolated from one another. Even if the application files and dependencies are identical, they consume space individually in each virtual guest. In Docker, three (or three hundred or three thousand) identical containers all start from the same image, using less space than their counterparts in the three virtual guests.[5]

Portability

Microsoft Word saves files in a standard format. I can share documents with others running Word on different operating systems or architectures and even with people using various word processing programs that recognize the standard.

Container *images* built with Docker (and similar technologies) adhere to the *Open Container Initiative* or *OCI*[6] (https://opencontainers.org). They're portable across hardware and operating systems and interchangeable across all OCI-compliant environments. Images built in Docker on Windows work identically on a Mac or Linux system and vice versa. Virtually every cloud vendor supports the OCI standard, too. A single, standard database image works the same on any cloud and is *portable* across clouds. Why is portability desirable, even essential?

Imagine we need to migrate several databases from on-premises systems to the cloud. Each database runs on dedicated hardware, with unique versions of Linux and different database software versions. Our cloud vendor offers pre-built compute images, but none are identical to our needs.

One option is to recreate each database environment in the cloud, manage and maintain multiple distributions and configurations, follow separate update and patching cycles, develop unique test and QA processes, etc.—all while adding overhead to operations.

Another option is to use a default compute image for every database host and run the databases in containers. Standard compute can be maintained identically across all infrastructure. Patching hosts doesn't affect the database containers—they're isolated, using their software. The abstraction and isolation containers offer facilitates and simplifies changing cloud vendors, running multicloud environments, and hybrid cloud/on-premises topologies.

---

[5] This concept is covered in detail in Chapter 12.
[6] Not to be confused with *Oracle Cloud Infrastructure*.

Reliability

When discussing reliability, we typically think of how stable a system is, how resilient it is to failure if its components are durable, and whether critical aspects are redundant. This describes systems, infrastructure, or hardware reliability. There's another aspect to reliability that's often overlooked but equally important to consider: *process reliability*.

Building reliable processes means assuring changes promoted from lower environments through production function predictably at each step. It also seeks to guarantee problem behaviors in production systems can be reproduced and confidently fixed elsewhere.

Automation, version control, and configuration management are the best means of achieving process reliability. Unfortunately, database environments tend to avoid these approaches, leaning more toward manual administration. The reasoning goes that the overhead and discipline applied to non-database infrastructure aren't justified when databases represent a minority of assets, and databases and hosts change too infrequently to benefit. Instead, a documented installation and configuration process substitutes to guarantee databases are consistent throughout the enterprise.

Relying on documentation alone is risky. Documentation is *descriptive*. It's a set of instructions that made sense to the authors when written but may be interpreted or understood differently by readers. It may be incomplete, particularly if the writer expects readers to understand certain things. Readers may even skip or miss steps. It's also only effective or correct if it's current.

Docker (and other automation tools) is Infrastructure as Code and lends itself naturally to centralized version control tools like *git*. Code is *procedural* and *instructive* and less open to misinterpretation. Incomplete procedures and incorrect syntax lead to failure. Coded processes are also more reliable and easier to test.

Images produced by Docker are *immutable*, meaning they can't be changed, and offer greater certainty that multiple database containers running from the same image are identical. It eliminates variables that might confuse troubleshooting efforts and cast doubt on findings from a process management perspective. It's easier to create (and keep) databases running in containers consistent and identical and achieve process reliability.

Cost

Services in containers occupy a smaller footprint than virtualized or bare-metal solutions. It's why containers are attractive—they do more with less. While the bottom line is undoubtedly important, it's not the only area where Docker and containers help reduce costs.

I saved cost for last because each prior argument includes or implies cost savings that are more difficult to quantify. Building simpler and faster solutions accelerates development pipelines. Database teams no longer spend as much time performing data refreshes. Developer and QA teams have greater autonomy over their environments. Both sides win in the war between DBAs and developers!

Operations teams use automation, configuration management, and version control to ensure consistency and simplify their environments. They help achieve efficiency. Databases often exist outside that envelope, eschewing standards and employing different or dedicated tools for monitoring and management. Docker introduces a way of bringing database teams into the operational fold and reducing the overhead associated with multiple techniques.

Container portability creates opportunities to leverage less powerful hardware and low-cost cloud services to host nonproduction database environments dedicated to database testing. The primary obstacles to restore and disaster recovery testing are preparation difficulty and hardware availability. Containers solve both, automating the setup and reducing the threshold for what constitutes acceptable test environments.

Finally, Docker creates predictable, reliable results. We solve problems with greater confidence and spend less time testing by reducing and eliminating doubts. When two systems behave differently, we typically begin looking for differences that may be to blame. For manually built databases, we can't dismiss the possibility of errors or missed steps. Two systems started from the same image have an identical heritage, and it's easier to locate where one diverges from the norm.

Use Cases

Let's get this out of the way: My Oracle Support note 2216342.1 outlines Oracle's support for Docker. Oracle certifies Docker for single-instance databases using 12.1.0.2 and later on hosts running

- Oracle Linux 7 UEK4 and later

- Red Hat Enterprise Linux 7

In October 2021, Oracle announced production support of RAC databases running Oracle Database 21c under My Oracle Support note 2488326.1.

Docker is an option for existing databases running on bare metal, a VM, or a cloud within these limitations.

Docker's small footprint, low resource demands, and speed make it a natural solution for sandbox and prototyping on limited hardware like laptops. But its architecture introduces the potential to work with Oracle in different and exciting ways.

One interesting feature is the ability to easily separate database and operating system software from data and configuration. It's easy to save the contents of a database as reference data, then share, restore, or provision new databases in seconds, using only basic OS commands—no Recovery Manager or Data Pump required. Let's examine a few ways of leveraging this.

Exchange Data

Running an Oracle database class or lab for anything more than a few students requires substantial horsepower. Docker's small footprint allows hardware to accommodate more students than a virtual guest solution. It also accelerates and simplifies the effort to provision the lab itself.

In either situation, instructors create a gold image of a database all students will use. A Vagrant solution saves the gold image as a custom box containing the operating system, database, and data. Students work on independent virtual guests started from the custom box.

In Docker, entire databases can be committed as new images and distributed. A second method creates two components: operating system and database software (host) and data and configuration (data). In this scenario, the host and data are shared or copied together or separately.[7] The advantage of this method may not be immediately apparent.

If the "host" piece in this example is a 19.10 database, it will work with *any* 19.10 "data." Different labs, with other data, can all use the same "host." Only the reference data changes.

---

[7] These methods are described in detail in Chapter 7.

A similar approach works for refreshing data in QA and development environments. Whenever reference data changes, copy the newer, self-contained version of the data and database configurations to the container's data volume and restart the container. The same technique is helpful for versioning data. Applications include A/B testing and side-by-side comparison of function or performance before and after application or parameter changes.

Modular Software

Docker images consist of a set of files that appear as a regular Linux filesystem. An image for an Oracle database will contain directories for the ORACLE_BASE, ORACLE_HOME, inventory files, and so on. These files appear in the image as part of a typical directory structure. Docker can read and copy some or all of an existing image to build new images, saving time and effort (and space!).

We can use images and parts of images as building blocks to construct more complex systems without duplicating effort. GoldenGate and database upgrades offer two scenarios illustrating ways to leverage a modular approach.

For GoldenGate, an existing database image is extended by adding and configuring the GoldenGate software and dependencies. The original database image provides a foundation. Docker adds *layers*[8] to the database image but leaves the original unchanged. The original image is untouched, and Docker can reuse identical portions of its filesystem to reduce the size of the final GoldenGate image.

Building an image to test database upgrades *can* be done the same way, adding a new database home to an existing database image. But there's another approach available, too. If I already have database images for my source and target versions, I can start with the source database image; *copy* the ORACLE_HOME from the target; attach or clone the new ORACLE_HOME to the existing inventory. The final image has source and target ORACLE_HOME directories and a complete inventory. There's no need to install the binaries, and Docker's storage deduplicates the shared content.

Database patching and upgrades are other applications that work like Oracle's *Rapid Home Provisioning*. Rather than patching software on an existing container, create a new image at the target release. The image produces consistent database containers, eliminating variations introduced by manual processes. To patch the database, stop the running container, start a new container using the updated image, and run any post-patching steps to modify database metadata.

---

[8] Layers are covered in Chapter 17, *Image Efficiency*.

Orchestration

Docker comes with its own orchestration solution, *Docker Compose*. Docker Compose (or simply Compose) typically coordinates two or more containers, manages cross-container dependencies, and facilitates networking and other shared resources. We can use Compose to run environments that use multiple databases, such as Data Guard.

Compose uses *YAML* (*Yet Another Markup Language*), a plain-text markup language, to define participating members or *services* in an orchestration. Besides describing the members, information passed to each service through the Compose specification can trigger conditional activities. Compose starts two Oracle 19.10 Enterprise Edition databases in the following example: DENVER and DALLAS. Each is assigned environment variables called ROLE and DB_UNQNAME. A script in the database image reads these values from each database container's environment and uses them to perform actions appropriate to each role.

Don't worry if you're unfamiliar with YAML or similar markup languages. What you should notice is the simplicity of the configuration. The orchestration needs just a few pieces of information to automatically provision two databases in a Data Guard configuration!

```
version: '3'
services:
  DENVER:
    image: oracledb:19.10-ee
    container_name: DENVER
    environment:
      ORACLE_SID: ORCL
      DB_UNQNAME: DENVER
      ROLE: PRIMARY

  DALLAS:
    image: oracledb:19.10-ee
    container_name: DALLAS
```

```
environment:
  ORACLE_SID: ORCL
  DB_UNQNAME: DALLAS
  ROLE: STANDBY
```

Compose simplifies the setup of complex environments and reduces the effort and time required to bring a fully configured set of interdependent databases online. Reduced startup cost makes building models for testing replication and disaster recovery systems easy. It also removes any reluctance to bend or break those systems. Once automation is in place, creating fresh models is straightforward.

Other Uses

As you work with Oracle in Docker, you will undoubtedly recognize new applications. Docker is my first thought when I need to troubleshoot anything, and my colleagues enjoy some good-natured teasing about it. Here are some additional ideas to consider:

- **Troubleshooting:** Isolating a bug in production can be difficult when the environment is restricted or prevents changes. Recreating a problem in Docker offers the freedom to tweak and test scenarios that allow better isolation and identification and, ultimately, faster resolutions.

- **Practice procedures:** Docker provides an excellent practice field for critical activities such as upgrades, migrations, database restores, and disaster recovery. It's an ideal place to become familiar with the process and perfect and document procedures and runbooks.

- **Monitoring systems:** Create a self-contained, portable monitoring repository in Docker and deploy it into any infrastructure.

- **Performance tuning:** Export statistics and metadata from a production database into a database running in Docker to model and tune optimizer behavior.

- **Hacking and penetration testing:** A local, isolated system is an excellent testbed to explore vulnerabilities and practice hacking skills!

- **Feature evaluations:** Every new release of Oracle introduces a plethora of new features and capabilities. Docker offers a risk-free setting where users can get acquainted with what's new and practice for certifications.

This is by no means an exhaustive list—hopefully, it sparks your imagination!

Objections to Docker

Over the years, I've heard many concerns about using Docker for databases, mainly Oracle. I shared many of these when I first began putting data into containers. Oracle officially supports Docker for production databases, but that doesn't mean Docker is an appropriate solution. To tackle that, let's address some of the myths, misconceptions, and misunderstandings about containers that exist, particularly in the database world:

- **I'll lose my data:** Containers are processes on a host, accessing the same storage as non-container processes. Take the same precautions to protect container and non-container databases.

- **Containers are ephemeral:** It's not unusual to see containers started to perform a service or function and destroyed when complete. There's no time limit, though, and containers exist until deliberately removed. They can be stopped and started, and their data persists across system restarts.

- **Images are immutable:** Yes, and that's good! Images are templates for starting new containers. They can't be changed, assuring us that every new container is a reliable copy of the original image. Just because an existing image is immutable doesn't prevent changing and saving it as a *new* image!

I think it's important to consider some of the opposition to Docker in a historical light. I've witnessed innovations over a long career in technology, including the introduction of RMAN, Enterprise Manager, virtualization, and the cloud. Each was met with resistance, not always rational. Humans don't deal well with change, and it's easy to dismiss new technology as a gimmick or marketing vaporware.

At the risk of dating myself, I remember the introduction of automatic undo management. Everyone I knew dismissed it, suggesting that undo management was too complex to automate. Today, I can't imagine manually tuning rollback. It's a primitive idea!

Summary

Containers are the new way of doing things, and some of the largest, most successful enterprises are all-in. Infrastructure consolidation saves money and improves manageability. While database administrators may try to resist it, it's only a matter of time before databases are the only things not in containers, at which point someone will ask, "Why not?" Justifying your answer to that question requires understanding how containers and databases coexist and operate and how they compare to the alternatives.

In the following chapters, I'll introduce you to container concepts relevant to databases and Oracle and walk you through the steps of building databases in Docker. We'll begin with simple examples to get Oracle up and running on a laptop or desktop and build confidence and familiarity. At each step, I provide practical recipes you can apply, customize, and build on in your environment!

## CHAPTER 2

Understanding the Container Landscape

Containers have their own language, and those new to Docker should understand some basic concepts and terminology before jumping in. This chapter introduces the vocabulary needed to navigate the terrain and a high-level view of how containers work. Let's begin by looking at containers in the context of another similar solution that readers may already be familiar with: virtual machines.

If you're already confident distinguishing between *images* and *containers* and recognize how containers and virtual machines differ, feel free to skip to Chapter 3.

Containers vs. Virtual Machines

Ask a group of IT professionals to describe Docker containers, and the chances are good that at least half will respond that they're "like lightweight virtual machines." Some might even make comparisons:

- VMs are like houses; containers are like apartments.

- VMs are like semi-tractor trailers; containers are like pickup trucks.

- VMs are like supermarkets; containers are like convenience stores.

- VMs are a bakery; containers are a slice of cake.

© Sean Scott 2023
S. Scott, *Oracle on Docker*, https://doi.org/10.1007/978-1-4842-9033-0_2

Virtual machines and containers are both valid solutions for addressing the challenges of cost, efficiency, scale, isolation, and portability, so it's natural to compare them. The misstep these analogies make is framing containers as a lesser, lighter, or trivial alternative. It perpetuates the myth that containers aren't capable or robust enough for production workloads.[1]

I'd like to reframe this for an Oracle database audience by looking at virtual machines and containers as *different ways of doing similar things*. Let's put Docker aside for a moment and put on our Oracle hat to consider ways to host three new database applications in an enterprise. Three possible approaches are as follows:

- **Three homes, three databases:** One database for each application, each with its own ORACLE_HOME. Individual Oracle software installations offer greater control over each application's database version at the expense of increased overhead. Each ORACLE_HOME takes up space and must be managed, patched, and supported separately.

- **One home, three databases:** One database for each application, all running from a single ORACLE_HOME, reduces the complexity of maintaining multiple software installations while separating each application. Each database has overhead associated with its memory structures, processes, and metadata (SYSTEM, SYSAUX, TEMP, and UNDO tablespaces).

- **One database, three schemas:** The most efficient approach is a single database with individual schemas for each application. All three schemas share one set of memory structures, background processes, and metadata. Smaller, less expensive hardware provides equal performance.

---

[1] To appreciate how capably containers handle production workloads and availability, consider that everything at Google runs on containers: Gmail, YouTube, even search! *cloud.google.com/ containers*

None of these solutions are right or wrong, good or bad, and there are scenarios where each is a better or more reasonable choice. Let's eliminate the first option[2] and narrow in on the second and third. These run from a single ORACLE_HOME and are therefore limited to running on a single host. Figure 2-1 compares these options side by side.

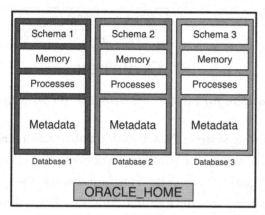
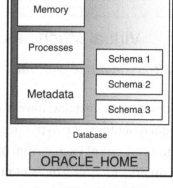

One ORACLE_HOME
Three Databases

One ORACLE_HOME
Three Schemas

Figure 2-1. *Alternatives for hosting three applications from a single ORACLE_ HOME—separate databases vs. separate schemas*

From a client standpoint, there is no *functional* difference. The choice is purely operational. Separate database instances offer greater flexibility but require more resources and management (with higher costs).

Spreading schemas across databases may *appear* to have security benefits and provide isolation. With a single ORACLE_HOME, vulnerabilities exploited in one database are there for others. More databases mean a larger attack surface. Security is a product of how well the infrastructure and schemas are protected.

Most works and explanations on containers compare the resource placement of containers and virtual machines using a diagram similar to Figure 2-2.

---

[2] Three homes and three databases in this example is analogous to running separate hosts. The latter two scenarios focus on methods that share infrastructure and resources of a single host and explore ways of isolating and presenting schemas and data to applications. Containers and virtual machines perform similar roles.

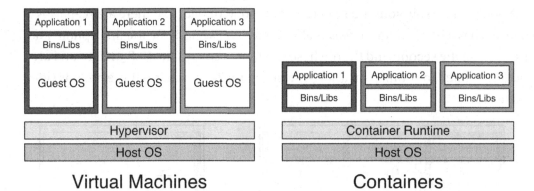

Figure 2-2.   *Resource placement comparison for virtual machines and containers*

Both run on a host and have host operating systems.[3] Each adds an abstraction layer: for virtual machines, the hypervisor; for containers, the runtime. Hypervisors allow the operating systems of each virtual machine guest to access host resources and isolate VMs from one another. The container runtime performs a similar function. The main takeaway from Figure 2-2 is that containers don't have a guest OS.

Dedicated vs. Shared

Note the parallels between Figures 2-1 and 2-2. Three databases mean three sets of duplicate metadata, each with process and memory requirements. The same applies to virtual machines. The guest operating systems are not shared. Independent virtual machines demand host resources to manage their environments as if they were running natively.

In contrast, multiple schemas in a single database share a data dictionary. Adding schemas doesn't increase the number of background processes or the amount of memory used. The only system resource affected when adding schemas is the storage needed by metadata and new objects. Similarly, containers share resources in the host kernel and environment. Containers enjoy smaller footprints by reducing or eliminating duplicate files and sharing administrative processes with the host operating system.

---

[3] Type 1 hypervisors combine the hypervisor and operating system. Type 2 hypervisors run atop a host operating system.

Performance

Other comparisons apply, too. There's more time and effort needed to add or start schemas assigned to individual databases. The same applies to virtual machines. Creating and starting databases and installing and booting operating systems in independent virtual machines are time- and resource-intensive activities.

Adding a schema is far less involved in the single database, a limited subset of creating a dedicated database for an application. There's also no concept of "starting" a schema in a database instance. If the database is up, the schema is available, too. The overhead of accessing a schema is just what's needed to establish a database connection.

We can look at containers the same way. There's no prerequisite installation, and since containers don't have an operating system, they don't need to boot. If the host is running, starting a container is just a matter of creating a process.

Capacity and Capability

The representation in Figure 2-2 doesn't provide a complete picture, though. Both run software at the host level—an OS and some software abstraction or emulation layer supporting guest interaction and isolation. Both solutions accommodate three applications. Besides the presence or absence of the operating system, they may *seem* to be relatively similar approaches.

Containers and virtual machines are sometimes referred to as "light" and "heavy," respectively. A VM's extra "weight" comes from the guest's operating systems. Identical applications (i.e., applications with the same binary, library, and application layers) duplicate components across virtual guests. In the virtual environment, the overhead of running parallel operating systems also adds load to the system.

Let's amend the original virtual machine vs. container comparison by adding a boundary to capture the relative *capacity* of the hosts, as shown in Figure 2-3. It's easier to understand that applications in the container solution have room to grow or that smaller and less powerful (and less expensive) hardware can be substituted without sacrificing capability.

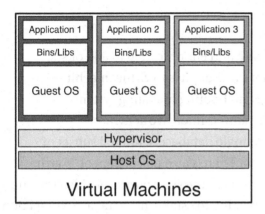 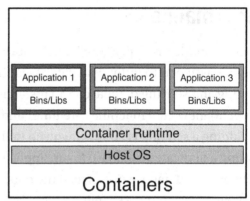

Figure 2-3. *Capacity requirement comparison of virtual machine and container infrastructure*

Virtual machines are the Oracle equivalent of running independent databases for every schema in an application, each with its own administrative, undo, and temporary tablespaces, memory structures, background processes, and so on.

Compare containers to running a single database instance with multiple schemas. Each schema contains only its unique objects. Common features are shared and managed centrally, reducing overhead and duplication and increasing capability and performance.[4]

Concepts and Terminology

Now that you know what containers are and where they fit in the enterprise, let's dive into some container concepts and terminology.

Images

An *image* is a package of files used to start and run containers. Images bear functional similarities to *Vagrant boxes* and *VirtualBox images*, and those comfortable with Oracle's multitenant architecture could even think of them as *seed databases*. Fundamentally, these are all starting points for working with technology and delivering reliable, identical starting points.

---

[4] Containers are even more efficient than shown here. Assuming the three applications hosted in these examples have similar foundations, most, if not all, of the binary, library, and application files of these containers are shared through overlay filesystems. This is discussed in greater detail in Chapter 17.

When Docker starts a new container from an image, it reads image metadata and presents a *filesystem* (including the binaries, libraries, and application files we discussed earlier) to the container. The next chapter goes into more detail on how containers use filesystems. In the meantime, let's look at some properties of images: *tags*, *portability*, *immutability*, and *statelessness*.

Tags

A *tag* (usually) identifies the *version* of an image in a *repository*. A repository is a collection of images, usually related, such as Linux or Python. Tagging an image differentiates each version and makes it easier to find and use a specific version. Tags combine with the repository name to create a human-readable or friendly image name with the form `repository-name:tag`.

Repository names and tags provide a convenient means for humans to work with images. There's even a special tag, `latest`, that references the current working version of an image without knowing its details. This highlights an important consideration. Tags are arbitrary conventions, not absolute identifiers.

Building images creates a unique *SHA256 hash* value. Images can exist in multiple repositories with different tags. The hash (sometimes referred to as its *digest*) identifies whether the images are the same and comes into play when considering immutability.

Portable

Docker images are *portable* because they run on any system that runs Docker—or, for that matter, any system with a compatible container runtime. This includes Docker alternatives like *Podman* and *LXC* and container services offered by cloud vendors.

Portability in this context is more than just *compatibility*. It guarantees users have *identical experiences* on every platform without changing the image or worrying about where it will run. If it works on one machine, it will work on *every machine*.

Portability lowers the threshold for various everyday challenges, including (but not limited to) building labs, teaching and experimenting, demonstrating new features, testing security, validating patches and fixes, and verifying procedures.

Immutable and Stateless

Images are *immutable*—they can't be changed. An image can be modified and saved as a new image and even updated to replace an image using the same tag, but its hash value changes.

Immutability goes hand in hand with the *stateless* nature of images. Information about an image's condition, or *state*, can't be saved *to the image*.[5] Images always start from the same, known place.

While tags offer a friendly mechanism for working with images, and portability lets us run an image anywhere, immutability guarantees images shared across multiple environments are the same. Statelessness assures that every image begins from the same starting point and delivers identical results.

Portability and immutability are key to sharing images, with hashes uniquely identifying their version. Docker and container technology are a way of building *Infrastructure as Code*. Infrastructure as Code produces reliable environments through version control and automation and reduces or eliminates manual configuration.

I recently helped troubleshoot a Data Guard issue. A new standby database added to an existing environment wasn't working as expected. The DBA team followed a documented procedure and felt confident the failing system was identical to the working one. Several hours later, a minor variation in the `sqlnet.ora` configuration was identified and fixed. Building from code avoids oversights, saving time and money (and frustration)!

Containers

A *container* is created by "running" an image. Containers perform work. From the host perspective, a container looks like a single process on the system. "Inside" a container, things appear differently! Once connected to a container, the environment seems to be a complete host with a filesystem, processes, users, and networking. Like virtual machines, things look and behave differently depending on whether you're "inside" or "outside."

Containers are *stateful* and *ephemeral* invocations of images. These characteristics are often misunderstood, particularly in the database world.

---

[5] This is an important difference between images and containers. Containers persist their state information.

Stateful

A container's condition, or *state*, is preserved. Nothing is lost when containers (or their host) are stopped and restarted. Files and content added and modified on the container's filesystem persist through the stop-start cycle. Directories and files deleted from the container don't reappear.

It's easy to confuse the ways images and containers manage state. Remember that images are like templates or seed databases. Their statelessness provides a reliable starting point to begin work. That work occurs (and is saved) in stateful containers. When working with databases, it's essential to understand that changes to data persist in containers just as in virtual machines or bare-metal environments.

Ephemeral

Containers usually do some work, then disappear. Generally speaking, containers are considered *ephemeral*, or temporary, processes. Based on this, it's easy to conclude containers are inappropriate for hosting long-lived applications like databases. However, containers don't expire, and nothing prevents them from running for days, months, or years.

Containers don't vanish on their own, either. They are no more or less permanent than virtual machines, yet there is a mistaken belief in the database world that containers are dangerous places to put your data.[6] Can you remove a container? Absolutely. You can also remove a virtual machine or delete its disks from the host. To be clear, these are operational matters and unrelated to the technology itself.

Resources

Like other processes running on a system, containers use the host's CPU, memory, and storage. Docker provides ways of managing and limiting resource use by individual containers and the Docker runtime. Chapter 16 covers this in more detail. But containers can interact with the host in other ways. The most common of these are accessing local storage and exposing network connectivity.

---

[6] Data in containers—including datafiles and configuration—can be persisted outside the container and protected by the same mechanisms used by databases running on bare-metal and virtual machines.

Volumes

Volumes are a mechanism for sharing filesystems from the local host with containers and separating data from software. Conceptually, volumes are like NFS filesystems visible to the host and container, allowing access to high-performance and resilient devices and shared data. They streamline operational activities that are difficult or impractical for Oracle databases running on other platforms, including

- **Patch and upgrade:** Stop and remove the running container, replace it with one using the upgraded version, run any post-upgrade steps, and start the database.

- **Move and migrate:** Containers are portable and run in any compatible environment. Whether it's moving to a newer, more powerful on-premises host or a lift and shift to the cloud, containers offer a consistent and controllable mechanism for transporting data and databases.

- **Clone databases:** Separating data and software makes cloning a database a matter of copying the data volume and starting a new container referencing the location of the data.

- **Create reference datasets:** Create gold images of data to distribute among QA and development teams. Stop a container, swap out its data, and restart it. Or drop and recreate the container using the new dataset to guarantee teams are testing with clean, consistent data.

Removing a container deletes its data—unless it's on a volume. Storing data and configuration files on volumes allows data to outlive containers and is key to these techniques. Oracle's official Docker image repository scripts build this capability into images, and it's easily accessed through the Docker API when creating a container.

Networking

Containers run in isolation by default, with connections limited to privileged users on the host. That isn't very useful for most applications. Fortunately, Docker can expose and map ports to the local host. Applications, users, and even other containers access a container using the mapped port on the host. Only ports deliberately opened in an image are mappable. Oracle's Docker images expose ports 1521 and 5500.

Figure 2-4 shows an example of connecting Oracle SQL Developer to an Oracle database running in a container. The database's listener port, 1521, is mapped to port 10000 on the local host. The hostname is `localhost` (or the hostname or IP address of the Docker host).

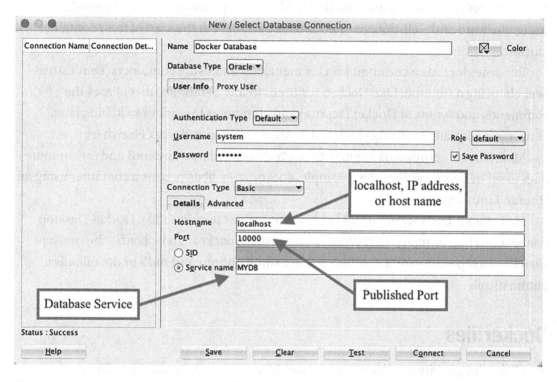

Figure 2-4. *Connecting SQL Developer to an Oracle database in a Docker container*

Most of the networking covered in this book uses port mapping for simplicity. There are more robust and scalable solutions suited to production environments. Chapter 9 covers a Docker-native solution. Tools like *Docker Compose* and *Kubernetes* have facilities for administering and securing connections to containers (and databases).

Additional Terminology

Readers should know a few additional terms and concepts to complete a basic understanding of Docker.

Runtimes

Container *runtimes* incorporate a suite of capabilities for building, managing, and running containers. *Docker Desktop* for Windows and Mac users and *Docker Engine* for Linux users are popular and free to download at www.docker.com and provide straightforward and well-documented avenues for users at the start of their container journey.

Runtimes include a command set for managing and using containers. Don't stress over choosing a runtime. Like Docker, runtimes follow a standard that aliases the commands and syntax of Docker Desktop and eliminates the risk of switching later. Simply put, virtually anything you run in Docker Desktop will work elsewhere.

Most Docker commands begin with *docker*, followed by a keyword and one or more flags to set or define options. For example, docker run ubuntu runs a container using an Ubuntu Linux image.

How does it know where to get the Ubuntu image? Runtimes like Docker Desktop connect to a hub or repository. When a user invokes docker run ubuntu, the runtime searches its repository for a certified image named ubuntu and *pulls* or downloads it automatically.

Dockerfiles

Recall that images are a collection of files and directories. A *Dockerfile* is the set of instructions, or code, used to populate the files in images. Dockerfiles run commands and call scripts for installing and configuring the final image. They also define the environment for containers that run the image, including variables, ports, and directories mapped to host resources. Dockerfiles also determine what scripts containers run when they start and define checks for reporting container health.

Builds

Building images executes the instructions in Dockerfiles. The build process steps through the Dockerfile sequentially. Builds always begin by pulling a base image.

The base image runs as a container, and changes are applied (remember, images can't be changed) as a *layer*. Each layer is a foundation for the following steps until the final image is complete.[7]

Summary

You now understand the language and concepts of Docker and containers and recognize how containers compare to virtual machines. For database administrators, it may be helpful to think of virtual machines as databases and containers as schemas. Adding a schema for a new application is far less costly than creating a new, dedicated database. There's nothing to start in a container or a schema, either.

You can differentiate between images and containers and understand that they're portable to any container environment to deliver reliable, identical results. You learned containers can share host resources, including network and storage. Most notably, volumes allow data—including Oracle databases—to persist independently from a container.

Next, we'll lift the veil and explore how containers work by building one, not in Docker, but at the command line, using Linux commands. This gives insight into concepts used in later chapters but, most importantly, eliminates some of the mystery and apprehension you may have when using Docker as a database platform!

---

[7] This is a basic example. Builds can involve multiple images and stages and may incorporate techniques to maximize layer reuse and minimize the size of the final image. A main objective of containers is efficiency—smaller images produce containers that pack more densely. Shared layers lower storage even further and take advantage of caching to improve overall performance. Techniques for building efficient images are covered in Chapter 17.

CHAPTER 3

Container Foundations

In the previous chapter, I covered some Docker terms and concepts. This chapter builds on that with more practical, hands-on examples that will help you understand Docker firsthand, how it works, and why it's grown so popular.

In addition to presenting basic Docker commands, I want to introduce fundamental concepts of images and containers. Images are *immutable*, and containers are *ephemeral* and *persistent*. I hesitate to type that because I know how academic and boring it sounds! When I started my container journey, I'll admit that I wrestled with wrapping my mind around these ideas or appreciating their importance. After a year or so, I saw them demonstrated and the how and why were immediately apparent! I will do my best to reproduce those "Aha!" moments and (hopefully) save you from repeating my struggles!

If you're already familiar with containers and these concepts, feel free to move on to Chapter 4. If not, I encourage you to take the extra time to follow along with the examples in this chapter in your environment because there's one thing you won't be able to pick up off the printed page.

Speed.

I can tell you containers are fast or that the Grand Canyon is big, but some things are best appreciated by *seeing for yourself.*

If you don't already have Docker Desktop installed, download and install it from `www.docker.com/products/docker-desktop`. The next chapter has details on installing Docker Desktop for Mac and Windows and configuring Docker on Linux systems.

Docker Command-Line Overview

Docker command-line instructions begin with the `docker` keyword. The list of commands is relatively brief, and, for the most part, they're plain and meaningful, even

© Sean Scott 2023
S. Scott, *Oracle on Docker*, https://doi.org/10.1007/978-1-4842-9033-0_3

to the uninitiated. `docker start` starts a container; `docker logs` displays container logs; `docker run` runs containers; and so on.

Docker has some synonymous commands. For example, `docker container run` and `docker run` are the same command, as are `docker image ls`[1] and `docker images`. The Docker community tends to use the shorter option when there's a synonym. I'll do the same throughout this book.

Docker alternatives, like Podman, include commands aliased to their Docker counterparts. I've worked in environments with Podman installed instead of Docker, and some users (including systems administrators) didn't notice for years!

You can always list all commands with `docker --help` (or just `docker`) at the prompt and get details for individual commands by typing `docker <COMMAND> --help`. (The Appendix includes a collection of common commands, with examples and recipes for running Docker and Oracle.)

Run Your First Container

Before jumping in and running an Oracle database, let's cover some basics using Ubuntu, a popular Linux distribution. It provides an opportunity to take a practical tour of Docker, explore some concepts behind images and containers, get comfortable with Docker commands, and demonstrate the essential properties of container environments.

List Images

Open a shell session on the computer where you've installed Docker Desktop and show the images available on the system by running `docker images`. Your output will show a heading but no containers:

```
> docker images
REPOSITORY    TAG      IMAGE ID    CREATED    SIZE
```

---

[1] A few Docker commands have origins in Unix/Linux commands for file and process management and may not be immediately obvious to Windows users. In Linux, `cp` copies files, `ls` lists files, `ps` lists processes, and `rm` removes files. Their Docker equivalents copy files to and from containers, list Docker objects, list containers, and remove Docker objects, respectively.

There's nothing listed indicating there are no images on the system. Recall that an image is like a template, and a container is a product of running an image. Before running a container, we need an image.

Run a Container

Can we run a container even if there are no images present? Let's check! Issue the following command at a shell prompt to run an Ubuntu Linux container:

```
docker run -it ubuntu
```

This runs an Ubuntu Linux image. The flags tell Docker to run the container in *interactive* mode using standard input and allocate a *TTY*.[2] Or, more simply, "start a container and give me a prompt." The -it flags, or modifiers, are shortcuts for --interactive and --tty (and much faster to type).

Even though there was no image on the system, the command completed successfully. You should see something like this:

```
> docker run -it ubuntu
Unable to find image 'ubuntu:latest' locally
latest: Pulling from library/ubuntu
7b1a6ab2e44d: Pull complete
Digest: sha256:626ffe58f6e7566e00254b638eb7e0f3b11d4da9675088f4781a50
ae288f3322
Status: Downloaded newer image for ubuntu:latest
root@4a9ddd43e0e2:/#
```

Let's break down the output and see what Docker did:

- Docker couldn't find an Ubuntu image locally, as expected.

- Without a local source for the image, it "*pulled*" or downloaded an image (I'll address where it came from shortly).

- Docker reported the hash value of the image it pulled and its status.

- It displayed a prompt.

All of this took just a few moments.

---

[2] TTY means teletype and dates to the "old days" before monitors were common. If you wanted human-readable output, it was shown on a teletype, or printer!

The last line is a Linux prompt for the root user and the interactive TTY session we requested, showing the root user logged in to host 4a9ddd43e0e2 and the current directory.

Explore the Container

The command prompt looks like a login to a physical Linux host or virtual machine. Let's confirm this by running some commands to interrogate the environment:

```
whoami
id
echo $$
head -2 /etc/os-release
```

The output of whoami and id confirms we're the root user. The result of echo $$ (showing the process ID or PID of the current session) says we're PID 1. And finally, the contents of the os-release file show we're logged in to an Ubuntu host. Your output (apart from the hostname in the prompt and the Ubuntu version) should match this:

```
root@4a9ddd43e0e2:/# whoami
root
root@4a9ddd43e0e2:/# id
uid=0(root) gid=0(root) groups=0(root)
root@4a9ddd43e0e2:/# echo $$
1
root@4a9ddd43e0e2:/# head -2 /etc/os-release
NAME="Ubuntu"
VERSION="20.04.3 LTS (Focal Fossa)"
```

Leave this session open and start a new shell on your computer. Rerun the docker images command from earlier. The result now shows an Ubuntu image is present:

```
> docker images
REPOSITORY     TAG       IMAGE ID      CREATED       SIZE
ubuntu         latest    ba6acccedd29  4 weeks ago   72.8MB
```

This image is what Docker pulled so it could run the Ubuntu container requested earlier. Where did it come from?

Image Registries

The Ubuntu image isn't part of Docker Desktop. Docker requested it from the *Docker Hub*, a registry of images built and shared by the Docker community. The Docker Hub includes *Official Images* published by Docker, *Verified Images* produced and maintained by commercial third parties (including Oracle), and everything else.

As I write this, there are nearly 8.5 million publicly available images on Docker Hub, mostly added by individuals and companies. Official and Verified Images are scanned and tested for vulnerabilities. There are no guarantees other images are well written or even safe. How do we know the Ubuntu image we're using is any good?

When we executed `docker run`, we requested an Ubuntu image but didn't specify a repository. Docker pulled from its library of Official Images. I'll cover registries in more detail in Chapter 16. For now, it's enough to know that Docker didn't pull something at random!

You may also notice that the image tag or version shows the latest in both the output of `docker run` and `docker images`. This is shorthand for the most recent version and the default if you don't request a specific tag (when there is more than one) for an image. This usually isn't important—you often want the most recent version of Ubuntu or Oracle Enterprise Linux 7 to guarantee the latest updates and bug fixes are present. You want to specify the version for applications where dependencies and versions are relevant. For example, to get a particular build of Node.js, you might call `docker run node:16` or `docker run node:17.1.0`, where the image tag follows a colon.

Minimalism

The information for the Ubuntu image from Listing 3-5 shows the image is a mere 72.8MB. That seems tiny, considering the ISO download from `www.ubuntu.com` is 1.2GB. The Docker image of Ubuntu is less than 6% the size of its installed counterpart. Why?

Images (typically) contain only what's *absolutely necessary* to perform their function. Reducing image footprint by excluding what's *not* needed has a slew of benefits:

- Less to transfer across networks.

- Effectively increases infrastructure capacity.

- Smaller images have smaller attack surfaces.

- Fewer dependencies reduce the potential for bugs and vulnerabilities.

Editors are among the things commonly excluded from images. Containers usually run autonomously, with lifetimes measured in hours or minutes. It's rare (even discouraged) to log in to containers in production environments. Editors simply aren't necessary and create security risks.

Return to the container prompt you used before and try running vi test.txt to edit a new file. It can't find the command. vi and nano aren't installed:

```
root@4a9ddd43e0e2:/# vi /etc/os-release
bash: vi: command not found
root@4a9ddd43e0e2:/# nano test.txt
bash: nano: command not found
```

There are other indications the Ubuntu image was trimmed down and not intended to be interactive. Try running man ls to display a *manpage*, Linux's built-in documentation. The OS responds with a message reminding us that this is not a complete OS:

```
root@ebb592e975f0:/# man ls
This system has been minimized by removing packages and content that are
not required on a system that users do not log into.

To restore this content, including manpages, you can run the 'unminimize'
command. You will still need to ensure the 'man-db' package is installed.
```

Modify the Container

Containers are stripped-down, functional systems for performing a narrow set of tasks, not running interactive environments. The base images Docker and other publishers provide are trimmed-down versions without the extra bells and whistles we're used to finding in physical and virtual systems.

Some publishers offer "slim" variants for common distributions. While there isn't a standard defining what is or isn't part of the nonslim variants, "slim" usually has the minimum required for a working system. In contrast, the nonslim versions may include additional standard or convenient functionality.

In Chapter 12, we'll see that container images for Oracle databases are built from "slim" versions of Oracle Enterprise Linux.

Nothing prevents us from updating the container OS to add functionality. Let's do that by running commands to add vi (or nano, if you prefer) to your container. Listing 3-1 shows the commands for installing vim-tiny, a distribution that doesn't require Python support.

Listing 3-1. Commands for installing the vim-tiny package on Ubuntu

```
apt-get update
apt-get install -y vim-tiny
```

Note that you need to run apt-get update to update the repository to include vim. Without the update, apt-get doesn't know the package exists!

Try creating the file using vi test.txt once again. This time, it works! You successfully modified the container to add features absent from the original image. Add some content to the file and save it—you'll use it again in the next section!

Persistence

Over the years I've talked and taught about Oracle and Docker, the most enduring (or persistent, pardon the pun!) misconceptions are *containers don't persist data* and *don't reliably save their contents*—particularly across restarts. Let's test this! Exit your Ubuntu container by typing exit at the prompt, just as you would if you'd logged in or connected to a host over SSH.

Check the Container State

We started the container using docker run and the -it option. It created an *interactive* container, tying its state to the session. Logging out of the container stopped it. We can see containers present on a system and their status using the docker ps command. At first, ps may not seem intuitive, but Unix and Linux users should recognize this as a command for reporting running processes on a system.

Recall that containers are just processes, and it begins to make sense. Type docker ps -a in your shell and examine the results:

```
> docker ps -a
CONTAINER ID IMAGE    COMMAND CREATED      STATUS
PORTS          NAMES
4a9ddd43e0e2 ubuntu   "bash"  2 hours ago Exited (0) 17 seconds ago
fervent_mendeleev
```

The -a flag is shorthand for --all and displays all processes (or containers) on the system, whether active or stopped. Without this option, docker ps reports only the running containers. A few other things to note in the output:

- The CONTAINER ID is a random string and matches the hostname we saw in the container's shell prompt.

- The COMMAND, bash, is the shell we used when the container started. A container's default command is defined in its *Dockerfile* and covered in Chapters 12 and 13.

- The STATUS shows the container exited normally, with an error code 0. (Anything other than 0 is technically an exception, though not always serious.)

- The randomly generated NAME, meant to be human-friendly, is customizable. I'll cover that shortly.

To confirm the container is stopped, run docker ps, without the -a option, to see only the active containers.

Start the Container

To start the container, type docker start, followed by either the NAME or CONTAINER ID from your system, then check the status by repeating the docker ps -a command:

```
> docker start fervent_mendeleev
fervent_mendeleev
> docker ps -a
CONTAINER ID    IMAGE    COMMAND    CREATED      STATUS
PORTS          NAMES
```

```
4a9ddd43e0e2   ubuntu   "bash"   2 hours ago  Up 3 seconds
fervent_mendeleev
```

Interactive vs. Detached

Notice you didn't reconnect to the container this time. When started this way, the container process runs as a *detached*, or background, process. Detached containers don't stop when users log out because their state isn't tied to an interactive session.

To run a container in detached mode at the outset, replace the -it options in docker run with -d or --detach.

Connect to the Container

Now that the container is active, reconnect to the prompt. There are different ways of doing this: *attaching* or *executing a command*.

- **Attaching** accesses a container's running process via the docker attach <CONTAINER NAME> command. In our case, that command is bash, as shown by the COMMAND column of docker ps. Only one session can attach at any given time. Running a container in interactive mode, as you did earlier, attaches to the container.

- **Executing** a command is akin to logging in to a remote host via ssh. Running docker exec <CONTAINER NAME> <COMMAND> allows you to specify a command or script. The execute command can run interactively or in the background and set the user, working directory, and environment. Multiple sessions can connect simultaneously with docker exec.

I've rarely needed docker attach when working with Docker and Oracle. I use docker exec almost exclusively in practice and in this book.

Connect to your container by running docker exec with the same -it options used when you first ran the container. Follow this with the container name and the command we want to run, bash, to start a shell:

```
> docker exec -it fervent_mendeleev bash
root@4a9ddd43e0e2:/#
```

Verify Persistence

Once you've reconnected to the container, list the contents of the directory where you created the file test.txt. The file is still there, and its contents are preserved, even after restarting the container.

Changes to the filesystem aren't the only thing that persisted in Docker. Session state survives, too. Use the keyboard up arrow from your container prompt to scroll the command history. Commands issued before stopping the container appear.

Remove the Container

Microservice architectures create containers to perform some work, then destroy them (more on this later). The container you created served its purpose: you learned how to run and modify a container, check its state, start and stop it, and connect. Now, we'll remove it.

Exit from the container prompt by typing exit as before. Remove the container by running docker rm -f <CONTAINER NAME> at your host prompt, substituting the name of the container on your system:

```
> docker rm -f fervent_mendeleev
fervent_mendeleev
```

The -f flag forces Docker to remove running containers. Without this option, you must stop the container before removing it.

Images Are Immutable

You modified the container by installing vi and adding a file, but it didn't change the image. Images are *immutable* and can't be changed. Every image has a digest or hash value, acting as a signature that guarantees the image contents. Every container started from a given image is identical. This is a desirable property, a foundation of operational reliability and repeatability, and something we'll use to our advantage in later chapters.

It does raise an obvious question, though. If you can't change an image, how can such a variety of images be present in Docker Hub? Saying images are immutable isn't the whole story. Images can't be changed, but the changes made in a container can be *saved as new images*. Building images is just a series of operations that start an image, run commands to modify the running container, and save the results as a new image.

Start a New Container

To demonstrate, start a new Ubuntu container, this time assigning a name with the --name option rather than letting Docker generate a "friendly" name:

```
> docker run -it --name my_container ubuntu
root@cadf21663737:/#
```

Notice how quickly this completed! There were no additional messages like those you saw the first time you ran an Ubuntu container. Docker didn't need to pull the image because it's already present on the system. It only needed to start a new Linux process on the local host—remember, with Docker, there's no initialization or boot cycle!

Save a New Image

The Ubuntu image we're using doesn't include the vi command. But what if we want an Ubuntu image that does? Installing vi on every new Ubuntu container isn't a practical solution. Instead, let's create a new image to include vi.

Install vi (or nano) in the new container, using the commands from Listing 3-1. Exit the container, and at the host command prompt, save the container as a new image using the docker commit command. You'll need to provide the name of the container you want to save and the name of the new image:

```
> docker commit my_container ubuntu_editor
sha256:be90b42f8ef0c5b8e343c7fd5d7aaa5d99f1e7e65dfac9020c4f362dade0410f
```

Docker responds with the hash value of the new image. Rerun docker images to confirm it created a new image, following the code in Listing 3-2.

Listing 3-2. Commit the modified container to a new image

```
> docker images
REPOSITORY        TAG       IMAGE ID        CREATED          SIZE
ubuntu_editor     latest    be90b42f8ef0    3 seconds ago    107MB
ubuntu            latest    ba6acccedd29    4 weeks ago      72.8MB
```

The new image, ubuntu_editor, is now available.

Notice the new image size compared to the original. Is vi that big? No! This is a by-product of how images and *layers* work, discussed later in this chapter.

Run the New Image

Start another container using this new image, using docker run -it ubuntu_editor, and confirm vi is present, as shown in Listing 3-3.

Listing 3-3. Create a container from the newly committed image and verify vi is present

```
> docker run -it ubuntu_editor
root@d3f700a3aae2:/# which vi
/usr/bin/vi
```

Union Filesystems

Listing 3-2 showed two images. The original Ubuntu image is 72.8MB. The modified version, with vi installed, is 107MB. Installing a simple editor increased the size by over 45%. Why?

Docker is very efficient, leveraging operating system features to improve speed and reduce footprint. One of these features, *union filesystems* (sometimes called *overlay filesystems*), "deduplicates" the contents of containers.

Logically, a system running five containers starting from a single 200MB image should use 1000MB—200MB per container. With union filesystems, the actual storage requirement is unrelated to the number of containers. In this example, it could be as little as 200MB, whether the host is running ten containers or a thousand.

Images provide all the files and dependencies the container needs, but they aren't copied from the image. *Containers are the image.*

How can containers use images in their filesystems if images can't be changed?

When starting a new container, Docker creates a union filesystem consisting of multiple layers: *lower*, *upper*, and *working*.

- **Lower layer:** Docker maps images to the lower layer. Every container sharing an image references the same immutable set of files in its lower layer.

- **Upper layer:** Docker creates a unique upper layer for each container. Creating and editing files adds them to the container's upper layer without altering the original copy in the lower layer.

- **Working layer:** The working layer is the union (hence the name) of the lower and upper layers. It merges unchanged files from the lower layer with new and modified files saved in the upper layer. Union filesystems handle deleted files as a particular file type, telling the working layer to block them from view.

To visualize this, imagine an image for playing out Tic-Tac-Toe game scenarios, shown in Figure 3-1. The image—the lower layer—holds the game board and the first few moves of the game. The starting moves are part of the image and appear on the game board whenever a container starts. Think of the upper layer as a transparent sheet where players mark their moves. The working layer is the view players see as if they were looking down, with the transparent upper layer superimposed onto the image beneath it. The working layer shows the complete game board—the merger of lower and upper layers.

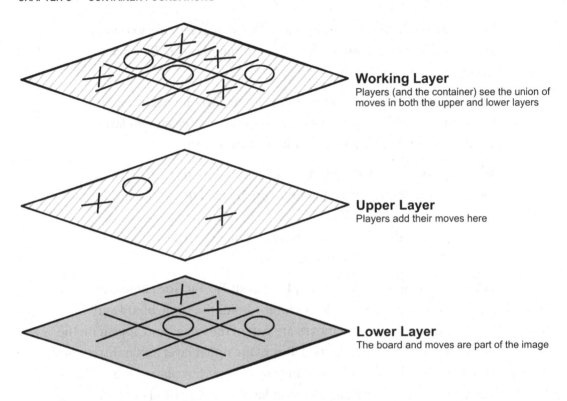

Figure 3-1. *The Tic-Tac-Toe moves in the lower layer are part of the image and are present at the start of every container. Moves added in the running container exist only in the upper layer. Players "looking down" from the perspective of the working layer see all the moves*

Figure 3-2 shows how this applies to a filesystem. Once again, the image supplies the lower layer with prepopulated files. Containers get their own upper layers, where they save local changes. Processes running in containers read the merged result from the working layer.

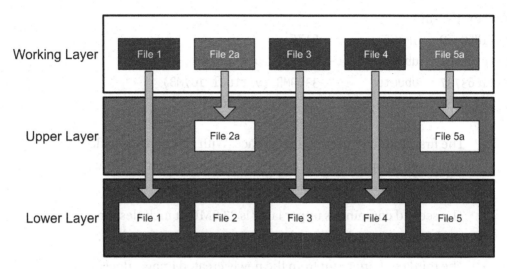

Figure 3-2. *Layers in a union filesystem*

In the working layer of Figure 3-2, the changed versions of files 2 and 5 overlay, or block, their original versions. Files 1, 3, and 4 are unobstructed and "visible" through the upper layer.

Under normal circumstances, most of the image—the binaries, libraries, and executables—are static and won't have copies in the container's upper layer.[3] The fewer the changes made in the container, the smaller its upper layer.

When you removed the Ubuntu container earlier, Docker deleted the upper layer of the union filesystem assigned to the container.[4] Changes made in the container were lost, but nothing happened to the underlying image.

Dozens or hundreds of containers started from the same image share a lower layer, leading to dramatic improvements in efficiency and cost-effectiveness at scale compared to their physical or virtual machine counterparts. We can see this by running the docker ps command with the -s or --size option. The following abridged output reports the real and virtual sizes of these containers:[5]

---

[3] Significant changes to a container's filesystem can lead to increased space use in overlay filesystems. See Chapter 12 for more details.

[4] Chapter 7 describes techniques for storing data beyond the container's union filesystem. Saving data outside the container decouples it from the container lifecycle, allowing databases in containers access to dedicated, high-performance storage.

[5] Source images are updated regularly, causing the sizes you'll see in this example to vary.

47

```
> docker ps -as
CONTAINER ID    IMAGE           SIZE
a5bf2c163d07    ubuntu          0B (virtual 72.8MB)
cadf21663737    ubuntu          33.9MB (virtual 107MB)
d3f700a3aae2    ubuntu_editor   0B (virtual 107MB)
```

- The first container uses no extra space. With no changes made in the container, its upper layer is empty, and the container's virtual size, 72.8MB, matches that of the original Ubuntu image.

- The second container's upper layer is 33.9MB. It includes the modifications needed to update the filesystem and install vi.

- The third container, run from the newly created image, doesn't include any changes to its environment. Like the first, the upper layer of this container is empty.

Commit vs. Build

That explains why the committed image is larger, but not the magnitude of the difference. That's a product of how much the container's layer changed when apt-get update and apt-get install ran. Those commands retrieved package lists, decompressed archives, and made incremental changes to files present in the lower layer. Every operation wrote something to the container's upper layer.

There is another way to create images. A *dockerfile* is a set of instructions for building images from scratch. docker commit is a convenient, albeit brute-force, method. Building images from scratch affords greater control and produces smaller, more efficient images.

Listing 3-4 shows a Dockerfile that creates an Ubuntu image with vi "baked in." Listing 3-5 shows the command for building an image using this file, followed by the operation's results.

Listing 3-4. A Dockerfile for creating a vi-enabled Ubuntu image

```
FROM ubuntu:latest AS base
RUN apt-get update \
 && apt-get install -y vim-tiny \
```

```
  && apt-get clean \
  && rm -rf /var/lib/apt/lists/*
CMD bash
```

Listing 3-5. The image build and results

```
> docker build --tag ubuntu_vi .
[+] Building 7.1s (6/6) FINISHED
 => [internal] load build definition from Dockerfile
 => => transferring dockerfile: 179B
 => [internal] load .dockerignore
 => => transferring context: 2B
 => [internal] load metadata for docker.io/library/ubuntu:latest
 => [1/2] FROM docker.io/library/ubuntu:latest
 => [2/2] RUN apt-get update && apt-get install -y vim-tiny && apt-get
clean && rm -rf /var/lib/apt/lists/*
 => exporting to image
 => => exporting layers
 => => writing image sha256:03545fa76800a4ed39a11c9e25aa184d1a60a2b1
cb889730961d47d8c8dde554
 => => naming to docker.io/library/ubuntu_vi
```

Don't worry about the syntax for now—we'll cover this in depth in Chapters 12 through 14. But note the difference in the size of the new image built from the Dockerfile:

```
> docker images
REPOSITORY        TAG        IMAGE ID        CREATED          SIZE
ubuntu_vi         latest     03545fa76800    15 seconds ago   75.1MB
ubuntu            latest     ba6acccedd29    4 weeks ago      72.8MB
```

The version built from scratch is only 2.3MB larger. A far more reasonable difference!

Summary

When I talk to people about running Oracle in Docker, I begin by demonstrating speed. It's a compelling opening argument and sets containers apart from competing technologies. Conversations with DBAs understandably turn to concerns about persistence and reliability. People hear containers are ephemeral and think the worst, dismissing the technology without taking time to understand. I'm not immune—these misunderstandings clouded my first experiences with Docker.

Containers' ephemeral labeling originates from their *typical* use cases, which have short lifespans. However, what counts as "short" is relative; when you think about it, everything is temporary! Nothing prevents long-lived applications, including databases, from running in containers.

You discovered additional distinctions between containers and their physical and VM counterparts in this chapter. Most of these differences originate in the different use cases. Physical and virtual hosts fill broad, multipurpose roles requiring various features and libraries. Their operating systems are often larger, and the extra features increase potential vulnerabilities. Containers are slimmer systems, purpose-driven to specific tasks, with filesystems that include only what's essential. Their smaller footprints are well suited for sharing across networks, as witnessed when creating your first container!

You should also be comfortable using Docker's command interface to run basic commands to report the images and containers present on your system and create, remove, stop, and start containers. You connected to a running container and updated the environment, adding an editor.

The foundation of Docker's speed and efficiency is how it uses union filesystems. Layers isolate the original image used for starting containers from the changes made over their lifecycle. Layers implement persistence for containers running on a system and contribute to the scalability of container infrastructure, all while appearing to defy common-sense mathematics! You'll see layers return in the second part of this book, in the chapters covering Dockerfiles, images, and builds. A deep understanding of layers isn't necessary to appreciate these topics, but it is an area I regret not learning sooner in my Docker journey.

Now that you're familiar with Docker's syntax and workflow, you're ready to begin working with database containers. We'll do that in the next chapter, with a quick-start tutorial covering the steps for running your first Oracle database in a container! Let's go!

CHAPTER 4

Oracle Database Quick Start

Whenever I give webinars and presentations about running Oracle on Docker, the top request from attendees is a set of step-by-step instructions to get a database up and running in a container. This chapter is a stand-alone collection of recipes for building images and running database containers.

Just as a pizza cookbook might offer instructions for making dough without describing how yeast makes dough rise, this chapter focuses on "how-to" and less on the "why" or "how." It covers downloading and building images, creating a basic container database, allowing client connections from applications outside the container (like SQL Developer), accessing a shell, and persisting data on the host. First, we must prepare our system and understand a few basic terms.

Access the Docker Environment

Continuing with the cooking theme, Docker Desktop is the kitchen where we prepare images and containers. Docker Desktop is available as a free download from www.docker.com. Appendix A covers setup and configuration.

Terminology

Getting a database up and running in Docker requires understanding some of the language used in the Docker environment. If you've jumped ahead to this chapter and aren't familiar with what *images*, *containers*, and *builds* are, how to access a command line on your system, or running basic Docker commands, spend a few moments

© Sean Scott 2023
S. Scott, *Oracle on Docker*, https://doi.org/10.1007/978-1-4842-9033-0_4

reviewing this section. If you're already comfortable with these concepts, feel free to skip to the next section, *"Obtaining an Image."*

Docker Commands

Docker commands begin with `docker` and a verb like `run`, `build`, `exec`, or `attach`, followed by flags, objects, and options. There are a handful of commands used in this tutorial. You'll likely use these commands most as you work with Docker. Years into my container journey, most of what I do still centers on these commands:

- **docker images:** Displays images available on the system, including their name, image ID, source, size, and age.

- **docker ps:** Lists running containers, name, status, source image, and age. Containers are processes on a system, and both Linux and Docker use `ps` to list processes. Adding the `-a` flag shows all containers, running and stopped.

- **docker run:** Creates a container from an image.

- **docker start:** Starts a running container.

- **docker stop:** Stops a container.

- **docker logs:** Displays log output from a container. For the Oracle database images we'll work with, it shows the output of startup operations, including starting the listener, the database, and the Database Configuration Assistant when the container runs the first time. Afterward, it displays output from the database alert log.

- **docker exec:** Executes commands in the container.

These are explained more fully elsewhere in this book.

Images and Containers

An *image* contains all the files needed to run an application or service. An Oracle database image includes its filesystem, operating system libraries and executables, prerequisite packages, settings, binaries, and configuration files.

Containers are processes started on a host from an image. Many containers can be started using the same image, and each container can perform work and make changes to its initial state independently of other containers. Containers can be stopped and started, and their contents persist across restarts.

Build and Run

Images are *built* using a set of instructions called a *Dockerfile*. Dockerfiles are the recipes Docker uses to collect ingredients (including files and other images) and prepare them into a final image. Containers *run* from an image.

It's not critical to understand the details of either process for this quick start. Still, it's important to recognize the relationships between the actions and objects since you will build an image and run a container as part of this tutorial.

The Docker Command Line

Most interactions with Docker Desktop occur through a command line. Windows users should use Windows Terminal.[1] In Mac and Linux environments, open a native terminal application.

Obtaining an Image

Before running a database container, we need an image. Like baking a pizza, there are a few options available for Oracle database images, including

- **Pre-built images:** This is the frozen pizza option. In a pre-built image, all the preparation is done for you. You only have to bake (or microwave) it and enjoy the results! In the container world, "baking"

---

[1] Windows command prompt and PowerShell may or may not work for some examples given here. Variations in the environment settings on individual machines, and the way they interpret certain environment variables, can lead to unexpected output and behavior. The same is true for third-party applications like PuTTY, Cygwin, and MobaXterm.

Windows and Docker both recommend running Docker on Windows using the Windows Subsystem for Linux, version 2. Appendix A includes instructions for installing and configuring WSL 2 and setting up an Ubuntu virtual environment, where you'll access Docker on the command line. It also has information on downloading Windows Terminal, a shell environment integrated with WSL.

the image is running a container. Pre-built images may not be exactly what you want. Configurations meet popular or general needs, and only one company makes pre-built images—Oracle.[2] Oracle's pre-built images include the database software, and users must accept a license agreement to download them.

- **Build from a repository:** If you want more control over images, consider a *repository*. A repository is a collection of scripts for building images. This is comparable to assembling a pizza from a ready-made crust, a jar of sauce, and ingredients you provide— including the Oracle database software and license. Oracle maintains an excellent repository for building a wide array of products beyond just the database. Since repositories don't include licensed software, organizations and community members can create and share repositories. Building from a repository is a bit more time-consuming but isn't difficult, much less so than creating images from scratch.

- **Build from a custom Dockerfile or repository:** Complete control and flexibility come from custom Dockerfiles or repositories. This is the pizza-making equivalent of preparing the sauce and hand-kneading dough from scratch. Writing custom Dockerfiles is covered in Chapter 13.

- **Database as a Service:** Cloud vendors may offer options for databases as a service or DBaaS. DBaaS is like ordering at a restaurant where the cloud vendor does the work and customers consume the results.

Let's begin with the most straightforward option: working from a pre-built image.

Pre-built Images

Pre-built images are the easiest way to get up and running. They're also the most limited regarding version and edition availability. Oracle maintains these images on their own

---

[2] There are pre-built Oracle database images available on the Web from sources other than Oracle. Distributing images that include Oracle database software is a violation of Oracle's licensing.

Oracle Container Registry site at `https://container-registry.oracle.com`.[3] They are not updated frequently, and you may encounter limited functionality.

As of this writing, the available options are

- Version 19.3.0.0 Enterprise Edition, Standard Edition

- Version 12.2.0.1 Enterprise Edition, Standard Edition 2 (SE2)

- Version 12.1.0.2 Enterprise Edition

If one of these options meets your needs, go to container-registry.oracle.com and navigate to the Database repository. Figure 4-1 shows the Oracle Container Registry and the Database repository where the pre-built database images reside.

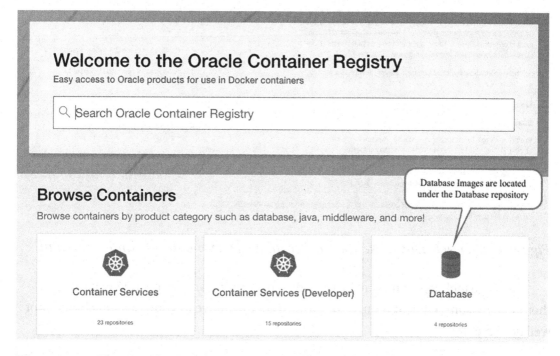

Figure 4-1. *The Oracle Container Registry and Database repository*

---

[3] There is a verified image from Oracle on the Docker Hub, hub.docker.com, but it hasn't been updated since 2017. It's for Enterprise Edition version 12.2.0.1. Images from unverified or unofficial sources that contain Oracle database software (on Docker Hub and elsewhere) likely violate Oracle licensing. They are also security risks; running an image from an unknown and unverified author is like opening an email attachment from an unknown sender!

There are separate Database repositories for Enterprise and Standard Editions (as well as Oracle Instant Client and RAC). Choose an edition to move on to the documentation and download page. For this example, I selected Enterprise Edition. Figure 4-2 shows the Oracle 19c Docker Image Documentation.

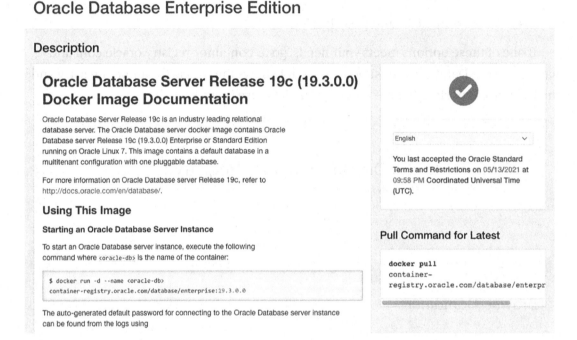

Database Repositories \

Oracle Database Enterprise Edition

Description

Oracle Database Server Release 19c (19.3.0.0) Docker Image Documentation

Oracle Database Server Release 19c is an industry leading relational database server. The Oracle Database server docker image contains Oracle Database server Release 19c (19.3.0.0) Enterprise or Standard Edition running on Oracle Linux 7. This image contains a default database in a multitenant configuration with one pluggable database.

For more information on Oracle Database server Release 19c, refer to http://docs.oracle.com/en/database/.

Using This Image

Starting an Oracle Database Server Instance

To start an Oracle Database server instance, execute the following command where <oracle-db> is the name of the container:

```
$ docker run -d --name <oracle-db>
container-registry.oracle.com/database/enterprise:19.3.0.0
```

The auto-generated default password for connecting to the Oracle Database server instance can be found from the logs using

English

You last accepted the Oracle Standard Terms and Restrictions on 05/13/2021 at 09:58 PM Coordinated Universal Time (UTC).

Pull Command for Latest

```
docker pull
container-
registry.oracle.com/database/enterpr
```

Figure 4-2. *Oracle Database 19c Docker Image Documentation and download*

This page includes complete instructions for running and using the image, and there's no reason to repeat them here. How to get the image to your local machine is not well documented!

Download an Image

First, log in to the site using your My Oracle Support (MOS) Single Sign-On (SSO) credentials and accept the license agreement. You should see a message in the upper right of Figure 4-2 indicating that you've accepted the license.

In Docker, downloading an image is done with the `pull` command, and the right sidebar has a promising element, "Pull Command for Latest." Unfortunately, copying/pasting produces an authentication error:

```
unauthorized: authentication required
```

We haven't authenticated to Oracle's repository. Log in with the following command:

```
docker login container-registry.oracle.com
```

Docker will ask for a username and password; these are your Oracle SSO credentials. Copy the `docker pull` command from the registry page and paste it into your shell. Docker will download the image's layers to your system. Listing 4-1 shows the abbreviated output from the `pull` command.

Listing 4-1. Running docker pull for a 19c Enterprise Edition image

```
> docker pull container-registry.oracle.com/database/enterprise:19.3.0.0
19.3.0.0: Pulling from database/enterprise
86607bb85307: Pull complete
...
5c2969cb34b8: Pull complete
Digest: sha256:ea9cd805ec49368fd288323e3f41d6c6e45698813e2ae89fd5d09
7c026ab5aa6
Status: Downloaded newer image for container-registry.oracle.com/database/
enterprise:19.3.0.0
container-registry.oracle.com/database/enterprise:19.3.0.0
```

That's it! You've successfully downloaded a Docker image to your host! Check the images on your system with the `docker images` command. You will see something similar to the output in Listing 4-2.

Listing 4-2. Running docker images after pulling the 19c Enterprise Edition image

```
> docker images
REPOSITORY                                            TAG
   IMAGE ID           CREATED           SIZE
container-registry.oracle.com/database/enterprise     19.3.0.0
   6ee1b2e4403f       6 months ago      7.87GB
```

The Repository column reflects the origin of the image. The *tag* is its version.

Download a Tag

Earlier, I listed that three versions were available for Enterprise Edition. Where are the others? Figure 4-3 shows the bottom of the Enterprise Edition repository page, where the tags from this repository are listed.

Tags

Tag	Size	Pull Command	Last Updated	Image ID
19.3.0.0	3 GB	docker pull container-registry.oracle.com/database/enterprise:19.3.0.0	6 months ago	6ee1b2e4403f414fd811a90fd7da8a96043200a3311ec1dff685095b64b88aff
latest	3 GB	docker pull container-registry.oracle.com/database/enterprise:latest	6 months ago	6ee1b2e4403f414fd811a90fd7da8a96043200a3311ec1dff685095b64b88aff
12.2.0.1	3 GB	docker pull container-registry.oracle.com/database/enterprise:12.2.0.1	3.8 years ago	12a359cd052828523d9e7479673c26c4c9c23cc628d7a4e7210ea7deae4994d7
12.2.0.1-slim	1 GB	docker pull container-registry.oracle.com/database/enterprise:12.2.0.1-slim	3.8 years ago	27c9559d36ec85fdaa42111ebc55076a63e842ddbe67e0849cdc59b4f6a6f7a1
12.1.0.2	5 GB	docker pull container-registry.oracle.com/database/enterprise:12.1.0.2	3.9 years ago	db889cfe1e903e8451353f518418878bcce8a5d2cf4eeab8e5310233133bda73

Figure 4-3. Tag listing for all versions available in the Enterprise Edition repository

Each tag represents a different version and has separate `docker pull` commands.

Notice there are two tags for version 12.2.0.1. The second, with the "`-slim`" suffix, is trimmed down to minimum capabilities. This is common for container images. Reducing the image to the bare minimum saves space and reduces the attack surface of containers—you can't attack software and features that aren't present. If you only need basic functionality, tags marked `-slim` are worth considering.

One final thing to pay attention to is the size. Figure 4-3 suggests the image 19.3.0.0 tag is 3GB, but that's the compressed download size. Listing 4-2 reports the proper size of the 19c image, 7.87GB.

Running Pre-built Images

Once complete, follow the directions on the documentation page or skip ahead to the section "*Running a Container*." The images in this registry use the same scripts discussed in the next section, and the same functionality *should* work. The container registry images are not updated frequently. Oracle's Docker repository is updated continuously with new features and capabilities. While unlikely, there is a possibility that images built from the current script repository will behave differently.

Pre-built Image Limitations

The images from Oracle's Container Registry offer convenience but sacrifice variety and functionality. With a frozen pizza, you can't change the toppings. With pre-built images, you can't change certain functionality built into the image. To illustrate why pre-built images might not satisfy your cravings, let's look at two limitations: editors and multitenancy.

Running Oracle in Docker on a desktop or laptop system is convenient. It's handy to have a "throwaway" database available for developing, testing, and experimenting on, and for most, that includes being able to view and edit files.

Users may be surprised that Oracle's database images do not contain a text editor, and the only file viewer included is more. This is by design—remember that containers typically run services, not interactive sessions, and don't need editors or file viewers. Leaving out unnecessary software makes containers smaller and reduces their attack surface.

Editors (and other utilities) were left out of the image when it was built. We can't change the image; manually installing the additional software is the only option. It's not difficult to do and isn't time-consuming to update the container until you find yourself doing it every time you run a new container! One reason for adopting containers is their ability to deliver self-contained environments that already include dependencies. Manually updating every container runs contrary to that purpose.

While you may not consider adding an editor as a compelling reason to build your own images, the type of database created in the container might.

When an Oracle database container starts, it checks to see if it already has a database. If not, it runs the *Database Configuration Assistant* (*DBCA*) and creates a new *container database*[4] (*CDB*) with a single *pluggable database* (*PDB*). CDB and PDB are still not widely adopted, and for those that want a traditional, non-CDB database, the alternative is to drop the database created by DBCA and create one by hand.

---

[4] Don't confuse Oracle's container database (CDB) with Linux containers. Container and pluggable databases are part of Oracle Multitenant, not Docker.

However, building an image from scripts makes it possible to amend Docker's instructions to include an editor, edit the response file for creating databases, and more. You may find this added control worth the extra minutes it takes to build your own images.

Building Images from a Repository

The authors of Oracle's script repository made building images using its script repository easy. A wrapper script handles the heavy lifting. Users only need to download the repository, place the Oracle database installation file in a directory, and run the script.

The repository has scripts for building images for versions:

- Oracle 11.2.0.2 Express Edition

- Oracle 12.1.0.2 Enterprise Edition, Standard Edition 2

- Oracle 12.2.0.1 Enterprise Edition, Standard Edition 2

- Oracle 18.3.0 Enterprise Edition, Standard Edition 2

- Oracle 18.4.0 Express Edition

- Oracle 19.3.0 Enterprise Edition, Standard Edition 2

The following examples use Oracle 19c. The steps are similar to other versions.

Oracle Docker GitHub Repo

GitHub is a popular version control, management, and distribution platform for code based on git. Oracle maintains an official repository of scripts on GitHub for building container images at github.com/oracle/docker-images. In addition to database images, you'll find directories here for many other Oracle products, from Instant Client to GoldenGate to REST Data Services. We need these files on the local machine where Docker Desktop is running. There are two ways to do this: direct download or using git. Figure 4-4 shows the dialog window after clicking the *Code* button.

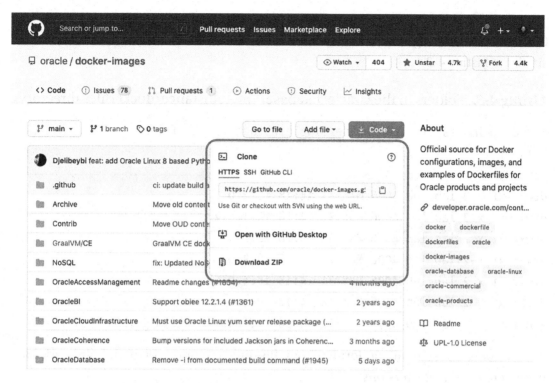

Figure 4-4. *GitHub options for cloning and downloading the repository*

Details for cloning or downloading the repository through git or *GitHub Desktop* are out of scope for this book. If you're using git, these should be familiar.

For readers who aren't comfortable with git or don't want to maintain these files in a repository, click the *Download ZIP* option at the bottom of the dialog. When the download completes, unzip the file on the local machine.

Tip   The paths beneath each subdirectory in the repository can be long. The repository scripts can be anywhere on your computer, but I prefer to keep the path short and place them in a directory near the root. Most examples in this book use $HOME/docker-images or $HOME/docker. As you work with containers, you may find yourself navigating to the repository often and appreciate the keystrokes saved by planning ahead!

Take a moment to navigate into a folder under the database subdirectory, OracleDatabase/SingleInstance/dockerfiles, then list the contents. You'll see a result similar to Listing 4-3.

Listing 4-3. Folders in the OracleDatabase/SingleInstance/dockerfiles directory

```
~/docker-images/OracleDatabase/SingleInstance/dockerfiles
> ls -l
total 32
drwxrwxr-x 2 lab lab 4096 Mar 31 14:18 11.2.0.2
drwxrwxr-x 2 lab lab 4096 Mar 31 14:18 12.1.0.2
drwxrwxr-x 2 lab lab 4096 Mar 31 14:18 12.2.0.1
drwxrwxr-x 2 lab lab 4096 Mar 31 14:18 18.3.0
drwxrwxr-x 2 lab lab 4096 Mar 31 14:18 18.4.0
drwxrwxr-x 2 lab lab 4096 Mar 31 14:18 19.3.0
-rwxrwxr-x 1 lab lab 6575 Mar 31 14:18 buildContainerImage.sh
```

The following steps are performed from this directory or one of the subdirectories for the different database versions.

Oracle Database Software

For Docker to install the Oracle database in the image, it needs the database software installation file. For Oracle 19c, the file is available from www.oracle.com/database/technologies/oracle-database-software-downloads.html. Other versions[5] are available from My Oracle Support, support.oracle.com, or the Oracle Software Delivery Cloud, edelivery.oracle.com.

Whichever version you choose, *be sure to download the installer for Linux x86-64.* The host operating system doesn't matter—whether running on Windows or Mac, Docker Desktop uses a Linux VM and the containers run in Linux. Be sure to download the ZIP file and not the RPM, if present. Figure 4-5 shows the relevant section of the download page highlighting the operating system and download to select Oracle Database 19c.

---

[5] The exception is Oracle 18.4.0 Express Edition, which downloads the RPM installation file automatically when building the image. There is no need to download it separately.

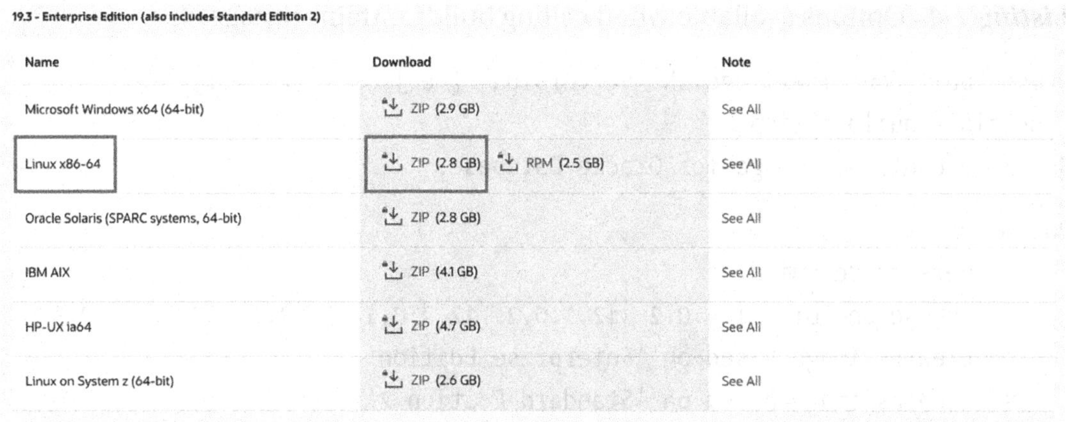

19.3 - Enterprise Edition (also includes Standard Edition 2)

Name	Download		Note
Microsoft Windows x64 (64-bit)	⬇ ZIP (2.9 GB)		See All
Linux x86-64	⬇ ZIP (2.8 GB)	⬇ RPM (2.5 GB)	See All
Oracle Solaris (SPARC systems, 64-bit)	⬇ ZIP (2.8 GB)		See All
IBM AIX	⬇ ZIP (4.1 GB)		See All
HP-UX ia64	⬇ ZIP (4.7 GB)		See All
Linux on System z (64-bit)	⬇ ZIP (2.6 GB)		See All

Figure 4-5. *Oracle 19c Database installer ZIP file download for Linux x86-64*

Download or copy the file into the subdirectory in the repository that matches the database version. For Oracle Database 19.3.0, the installation needs to be copied into OracleDatabase/SingleInstance/dockerfiles/19.3.0.[6]

Note   Do not unzip the installation file! Docker's build process looks for the ZIP file and copies it into its *build context*. Builds run intermediate containers to do work, including unzipping the installation file.

We're ready to build a database image with the repository and installation file in place!

Build an Image

The buildContainerImage.sh[7] script in the OracleDatabase/SingleInstance/ dockerfiles directory handles the heavy lifting and accepts parameters, as shown in Listing 4-4.

---

[6]The installer file must be physically present in the directory for Docker to include in the image. Docker does not recognize linked files.

[7]In older versions, the script was called buildDockerImage.sh.

Listing 4-4. Options available when calling buildContainerImage.sh

```
Usage: buildContainerImage.sh -v [version] [-e | -s | -x] [-i] [-o]
[container build option]
Builds a container image for Oracle Database.

Parameters:
    -v: version to build
        Choose one of: 11.2.0.2  12.1.0.2  12.2.0.1  18.3.0  18.4.0  19.3.0
    -e: creates image based on 'Enterprise Edition'
    -s: creates image based on 'Standard Edition 2'
    -x: creates image based on 'Express Edition'
    -i: ignores the MD5 checksums
    -o: passes on container build option

* select one edition only: -e, -s, or -x
```

For now, we need only be concerned with those for version and edition. For this example, I'll build an image for a 19c Enterprise Edition database by calling the script with the -e flag and passing 19.3.0 to the version flag, -v:

```
./buildContainerImage.sh -e -v 19.3.0
```

This starts the build process and usually takes 8–15 minutes on most laptops. Docker displays the output of each step, and you may spot some familiar messages as it updates the filesystem with prerequisites and installs Oracle software. You should see a message indicating the image name, tag, and total build time when it completes. Run docker images and verify your output appears similar to the following:

```
> docker images
REPOSITORY        TAG         IMAGE ID       CREATED       SIZE
oracle/database   19.3.0-ee   c0d1669287ad   2 hours ago   6.68GB
```

We now have an image to use for running database containers!

Running a Container

Congratulations! You've created an image and are just a few minutes away from enjoying the fruits of your labor! Running a container is like baking our pizza—the steps are the same whether it's fresh or frozen! And just like our pizza, the commands for running a container are the same no matter the source of the image: Oracle Container Registry, Oracle's repository scripts, or a custom image.

Container Properties

docker run starts a container for the first time. It also sets properties for the container that can't be changed later, including how it interacts with its environment. Essential elements of this first database container are the environment variables, port publishing, volume mounting, and name.

Port Publishing

Containers are isolated processes on the host; what occurs inside a container is generally invisible to other applications on the host. Sometimes, we want to interact with containers, and a prime example is connecting to an Oracle database listener, typically over port 1521. Mapping, or *publishing*, this port to one on the host allows other processes in the host environment to communicate with the database inside the container.[8]

Port mapping is controlled by the -p or --publish flag, followed by the host and container ports. For example, "-p 10000:1521" maps port 1521 in the container to port 10000 on the host.

Volume Mounting

Just as we may want to communicate across the host-container boundary using port mapping, there are situations where we need to allow the host and container to share files or directories. Volume mapping accomplishes this by mapping a filesystem inside the container to a volume or directory on the local host. For now, think of mapped volumes as NFS mounts.

---

[8] For security, ports must be explicitly exposed. This is covered more fully in Chapter 14.

In Oracle database images, database configuration and datafiles are located at /opt/ oracle/oradata. Mapping this directory to the local machine allows the database to utilize high-performance storage, external redundancy, and *persistence*.

Deleting a container deletes its contents, but the contents of bind-mounted volumes mapped to host directories remain outside the container. There are many situations where we want to delete containers but save the data, including database cloning, patching, and upgrades.[9]

Volume mounting, or bind mounting, is handled by the -v or --volume flag, followed by mapping the host directory to the container directory. For example, "-v $HOME/my_ container:/opt/oracle/oradata" maps the container's oradata directory to a directory called my_container under the user's home directory on the host.

Permissions Issues in Linux and Windows WSL Environments

On Linux and Linux guests in Windows WSL environments, the target directory on the host must be owned by the oracle user or have permissions that permit the oracle user to write the directory.

This will likely confuse Windows users due to the different permissions structures in Linux and Windows environments. Containers created in Docker Desktop, in PowerShell, or from a command prompt, run under the Windows filesystem. The Windows user owns both the files and the process, and there's no conflict when Docker creates files on the local filesystem.

The --volume or -v options of docker run creates the mapped directories on the host if they don't exist. In a Linux environment—including WSL on Windows—they're made by and inherit ownership from the calling process. The Docker daemon runs (and creates directories) as root, as in Figure 4-6. This was captured on a Windows WSL system after running the following command:

```
docker run -d --name MYDB \
      -v $HOME/oradata/MYDB:/opt/oracle/oradata \
      oracle\database:19.3.0-ee
```

---

[9] Persistence and use cases are discussed in depth in Chapter 5.

```
> ls -l $HOME/
total 8
drwxr-xr-x 32 docker docker 4096 Sep 10 16:38 docker-images
drwxr-xr-x  3 root   root   4096 Sep 11 14:46 oradata
```

Figure 4-6. *Directories created by docker run on Linux systems inherit ownership from the Docker daemon,* `root`

The `$HOME/oradata` directory path didn't exist, so Docker created it—as `root`. But, when the Database Configuration Assistant ran inside the container as the `oracle` user,[10] it attempted to write files to directories on the container's volume. Still, it's mapped to a directory on the local filesystem the `oracle` user can't access. Unable to create the necessary directories or write files in Figure 4-7, DBCA fails.

```
△ Ubuntu          ×  + ⌄                                              —  □  ×
  (DESCRIPTION=(ADDRESS=(PROTOCOL=tcp)(HOST=0.0.0.0)(PORT=1521)))
The listener supports no services
The command completed successfully
Prepare for db operation
Cannot create directory "/opt/oracle/oradata/MYDB".   ◄——     DBCA failed because the
8% complete                                                   container has no permission
Copying database files                                        to create resources on the
31% complete                                                  directory mapped to the volume.
100% complete
[FATAL] Recovery Manager failed to restore datafiles. Refer logs for details.
8% complete
0% complete
```

Figure 4-7. *The /opt/oracle/oradata directory in the container was mapped to a directory that didn't exist. The Docker daemon created the directory on the host as the root user. The container doesn't have permission to write files there, and DBCA failed*

There are a variety of options for avoiding this. Perhaps the simplest is adding the `oracle` user and `oinstall` group in the Linux system:

```
sudo groupadd -g 54321 oinstall
sudo useradd -u 54321 -g oinstall oracle
```

Precreate directories to be mapped to volumes and set their ownership to `oracle:oinstall`:

```
sudo mkdir -p $HOME/oradata/MYDB
sudo chown -R oracle:oinstall $HOME/oradata/MYDB
```

---

[10] If the container user isn't present on the container host, interaction between container processes and host resources run with a user and group ID of 1000.

Whenever I see a failed Oracle database container on a Windows or Linux system, I first check whether the logs contain a "Cannot create directory" error. It usually leads back to a permissions issue, where ownership on a mapped volume was incompatible with the user requesting the resource inside the container.

Environment Variables

Containers inherit default environment settings from the parent image, including the database and pluggable database names, typically ORCLCDB and ORCLPDB1. When a container runs for the first time, a startup script checks to see if a database exists and, if not, creates one based on these values. We can override the defaults to customize the database name with the -e or --env flags, followed by a variable-value pair. For example, "-e ORACLE_SID=TEST -e ORACLE_PDB=TESTPDB" overrides the default database names and creates a database called TEST with a pluggable database named TESTPDB.

This illustrates how to set multiple environment variables using separate -e flags. The same pattern applies to multiple port and volume mappings.

Container Name

The --name flag sets a "friendly" name for a container. If not specified, Docker generates a random name like "*quirky_elbakyan*" or "*nifty_buck*." Defining a name is a good practice. You won't have to query Docker to find the name of your container, and you're more likely to remember the purpose of a container when it has a meaningful name.

Note   Container names are case sensitive.

A Full Run Command

Let's run a new container using the command in Listing 4-5.

Listing 4-5. A practical docker run command for a basic Oracle database container

```
docker run -d --name MYDB  \
        -p 10000:1521  \
        -v $HOME/oradata/mydb/data:/opt/oracle/oradata \
```

```
-v $HOME/oradata/mydb/diag:/opt/oracle/diag \
-e ORACLE_SID=MYDB \
-e ORACLE_PDB=MYPDB \
oracle/database:19.3.0-ee
```

There's a new flag, -d, that we haven't covered. It tells Docker to run the container as a detached background process. Without this flag, the container runs interactively in the local session. Exiting the container causes it to stop.

The command ends with the image Docker should use to start the container. The image combines the repository and tag fields reported by docker images, connected with a colon.

Submitting this command causes Docker to start the container and run startup scripts embedded in the image. There's no existing database, so the startup script calls DBCA to create a database called MYDB, with a pluggable database called MYPDB. The datafiles and configurations are written to a directory under the user's home. We can connect to the database listener over port 10000 on the local host.

When running this command on a Linux system or from a Linux shell on a Windows WSL host, be sure to create the necessary directories first:

```
sudo mkdir -p $HOME/oradata/mydb/{data,diag}
sudo chown -R oracle:oinstall $HOME/oradata/mydb
```

The values inside the curly braces—{data,diag}—tell Linux to create two subdirectories under $HOME/oradata/mydb. I'm assigning them to two volumes in the container. The first, mapped to /opt/oracle/oradata, is the target for the database's datafiles and configurations. The second, mapped to /opt/oracle/diag, receives the database diagnostic directory.

Mapping Oracle's diagnostic directory has two benefits. First, this is a volatile directory. Without a volume, Oracle writes these files into the container's union filesystem, causing it to grow. Container layers are managed inside Docker's private filesystem. Growing that filesystem can be painful, so saving the files externally from container layers helps prevent problems later. Second, having them on a volume preserves them if the container is deleted and makes them more accessible for review.

View Container Logs

Creating the database will take a few minutes. We can monitor progress in the container with the docker logs command. Follow the log activity of the MYDB container we just created using the -f flag:

```
docker logs -f MYDB
```

The initial output shows the database creation process. When complete, the startup scripts report that the database is ready to use, and the content switches to showing the contents of the alert log, as shown in Listing 4-6.

Listing 4-6. Log output reporting database availability

```
########################
DATABASE IS READY TO USE!
########################

Datafiles are already patched. Skipping datapatch run.

The following output is now a tail of the alert.log:
ORCLPDB1(3):
ORCLPDB1(3):XDB initialized.
2021-03-01T17:32:38.353181+00:00
ALTER SYSTEM SET control_files='/opt/oracle/oradata/MYDB/control01.ctl'
SCOPE=SPFILE;
```

The database creation is complete! We can use the database interactively through the container shell and connections from host applications like SQL Developer.

Access and Use the Container

Let's explore ways of accessing and using the database and container environment. We can interactively connect to the container shell, run scripts, and connect from remote clients using a mapped port.

Access a Container Shell

docker exec executes commands, interactively or in the background, in container environments. Start an interactive shell in the MYDB container we just created with the following command:

```
docker exec --interactive --tty MYDB bash
```

The --interactive flag instructs docker exec to run interactively; the --tty flag opens a TTY session. These flags have shorthand options, -i and -t, respectively, and can be combined into a shorter, equivalent command:

```
docker exec -it MYDB bash
```

Running either command executes (opens) a bash shell in the container. It may be helpful to think of this as ssh-ing into a remote server—we're now in the container environment. Any commands we run are executed in the container as if we'd connected to a different host, until we exit the connection.

Once connected, we're effectively on a different machine—an Oracle database server. To prove that, run sqlplus / as sysdba at the container prompt and perform some queries. The result will appear much like Listing 4-7.

Listing 4-7. Starting SQL*Plus in the database container

```
[oracle@9fc6a7a36152 ~]$ sqlplus / as sysdba

SQL*Plus: Release 19.0.0.0.0 - Production on Mon Mar 1 19:51:55 2021
Version 19.3.0.0.0

Copyright (c) 1982, 2019, Oracle.  All rights reserved.

Connected to:
Oracle Database 19c Enterprise Edition Release 19.0.0.0.0 - Production
Version 19.3.0.0.0

SQL> select name from v$database;

NAME
---------
MYDB

SQL>
```

To be clear, this is a fully functional Oracle database, limited only by its host resources. All commands in a "normal" database installation are present in the container database (unless removed to reduce image size).

Run SQL*Plus

SQL*Plus, like bash, is an executable and can be invoked by the docker exec command in the same way. Listing 4-8 demonstrates how to open an SQL*Plus session directly.

Listing 4-8. Execute SQL*Plus in a container

```
> docker exec -it MYDB sqlplus / as sysdba

SQL*Plus: Release 19.0.0.0.0 - Production on Mon Mar 1 20:09:25 2021
Version 19.3.0.0.0

Copyright (c) 1982, 2019, Oracle.  All rights reserved.

Connected to:
Oracle Database 19c Enterprise Edition Release 19.0.0.0.0 - Production
Version 19.3.0.0.0

SQL> select name from v$database;

NAME
---------
MYDB

SQL>
```

The same pattern holds for running other commands in the container.

Run Scripts

Calling docker exec without the -it flags runs commands and reports the output. Listing 4-9 illustrates how to list files from a directory in the container.

Listing 4-9. List the contents of the /opt/oracle/oradata/MYDB directory in the MYDB container

```
> docker exec MYDB ls /opt/oracle/oradata/MYDB
MYPDB
control01.ctl
control02.ctl
pdbseed
redo01.log
redo02.log
redo03.log
sysaux01.dbf
system01.dbf
temp01.dbf
undotbs01.dbf
users01.dbf
```

The Oracle images include scripts for managing the database in the container environment. Among these is `setPassword.sh`, for changing the passwords of the SYS, SYSTEM, and PDBADMIN users. Listing 4-10 shows how to call the setPassword.sh script to update these user passwords.

Listing 4-10. Run setPassword.sh on the MYDB container to change passwords

```
> docker exec MYDB ./setPassword.sh NewPassword1
The Oracle base remains unchanged with value /opt/oracle

SQL*Plus: Release 19.0.0.0.0 - Production on Mon Mar 1 20:25:55 2021
Version 19.3.0.0.0

Copyright (c) 1982, 2019, Oracle.  All rights reserved.

Connected to:
Oracle Database 19c Enterprise Edition Release 19.0.0.0.0 - Production
Version 19.3.0.0.0

SQL>
User altered.
```

```
SQL>
User altered.

SQL>
Session altered.

SQL>
User altered.

SQL> Disconnected from Oracle Database 19c Enterprise Edition Release
19.0.0.0.0 - Production
Version 19.3.0.0.0
```

These examples should be enough to get you started.

Connect from Host Applications

If the container's listener port is published, database clients on the local host can access the container database using these port mappings. This includes SQL Developer and SQLcl (www.oracle.com/tools/downloads/sqldev-downloads.html), Oracle Instant Client (www.oracle.com/database/technologies/instant-client.html), and third-party tools like Quest Toad (www.quest.com/products/toad-for-oracle/software-downloads.aspx). The port is the only thing that's different when connecting to databases running in containers. Use localhost when connecting to containers on the local machine or the IP or hostname of the system where the container is running.

Figure 4-8 shows the database connection dialog from SQL Developer, with entries for the host, port, and service name populated for the MYDB database.

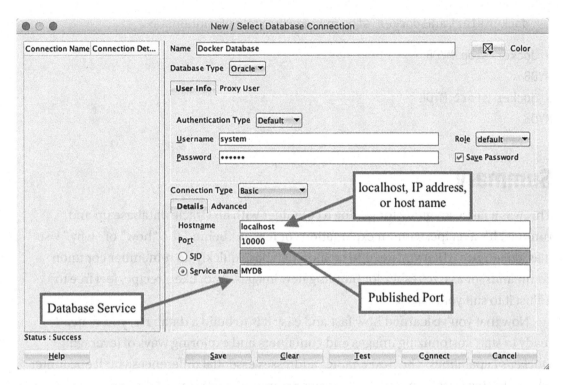

Figure 4-8. *Adding a connection to a database running in a Docker container in SQL Developer*

If you don't know or remember the port mapping, the docker container ports command reports this information for containers (it's also part of the docker ps output):

```
> docker container port MYDB
1521/tcp -> 0.0.0.0:10000
```

Manage the Container

When it comes to managing the new container database, there isn't much to do. Databases created from Oracle's repository and container registry images are set to NOARCHIVELOG mode by default, so there are no archive logs to manage. There's no need to stop the container or its database when shutting down or rebooting the host. If the host or Docker Desktop restarts, start the container once the system is up. The database and listener start automatically as part of the process.

docker start and docker stop manage the state of containers:

```
> docker stop MYDB
MYDB
> docker start MYDB
MYDB
```

Summary

This was a fast-start guide for getting a container with an Oracle database up and running. It's a recipe, without explanations or reasons behind the "how" or "why." Use it as a reference when you need to create a database quickly, to remember common commands, or as a refresher for building new images. And, like a recipe, feel free to adjust it to suit your tastes.

Now that you've learned how fast and easy it is to build a database, you're nearly ready to start customizing images and containers and exploring ways of leveraging Docker's capabilities. The next chapter addresses essential differences you'll encounter when running Oracle containers. Chapter 6 introduces ways of modifying the basic container we just created to suit different requirements.

CHAPTER 5

Differences in Database Containers

I'm old enough to remember the days when Oracle database administrators managed rollback segments by hand. When Oracle introduced automatic undo retention, people (myself included) balked at the idea, confident that it couldn't manage rollback appropriately. Years later, I can't imagine a world without that feature!

Database administrators have expressed skepticism toward other new features and advances over the years, including Recovery Manager, Automatic Shared Memory Management, and virtual machines. Each introduced new ways of doing things, different from familiar methods. Over time, our understanding and acceptance grew until these (and other new features) became the routine we now take for granted.

Change isn't easy. The mainstream rejects advances initially, often without reason or understanding, simply because we're not used to them. They're called *advances* for a reason, though; containers are no exception. Google, for instance, boasts that they run everything in containers, as shown in the screen capture from *https://cloud.google.com/containers* in Figure 5-1.

77

© Sean Scott 2023
S. Scott, *Oracle on Docker*, https://doi.org/10.1007/978-1-4842-9033-0_5

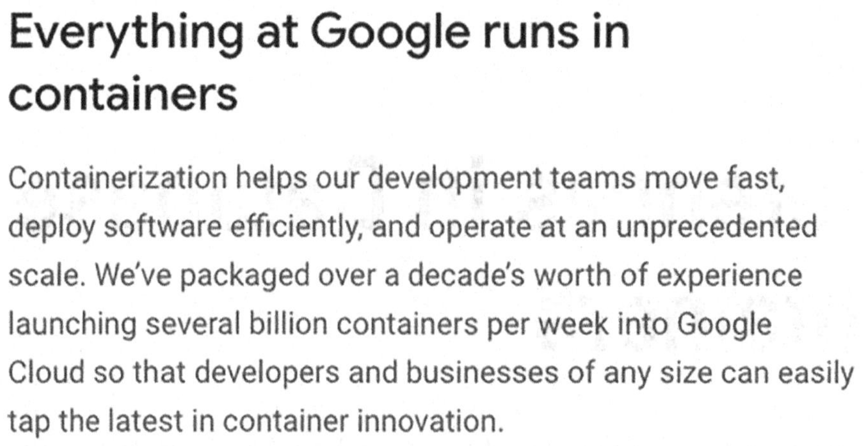

Everything at Google runs in containers

Containerization helps our development teams move fast, deploy software efficiently, and operate at an unprecedented scale. We've packaged over a decade's worth of experience launching several billion containers per week into Google Cloud so that developers and businesses of any size can easily tap the latest in container innovation.

Figure 5-1. *Google runs everything in containers*

Change may be uncomfortable, but it's necessary, even vital, for organizations and individuals wanting to advance or improve. So far, we've covered basic Docker concepts and demonstrated how to get started building and running Oracle database images. These are sufficient if your intentions are limited to running a simple database in a local environment. In this chapter, I introduce some ways containers differ from traditional database platforms. Understanding these concepts is essential for integrating containers into your practice and adapting and customizing them to suit your current and future needs.

Before we start modifying things, it's vital to understand how environments in Oracle containers compare to those of "normal" databases running natively on Linux systems. To that end, we'll examine default containers built from Oracle's repository and explore unique aspects and features that set them apart.

Readers already comfortable with containers but who haven't run containerized Oracle databases should start here. Some concepts may be familiar, but it's valuable to see how Oracle databases are adapted and implemented in containers.

Start an Oracle Database Container

We'll begin with a basic container built from Oracle's GitHub scripts (`https://github.com/oracle/docker-images`) using a very basic command:

```
> docker run -d --name ORCL oracle/database:19.3.0-ee
```

Let's break down that command to understand it better:

- **docker run:** Instructs Docker to "run" an image

- **-d flag:** Informs Docker that we want to run the container *detached* (not interactively) in the background

- **--name flag:** Assigns a name, *ORCL*, to the container

- **oracle/database:19.3.0-ee:** Identifies the image Docker will use

Docker responds with a unique hash value identifying the container:

```
> docker run -d --name ORCL oracle/database:19.3.0-ee
8facfd649aa4fcdbf27ae6908a573c2a16db0be7cba73c3093593507ac12b93f
```

That doesn't tell us much! The docker logs command reports what's happening inside containers. In Listing 5-1, I ran docker logs, passing the container name along with an optional flag, -f, to actively "follow" the progress and see events as they occur. Without this flag, Docker would have reported only the most recent lines in the log.

Listing 5-1. Following or "tailing" a container log with the docker logs command. When run with the -f option, docker logs runs continuously—type ctrl-c to exit the log session

```
> docker logs -f ORCL
ORACLE EDITION: ENTERPRISE
ORACLE PASSWORD FOR SYS, SYSTEM AND PDBADMIN: 2Fy7ZqtWS9U=1

LSNRCTL for Linux: Version 19.0.0.0.0 - Production on 06-MAR-2022 22:04:37

Copyright (c) 1991, 2019, Oracle.  All rights reserved.

Starting /opt/oracle/product/19c/dbhome_1/bin/tnslsnr: please wait...

TNSLSNR for Linux: Version 19.0.0.0.0 - Production
System parameter file is /opt/oracle/product/19c/dbhome_1/network/admin/
listener.ora
Log messages written to /opt/oracle/diag/tnslsnr/8facfd649aa4/listener/
alert/log.xml
Listening on: (DESCRIPTION=(ADDRESS=(PROTOCOL=ipc)(KEY=EXTPROC1)))
```

Listening on: (DESCRIPTION=(ADDRESS=(PROTOCOL=tcp)(HOST=0.0.0.0)
(PORT=1521)))

Connecting to (DESCRIPTION=(ADDRESS=(PROTOCOL=IPC)(KEY=EXTPROC1)))
STATUS of the LISTENER

Alias   LISTENER
Version   TNSLSNR for Linux: Version 19.0.0.0.0 -
Production
Start Date   06-MAR-2022 22:04:46
Uptime   0 days 0 hr. 0 min. 8 sec
Trace Level   off
Security   ON: Local OS Authentication
SNMP   OFF
Listener Parameter File /opt/oracle/product/19c/dbhome_1/network/admin/
listener.ora
Listener Log File   /opt/oracle/diag/tnslsnr/8facfd649aa4/listener/
alert/log.xml
Listening Endpoints Summary...
  (DESCRIPTION=(ADDRESS=(PROTOCOL=ipc)(KEY=EXTPROC1)))
  (DESCRIPTION=(ADDRESS=(PROTOCOL=tcp)(HOST=0.0.0.0)(PORT=1521)))
The listener supports no services
The command completed successfully
Prepare for db operation
8% complete
Copying database files
Creating and starting Oracle instance
32% complete
...
46% complete
Completing Database Creation
54% complete
Creating Pluggable Databases

The repository authors thoughtfully included extensive log output in the container scripts! The first two lines show the database edition (Enterprise, in this case) and the (randomly generated) password for privileged database accounts. Recall that I mentioned these are not production-ready images; this is one example—credentials displayed in the log output! Anyone with access to the host or container can view this information!

The container next starts the listener, after which the startup scripts (discussed in the next chapter) check to see whether a database exists. If so, it starts the database. If not, it calls the Oracle *Database Configuration Assistant*, *DBCA*, to create a new database. This is the first time we've run this container, so DBCA starts building the database.

Creating a database is time-consuming and resource intensive. Depending on the host's capabilities, this may take a few minutes to an hour. Later in this book, we'll discuss methods for bypassing database creation—even for new containers—that allow rapid, near-instantaneous database provisioning. For now, monitor the logs as Oracle creates a database until you see the message in Listing 5-2, "DATABASE IS READY TO USE," indicating DBCA completed successfully.

Listing 5-2. The output of docker logs shows DBCA finished, and the database is ready to use

```
77% complete
Executing Post Configuration Actions
100% complete
Database creation complete. For details check the logfiles at:
 /opt/oracle/cfgtoollogs/dbca/ORCLCDB.
Database Information:
Global Database Name:ORCLCDB
System Identifier(SID):ORCLCDB
Look at the log file "/opt/oracle/cfgtoollogs/dbca/ORCLCDB/ORCLCDB.log" for
further details.
...
#########################
DATABASE IS READY TO USE!
#########################
The following output is now a tail of the alert.log:
ORCLPDB1(3):
ORCLPDB1(3):XDB initialized.
```

Great! The database is ready. Now what? It's time to connect to the container and see what things look like "inside" the container!

Connect to the Container

Connecting to containers is like making *SSH* connections to remote hosts. Once established, we navigate the container's operating system using familiar shell commands as if connected to an external machine. Commands run in the container don't affect the local environment.

We'll connect to the container using the *docker exec* command. The *exec* in docker exec stands for execute, and the basic syntax is

```
docker exec <CONTAINER NAME> <COMMAND>
```

The container name is the target container, and the command is any executable script or command present in the container. To start an interactive session in a container, we'll execute a shell—in this example, bash:

```
> docker exec -it ORCL bash
[oracle@8facfd649aa4 ~]$
```

Let's break down this command:

- **The -it flags are a shorthand way of passing multiple flags to Docker.** They represent --interactive (-i) and --tty (-t) and are used in combination to keep *standard input* (*STDIN*) open while allocating a *pseudo-TTY* or terminal-like session to the container. Translated, it just means you get an interactive session. (The order of the flags doesn't matter. They can occur individually or combined, and you can mix and match long and short flags.)

- **ORCL is the name of the container.**

- **bash is the command Docker runs in the container.** *bash*, the *Bourne Again SHell*, is the default shell for many Linux operating systems, including Oracle Enterprise Linux.

Docker responds to this with a prompt, [oracle@8facfd649aa4 ~]$. The default prompt displays the user (oracle), the hostname (8facfd649aa4), and the current working directory (~, a special shorthand character representing the user's home).

The container name is ORCL, so shouldn't the hostname be ORCL, too? Where does the 8facfd649aa4 originate?

If you open a new session on your host and look at the running containers using the docker ps command, you'll see that the hostname, 8facfd649aa4, is also the container ID:

```
> docker ps
CONTAINER ID    IMAGE                       NAMES
8facfd649aa4    oracle/database:19.3.0-ee   ORCL
```

Docker still recognizes the "friendly" container name we assigned, and we can use both the container ID and container name to reference the container when calling commands. Docker creates unique identifiers for containers and uses them as the hostname to avoid issues caused by user-assigned names that might violate host-naming conventions.

You can log in to a container using different shells, as long they're part of the image, for instance, substituting sh instead of bash:

```
> docker exec -it ORCL sh
sh-4.2$
```

docker exec is the primary method we'll use for connecting to and running commands in containers throughout this book.

Navigate the Oracle Database Container

Now that you're connected to the database container, let's look at the environment. At first glance, it doesn't seem different than a typical database host running natively in Linux. Listing 5-3 shows the result of some basic commands to query the environment. They seem to indicate this is a Linux machine running RHEL 7.8. The oracle user is there, along with Oracle's PMON process. An entry for the database is in the /etc/oratab file. Everything looks normal!

Listing 5-3. Review basic information about the container's user, operating system, and database

```
[oracle@8facfd649aa4 ~]$ id
uid=54321(oracle) gid=54321(oinstall) groups=54321(oinstall),54322(dba),
54323(oper),54324(backupdba),54325(dgdba),54326(kmdba),54330(racdba)

[oracle@8facfd649aa4 ~]$ cat /etc/redhat-release
Red Hat Enterprise Linux Server release 7.8 (Maipo)

[oracle@8facfd649aa4 ~]$ ps -ef | grep pmon | grep -v grep
oracle      2464      1  0 22:42 ?        00:00:00 ora_pmon_ORCLCDB

[oracle@8facfd649aa4 ~]$ egrep -v "^$|^#" /etc/oratab
ORCLCDB:/opt/oracle/product/19c/dbhome_1:N
```

Indeed, most things seem ordinary. That's part of the magic of containers—for all (or most) intents and purposes, they're indistinguishable from full-fledged, native hosts. If they weren't, we'd have to work around those differences to get applications—like Oracle databases—to work as expected!

Container Differences

We've already seen one hint of differences in containers—the hostname. Let's look at this and others in greater depth.

Hostname

Listing 5-4 digs deeper into the host naming we saw earlier. After displaying the contents of the /etc/hosts file in the container, I tried (and failed) to change the hostname to something more user-friendly.

Listing 5-4. The oracle user can't change the hostname

```
[oracle@8facfd649aa4 ~]$ hostname
8facfd649aa4

[oracle@8facfd649aa4 ~]$ cat /etc/hosts
127.0.0.1       localhost
```

```
::1      localhost ip6-localhost ip6-loopback
fe00::0     ip6-localnet
ff00::0     ip6-mcastprefix
ff02::1     ip6-allnodes
ff02::2     ip6-allrouters
172.17.0.7     8facfd649aa4

[oracle@8facfd649aa4 ~]$ hostname ORCL
hostname: you must be root to change the host name
```

Naturally, the oracle user can't change the hostname! But it turns out root can't change the hostname in a container, as shown in Listing 5-5. I logged in to the container with docker exec, adding the -u (or --user) flag to define the user as root. After confirming I logged in as root, I still couldn't change the hostname. (I'll show a workaround for this later. For now, chalk this up as the first of several differences to keep in mind when working in containers!)

Listing 5-5. The root user can't change the hostname, either!

```
> docker exec -it -u root ORCL bash
bash-4.2# whoami
root

bash-4.2# hostname ORCL
hostname: you must be root to change the hostname
```

cron

Containers don't typically include *cron*, the Linux scheduling system, either. While containers have an operating system,[1] they aren't full-fledged systems. Containers call binaries and reference libraries in that directory structure but rely on the host to perform system-level actions. The host kernel handles CPU, storage, and networking interactions like any process. It doesn't make sense that application processes would duplicate these tasks!

---

[1] Remember that the operating system in a container isn't really an operating system. A container's operating system is just a filesystem with the binaries and libraries necessary to make it look and behave like an operating system, for the purpose of performing a specific, limited set of tasks.

Containers are no different, and cron is one such system-managed process. Look at Listing 5-6 to see the processes containing the text "system" in my container. Compare that with the output in Listing 5-7, showing the system processes on my host running a complete Ubuntu Linux operating system.

Listing 5-6. Processes containing "system" in the container

```
[oracle@8facfd649aa4 ~]$ ps -ef | grep system
oracle     6486    4347  0 23:56 pts/0   00:00:00 grep --color=auto system
```

Listing 5-7. Processes containing "system" on the host

```
> ps -ef | grep system
root          486       1  0 Feb14 ?        00:00:10 /lib/systemd/
                                                     systemd-journald
root          520       1  0 Feb14 ?        00:00:14 /lib/systemd/
                                                     systemd-udevd
systemd+      741       1  0 Feb14 ?        00:00:05 /lib/systemd/systemd-
                                                     timesyncd
systemd+      750       1  0 Feb14 ?        00:00:10 /lib/systemd/
                                                     systemd-networkd
systemd+      753       1  0 Feb14 ?        00:00:11 /lib/systemd/
                                                     systemd-resolved
message+      792       1  0 Feb14 ?        00:00:32 /usr/bin/dbus-daemon
                                                     --system --address=systemd:
                                                     --nofork --nopidfile --systemd
                                                     -activation --syslog-only
root          809       1  0 Feb14 ?        00:00:14 /lib/systemd/
                                                     systemd-logind
root          812       1  0 Feb14 ?        00:04:09 /usr/sbin/thermald
                                                     --systemd --dbus-enable
                                                     --adaptive
lab        744954       1  0 Feb26 ?        00:01:05 /lib/systemd/
                                                     systemd --user
lab       2348206 2334483  0 23:56 pts/6    00:00:00 grep --color=auto
                                                     system
```

There are no system processes in the container. This includes any needed to schedule and run cron. Yet the *crontab* command, used to manage cron jobs, is present, and the oracle user can run it:

```
[oracle@8facfd649aa4 ~]$ ls -l /bin/crontab
-rwsr-xr-x 1 root root 57656 Jun  9  2019 /bin/crontab

[oracle@8facfd649aa4 ~]$ crontab -l
no crontab for oracle
```

Let's try editing the crontab by adding an entry:

```
[oracle@8facfd649aa4 ~]$ crontab -e
no crontab for oracle - using an empty one
/bin/sh: /usr/bin/vi: No such file or directory
crontab: "/usr/bin/vi" exited with status 127
[oracle@8facfd649aa4 ~]$
```

It fails—but not for the reason you might expect! crontab -e (for edit) calls the vi (*visual*) editor, but *vi isn't there*! To solve that, I logged in to a new session using the -u root option and installed vi using yum:

```
> docker exec -it -u root ORCL bash
bash-4.2# yum install -y vi
Loaded plugins: ovl
ol7_latest                           | 3.6 kB  00:00:00
(1/3): ol7_latest/x86_64/group_gz    | 136 kB  00:00:00
(2/3): ol7_latest/x86_64/updateinfo  | 3.4 MB  00:00:03
(3/3): ol7_latest/x86_64/primary_db  |  39 MB  00:00:08
Resolving Dependencies
--> Running transaction check
---> Package vim-minimal.x86_64 2:7.4.629-8.0.1.el7_9 will be installed
--> Finished Dependency Resolution
...
Install  1 Package
```

```
Total download size: 443 k
...
Installed:
  vim-minimal.x86_64 2:7.4.629-8.0.1.el7_9
```

Complete!

Now that `vi` is present, I should be able to return to my original session and add an entry to the `oracle` user's crontab. I added this line:

```
* * * * * touch /home/oracle/added_by_cron
```

For those unfamiliar with `cron` syntax, the job will run every minute of every hour of every day and "touch," or create, an empty file called /home/oracle/added_by_cron. If the file isn't present, `cron` will create it. When I check the `oracle` user's `crontab`, the line is present:

```
[oracle@8facfd649aa4 ~]$ crontab -l
* * * * * touch /home/oracle/added_by_cron
```

Or rather, `cron` should create it, but it doesn't. Listing 5-8 shows that, even after 30 minutes, the file still isn't there!

Listing 5-8. cron inside the container doesn't behave as expected!

```
[oracle@8facfd649aa4 ~]$ date
Mon Jan  7 00:10:01 UTC 2022
[oracle@8facfd649aa4 ~]$ ls -l /home/oracle
total 0
lrwxrwxrwx 1 root root 26 Apr 10  2021 setPassword.sh -> /opt/oracle/
setPassword.sh

[oracle@8facfd649aa4 ~]$ date
Mon Jan  7 00:44:26 UTC 2022
[oracle@8facfd649aa4 ~]$ ls -l /home/oracle
total 0
lrwxrwxrwx 1 root root 26 Apr 10  2021 setPassword.sh -> /opt/oracle/
setPassword.sh
```

Interesting! Perhaps the `cron` service isn't running. In Listing 5-9, I returned to the `root` session I started earlier, checked the status, and tried starting the service.

Listing 5-9. The root user can't start cron inside the container

```
bash-4.2# service crond status
Redirecting to /bin/systemctl status crond.service
Failed to get D-Bus connection: Operation not permitted

bash-4.2# service crond start
Redirecting to /bin/systemctl start crond.service
Failed to get D-Bus connection: Operation not permitted
```

This is intentional. `cron` is a system process, and containers expect the host OS to handle them. While the binaries are present in the container filesystem—even executable—there is no system process running in the container to identify and run jobs.

The absence of running `init.d` or `system.d` processes in containers raises legitimate concerns, particularly for Oracle databases. How do we schedule backups in containers? Better yet, how do products like *Oracle Grid Infrastructure*, *Oracle Real Application Clusters*, and *Oracle Restart*—which depend extensively on `init.d` or `system.d`—work in containers? Fortunately, there are ways to add this functionality to containers.

Let's now revisit the `vi` editor issue we encountered earlier and see why it was missing!

Binaries

Containers are frequently deployed at scale. Smaller containers maximize infrastructure capacity and take less time to copy across networks. When building container images, the objective is to eliminate anything that isn't necessary. Editors, like `vi`, are not needed.

Without editors, how can anyone change files in containers? The simple answer is that it's not something done in *most* containers. Unlike virtual and physical hosts, images provide ready-made filesystems that perform specific services or functions. They're not multipurpose, interactive systems. If something needs editing, it's done during the build and baked into the image, not after the container runs. Automation-friendly editors like `sed` are better suited if files in containers require modification.

You learned in Chapter 3 that changes made in containers write to a layer in a union filesystem. Union filesystems evaluate the differences between lower and upper layers, projecting the result to the container. Besides adding space in the container's layer, calculating those differences requires a CPU, and limiting changes in a container has performance implications.

It's not just about space and performance, though. You'll discover that the binaries and tools missing from container images extend beyond editors. *Anything* unnecessary adds an *attack surface* that bad actors can exploit. Attackers can't take advantage of what isn't there.

A system's attack surface is the collection of possible vectors or points an unauthorized user might exploit to gain access to the system. Limiting the software installed on containers reduces what's available to attackers and highlights another difference between containers and physical or virtual hosts. Complete operating systems tend to include tools and utilities that users *might* need. Container images have a more limited scope and include only what's required.

Linux distributions for Docker are often available with a "*-slim*" option, indicating a minimized distribution. There's no convention defining what is and isn't included (or, more accurately, excluded from) a slim version, which varies across vendors and versions. Production-savvy images usually start with a slim version and add what's necessary. As we'll see in Chapter 12, Oracle's database images follow suit, using a "slim" distribution of Oracle Enterprise Linux 7 as their foundation.

For most of us, though, the first use case for putting databases in containers includes some interaction, which implies editors and diagnostic tools. Fortunately, modifying build scripts to include binaries is easy, as discussed in the next chapter.

Oracle Directories

Another difference peculiar to Oracle's container registry images is the location of some Oracle-specific files. In Listing 5-10, I navigated to the ORACLE_BASE directory and listed its contents.

Listing 5-10. Contents of `ORACLE_BASE` in an Oracle database container

```
[oracle@8facfd649aa4 opt]$ cd $ORACLE_BASE
[oracle@8facfd649aa4 oracle]$ pwd
/opt/oracle

[oracle@8facfd649aa4 oracle]$ ls -l
total 92
drwxr-x--- 3 oracle oinstall 4096 Mar  6 22:04 admin
drwxr-x--- 2 oracle oinstall 4096 Mar  6 22:04 audit
drwxr-x--- 4 oracle oinstall 4096 Mar  6 22:15 cfgtoollogs
-rwxrwxr-x 1 oracle dba      1040 Mar 31  2021 checkDBStatus.sh
drwxr-xr-x 2 oracle dba      4096 Apr 10  2021 checkpoints
-rwxrwxr-x 1 oracle dba      4121 Mar 31  2021 createDB.sh
-rw-rw-r-- 1 oracle dba      9204 Oct 11  2020 dbca.rsp.tmpl
drwxrwxr-x 1 oracle dba      4096 Apr 10  2021 diag
drwxrwx--- 1 oracle dba      4096 Mar  6 23:32 oraInventory
drwxr-xr-x 1 oracle dba      4096 Mar  6 23:33 oradata
drwxr-xr-x 1 oracle dba      4096 Apr 10  2021 product
-rwxrwxr-- 1 oracle dba      1941 Oct 11  2020 relinkOracleBinary.sh
-rwxrwxr-x 1 oracle dba      6488 Mar 31  2021 runOracle.sh
-rwxrwxr-x 1 oracle dba      1015 Oct 11  2020 runUserScripts.sh
drwxr-xr-x 1 oracle dba      4096 Apr 10  2021 scripts
-rwxrwxr-x 1 oracle dba       758 Oct 11  2020 setPassword.sh
-rwxrwxr-x 1 oracle dba       678 Oct 11  2020 startDB.sh
```

Ignore the shell scripts for the time being. I want you to look closely at the *directories*. Much of what's here is what we expect to find. Admin, audit, and diagnostic directories—check! The product directory that forms the root of the `ORACLE_HOME` installed on the system—check! The `oradata` directory, where Oracle stores database files—check! But, oraInventory?

Oracle's database inventory is a collection of metadata for different Oracle products installed on a host, and Oracle doesn't recommend installing in or under the `ORACLE_BASE`, yet here it is. Why?

It's linked to the way containers use union filesystems for efficiency. For more on that, let's look at the `oradata` directory.

Configuration Files

Navigating further into the ORACLE_BASE/oradata directory, you'll notice two
subdirectories, ORCLCDB and dbconfig:

```
[oracle@8facfd649aa4 oradata]$ pwd
/opt/oracle/oradata

[oracle@8facfd649aa4 oradata]$ ls -l
total 8
drwxr-x--- 4 oracle oinstall 4096 Mar  6 22:15 ORCLCDB
drwxr-xr-x 3 oracle oinstall 4096 Mar  6 23:33 dbconfig
```

The ORCLCDB directory here is expected. It's part of the *Optimal Flexible Architecture,*[2]
or *OFA*, and forms the root directory containing the *control, data,* and *redo log* files
belonging to the ORCLCDB database instance running on the host.

In Listing 5-11, I listed the contents of the ORCLCDB subdirectory. As anticipated,
there are database files and subdirectories for the pluggable database ORCLPDB1 and
PDB seed files. This is consistent with Oracle database installations in non-container
environments.

Listing 5-11. Contents of $ORACLE_BASE/oradata/$ORACLE_SID in a container

```
[oracle@8facfd649aa4 oradata]$ ls -l ORCLCDB
total 2341684
drwxr-x--- 2 oracle oinstall      4096 Mar  6 23:32 ORCLPDB1
-rw-r----- 1 oracle oinstall  18726912 Mar  7 01:44 control01.ctl
-rw-r----- 1 oracle oinstall  18726912 Mar  7 01:44 control02.ctl
drwxr-x--- 2 oracle oinstall      4096 Mar  6 22:37 pdbseed
-rw-r----- 1 oracle oinstall 209715712 Mar  7 00:38 redo01.log
-rw-r----- 1 oracle oinstall 209715712 Mar  7 01:44 redo02.log
-rw-r----- 1 oracle oinstall 209715712 Mar  6 23:32 redo03.log
-rw-r----- 1 oracle oinstall 545267712 Mar  7 01:41 sysaux01.dbf
-rw-r----- 1 oracle oinstall 933240832 Mar  7 01:41 system01.dbf
-rw-r----- 1 oracle oinstall  33562624 Mar  6 22:44 temp01.dbf
```

---

[2] *Optimal Flexible Architecture* is an organizational and naming convention that separates files of
multiple databases into distinct directories.

```
-rw-r----- 1 oracle oinstall 246423552 Mar  7 01:43 undotbs01.dbf
-rw-r----- 1 oracle oinstall   5251072 Mar  7 00:43 users01.dbf
```

The *dbconfig* directory, however, is unexpected. Listing 5-12 shows the contents of the dbconfig directory. There's a subdirectory for the ORACLE_SID and, beneath that, some unexpected files!

Listing 5-12. Contents of $ORACLE_BASE/oradata/dbconfig/$ORACLE_SID

```
[oracle@8facfd649aa4 oradata]$ ls -l dbconfig
total 4
drwxr-xr-x 2 oracle oinstall 4096 Mar  6 23:33 ORCLCDB

[oracle@8facfd649aa4 oradata]$ ls -l dbconfig/ORCLCDB
total 24
-rw-r--r-- 1 oracle oinstall  234 Mar  6 22:04 listener.ora
-rw-r----- 1 oracle oinstall 2048 Mar  6 22:15 orapwORCLCDB
-rw-r--r-- 1 oracle oinstall  784 Mar  6 23:33 oratab
-rw-r----- 1 oracle oinstall 3584 Mar  6 23:33 spfileORCLCDB.ora
-rw-r--r-- 1 oracle oinstall   53 Mar  6 22:04 sqlnet.ora
-rw-r----- 1 oracle oinstall  211 Mar  6 23:33 tnsnames.ora
```

These configuration files are customarily saved under the ORACLE_HOME or /etc. What are they doing here?

To answer that, look first at the default location for the three networking files—listener.ora, sqlnet.ora, and tnsnames.ora—the ORACLE_HOME/network/admin directory, in Listing 5-13. These network configuration files *link* to the files in ORACLE_BASE/oradata/dbconfig/ORCLCDB!

Listing 5-13. Contents of $ORACLE_HOME/network/admin in a container. The listener, SQL*Net, and TNS configurations link to the files under the dbconfig directory

```
[oracle@8facfd649aa4 oradata]$ ls -l $ORACLE_HOME/network/admin
total 8
lrwxrwxrwx 1 oracle oinstall   49 Mar  6 23:33 listener.ora -> /opt/oracle/
oradata/dbconfig/ORCLCDB/listener.ora
drwxr-xr-x 2 oracle dba       4096 Apr 17  2019 samples
```

```
-rw-r--r-- 1 oracle dba        1536 Feb 14   2018 shrept.lst
lrwxrwxrwx 1 oracle oinstall   47 Mar   6 23:33 sqlnet.ora -> /opt/oracle/
oradata/dbconfig/ORCLCDB/sqlnet.ora
lrwxrwxrwx 1 oracle oinstall   49 Mar   6 23:33 tnsnames.ora -> /opt/oracle/
oradata/dbconfig/ORCLCDB/tnsnames.ora
```

Listing 5-14 shows the *password file* (orapwORCLCDB) and *server parameter file*, or *spfile* (spfileORCLCDB.ora) in their "proper" location, ORACLE_HOME/dbs, are also linked to ORACLE_BASE/oradata/dbconfig/ORCLCDB!

Listing 5-14. Database configuration files in $ORACLE_HOME/dbs link to their counterparts in dbconfig

```
[oracle@8facfd649aa4 oradata]$ ls -l $ORACLE_HOME/dbs
total 12
-rw-rw---- 1 oracle oinstall 1544 Mar   6 23:32 hc_ORCLCDB.dat
-rw-r--r-- 1 oracle dba       3079 May 14   2015 init.ora
-rw-r----- 1 oracle oinstall   24 Mar   6 22:10 lkORCLCDB
lrwxrwxrwx 1 oracle oinstall   49 Mar   6 23:33 orapwORCLCDB -> /opt/oracle/
oradata/dbconfig/ORCLCDB/orapwORCLCDB
lrwxrwxrwx 1 oracle oinstall   54 Mar   6 23:33 spfileORCLCDB.ora -> /opt/
oracle/oradata/dbconfig/ORCLCDB/spfileORCLCDB.ora
```

Finally, in Listing 5-15, we see the oratab file, /etc/oratab, is not linked but identical to the mysterious file in the special dbconfig directory.

Listing 5-15. The /etc/oratab and /opt/oracle/oradata/dbconfig/ORCLCDB/ oratab files are identical

```
[oracle@8facfd649aa4 oradata]$ ls -l /etc/oratab
-rw-rw-r-- 1 oracle oinstall 784 Mar   6 23:33 /etc/oratab

[oracle@8facfd649aa4 oradata]$ md5sum /etc/oratab
31f3633542a9883ebd7f0eaac771ec7b  /etc/oratab

[oracle@8facfd649aa4 oradata]$ md5sum $ORACLE_BASE/oradata/dbconfig/
ORCLCDB/oratab
31f3633542a9883ebd7f0eaac771ec7b  /opt/oracle/oradata/dbconfig/
ORCLCDB/oratab
```

What's the explanation for this? Layers and volumes.

Volumes

In Chapter 3, you learned how containers use union filesystems to store local data. Union filesystems allow multiple containers running from the same image to use the same files. Two containers don't take up twice the space because both *share* the original image. It's why containers start so quickly, and every container behaves identically. *Creating a container doesn't copy or change the contents of the image.* Every container uses (and reuses) the directory structure from the image itself!

The image provides the lower layer of the union filesystem. A layer "above" that saves the changes made in each container. By "looking down" into the layers, each container sees either the unchanged files in the lower layer (the image) or the local changes held in the upper layer. (Refer back to the discussion in Chapter 3 about layers and union filesystems.)

This arrangement works well for short-lived applications that don't write much data. On more durable systems with longer lifespans—like databases—activity in the container may add considerably to the individual container layers. Figure 5-2 shows this for an Oracle database container. The drawing on the left shows the system immediately after starting two database containers. Docker adds layers dedicated to each container. They sit atop the image, and, initially, they're empty. But soon, Oracle begins creating databases in the containers. Datafiles added during this step aren't part of the image, so they're written into the container's layers. (Even if they were in the image, the container layer would capture the changes to image files.) The drawing on the right shows how the container layers grew to hold the additional content.

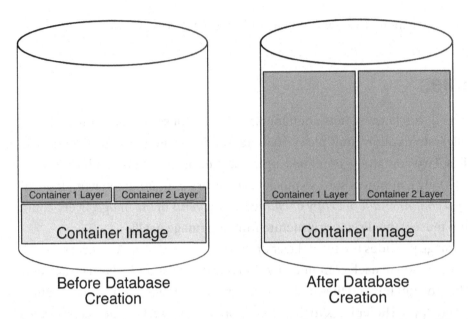

Before Database
Creation

After Database
Creation

Figure 5-2. *Representations of a host running two database containers. The image on the left represents the situation immediately after the containers start. The layers are empty. The right-side image shows the result after database creation completes. The layers grew substantially to hold the files added and changed during database provisioning*

This isn't an ideal situation for several reasons. Computing the differences between the upper and lower layers of union filesystems loads the host CPU. The database is limited, too—the container layers are on the host filesystem, which may not be large enough to accommodate a growing database nor fast enough to satisfy the database's performance requirements.

There's another drawback to saving data in the container layer: durability. The upper layer assigned to the container *is* the container. Deleting the container removes the layer—and with it, the database!

Fortunately, Docker offers a solution called a *volume*. Container volumes assign directories *inside* the container to storage *outside* the layered filesystem on the local host. When the container saves data to the mounted directory, it's writing it to persistent storage on the local host.

Figure 5-3 shows the same database containers, now using volumes for the /opt/ oracle/oradata directories. Now, container operations writing into this directory are saved to the host filesystem, not the container layers. All other directories inside the container behave as they did before.

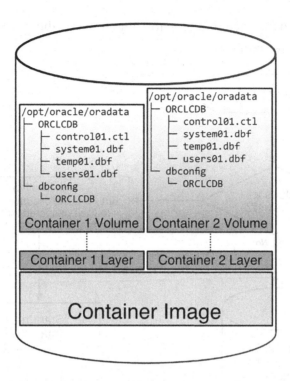

Figure 5-3. *Database containers use volumes to store the contents of the /opt/ oracle/oradata directory to the local filesystem*

Deleting containers removes the upper and working layers and, along with them, all the changes they hold. Once the layer is gone, it can't be recovered or recreated. Volumes are independent of the container and unaffected when deleting their parent container. Volumes can act like network filesystems, too, sharing files between the container and host and even between containers. They can take advantage of high-performance storage for data, too.

This brings us back to the `oradata` directory and the mystery behind the placement of the Oracle database configuration files.

Mounting the `oradata` directory as a volume keeps Oracle's volatile datafiles off the union filesystem, avoiding performance penalties. But configuration files aren't changed frequently enough to hamper performance. There's another explanation.

When database containers first start, there's a check to see if a database exists, as shown in Figure 5-4. If the review finds a database, it next looks in the `dbconfig` directory, links the configuration files it finds to their expected locations, then starts the database. Otherwise, it creates a new database. When it finishes, it copies the

configuration files into the dbconfig directory and replaces them in their usual locations
with links pointing to the copies.

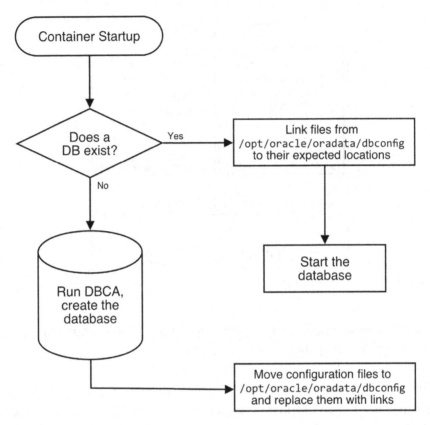

Figure 5-4. *Actions performed when starting Oracle database containers.
Whether the database is old or new, it saves configuration files in the dbconfig
directory*

With volumes, the data in the /opt/oracle/oradata directory is written to the
local host. Configuration files under ORACLE_BASE and ORACLE_HOME, the /etc/oratab
file, and the database inventory—saved in the container's ephemeral layers—are lost
when dropping the container. In this case, it deletes *links*[3] to those files, not the files
themselves. The database configuration files are safely preserved on the volume, as
shown in Figure 5-5.

---

[3] The /etc/oratab file on the container isn't linked to the volume, it's copied. The /etc directory
is owned by root, and the oracle user lacks permission to create links there.

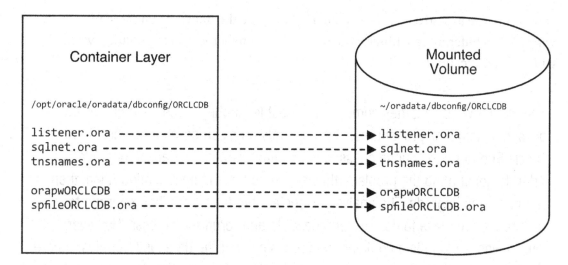

Figure 5-5. *The database configuration files under the ORACLE_HOME in the container aren't physically there. They're links, referencing files under* /opt/ oracle/oradata/dbconfig

The volume is a snapshot of everything necessary for recreating the database. When I delete the container, the volume remains behind. What happens when I start a new container and map its oradata volume to the directory left over from the prior container?[4]

The startup script checks to see if a database exists, and—even though it's brand new—*it discovers the files from the existing database!*[5] The container doesn't know the files came from a now-deleted container. All it sees are the files it needs for a database. Instead of creating a new database, it starts the one it discovered.

Every time the startup script runs, it checks for a database and, if found, recreates the links, if necessary, from their expected locations to the files in the /opt/oracle/ oradata/dbconfig/$ORACLE_SID directory.

We can leverage this feature to provision database clones very quickly. Nothing ties data on a volume to a specific container. Taking a copy of an existing oradata directory and using it in a new container lets Oracle skip the database creation process entirely! Provided the ORACLE_SID and other database-specific environment variables passed during container creation match the values used in the database on the volume, the

---

[4] Mounting volumes is covered in detail in Chapter 7.

[5] The ORACLE_SID and certain other environment variables must match.

contents of the oradata volume can be used to clone the database on the same system, copy data to different machines, and even share them across host operating systems—without modification!

The real power of volumes comes when troubleshooting issues and practicing or refining complex procedures. I was recently on a screen-sharing session with Oracle Support to diagnose an issue happening deep in a database upgrade. After demonstrating the problem, they suggested changing a configuration, then rerunning the upgrade. The analysts expected it to take a few hours for me to restore the database to its pre-upgrade state and rerun the process. However, since I was working in a container and had a copy of the database from just before the failure, it only took a few minutes to stop the container, restore a copy of the snapshot, and restart the container!

Volumes are a unique and powerful feature exclusive to databases running in containers. Restoring and cloning databases in Docker doesn't require a DBA or knowledge of RMAN. It's a straightforward directory copy. Treating *data* as a self-contained set of files on a volume, separate from the database *software* in the container, transforms the way development teams work. Treating data as a freestanding asset means organizations can version and share data with little or no dependency on specialized database skills.

Summary

Different isn't good or bad. It's just *different*. It's how we embrace "different" that matters. That may be as simple as picking something new from the menu or opening yourself to the possibilities introduced by technological evolution!

In this chapter, you learned the basic commands for starting a container and monitoring activity and how to connect to and navigate a database container. Once logged in to the container system, you explored some distinctions that set containers apart from traditional systems, including the absence of certain binaries and features, like cron. Remember that containers are not the comprehensive environments we're accustomed to and may force us to rethink how we accomplish specific tasks. These differences aren't without reward, however. Using minimal or slimmed-down filesystems improves performance and reduces containers' attack surface.

You also discovered how to use volumes to persist data outside the container, where it's independent of the container's lifecycle. Volumes also make durable, high-performance, network-attached storage accessible to databases hosted in containers.

Perhaps the most vital concept from this chapter is Oracle's method for relocating the database configuration files used in container databases. Saving these files to a volume, alongside the database's control, data, and redo log files, separates the database software from the database itself. These distinct boundaries are crucial to managing each component independently. Organizations running containerized databases can manage data as a versioned, portable asset, integrate data into DevOps processes, and accelerate development lifecycles.

With an enhanced appreciation for some of Docker's internals, you're ready to move on to the next chapter and begin customizing containers!

CHAPTER 6

Customize Container Environments

Running containers is comparable to calling a sophisticated shell script. Containers and shell scripts both perform a scoped set of tasks. Scripts can be explicit, with hard-coded values, but adding some flexibility makes them more portable and valuable. That might mean deriving specific values from the environment or interpreting parameters passed to the script at runtime. Take an RMAN backup script as an example. Hard-coding the database name prevents its use on other databases. Pass the database name as a variable, and the same script works across an enterprise. Adding additional options for the backup destination, degree of parallelism, and incremental level makes the script much more flexible and valuable over various implementations.

Docker is similar in this regard, and in this chapter, we'll dive into an option to the `docker run` command that passes variables and values to the container's private environment. Those environment variables act like shell script parameters and allow one image to work dynamically, supporting various needs or applications. When an Oracle database container starts, it evaluates the container environment—as the backup script reads parameters—and applies changes to the container to create and run a database to match.

The magic behind this is a special instruction Docker runs automatically whenever a container starts.

© Sean Scott 2023
S. Scott, *Oracle on Docker*, https://doi.org/10.1007/978-1-4842-9033-0_6

The Startup Process

I've mentioned the startup process previously. At a very high level, it checks to see if a database exists and, if found, starts it. If not, it runs the *Database Configuration Assistant (DBCA)* to create a new database in the container. The startup instruction[1] for the Oracle container repository images we're working with is a `bash` shell script called `runOracle.sh`. (For reference, all examples in this chapter are based on a default Oracle Database 19c image built using the Oracle-authored repository at `https://github.com/oracle/docker-images` but are valid for other database versions as well.) Figure 6-1 adds some detail to the startup process of an Oracle database container.

---

[1] Chapter 11 describes this and other scripts, including example modifications.

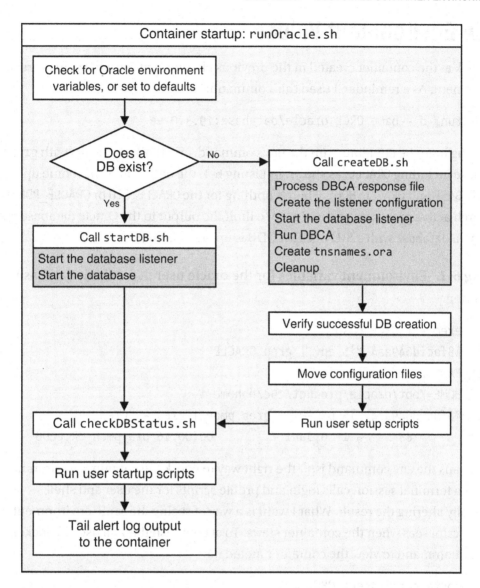

Figure 6-1. *Flowchart of the startup process for an Oracle database container*

The `runOracle.sh` script reads values from the environment, and one of the first things it looks for is the `ORACLE_SID` and `ORACLE_PDB`. If they're not defined, it assigns defaults. Only then will it check whether a database matching the SID is present.

View Environment Values

Let's look at the container created in the previous chapter and see what values are in its environment. As a reminder, I used this command:

```
docker run -d --name ORCL oracle/database:19.3.0-ee
```

If I log in to the container, run the env command, and limit the results with grep to just those including ORACLE, as shown in Listing 6-1, the only values that come up are the ORACLE_BASE and ORACLE_HOME. There's nothing for the ORACLE_SID or ORACLE_PDB. Yet if I search active processes and use grep to limit the output to the Oracle database pmon process, a database with a SID of ORCLCDB is up and running.

Listing 6-1. Environment variables for the oracle user in a default database container

```
docker exec -it ORCL bash
[oracle@8facfd649aa4 ~]$ env | grep ORACLE
ORACLE_BASE=/opt/oracle
ORACLE_HOME=/opt/oracle/product/19c/dbhome_1
[oracle@8facfd649aa4 ~]$ ps -ef | grep pmon | grep -v grep
oracle        88        1  0 Jan1 ?        00:00:16 ora_pmon_ORCLCDB
```

Perhaps the env command isn't the right way to check the container environment. Starting a terminal session calls login and profile scripts for the user and shell, potentially altering the result. What I want is a way of seeing the same environment the startup script sees when the container starts. To accomplish that, I'll use the docker inspect command to view the container metadata:[2]

```
docker container inspect ORCL
```

docker inspect for my container produces nearly 300 lines of JSON output and isn't very user-friendly. It's a lot to pick through just to see the environment settings! Fortunately, the inspect command (and many others) have a helpful --format option we can use to limit and structure its output. In Listing 6-2, I added formatting to confine

---

[2] docker inspect works against a wide range of Docker objects, including images, containers, volumes, and networks. The JSON output for each object type is different, but the formatting examples shown here can be adapted to suit your needs!

the result to the environment values in the configuration output, `--format='{{.Config.`
`Env}}'`. Unfortunately, it sacrifices brevity for clarity. It puts everything onto a single line
rather than a nice, clean list of variables!

Listing 6-2. Limiting the result with the --format option places all the output on
a single line with no formatting

```
> docker container inspect --format='{{json .Config.Env}}' ORCL
[PATH=/opt/oracle/product/19c/dbhome_1/bin:/opt/oracle/product/19c/
dbhome_1/OPatch/:/usr/sbin:/usr/local/sbin:/usr/local/bin:/usr/sbin:/usr/
bin:/sbin:/bin ORACLE_BASE=/opt/oracle ORACLE_HOME=/opt/oracle/product/19c/
dbhome_1 INSTALL_DIR=/opt/install INSTALL_FILE_1=LINUX.X64_193000_db_home.
zip INSTALL_RSP=db_inst.rsp CONFIG_RSP=dbca.rsp.tmpl PWD_FILE=setPassword.
sh RUN_FILE=runOracle.sh START_FILE=startDB.sh CREATE_DB_FILE=createDB.
sh SETUP_LINUX_FILE=setupLinuxEnv.sh CHECK_SPACE_FILE=checkSpace.sh CHECK_
DB_FILE=checkDBStatus.sh USER_SCRIPTS_FILE=runUserScripts.sh INSTALL_DB_
BINARIES_FILE=installDBBinaries.sh RELINK_BINARY_FILE=relinkOracleBinary.sh
SLIMMING=true LD_LIBRARY_PATH=/opt/oracle/product/19c/dbhome_1/lib:/usr/lib
CLASSPATH=/opt/oracle/product/19c/dbhome_1/jlib:/opt/oracle/product/19c/
dbhome_1/rdbms/jlib]
```

To get more human-friendly output, I sent the result through the jq[3] utility to parse
the JSON block into something more readable in Listing 6-3. I used additional formatting
options in Listing 6-4 to print entries on separate lines. I like the formatting output from
the second example. I find it more readable, but the command is more verbose and
harder to remember than piping the result through jq.[4]

Listing 6-3. Parsing environment information with jq

```
> docker container inspect --format='{{json .Config.Env}}' ORCL | jq
[
```

---

[3] jq formats, or "pretty prints" JSON output in more human-readable form. On Ubuntu systems
(the default Linux flavor in Windows WSL), install it with `sudo apt-get install jq`.

[4] Aliases and functions are alternatives to remembering verbose syntax. In Appendix B, I've
included examples of what I use in my environment to simplify complex commands.

```
  "PATH=/opt/oracle/product/19c/dbhome_1/bin:/opt/oracle/product/19c/
  dbhome_1/OPatch/:/usr/sbin:/usr/local/sbin:/usr/local/bin:/usr/sbin:/usr/
  bin:/sbin:/bin",
  "ORACLE_BASE=/opt/oracle",
  "ORACLE_HOME=/opt/oracle/product/19c/dbhome_1",
  "INSTALL_DIR=/opt/install",
  "INSTALL_FILE_1=LINUX.X64_193000_db_home.zip",
  "INSTALL_RSP=db_inst.rsp",
  "CONFIG_RSP=dbca.rsp.tmpl",
  "PWD_FILE=setPassword.sh",
  "RUN_FILE=runOracle.sh",
  "START_FILE=startDB.sh",
  "CREATE_DB_FILE=createDB.sh",
  "SETUP_LINUX_FILE=setupLinuxEnv.sh",
  "CHECK_SPACE_FILE=checkSpace.sh",
  "CHECK_DB_FILE=checkDBStatus.sh",
  "USER_SCRIPTS_FILE=runUserScripts.sh",
  "INSTALL_DB_BINARIES_FILE=installDBBinaries.sh",
  "RELINK_BINARY_FILE=relinkOracleBinary.sh",
  "SLIMMING=true",
  "LD_LIBRARY_PATH=/opt/oracle/product/19c/dbhome_1/lib:/usr/lib",
  "CLASSPATH=/opt/oracle/product/19c/dbhome_1/jlib:/opt/oracle/product/19c/
  dbhome_1/rdbms/jlib"
]
```

Listing 6-4. "Pretty-printing" environment information with an extended format command

```
> docker container inspect --format '{{range .Config.Env}}{{printf "%s\n"
.}}{{end}}' ORCL
PATH=/opt/oracle/product/19c/dbhome_1/bin:/opt/oracle/product/19c/dbhome_1/
OPatch/:/usr/sbin:/usr/local/sbin:/usr/local/bin:/usr/sbin:/usr/bin:/
sbin:/bin
ORACLE_BASE=/opt/oracle
ORACLE_HOME=/opt/oracle/product/19c/dbhome_1
INSTALL_DIR=/opt/install
```

```
INSTALL_FILE_1=LINUX.X64_193000_db_home.zip
INSTALL_RSP=db_inst.rsp
CONFIG_RSP=dbca.rsp.tmpl
PWD_FILE=setPassword.sh
RUN_FILE=runOracle.sh
START_FILE=startDB.sh
CREATE_DB_FILE=createDB.sh
SETUP_LINUX_FILE=setupLinuxEnv.sh
CHECK_SPACE_FILE=checkSpace.sh
CHECK_DB_FILE=checkDBStatus.sh
USER_SCRIPTS_FILE=runUserScripts.sh
INSTALL_DB_BINARIES_FILE=installDBBinaries.sh
RELINK_BINARY_FILE=relinkOracleBinary.sh
SLIMMING=true
LD_LIBRARY_PATH=/opt/oracle/product/19c/dbhome_1/lib:/usr/lib
CLASSPATH=/opt/oracle/product/19c/dbhome_1/jlib:/opt/oracle/product/19c/
dbhome_1/rdbms/jlib
```

No matter how it's formatted, there's still no ORACLE_SID or ORACLE_PDB.

I'll see similar results by navigating to the container details in Docker Desktop and selecting the Inspect tab, as in Figure 6-2. The screen lists the container's environment variables (but lacks sorting and filtering on the results).

Figure 6-2. *The Inspect tab in Docker Desktop's container detail page lists all the environment variables set in the container. But the ORCL container, created without specifying values for ORACLE_SID or ORACLE_PDB, doesn't report either variable in its environment*

There are several additional variables we don't see in "normal" database environments, like SLIMMING and those identifying directories, files, and scripts. Notice our startup script is there, too:

```
RUN_FILE=runOracle.sh
```

These values come from the parent image and represent the baseline configuration of any container started from the image. The results of the following commands that report environment configurations of the container and image are identical:

```
docker container inspect --format '{{range .Config.Env}}{{printf "%s\n" .}}
{{end}}' ORCL
docker image inspect --format '{{range .Config.Env}}{{printf "%s\n" .}}
{{end}}' oracle/database:19.3.0-ee
```

Containers inherit environment settings from their parent image. Just as an RMAN backup script might set default values if not overridden, the database container assigns defaults for the ORACLE_SID and ORACLE_PDB if not provided when creating a container with docker run.

docker run

The command used to create the ORCL database container in the examples so far was

```
docker run -d --name ORCL oracle/database:19.3.0-ee
```

Once created, its environment is static, at least from the standpoint of automation. I could open a session in the container and set environment variables, but they won't alter the environment values in the metadata. It's that metadata the startup script sees and reads each time the container starts. The only opportunity to change the metadata, potentially overriding defaults present in the image, is during container creation. (This is true for other container properties like volumes and networking, as we'll see in the coming chapters.)

A few methods pass environment variables[5] to the docker run command: via the command line, the host environment, or a file. Each passes a value to the container's metadata, making them available to scripts (including startup commands) and processes.

---

[5] Docker only allows simple values—no arrays!

Command-Line Option

Use the -e flag or its long form, the --env flag, followed by a single *key=value* pair, for example:

```
docker run ... -e ORACLE_SID=TEST ...
docker run ... --env ORACLE_PDB=TESTPDB1 ...
```

Pass multiple values using the -e flag separately for each:

```
docker run ... -e ORACLE_SID=TEST -e ORACLE_PDB=TESTPDB1 ...
```

The value (the part after the equal sign) can also be a variable from the local environment. It's useful for provisioning multiple containers. Listing 6-5 shows an example of using a for loop in a Linux environment for deploying multiple containers from a list of values—DEV, TEST, and STAGE—assigning a different database name to each from the loop variable.

Listing 6-5. Automatically deploying three Oracle 19c database containers, passing the ORACLE_SID to each from the environment

```
for dbname in DEV TEST STAGE
  do docker run -d --name $dbname -e ORACLE_SID=$dbname oracle/
database:19.3.0-ee
done
```

Values from a File

Environment files are text files, with each *key=value* pair on a separate line, making it easier to share multiple values with docker run. Docker ignores lines starting with pound signs (#) as comments. Use the --env-file option with the file's name when calling docker run. Listing 6-6 shows a sample environment file, named db.env, for an Oracle database, along with an example of using the --env-file option in the docker run command.

Listing 6-6. An example environment file for passing multiple key-value pairs to docker run

```
ORACLE_SID=TEST
ORACLE_PDB=TESTPDB1
ORACLE_EDITION=EE
ENABLE_ARCHIVELOG=true
```

Passing that file to the `--env-file` option of `docker run` populates the variables listed in the file into the container environment:

```
> docker run ... --env-file db.env ...
```

Values from the Host Environment

There's a particular case for sharing environment variables from the host with a container. If the variable exists on the host with the same name as the container, it's only necessary to provide the variable name (without the equal sign or value). This works for both the command line and environment file options.

In Listing 6-7, I modified the earlier loop example by changing the loop variable from dbname to `ORACLE_SID`. Because the container has a matching variable, I can use the variable name on its own. Docker interprets the variable and value for me.[6]

Listing 6-7. Implicit variable assignment to a container using a host variable

```
for ORACLE_SID in DEV TEST STAGE
   do docker run -d --name $ORACLE_SID -e ORACLE_SID oracle/
database:19.3.0-ee
done
```

It isn't necessary to write `ORACLE_SID=$ORACLE_SID` in this case. To use a host variable in an environment file, include the variable on a separate line without an equal sign or value. Docker reads the value from the host environment.

---

[6] The value in the container is set to the host value at the time `docker run` is executed. It's written to the container metadata, and changes to the value on the host won't alter the value in the container once the container is created.

Overwriting and Creating Variables

Assigning variables with docker run overwrites values from the image. Refer to Listings 6-3 and 6-4, which list variables and values the example container inherited from its parent. If I issue a slightly different command and create a new container, seen in Listing 6-8, this time changing the ORACLE_HOME, the container breaks when the startup script can't locate the necessary files.

Listing 6-8. Overriding the ORACLE_HOME in a container breaks things!

```
> docker run -d -e ORACLE_HOME=/home/oracle --name OOPS oracle/
database:19.3.0-ee
1c32eb9d016e723256e47199e5801d3bcd4cc64c87099cc40057028cd0177eba

> docker logs -f OOPS
/opt/oracle/relinkOracleBinary.sh: line 13: /home/oracle/bin/oraversion: No
such file or directory
/usr/bin/ar: /home/oracle/lib/libedtn.a: No such file or directory
ORACLE EDITION:
touch: cannot touch '/home/oracle/install/.docker_': No such file or
directory
ORACLE PASSWORD FOR SYS, SYSTEM AND PDBADMIN: vXy8JX7aiE4=1

LSNRCTL for Linux: Version 19.0.0.0.0 - Production on 11-JAN-2022 21:52:59

Copyright (c) 1991, 2019, Oracle.  All rights reserved.

Message 1070 not found; No message file for product=network,
facility=TNSTNS-12545: Message 12545 not found; No message file for
product=network, facility=TNS
 TNS-12560: Message 12560 not found; No message file for product=network,
facility=TNS
  TNS-00515: Message 515 not found; No message file for product=network,
facility=TNS
   Linux Error: 2: No such file or directory
cat: /opt/oracle/cfgtoollogs/dbca/ORCLCDB/ORCLCDB.log: No such file or
directory
cat: /opt/oracle/cfgtoollogs/dbca/ORCLCDB/ORCLCDB.log: No such file or directory
```

If a variable/value given in docker run isn't part of the image, Docker adds it to the container environment (and its metadata). Instead of changing the ORACLE_HOME, Listing 6-9 shows what happens when I create a container, this time assigning nondefault values for ORACLE_SID and ORACLE_PDB.

Listing 6-9. The container environment when using nondefault values for ORACLE_SID and ORACLE_PDB

```
> docker run -d -e ORACLE_SID=ORA19C -e ORACLE_PDB=PDB1 --name ORA19C
oracle/database:19.3.0-ee
aba0514d7fb36e70777c69ca4a6b619e3fbdca1f8a13a95935fed8e48c7722c3

> docker container inspect --format '{{range .Config.Env}}{{printf "%s\n"
.}}{{end}}' ORA19C | grep ORACLE
ORACLE_BASE=/opt/oracle
ORACLE_HOME=/opt/oracle/product/19c/dbhome_1
ORACLE_PDB=PDB1
ORACLE_SID=ORA19C

> docker exec -it ORA19C bash
[oracle@aba0514d7fb3 ~]$ env | grep ORACLE
ORACLE_SID=ORA19C
ORACLE_BASE=/opt/oracle
ORACLE_PDB=PDB1
ORACLE_HOME=/opt/oracle/product/19c/dbhome_1
[oracle@aba0514d7fb3 ~]$ ps -ef | grep pmon
oracle      5072       1  0 21:21 ?        00:00:00 ora_pmon_ORA19C
```

The original container didn't have ORACLE_SID or ORACLE_PDB in its environment, and those variables aren't included or assigned in the parent image. When the startup script, runOracle.sh, runs, it checks the environment and assigns a default value if they aren't set. docker run added the new variables and values to the container in the newly created container. docker inspect shows them in the container metadata, and they're in the oracle user environment. And—last but not least—the startup script created a database with an ORACLE_SID of ORA19C.

ORACLE_SID is ubiquitous in Oracle database settings, and ORACLE_PDB is part of multitenant installations. Being common to traditional Oracle database environments, we can make an educated guess they're meaningful to container environments, despite being absent from the predefined database image environment. But are there other, less obvious, or conventional values used in container environments?

Environment Options in Oracle Images

Oracle's container image repository has extensive documentation at `https://github.com/oracle/docker-images/tree/main/OracleDatabase/SingleInstance`, including environment options for customizing database startup and creation.

Environment options for customizing Oracle database creation in containers (defaults shown in brackets [])

- **ORACLE_SID:** The Oracle Database SID [ORCLCDB]

- **ORACLE_PDB:** The Oracle Database PDB name [ORCLPDB1]

- **ORACLE_EDITION:** The Oracle Database Edition[7,8]

- **ORACLE_CHARACTERSET:** The database character set [AL32UTF8]

- **ORACLE_PWD:** The Oracle Database SYS, SYSTEM, and PDB_ ADMIN password [randomly generated during database creation]

- **ENABLE_ARCHIVELOG:** Enable archive logging [False][7]

---

[7] Options for setting the database edition, enabling archive logging, SGA, PGA, and automatic memory calculation are available for database 19.3 onward.

[8] This parameter changes the Oracle Database Edition in the container by relinking the binaries in the Oracle Home. It reconfigures images with Enterprise Edition homes to use Standard Edition, and vice versa. The feature is used to start a container using preexisting datafiles created using a database edition that's different from the image.

Optional environment options available for managing memory in Oracle database containers.

- **INIT_SGA_SIZE:** The total memory, in MB, for the SGA components.[7]

- **INIT_PGA_SIZE:** The target aggregate PGA size, in MB.[7]

- **AUTO_MEM_CALCULATION:** Calculates total memory allocation based on the container's available memory during database creation. When set to false, the total memory allocation is 2GB. This option is ignored when either INIT_SGA_SIZE or INIT_PGA_SIZE are set. [True][7]

These options cover the most common modifications for creating databases. Chapter 13 offers examples and ideas for additional customizations, extending the possibilities further!

Summary

In this chapter, you learned that containers inherit environment settings from their parent images, storing them as metadata. Each time an Oracle database container starts, the runOracle.sh runs automatically, governing activity in the container and its database. The startup script evaluates environment variables to customize database creation and startup—much as a shell script accepts command-line parameters to alter its default behavior.

You learned different methods for passing environment variables to containers and can now use docker inspect to report and format metadata from containers. Finally, you discovered how to create an Oracle database in a Docker container using custom CDB and PDB names and learned about additional options for adjusting the database memory allocation, database edition, and archive logging state.

In the following two chapters, you'll explore additional options of the docker run command that allow interaction between hosts and containers. Chapter 7 introduces techniques for sharing host storage with containers and its implications for performance, data persistence, and efficiency. Chapter 8 covers communication between hosts and containers and configuring containers to serve clients, whether on the host or in other containers.

CHAPTER 7

Persistence

As I began looking for information on running Oracle in containers back in 2014, the consensus among Oracle experts wasn't very promising. Most database administrators dismissed Docker as the latest *technology-de-jour* among developers and not something capable of handling the demands of a database. They cited dire warnings about instability, poor performance, and data loss. Peers shared horror stories of various disasters rooted in the immaturity or fragility of Docker.

Those criticisms shared a common theme. Each was an anecdote involving some vague "friend of a friend" and echoed the warnings made for other new technologies over the years—technologies we take for granted today, like Recovery Manager (RMAN), automatic undo management,[1] and even virtual machines. It's also curious that these disasters were each blamed on a still-new technology used in production environments, which seemed unlikely. That's when I understood these stories were by-products of apprehension surrounding the unknown, even fear that containers might change how we do things.

If there was one objection at the forefront, then it was data persistence. The (mistaken) belief was since containers are ephemeral, anything associated with containers was, too. Indeed, a container's filesystem is linked to the container. Deleting a container permanently removes its data.

Unless that data is mounted *externally*.

Docker can save (and persist!) data outside containers using mounted storage because it's separate from the container. Deleting a container doesn't affect the data stored externally. Thoughtful use of database mounts offers greater control and visibility and sets the foundation for running efficient, reliable, consistent, and modular database environments. And mounts are the critical component behind powerful capabilities unique to Linux containers.

---

[1] I'm guilty of this attitude myself. Not only am I old enough to remember the joys of manually managing undo segments, I was among those who claimed they were too complicated and important to trust to one of Larry's algorithms. I even gave a conference presentation where I advised against the feature. I can't imagine how much time I wasted through my stubborn refusal to accept the newer, better way of doing things!

S. Scott, *Oracle on Docker*, https://doi.org/10.1007/978-1-4842-9033-0_7

Container Storage

We've seen how containers take advantage of union filesystems to deliver reliable, consistent results. It's tempting to say that every container run from a given image starts with identical filesystems. But containers don't use exact *copies*. Throughout their lifecycle, they all share the *same* filesystem—the image itself. Starting a container creates a dedicated *union filesystem* (sometimes called an *overlay filesystem*), using the parent image as a foundation. Figure 7-1 visualizes how container layers work for playing a game of Tic-Tac-Toe. The image contains the game board and the opening moves, filling the top row and center square. Every container uses the image as the *lower layer* but can't "touch" or change its contents. Instead, Docker writes container changes to each container's private *upper layer*. The two containers in Figure 7-1 start with the same board, moves, and an empty upper layer. Docker adds new moves to the upper layers as the games in each container progress. The view inside the container, provided by the *working layer*, is a composite or merger of the lower and upper layers. Looking "down" through the layers from the container's perspective, the filesystem appears "flat."

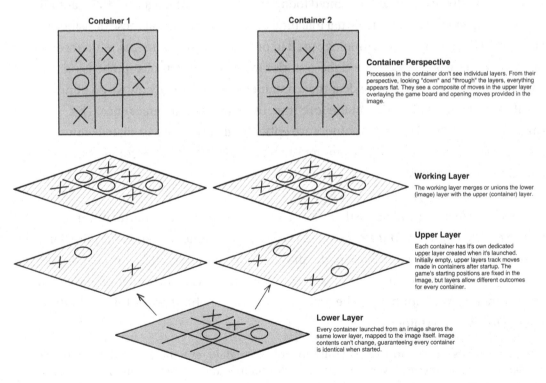

Figure 7-1. Containers use union filesystems to project local changes over the base filesystem provided by their parent image

Union filesystems make containers fast and efficient. It doesn't matter if an image is a few megabytes or several gigabytes in size because containers aren't copying them on startup. They're just initializing a new union filesystem and adding an initially empty layer atop the existing image. Running ten containers from a 1GB image doesn't require 10GB of space. They all use the same 1GB image, so their storage requirement is only the sum of the space used by changes in each container's private layer.

Docker Internal Storage

These images and layers still occupy space on disk in Docker's /var/lib/docker directory. The directory is part of the Linux virtual machine running under the covers on Windows and Mac systems running Docker Desktop. On Linux systems, it's the default location for Docker installations.[2] In either case, only privileged (root) users can navigate the directory, and with good reason. Its contents need to be protected to guarantee the health of container ecosystems.

The only practical way to view information and contents of the /var/lib/docker directory is indirectly, either through Docker CLI commands to report metadata or connecting to a container and inspecting its filesystem. It's not always the most convenient way of doing things, particularly when sharing information between host and container.

Consider a troubleshooting scenario using a Docker container running an Oracle database to isolate a potential software bug. At some point, I'll need to get files from the container to share with Oracle. How?

Assuming SMTP is configured, I could email or copy-paste them from a container shell to files on my local host. Neither is very practical. I could sudo into the /var/lib/ docker directory and try to locate the files in their layers and copy them to my home directory—again, perhaps not the best solution.

A more realistic alternative is the docker cp command. Like its Linux namesake, cp, docker cp lets me copy files between hosts and containers. I visualize containers as remote hosts and think of docker cp as equivalent to scp or sftp. The structure of docker cp is comparable to the scp command:

```
scp [source file] [destination]
docker cp [source file] [destination]
```

---

[2] The /var/lib/docker directory on a Linux host typically exists on the host boot volume. It can be relocated to a dedicated partition

The conventions are similar, too. The remote component is the host or container, followed by a colon and ending with a path or file name:

```
scp [host or IP address]:[source file] [destination]
docker cp [container name]:[source file] [destination]
```

That's certainly a more accessible and better way of transferring files, but for one thing. docker cp doesn't honor wildcards. With docker cp, operations are limited to entire directories or individual files. Moving files between hosts and containers is inconvenient at best. There are other limitations to union filesystems, particularly for databases.

Drawbacks of Union Filesystems

Union filesystems are a significant piece of the magic behind containers, but they are not an ideal storage mechanism for databases:

- **They're temporary**. Any data written to the container's private layer is lost when removing the container. If I delete one of the containers shown in Figure 7-1, I'm removing its union filesystem and the upper and working layers along with it.

- **The efficiency of union filesystems drops as the container's private layer changes grow**. Every modification made against a file that's part of the parent image adds to the work the host system must perform to generate the working view seen by the container. Getting the functional result involves reading files in the base and intermediate directories, then computing the difference. The overhead isn't significant when the container remains close to the original image. Applications that write considerable amounts of data—like databases—add to the container's upper layer, drawing resources to calculate results.

- **Layers in /var/lib/docker are limited to a single filesystem, by default, the boot volume**. Database capacity, performance, and redundancy are limited to the capabilities of this one disk, with no option to spread activity across multiple devices.

Adding an Oracle spin on this is like running an Oracle database using the host's boot volume for the ORACLE_HOME and data. Disk performance isn't critical for the database software—once binaries are cached in memory after startup, activity is limited. The size of the database home remains reasonably stable over its lifetime, so capacity isn't a concern, either.

However, collocating data and archive log files on the same disk is a problem. The database can only grow to the physical limits of one disk. Adding RAID to protect database files applies to everything on the disk, whether or not that protection is warranted. Fortunately, Oracle gives us control over the placement of those database files, and mounts in Docker have a similar purpose for containers: mounted storage.

Mount Concepts

Mounts expand container storage beyond the union filesystem. Think of them as networked attached storage or shared filesystems (and containers can use network storage, too). They're separate objects, independent of containers and their lifecycles. With mounts, containers can

- Use local storage on the host for persistence, better performance, and increased capacity

- Share files with the host or other containers

- Avoid the overhead of union filesystems for volatile directories

- Access files and directories that aren't part of their parent image

- Distribute database files across multiple disks, improving performance, increasing capacity, and controlling redundancy

As you work with mounts, particularly with databases, you'll see how they expose differences between software, configuration, and data. The container in Figure 7-2 uses mounts to separate relatively static components of an Oracle database from its data, configuration, logs, and scripts. The advantages of such an approach are significant:

- The database software and its dependencies are built into an image. Database software doesn't change much, and an immutable image is the most appropriate and efficient provisioning method. Any database started from this image is guaranteed to have the same version and patches baked in.[3] The few changes that might appear in these directories aren't significant to the performance of the container's union filesystem.

- Files that combine to make up the database instance—data, temp, control, redo, and archive log files—exist on dedicated storage, taking advantage of high-performance and redundant disks. Configuration files needed to start and operate a database—including the password, parameter, oratab, and networking configurations—are separate from software and data. This and the data are the most necessary parts of an Oracle database. Cloning or copying these files is all that's needed to create an identical copy of the database. Thanks to Docker's portability, that copy can be on the same system, a colleague's machine running a different operating system, or the cloud.

- Saving diagnostic directories to disk makes them visible to processes on the host and remains available even if the database container is stopped. Log monitoring and rotation can run from the container host rather than on the database.

- Using mounts for shared support scripts is more sensible than adding them to the parent image. While these scripts might remain unchanged, sharing them among containers over a mount is better. Leaving them out of the image leads to smaller images that don't need updating to include modified scripts, nor do those changes have to be propagated to running containers.

Oracle adopted a similar approach with *Read-Only Homes*, a feature introduced in Oracle Database 18c. Once mixed into the software directories, configuration files, like the password and parameter files and network configurations, are now stored separately from the ORACLE_HOME. It makes cloning and restoring databases easier and increases the distinction between the database instance and the database software.

---

[3] But what about patching and upgrades? Rather than patching a container, it's better to build a new image for the patched version. The time and effort of patching is spent just once—during image build—and every container started from that image benefits. In a container environment, the patching process consists of stopping and removing the container running the old database version, then starting a new container using a patched image and pointing it at the data on a mount.

Read-Only Homes and mounts lend themselves to a more modular way of thinking about database components. Look at Figure 7-2 and note how different types of files are divided between the container's union filesystem and mounts.

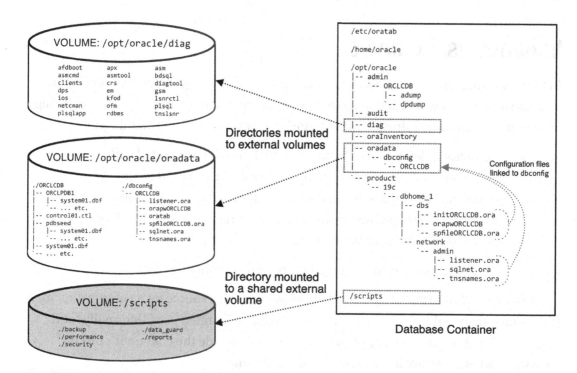

Figure 7-2. *An Oracle database running in a container, with relatively static content built into the image. The data, logs, and configuration files are separated onto mounts dedicated to the database(s) running in the container. The scripts directory is mounted to a filesystem shared with multiple containers*

Notice that the relatively static content, including the database software home and inventory directories, are in the container's filesystem. Volatile content, like datafiles and logs under Oracle's diagnostic directory in /opt/oracle/diag, are separated onto volumes. Configuration files under $ORACLE_HOME/dbs and $ORACLE_HOME/network/admin are linked from their expected locations to a subdirectory under /opt/oracle/oradata, too, which in turn saves them to the database volume.

Mounts aren't limited to data and configuration. The /scripts directory in this example is mounted to a shared filesystem, giving every container access to a common library of scripts and utilities.

Volumes vs. Volumes

Before venturing any further, I want to clarify some terminology. In Docker, *volume* has multiple meanings and is often used loosely to describe or reference any external storage mounted to a container. Officially, a "volume" in Docker describes two things:

- A directory, defined in a *Dockerfile*, which may be associated with a container host resource. The path of the volume is part of the image metadata. You can assign persistent storage for the volume when creating a new container. Oracle's container repository images define a volume at /opt/oracle/oradata.

- A Docker object used as a target for persisting container data.

A *Docker Volume* (the latter, object definition) can be a source for a volume directory (the former, path in the image metadata). But "volume" is often used informally (and incorrectly) to describe *any* type of storage mounted outside the container's union filesystem, whether or not it's actually a Docker Volume.

If that's not already confusing enough, the docker run command has a -v or --volume option that maps storage to a container. So, we use the --volume option to map *Docker Volumes* to *volumes* when creating containers!

Let's break down the different methods of storage attachment to help navigate these overlapping terms.

Mount Types

The only time for attaching storage to containers is during initial creation, using options in the docker run command. There's no going back to edit or add it later, so it's essential to get it right! That means understanding the types of storage, their purpose, and their advantages or limits. The two types used most with our databases are *bind mounts* and *volumes*. Two additional types, *tmpfs*, and a special case, *secrets*, are less common.

Bind Mount

You've already seen *bind mounts* used to persist data to the local filesystem. Bind mounts map files and directories in containers to files and directories on hosts. They're arguably more familiar and comfortable for anyone new to Docker and containers, and the method Oracle demonstrates in their container repository documentation. The advantage of bind mounts is convenience and, ostensibly, visibility. Using the /opt/oracle/oradata volume directory of an Oracle database container as an example, I can navigate to the directory on my local machine to view and manage its contents:

```
~/oradata> du -sh ./*
1.5G    ./ORA11G
2.0G    ./ORA12C
2.9G    ./ORA19C
4.8G    ./ORA21C
```

I mapped multiple containers to separate subdirectories under $HOME/oradata and can use standard Linux commands to view and manage those directories. Their space consumption is readily visible using the du command.

Assigning bind mounts to containers during docker run is straightforward, and the host directory doesn't even have to exist! The directory is part of the host filesystem,[4] and the same familiar Linux commands used elsewhere on the Docker host work in the mapped directory. There are no extra commands or prerequisites needed to use bind mounts. What's not to love?

Docker Volumes

Docker Volumes are similar to bind mounts in some regards: each persists data outside the container's union filesystem. The differences lie in capabilities and management. While bind mounts are directories on the host filesystem, Docker Volumes are Docker

---

[4]Windows systems running Windows Subsystem for Linux version 2 are a special case. Where the container and volume are created—in the native, Windows OS, or in the Linux subsystem—affects their visibility. More on this later in the chapter!

objects and must be created ahead of time,[5] adding a step to container creation. The *default* location for Docker Volumes is the host's private `/var/lib/docker` area.

Using the `/var/lib/docker` for storage was one of the indictments against union filesystems, though! If volumes use this location, we're back in the same boat, putting data in a limited destination! But that's merely the *default* location. We have the opportunity to create volumes on the local filesystem, just like bind mounts. Volumes can also reference storage beyond the reach of binds, including Object Storage buckets on cloud sources.

Docker Volumes are *objects* in the Docker environment, managed through the Docker CLI, primarily the `docker volume` command. In some ways, Docker Volumes parallel *Oracle Automatic Storage Management* (ASM)—both provide integrated, application-aware storage and extended features and capabilities, but with the addition of dedicated commands. A volume must exist before mapping it to a container, just as DBAs need to create ASM disks before assigning them to a database. Listing 7-1 offers examples of creating a volume, listing volumes on the system, inspecting volume metadata, and removing the volume.[6] Docker Desktop provides volume management, too. Figure 7-3 shows the volume management tab in Docker Desktop for the `oradata` volume in this example.

Listing 7-1. Examples of Docker commands for creating a volume, listing volumes on a system, displaying volume metadata, and removing a volume

```
> docker volume create oradata
oradata

> docker volume ls
DRIVER     VOLUME NAME
local      oradata
```

---

[5] Volumes created "on the fly" when calling docker run are called anonymous volumes. They're assigned uniquely generated names, making them more difficult to associate with specific containers. For clarity, the examples in this book use named volumes.

[6] Good news! Docker returns an error if you attempt to remove a volume that's used by any containers—whether or not they're running. The same isn't true of manually managed directories!

```
> docker volume inspect oradata
[
    {
        "CreatedAt": "2022-01-01T12:00:00Z",
        "Driver": "local",
        "Labels": {},
        "Mountpoint": "/var/lib/docker/volumes/oradata/_data",
        "Name": "oradata",
        "Options": {},
        "Scope": "local"
    }
]

> docker volume rm oradata
oradata
```

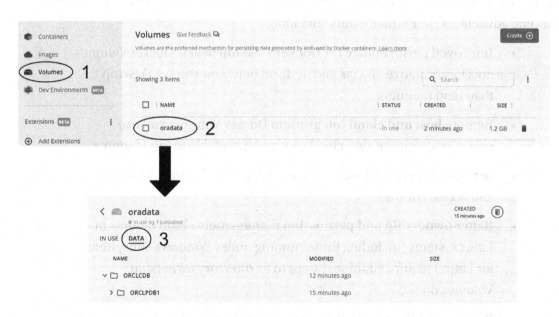

Figure 7-3. *The Docker Desktop view for the oradata volume. Under the "Volumes" view (1), I selected the oradata volume (2) to navigate to the volume details page. Under the "Data" tab (3), I can see the volume's files and directories*

tmpfs and Secrets

The remaining mount types see more limited and specific use.

The *tmpfs* type saves data to memory but never writes to the host filesystem. They're suitable for application or session data used while the container is running that doesn't require persistence. A `tmpfs` mount can share sensitive information with containers, such as keys and passwords.

Runtime secrets[7] are a special type of mount available in *Podman*, an alternate container engine. Runtime secrets offer a better, safer way of sharing credentials with containers. Absent runtime secrets, the options for passing passwords and other sensitive information to containers may leave visible artifacts threat actors can leverage.

Volumes vs. Bind Mounts

Docker Volumes are the preferred means for persisting data, per Docker, and enjoy several advantages over bind mounts, including

- **Improved performance for Docker Desktop users:** Docker Volumes are Docker-native objects and perform better on Docker Desktop than bind mounts.

- **Remote host and cloud integration:** Docker Volumes can use specialized, remote, and cloud storage unavailable to bind mounts.

- **Increased security:** Plugins and drivers allow volume encryption and access control.

- **Better ownership and permission management:** Bind mounts in Linux systems (including those running under Windows Subsystem for Linux) require additional steps to fix directory ownership. Volumes do not.

- **Backup and sharing:** Volumes are easier to back up and migrate and safer to share across multiple containers.

---

[7] There are two types of secrets: runtime and build. Build secrets are available in Docker via Buildah.

For those new to containers, it's easy to forget to manage the volume resources. Deleting a container orphans its volumes. Over time, starting and dropping database containers without cleaning up volumes adds space pressure on the host. It's especially true for volumes in the Docker's private /var/lib/docker directory, which can easily fly under the radar. Only privileged users can identify what's using the space on Linux systems. For Docker Desktop users, that space is hidden in a virtual machine.

What happens once volumes[8] fill the disk depends on the environment. For Docker Desktop users, when the Docker VM runs out of space it stops working or reports errors. On Linux systems, users may observe anything from odd behavior to failures.

The attraction and apparent advantage of bind mounts was their accessibility from the host. They're regular directories, and discovering their space use is straightforward. But volumes can be bind mounts, too! Listing 7-2 shows how I created a volume called oradata_ORA11G, then listed and inspected its metadata. The volume create command uses additional options, instructing Docker to bind the volume to a directory on my local filesystem. In the end, I have a volume using a local directory, just like a bind mount!

Listing 7-2. Creating a volume that binds to a directory on the local host

```
> docker volume create --opt type=none --opt o=bind --opt device=/oradata/
ORA11G oradata_ORA11G
oracle_data
> docker volume ls
DRIVER              VOLUME NAME
local               oradata_ORA11G
> docker volume inspect oradata_ORA11G
[
    {
        "Driver": "local",
        "Mountpoint": "/var/lib/docker/volumes/oradata_ORA11G/_data",
        "Name": "oradata_ORA11G",
        "Options": {
            "device": "/oradata/ORA11G",
            "o": "bind",
```

---

[8] Images and build artifacts can grow to fill disk, too. See the section on space management toward the end of this chapter.

```
        "type": "none"
    },
    "Scope": "local"
  }
]
```

Now I have the best of both worlds! My volume is visible through Docker's CLI and uses a directory on the host I can navigate with regular Linux commands![9] The next step is using this volume to mount the `oradata` volume in a new container called *ORA11G*.

There's a relationship between containers and external data. Docker has a better understanding of that relationship through volumes. In a simple environment with one or a few containers and volumes, it's not that important. With growing complexity, it's more critical to understand what's used and where.

When I first started running Oracle databases in containers, I used a directory called `oradata` as the root for all my containers. Each container was bind-mounted to its own subdirectory, and I managed everything manually. If I had a subdirectory called `TEST123` but no matching container, I knew it was safe to remove that subdirectory to reclaim space.

It wasn't long before I mounted multiple directories to a container or shared directories among numerous containers. Keeping track grew more difficult, and the ramifications of deleting a directory were more severe.

Oracle databases running in production face similar problems. They'll likely use more than one volume per container—one for the diagnostic directory, others for configuration files and shared scripts, and one or more for data. Keeping track of these associations is easier when Docker itself understands which volumes are used where.

Creating volumes is a little more trouble. It's an extra step with some additional complexity. Developing the habit early in your Docker experience makes it second nature and puts the benefits of volumes within reach when container projects begin demanding more from storage.

If you're still not convinced, there are things bind mounts simply can't do, for instance, accessing cloud storage. Listing 7-3 shows an example of a Docker Volume created for an Object Storage bucket in Oracle Cloud Infrastructure.

---

[9] The mount point is still in /var/lib/docker—it's Docker's internal reference telling the container where to find the volume.

Listing 7-3. A volume backed by an Oracle Cloud Infrastructure Object Storage bucket

```
docker volume inspect docker_bucket
[
    {
        "CreatedAt": "0001-01-01T00:00:00Z",
        "Driver": "s3fs:latest",
        "Mountpoint": "",
        "Name": "docker_bucket",
        "Options": {},
        "Scope": "local",
        "Status": {
            "args": [
                "-o",                        "nomultipart,use_path_request_
                                             style,url=https://ocid1.tenancy.oc1..
                                             XXXXX.compat.objectstorage.XXXXX-1.
                                             oraclecloud.com/,bucket=docker_bucket"
            ],
            "mounted": false
        }
    }
]
```

Oracle's container registry documentation uses a bind mount (not a volume) for the /opt/oracle/oradata directory. I suggest mounting two additional directories in your Oracle containers for diagnostic and audit data. Both have the potential to grow over time. When saved within the container's union filesystem, they add to the /var/lib/docker filesystem.

Docker recommends volumes over bind mounts due to their flexibility and capabilities. Examples in the following chapters, therefore, use volumes unless otherwise noted.

Mounting Storage

With an understanding of the different methods of mounting storage in containers, we're ready to dig into the syntax. The images in Oracle's container repository use the /opt/oracle/oradata directory as a volume. This directory is the default root for datafiles, and I'll use it as an example to illustrate options for mapping mounts to containers. (For simplicity, I didn't include diagnostic and audit directories in these initial examples.)

Mapping storage to containers occurs during container creation through options in the docker run command. Oracle's container repository documentation uses the legacy -v (long form: --volume) option in its examples, but Docker recommends using --mount instead. Generally speaking, both the --mount and -v options offer the same capabilities.[10] The significant difference lies in the expressions for defining each component. -v uses an ordered format, while --mount separates elements into named components.

Both methods share two things:

- A *source* directory or volume on the host

- A *target* path in the container

Using -v or --volume

Ultimately, we're mapping a target path in a container to write data to a source on the host. For the -v or --volume option, they're passed as an ordered pair separated by a colon, source first, followed by the target. For bind mounts, the *source* is a *directory*:

```
docker run ... \
       -v /oradata/ORA19C:/opt/oracle/oradata \
...

docker run ... \
       --volume /oradata/ORA19C:/opt/oracle/oradata \
...
```

For volumes, the *source* is the *volume name*:

```
docker run ... \
       -v oradata_ORA19C:/opt/oracle/oradata \
...

docker run ... \
       --volume oradata_ORA19C:/opt/oracle/oradata \
...
```

---

[10] The --mount flag allows added capabilities for some special cases.

Using --mount

The --mount option separates elements into named, comma-delimited lists. The order of elements doesn't matter. The --mount equivalent for bind-mounting a directory is

```
docker run ... \
        --mount type=bind,source=/oradata/ORA19C,target=/opt/oracle/
oradata \
...
```

For attaching a volume:

```
docker run ... \
        --mount type=volume,target=/opt/oracle/oradata,source=oradata_
ORA19C \
...
```

Note the additional field, type, in the --mount syntax. It tells Docker whether we're using a volume or bind mount. The type is understood in the -v option based on whether the source is a Docker Volume or a directory. The first command uses the same order—source, then target—as the -v option. The second demonstrates that order doesn't matter by reversing the elements.

Another difference between -v and --mount is how Docker handles nonexistent source directories. If the source directory in these examples, /oradata/ORA19C, isn't present on the host, -v creates the directory during docker run.[11] The --mount option doesn't and fails with an error.

According to Docker's research, the field names in --mount, source and target, make the command more understandable,[12] and they recommend the --mount option. Oracle's container registry uses the -v flag in their documentation. Whether you use -v or --mount is up to you.

---

[11] Linux users (including those running Windows Subsystem for Linux, or WSL) may discover issues with directory ownership. See the section "*Which Type of Volume Is Best*" at the end of this chapter for more details.

[12] See: https://docs.docker.com/storage/bind-mounts/

Undefined Volumes

So far, I've covered mounting storage to a known volume in the container, the /opt/ oracle/oradata directory. That directory is defined as a volume in the Dockerfile, and the image metadata understands it's special. It's a directory that *can* be associated with a host resource, whether a bind mount or a Docker volume.[13]

What happens if I try to map a host directory to something that doesn't exist in the container? How will Docker handle a nonexistent volume? Docker creates the directory in the container, as shown in Listing 7-4. It's a convenient way of sharing files between the Docker host and container!

Listing 7-4. When mounting a local directory to a nonexistent path in the container, Docker creates the directory in the container and maps it to the host!

```
> docker run --rm -it \
>           -v $HOME:/not/a/real/directory alpine

/ # ls -l /not/a/real/directory/
total 8302776
drwx------    7 sean.scott   staff        224 Mar 26 11:44 Applications
drwx------@  88 sean.scott   staff       2816 Apr  8 16:57 Desktop
drwx------+  49 sean.scott   staff       1568 Mar 16 08:31 Documents
...
```

Docker created a new directory inside the container in this example. You can also mount directories to existing paths in containers. If the container path includes files, Docker hides the contents of the container's target directory, projecting the source directory contents on top. It's a neat trick to replace an image's contents for testing. For example, I can mount an updated or patched copy of an ORACLE_HOME or scripts to a container for testing purposes—without rebuilding the image!

A word of warning, though: Mounting existing, nonempty directories in containers can have unexpected and undesirable results if the source directory lacks the files the container needs. In the previous example, mounting an empty host directory to the container's ORACLE_HOME prevents Oracle from starting in the container.

---

[13] Volumes don't have to be attached to a host resource. If a mapping isn't given, Docker puts the files in the container's private layer, as part of the union filesystem. In my experience, creating an Oracle database container without a volume for /opt/oracle/oradata is a bad idea—database creation is orders of magnitude slower!

Entrypoint Directories

Images define *startup commands*, similar to the boot or initialization processes on physical or virtual hosts. Startup commands run when creating and starting containers, directing them to perform predefined work. (Review the Oracle database image startup procedures in Chapters 5 and 6 if you need a refresher.) When an Oracle database container starts, it calls a script to discover whether a database exists. If it finds one, it starts the listener and database. If not, it creates a new database.

An *entrypoint directory* (not to be confused with *container entrypoints*, discussed in Chapter 12) is a special type of empty directory. The startup command scans the directory for additional scripts and processes them programmatically. The directory location and how startup evaluates the contents are purely dependent on the startup command or script.

The startup script in the Oracle database images we're using looks for these scripts in either /docker-entrypoint-initdb.d[14] or /opt/oracle/scripts, where it expects to find two subdirectories, `setup` and `startup`. It runs shell (.sh) and SQL (.sql) scripts in the `setup` directory after initial database creation; those in the `startup` directory every time the container starts, including after database creation.

Mounting a volume or local directory to the entrypoint directory, and populating it with custom scripts, allows greater control of container databases. A caution is in order, however. Since this directory exists outside the container, changes to its contents affect future startups, potentially leading to unexpected results.

Listing 7-5 shows how to mount a local directory to the entrypoint directory. It uses a single path that has existing `setup` and `startup` subdirectories. When Docker mounts this directory to the container, these directories match those expected by the startup script.

Listing 7-5. Mounting an entrypoint directory to an Oracle database container

```
docker run ... \
        --mount type=bind,source=$HOME/dbscripts,target=/docker-entrypoint-
        initdb.d \
...
```

---

[14] The /docker/entrypoint-initdb.d directory is used by multiple database vendors as an entrypoint for custom scripts.

The example in Listing 7-6 mounts two separate directories, one for setup and another for startup, to their respective targets.

Listing 7-6. Mounting separate startup and setup entrypoints to a container

```
docker run ... \
      --mount type=bind,source=$HOME/dbstartup,target=/opt/oracle/scripts/
      startup \
      --mount type=bind,source=$HOME/dbsetup,target=/opt/oracle/
      scripts/setup \
...
```

When multiple scripts exist in these directories, Oracle recommends adding a numerical prefix to ensure the order of execution, for example:

```
01_first_step.sql
02_second_step.sh
03_last_step.sql
```

Manage Space

To see what Docker objects use space on a system, run the `docker system df` command:

```
> docker system df
TYPE            TOTAL   ACTIVE   SIZE       RECLAIMABLE
Images          29      2        157.3GB    143.7GB (91%)
Containers      2       2        540.6MB    0B (0%)
Local Volumes   8       0        15.42GB    15.42GB (100%)
Build Cache     138     0        41.05MB    41.05MB
```

The output reports a summary of the object types using space in Docker's private, /var/lib/docker directory. *Images* are just that—images built or downloaded on this system. The *Containers* line displays the space used by the container's *upper layers*. The last line, *Build Cache*, lists the size of content cached by build activity.

The third line reports eight *Local Volumes* that take up 15GB of space. None are active. Remember that local volumes are those created *without* drivers and save data in Docker's private, /var/lib/docker directory. This does *not* include volumes associated to bind mounts on the system, created with an --opt o=bind or similar option.

Prune Volumes

It's easy to confuse *local volumes* with volumes that *use a local driver*, as shown in the output of docker volume ls:

```
> docker volume ls
DRIVER   VOLUME NAME
local    2ac7d7486083a10a4ed313699e06eba017e63ba
local    4efabdab067033c973d00e73de9a05121e0cb70
local    9fc0fdc81eabd71a07f28a8d79fd2c1a5606747
local    84c91dc6a3f0cb354243cb9ee2ca5a79933ca67
local    ORA216_data
local    ORA216_diag
local    ORA216_audit
local    ORA1915_data
local    ORA1915_diag
local    ORA1915_audit
local    oradata_ORCL1_data
local    oradata_ORCL1_diag
local    oradata_ORCL1_audit
local    b26d713b83be8ac8f549f825d19cc2b6e6f19a6
```

All the volumes use a local driver. The six beginning with "ORA" are bind-mounted to directories on the host. I can confirm this by inspecting the volumes and looking for the presence of a device. The output for the ORA216_data volume shows the device in the Options section:

```
> docker volume inspect ORA216_data
[
    {
        "Driver": "local",
        "Mountpoint": "/var/lib/docker/volumes/ORA216_data /_data",
        "Name": "ORA216_data",
        "Options": {
            "device": "/oradata/ORA216_data",
            "o": "bind",
            "type": "none"
        },
```

```
        "Scope": "local"
    }
]
```

The Options section from the oradata_ORCL1_data volume is empty:

```
> docker volume inspect oradata_ORCL1_data
[
    {
        "Driver": "local",
        "Mountpoint": "/var/lib/docker/volumes/oradata_ORCL1_data/_data",
        "Name": "oradata_ORCL1_data",
        "Options": {},
        "Scope": "local"
    }
]
~
```

I know that all eight local volumes are orphaned based on the zero under the "ACTIVE" column. Since they're unused by any containers, it's safe to remove them using the docker volume prune command:

```
> docker volume prune
WARNING! This will remove all local volumes not used by at least one
container.
Are you sure you want to continue? [y/N] y
Deleted Volumes:
84c91dc6a3f0cb354243cb9ee2ca5a79933ca67
oradata_ORCL1_data
oradata_ORCL1_diag
4efabdab067033c973d00e73de9a05121e0cb70
9fc0fdc81eabd71a07f28a8d79fd2c1a5606747
oradata_ORCL1_audit
b26d713b83be8ac8f549f825d19cc2b6e6f19a6
2ac7d7486083a10a4ed313699e06eba017e63ba
```

It's reassuring knowing Docker won't remove volumes used by containers (whether running or stopped)!

After running the prune command, I checked the space use a second time:

```
> docker system df
TYPE            TOTAL   ACTIVE   SIZE      RECLAIMABLE
Images          29      2        157.3GB   143.7GB (91%)
Containers      2       2        540.6MB   0B (0%)
Local Volumes   0       0        0B        0B
Build Cache     138     0        41.05MB   41.05MB
```

Docker removed the inactive volumes and reclaimed the space. docker volume ls confirms the prune didn't affect the bind-mounted volumes on the host:

```
> docker volume ls
DRIVER   VOLUME NAME
local    ORA216_data
local    ORA216_diag
local    ORA216_audit
local    ORA1915_data
local    ORA1915_diag
local    ORA1915_audit
```

Prune Images

There are prune options for images, too:

```
docker image prune
```

The *image prune* command removes "dangling" images—those unused by any container and not tagged with a name:

```
> docker image prune
WARNING! This will remove all dangling images.
Are you sure you want to continue? [y/N] y
Total reclaimed space: 0B
```

Dangling images typically result from rebuilding an existing image and using the same tag. If any containers use the old image, it's untagged by Docker. This abbreviated output of docker ps shows two containers, one using the old (untagged) image identified only by its Image ID, the other using the newer, tagged version:

```
> docker ps
NAMES          IMAGE
ORA19c_old     f53962475832
ORA19c_new     oracle/database:19.3.0-ee
```

In the output of docker images, the dangling image has no repository or tag:

```
# docker images
REPOSITORY       TAG         IMAGE ID       CREATED        SIZE
oracle/database  19.3.0-ee   94d27a821d52   4 weeks ago    6.67GB
<none>           <none>      f53962475832   4 months ago   6.53GB
```

docker image prune won't remove the dangling image—provided any containers still use it. After removing all dependencies on a dangling image, docker image prune deletes them.

Prune Containers

Pruning images is relatively safe. However, you should use docker container prune with caution! Pruning containers removes all *stopped* containers from the system:

```
> docker container prune
WARNING! This will remove all stopped containers.
Are you sure you want to continue? [y/N] y
Total reclaimed space: 0B
```

Stopped containers aren't necessarily obsolete! Be careful with this command!

Prune the System

If you *really* want to clean up *everything* on the system in a single command, there's docker system prune. It removes stopped containers, dangling images, unused networks, and build cache:

```
> docker system prune
WARNING! This will remove:
  - all stopped containers
  - all networks not used by at least one container
```

```
- all dangling images
- all dangling build cache
```

```
Are you sure you want to continue? [y/N] y
Total reclaimed space: 0B
```

The same cautions raised for docker container prune apply to the system prune command.

Which Type of Volume Is Best?

You've seen several methods for saving and preserving database contents outside containers, but which is best? There are several criteria affecting container storage choices:

- **Access and navigation:** Is container data saved to the volume visible to users on the local operating system?

- **Docker managed:** Does Docker manage the storage as an object, associate it with containers, and report whether the volume is used?

- **Directory creation:** Will Docker automatically create nonexistent directory paths on the host?

- **Directory ownership:** For automatically created directories, is ownership set correctly?

- **Backup and save data:** What mechanisms are available for copying and saving data?

- **Consistent across platforms:** Does the solution behave identically on all platforms (Windows, Mac, and Linux)?

Let's examine how each storage option handles these scenarios. I want to focus on ramifications for Oracle databases and users, including the steps necessary to create the container and supporting objects and ease of backing up or copying the contents of a database's oradata volume.

No Volume

Containers created with no volume store data in the upper layers of their union filesystems. Container creation is easy. There are no concerns related to directory creation or ownership, and it works the same on every OS. However, users lack practical access to the database's oradata volume.

Containers run with no volume options keep data in Docker's private storage. As databases grow, adding space isn't a simple task, and it's a single bucket that may not meet performance requirements. The space is also shared by all containers on the host, disqualifying it as a method for anything beyond local implementations and environments with low expectations for I/O performance.

Bind Mounts

Bind mounts improve things considerably by mapping a container directory to storage on the host. Files saved to the host OS are visible to users, and we can back up and copy the contents of the oradata volume. However, bind mounting fails four of the test criteria outlined earlier.

Container Association and Orphans

Bind-mounting directories doesn't explicitly associate them with a container. Running docker container inspect shows the source and target of the bind mount, as in this example formatted to show only the mount information:

```
> docker inspect -f "{{ .Mounts }}" ORCL
[{bind  /oradata/ORCL /opt/oracle/oradata   true rprivate}]
```

However, there's no good method for identifying whether /oradata/ORCL is used by any containers, short of inspecting all containers on the system. Bind mounting makes it easy to lose track of orphaned directories.

Mounting Method

The mounting method affects whether Docker automatically creates nonexistent directories. When I use the --volume or -v option, Docker creates the directory. Here, I'm creating an Alpine container, mounting a directory called $HOME/test_volume that doesn't already exist, and listing the contents:

```
> docker run \
        --volume $HOME/test_volume:/test_volume \
        alpine ls -l /test_volume
total 0
> ls -l $HOME
drwxr-xr-x  2 root root        4096 Sep 18 19:36  test_volume
```

However, if I run the same command, this time using the --mount option for a different, nonexistent directory, $HOME/test_mount, it fails:

```
> docker run \
        --mount type=bind,source=$HOME/test_mount,target=/test_mount \
        alpine ls -l /test_mount
docker: Error response from daemon: invalid mount config for type "bind":
bind source path does not exist: /home/sean/test_mount.
See 'docker run --help'.
```

Directory Ownership

The preceding --volume example ran on a Linux machine and created the directory, $HOME/test_volume, for me. But look at the contents of my $HOME folder after running the container:

```
> ls -l $HOME
drwxrwxr-x 32 sean sean        4096 Aug 20 17:06  docker-images
drwxr-xr-x  2 root root        4096 Sep 18 19:36  test_volume
```

Notice anything odd?

The newly created directory, test_volume, is owned by root.

I called docker run as a non-root user without using sudo. How, then, did I manage to create the new directory owned by root in my home directory?

Docker creates nonexistent directories within its daemon, and they inherit their ownership from the user running the daemon process. On Linux systems, the daemon runs as the root user. root, therefore, owns the newly created directories.

This creates problems for Oracle database containers on Linux systems and those initiated from a Linux command prompt in Windows Subsystem for Linux. Docker creates the directory as root. Oracle processes running within the container can't write to the directory, and if that happens to be the mount point for /opt/oracle/oradata, the Database Configuration Assistant fails!

This isn't an issue for Mac or Windows, provided you issue the docker run command within a session running from the native Windows operating system. In these cases, the daemon runs as the local user, and the Oracle processes in the container have permission to add files in the newly created directories. Starting containers from Docker Desktop circumvents this issue, too. The "Run a new container" dialog in Figure 7-4 lets users create a mount, assigning a host directory to a container target. (Despite how it may appear, defining a Host path under the Volumes section of the dialog does *not* create a Docker Volume.)

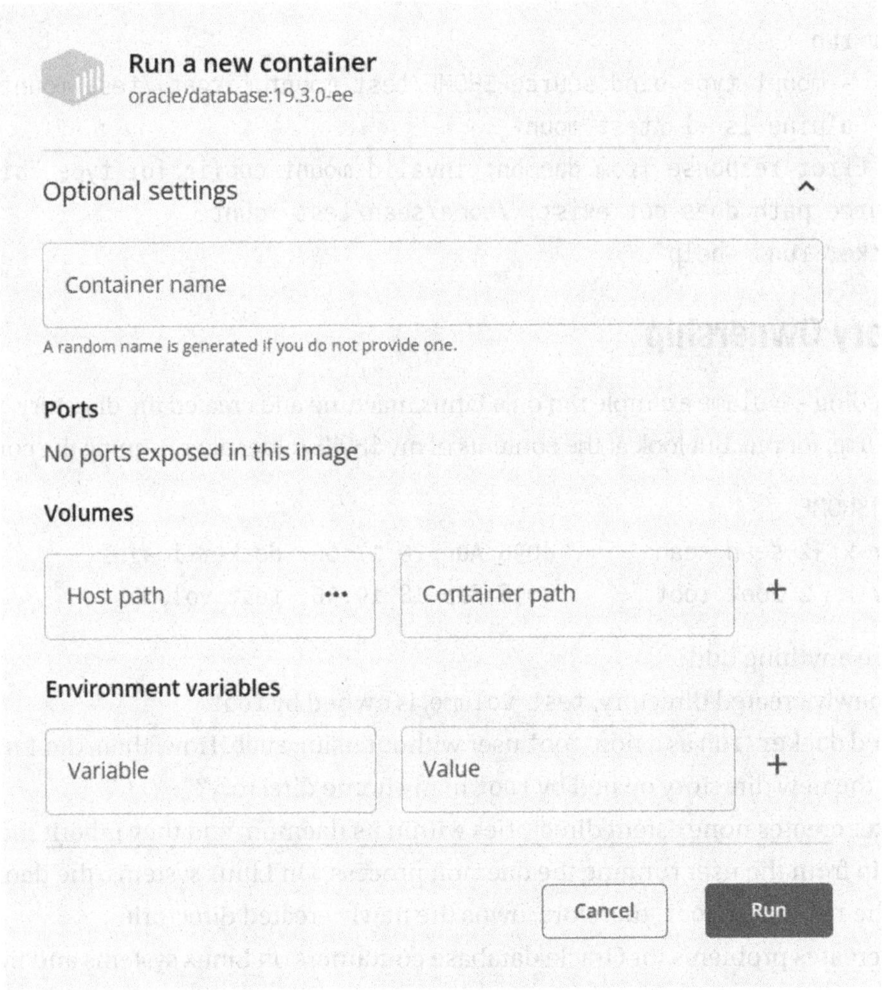

Figure 7-4. *The Docker Desktop "Run a new container" dialog allows users to assign a local directory to a target in the new container*

Users in Linux and WSL environments can work around this by precreating the directories and setting directory ownership:

```
sudo mkdir -p /oradata/ORCL
sudo chown oracle:oinstall /oradata/ORCL
```

Setting ownership to oracle:oinstall means the user and group must exist, with the same user and group ID specified in containers by the Linux preinstall RPMs:

```
sudo groupadd -g 54321 oinstall
sudo useradd -u 54321 -g oinstall
```

Alternately, you can assign the directory ownership to the Docker process ID, 1000:

```
sudo chown 1000 /oradata/ORCL
```

Bind mounts are a good, but not great, solution for database storage, mainly if you're using a Mac or running everything from Docker Desktop. Users working on multiple operating systems or environments will likely encounter limitations and peculiar or annoying behaviors.

Local Volumes

With local volumes, users graduate onto objects fully managed by Docker. Whether in Docker Desktop or at the command line, containers and their volumes are visibly associated, making the relationships more manageable.

Recall from the section on volume pruning that local volumes are created without any type and show nothing in the Options output of docker volume inspect.

Local volumes are Docker objects and behave consistently on all operating systems. Docker provides tools for saving directories and files on volumes and sharing volume contents among containers.

However, since local volumes save data inside Docker's private directory, they suffer many of the same shortcomings as saving data with no mount or volume. Data in local volumes isn't visible from the local operating system, and they're subject to the same limitations to performance and space.

Bind-Mounted Volumes

Bind-mounting volumes combines the best of bind mounts with the advantages of Docker-managed objects. Files saved to the host filesystem are visible to users and processes—including backups. Docker Desktop or the Docker CLI manages relationships between containers and bind-mounted volumes, as with local volumes.

Unfortunately, Docker Desktop doesn't currently offer an option for creating volumes with bind mounts, forcing us to perform at least this step from the command line.

Let's compare behaviors between regular bind mounts and volumes that use bind mounts.

Directory Creation

I'll first create a bind mount using the directory $HOME/test_bind:

```
> docker volume create --opt type=none --opt o=bind \
        --opt device=$HOME/test_bind test_bind
test_bind
```

So far, so good. Now I try running a test similar to the one I performed before, this time mapping a directory in the container to the volume:

```
> docker run \
>        --volume test_bind:/test_bind \
>        alpine ls -l /test_bind
docker: Error response from daemon: error while mounting volume '/docker/
volumes/test_bind/_data': failed to mount local volume: mount /home/docker/
test_bind:/docker/volumes/test_bind/_data, flags: 0x1000: no such file or
directory.
ERRO[0000] error waiting for container: context canceled
```

Creating the bind-mounted volume didn't make the directory! Let's take care of that and try again:

```
> mkdir -p $HOME/test_bind

> docker run \
>        --volume test_bind:/test_bind \
>        alpine ls -l /test_bind
total 0
```

This time it works! I created the directory as the local user on the system, meaning it's not owned by root. But how will this affect our database containers?

Directory Ownership and Permissions

Remember in the earlier bind mount example that Oracle database processes running inside containers on Linux systems needed specific permissions on the host directory. Else, the Database Configuration Assistant fails with "permission denied" errors when creating a database. I'll test this, creating a new directory and volume for an Oracle database container:

```
> docker volume create --opt type=none --opt o=bind \
>         --opt device=$HOME/oracle_bind oracle_bind
oracle_bind

> mkdir -p $HOME/oracle_bind
```

There's nothing unusual about the ownership on the new directory:

```
> ls -l $HOME
total 7386868
drwxrwxr-x 32 sean sean       4096 Aug 20 17:06  docker-images
drwxr-xr-x  3 sean sean         21 Sep 18 22:11  oracle_bind
```

Without doing anything special with the newly created $HOME/oracle_bind directory, I start a container, mapping the oradata directory to the volume:

```
> docker run -d --name bind_test \
>         -v oracle_bind:/opt/oracle/oradata \
>         oracle/database:19.3.0-ee
d2b25b1f661d7f243984fdcbd77177beb14dc61be9525d421426e0d609917f31
```

However, once DBCA starts in the container, something unusual happens to this directory:

```
> ls -l $HOME
total 7386868
drwxrwxr-x 32 sean    sean       4096 Aug 20 17:06  docker-images
drwxr-xr-x  4 oracle  54322        61 Sep 18 22:26  oracle_bind
```

Docker changed the directory ownership! While the Docker daemon runs as root, processes inside the container propagate the expected ownership to the daemon, which makes the necessary changes on the container host.

Mounting Method

With regular bind mounts, the `--volume` and `--mount` options treated nonexistent directories differently. Because the directories used by bind-mounted volumes must be precreated, the `--volume` and `--mount` options are both valid.

Despite the additional effort needed to create the volume and source directory before running containers, bind-mounted volumes are the best option for databases. Data on the volumes are accessible from the OS, and we can back up the data using either operating system commands or Docker's volume management tools. We see consistent behavior and operation across platforms and don't need to worry about setting permissions or ownership!

Summary

Understanding storage is arguably among the most important concepts when implementing database infrastructure in containers. In this chapter, you discovered the advantages and limitations of container union filesystems and how externally mounted storage extends capabilities and improves containers' performance.

You learned the differences between bind mounts and volumes. You now understand the multiple meanings of *volume* in Docker circles, as a target directory in an image, an object for storing data, and how it's inaccurately used to reference any storage attached to a container. Finally, you recognize the differences and benefits of different storage methods and know how to create volumes and mount storage to new containers.

Exploring container storage offered a glimpse into how well-planned images lead to highly modular, efficient, and portable implementations. In the next chapter, you'll learn how to set up communication between hosts and containers. It's the second half of the puzzle, joining host resources to containers.

CHAPTER 8

Basic Networking

In the early days of Unix, compute resources were expensive. Getting the most from these costly systems meant finding ways to support many simultaneous connections. Users from different companies and those working with sensitive information needed assurance their processes and data were safe. This was a driver behind the Unix Time Sharing System, or UTS, and provides session isolation and security, the foundation of modern container implementations.

Insulating and securing containers is the backbone of modern high-density infrastructure. Service-based and cloud-native computing concentrates the work of dozens or hundreds of individual systems onto individual servers. Each remains unaware they're sharing resources. But what happens when you *want* containers to interact? Enterprises aren't solitary systems cut off from the world, so there must be a mechanism for describing and managing access.

Container networking builds on "normal" networking concepts. The container boundary—where packets cross from inside to outside the container—is a network interface. It follows the same rules, and we can use the same techniques to control and manipulate traffic. Virtual networks handle communication between a container and its host, other local containers, and remote resources (including containers on different machines) in container environments. You'll see that creating network resources is very similar to what you learned about defining volumes in the last chapter. There's a quick, easy, but limited way of doing things or a more involved method that offers greater flexibility.

If you're running a few database containers on a local system and only plan to connect with command-line or database clients like *SQL Developer*, the quick and easy way is probably all you need. Orchestrations and shared environments benefit from more structured approaches, which deliver more advanced networking capabilities like DNS. The extra effort spent planning network topologies of more complex, multicontainer projects (think RAC, GoldenGate, and Data Guard) is well worth the convenience and time savings once they're in use.

© Sean Scott 2023
S. Scott, *Oracle on Docker*, https://doi.org/10.1007/978-1-4842-9033-0_8

With that in mind, this chapter covers the quick, easy method—*port publishing*—and demonstrates how to connect clients to a container database. The next chapter digs into the more formal subject of *container networks* and their advantages, some practical examples for creating and managing different network resources, and adding containers to networks.

Port Publishing

Port publishing is the simplest way of establishing communication with containers. It's perfectly suitable for local desktop systems but lacks container networks' scalability, flexibility, and controls. However, if all you want is to connect to an Oracle database on your desktop or laptop with a client like SQL Developer, the extra time and effort of creating a dedicated network are academic. Port publishing is all you need.

For Oracle databases, we're usually interested in port 1521, the default for *SQL*Net* traffic to and from the database listener. I'll use port 1521 as an example while introducing port mapping (and container networking) in the following examples.

Port publishing binds a port on the local host to a port on the container. For a container running an Oracle database, traffic to and from the container's port 1521 is redirected to a port on the host and vice versa. I'll use port 51521 as the host port (for reasons I'll get to shortly). So, packets leaving the container on port 1521 are mapped and visible at port 51521 on the host. Anything we want to connect to the listener inside the container should go to the host's port 51521, as shown in Figure 8-1.

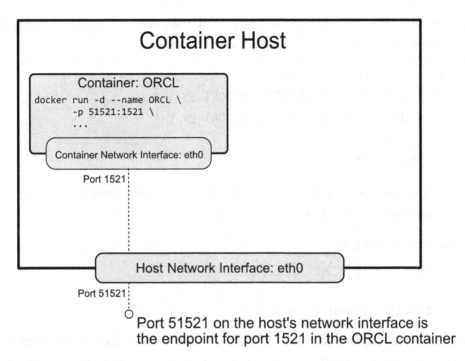

Figure 8-1. *Traffic from port 1521 in the container is redirected over port 51521 on the host's network interface*

The docker run command's -p (long-form --publish) option defines mappings. The syntax, shown in Listing 8-1, follows the same pattern as mapping volumes in the previous chapter:

- The local resource first

- Then the container resource, separated by a colon

Listing 8-1. The docker run syntax for publishing ports with the -p and --publish flags

```
docker run --name <CONTAINER NAME> \
        -p <HOST PORT>:<CONTAINER PORT> \
...
        <IMAGE NAME>

docker run --name <CONTAINER NAME> \
        --publish <HOST PORT>:<CONTAINER PORT> \
...
        <IMAGE NAME>
```

Just as you map multiple volumes by using more than one -v flag, create multiple port mappings with separate -p (or --publish) declarations:

```
docker run --name <CONTAINER NAME> \
          -p <HOST PORT 1>:<CONTAINER PORT 1> \
          -p <HOST PORT 2>:<CONTAINER PORT 2> \
...
          <IMAGE NAME>
```

Here, I'm mapping port 51521 on the host to port 1521 in the container while creating a new Oracle 19c database:

```
docker run --name ORCL \
          -p 51521:1521 \
...
          oracle/database:19.3.0-ee
```

When the traffic is local—where the client and container are both on the same host—the port is all that's necessary. There's no need for hostnames (or anything other than localhost or its equivalent). The container "sees" incoming traffic arrive at port 1521. Clients typically connecting to the database on port 1521 will use port 51521 on localhost instead.

Publishing Container Ports

The only opportunity for publishing ports is during container creation. You can't add a port mapping to an existing container later.[1]

Following the advice from the previous chapter, I'll create a volume to hold my database files. Then, I'll start a container, assigning a name, mounting the volume, and mapping container port 1521 to host port 51521. Listing 8-2 shows these commands and their results.

---

[1] I'll show you a trick to get around that a bit later!

Listing 8-2. Creating the new volume and container we'll use to demonstrate client connectivity

```
> docker volume create \
>       --opt type=none \
>       --opt o=bind \
>       --opt device=/Users/sean.scott/oradata/ORCL \
>       oradata_ORCL
oradata_ORCL

> docker run -d \
>       --name ORCL \
>       --mount type=volume,target=/opt/oracle/oradata,source=oradata_ORCL \
>       -p 51521:1521 \
>       oracle/database:19.3.0-ee
f502c53c3c272463f6b40860784c95f0c2f0cbf9893e503a7cce83bf2ccd35e6
```

After starting the container, I see the port mapping listed in the output of docker ps:

```
NAMES   IMAGE                     PORTS                       STATUS
ORCL    oracle/database:19.3.0-ee  0.0.0.0:51521->1521/tcp    Up 6 minutes
(healthy)
```

Publishing ports does more than just redirect traffic. The mapping, `0.0.0.0:51521->1521/tcp`, acts as a firewall rule that opens port 1521 on the container and allows traffic to pass. Unpublished ports aren't accessible. Since you can't go back and add ports to existing containers, it reinforces the importance of anticipating networking needs during container creation!

Limits of Container Port Mapping

My container is running and listening for database traffic on host port 51521. Let's see what happens when I try adding a second container using the same port mapping:

```
> docker run -d \
>       --name ORCL1 \
>       -p 51521:1521 \
>       oracle/database:19.3.0-ee
```

```
8ab4c0a09137cebcd99fda61a20942aa4c45350070d5af8d69f3dc2605b6ae9d
docker: Error response from daemon: driver failed programming external
connectivity on endpoint ORCL1: Bind for 0.0.0.0:51521 failed: port is
already allocated.
```

Port 51521 is already in use! Starting the second container failed because container-port combinations must use unique, unassigned ports on the host.

The preceding output shows the container was *created* (as evidenced by its hash, the string beginning 8ab4… reported before the error message). Listing containers on my system, using docker ps, confirms this and shows no mapped ports:

```
NAMES   IMAGE                        PORTS                     STATUS
ORCL1   oracle/database:19.3.0-ee                              Created
ORCL    oracle/database:19.3.0-ee    0.0.0.0:51521->1521/tcp   Up 23 minutes
(healthy)
```

Before rerunning a corrected docker run command for this container, I need to remove it.

Keeping track of ports isn't difficult in small environments, like those running on laptops for experimentation. As the number of containers (or the number of ports mapped to the host) grows, port mapping becomes impractical. Ports are a finite resource, and, eventually, capacity on the host runs out.

Tracking what port goes with what container is more complicated, too. When assigning host ports, I typically prefix the container's port with a digit, for example, using ports 51521 and 55500 for one container, 61521 and 65500 in the next, and so on.

Ports below 1024 are the *well-known* ports, usually assigned to standard system or root-owned processes. Mapping container ports to anything below 1024 risks conflict with these registered processes and can prevent host services (or the system) from running normally.

Assigning ports in the 1024 to 49151 range isn't always safe, either. These are the *registered ports*, and while not strictly controlled, registration reduces the chances that vendors duplicate one another. Oracle networking on port 1521 is an example. Other vendors and services *could* use it, but it would create conflicts on systems also running an Oracle database listener.

Dynamic or *nonreserved* ports in the 49152 to 65535 range aren't assigned, controlled, or registered and are generally considered safe for private or temporary use. It's why I chose port 51521 earlier. Ideally, only use ports in the dynamic range for port publication.

Automatic Port Publication

Rather than defining individual, explicit host-to-container port mappings, there's an option to expose ports in the container and let Docker map them to unassigned ports in the dynamic range by using the -P (or --publish-all) option of docker run.

The help menu for docker run states the --publish-all flag will "*Publish all exposed ports to random ports.*" We haven't covered Dockerfiles yet, but they include an option that *exposes* ports in the image metadata. Running docker inspect against an *older* version of an Oracle database container image shows it exposes ports 1521 and 5500:

```
> docker inspect -f '{{.Config.ExposedPorts}}' oracle/database:19.3.0-ee
map[1521/tcp:{} 5500/tcp:{}]
```

Running that image with the -P flag will randomly assign the exposed ports to available ports in the dynamic on the host:

```
> docker run -d \
      --name TEST \
      -P oracle/database:19.3.0-ee
639c6770dacd207f1d9b0a5fa301c9a9d1dc6dac420047ca6c0a41598b9a0203
```

After starting the container, use docker ps to reveal the port assignments Docker made for the image's exposed ports:

```
> docker ps -a \
      --format "table {{.Names}}\t{{.Ports}}"
NAMES     PORTS
TEST      0.0.0.0:32771->1521/tcp, 0.0.0.0:32770->5500/tcp
```

I noted that this was from an older image. The -P option only works when ports are *explicitly* exposed in the image, as in images created from older versions of Oracle's container repository scripts. Somewhere along the line, they removed this from the images:

```
> docker inspect -f '{{.Config.ExposedPorts}}' oracle/database:19.3.0-ee
map[]
```

The -P option has nothing to map if ports aren't exposed in the image.

Explicitly exposing ports in the image isn't necessary, though. The capability is available via docker run's --expose flag. It does at the container level what the EXPOSE option in a Dockerfile does for an image and offers more flexibility to define a list of exposed ports at runtime rather than fixing them into the image. Passing a list or range of ports to --expose tells Docker what ports to open on the container. When given alongside the -P option, Docker assigns ports as if they were exposed in the image.

Listing 8-3 shows how --expose and -P work together with a current Oracle database image, opening and assigning ports 1521 and 5500.

Listing 8-3. Running an image using --expose and -P to open and publish ports 1521 and 5500, even though no ports are defined in the image

```
> docker run -d \
      --name TEST \
      --expose 1521 \
      --expose 5500 \
      -P oracle/database:19.3.0-ee
0d34bb1d59f85b67b90f19db16d0ab09b91ee000c81187f8847c4fe2f6c186eb

> docker ps -a \
      --format "table {{.Names}}\t{{.Ports}}"
NAMES      PORTS
TEST       0.0.0.0:49157->1521/tcp, 0.0.0.0:49156->5500/tcp
```

Now that you understand how to open and map ports from the container to the host, let's put the knowledge to practical use and connect clients to the database inside the container!

Connect to a Database in a Container

Whether adding a new database connection in SQL Developer, building an *EZConnect* string, or creating a tnsnames.ora entry, we need the same basic information:

- **A hostname:** Local clients will use the host localhost or IP address 0.0.0.0.

- **The listener port:** For these examples, I'll switch back to the ORCL container I created at the beginning of the preceding section. If you recall, I mapped the container's listener port, 1521, to port 51521 on my host.

- **The database service or SID:** The default service names created by the Oracle 19c database image I ran earlier are ORCLCDB (for the CDB or container database—not to be confused with the database running in the Docker container!) and ORCLPDB1 (for the PDB, or pluggable database).

- **A username and password:** For demonstration purposes, I changed the system user's password to `oracle`.

Set Up Connections in SQL Developer

SQL Developer is Oracle's versatile, popular, and easy-to-use graphical development utility. It's free to download from *www.oracle.com/tools/downloads/sqldev-downloads.html*. There are dozens of other development tools compatible with Oracle databases, but the procedure for adding a new connection is similar. They all need the same four pieces of information, and what's shown here is adaptable to other products.

After opening SQL Developer, navigate to the connections panel in the upper left and click the green plus symbol to open the New Connection dialog shown in Figure 8-2.

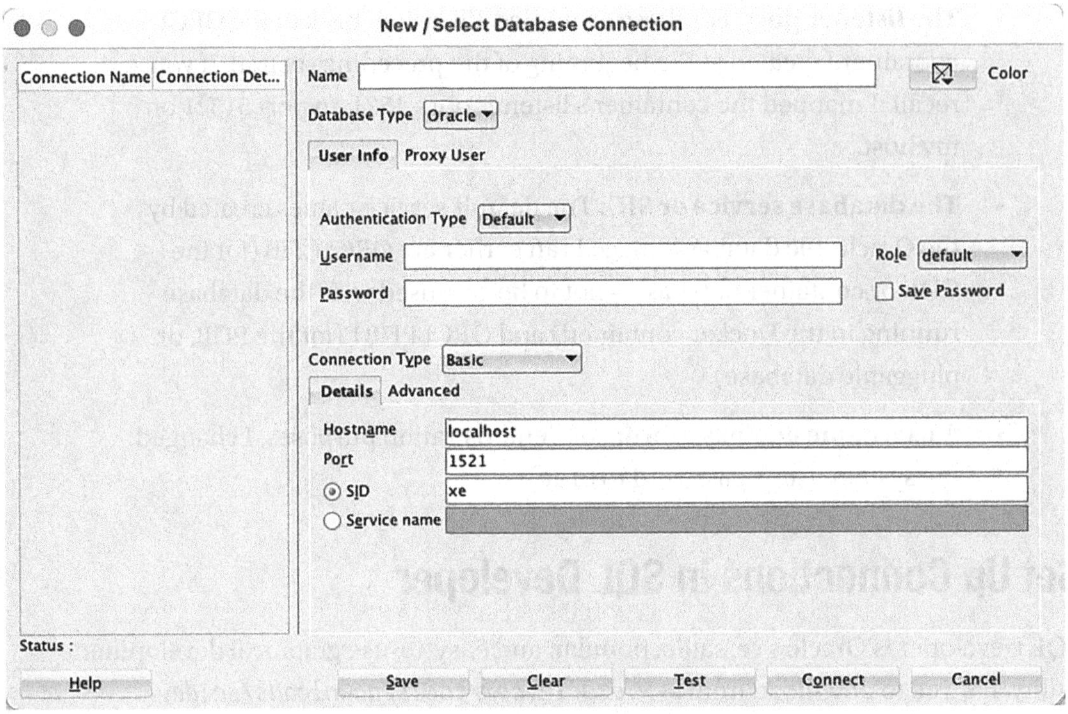

Figure 8-2. *The Oracle SQL Developer New Connection dialog*

Give the new connection a name and enter the username and password, as shown in Figure 8-3. Optionally, mark the "*Save Password*" checkbox.

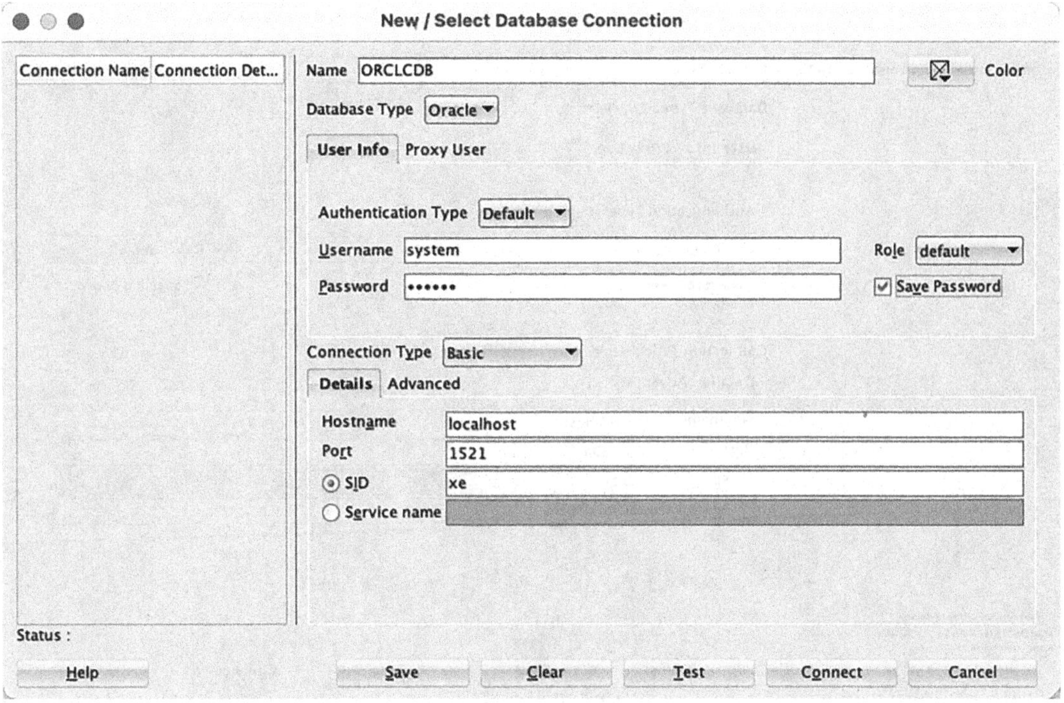

Figure 8-3. *Enter a connection name and the username and password of a database user*

In the *Details* tab, leave the connection type set to *Basic* and *Hostname* at the default, localhost. Change the *Port* to the mapped host port assigned to the container. I'm using 51521 on my system, but yours may be different, notably if you opted to use the -P option to let Docker assign ports automatically.

Next, check the radio button for "*Service name*" and enter the service name of the database running in the container. In Figure 8-4, I provided the default CDB service, ORCLCDB. Finally, click the "*Test*" button at the bottom of the dialog and confirm that the "*Status*" displayed at the lower left reports "*Success.*"

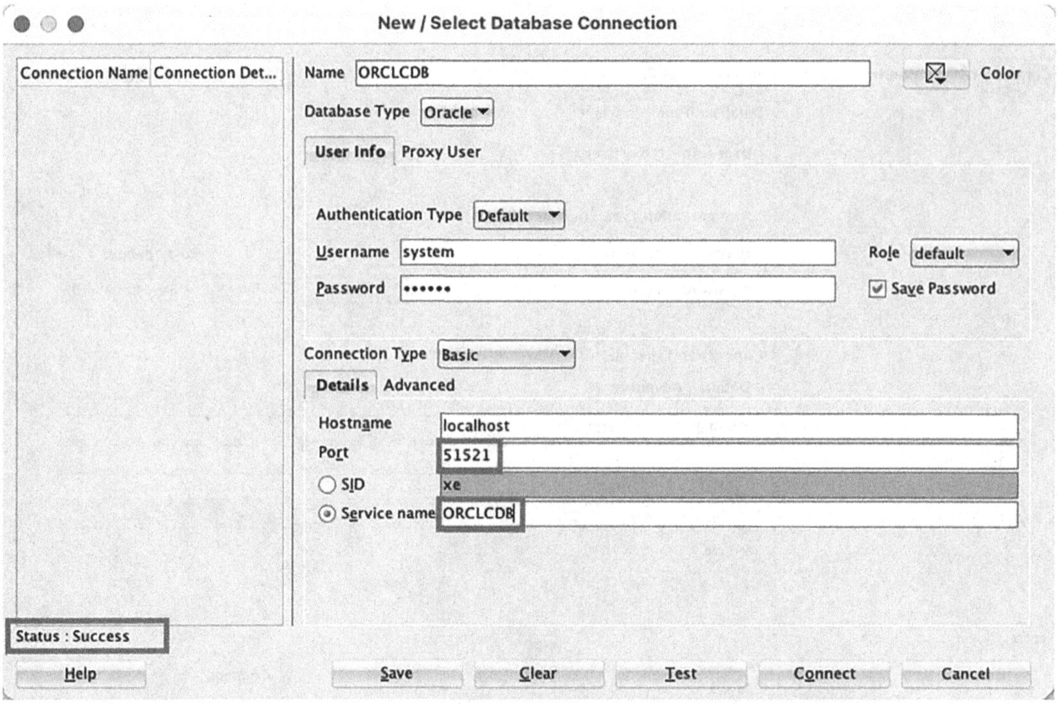

Figure 8-4. *Change the port and service name, then test the connection*

Finally, click the "*Save*" button at the bottom of the dialog to save the connection settings.

Congratulations! You created a connection to a database in a Docker container! Feel free to take a few minutes to explore the environment or connect to a user in the pluggable database, too!

EZConnect

Oracle's *EZConnect*, or *Easy Connect*, is a simplified method of connecting to Oracle databases without performing service lookups in traditional tnsnames.ora files. The basic syntax is

username/password@//host:port/service_name

Plugging in the same information used to build the SQL Developer connection earlier, I get a working connection string:

system/oracle@//localhost:51521/ORCLCDB

I can use this string to connect to the database from command-line clients like Oracle's *SQLcl*, a command-line tool similar to SQL*Plus, but with many more developer-friendly features. It's free to download from *www.oracle.com/tools/ downloads/sqlcl-downloads.html*.

This connection string works for any client *in my local environment* because it tells the client to connect to a database listening on port 51521 on the localhost. It will not work *inside the container itself.* Why not?

The listener runs on port 1521 in the container and doesn't know about the outside world. Nor does it see port mappings added by Docker between container and host. Inside the container, I connect to the database "normally" using an EZConnect string that includes the host, port, and service. EZConnect assumes port 1521, meaning I can use just the host and service, too:

```
SQL> conn system/oracle@//localhost:1521/ORCLCDB
Connected.

SQL> conn system/oracle@//localhost/ORCLCDB
Connected.
```

Connections from the container host (in this case, my laptop) and clients inside the container (here, SQL*Plus running in container ORCL) use `localhost` as the host. `localhost` is an alias for "my local host," but it doesn't represent *the same hosts* in the container and host!

To illustrate this, I ran the Linux hostname command in the container in Listing 8-4, exited the container environment, and reran it on the host.

Listing 8-4. The localhost references different hosts inside and outside the container environment

```
[oracle@f502c53c3c27 ~]$ hostname
f502c53c3c27

[oracle@f502c53c3c27 ~]$ exit
exit

> hostname
SSCOTT-C02QP2DJG8WN
```

I've confused this myself and once spent more time than I'd like to admit trying to reason why an EZConnect string that worked *outside* the container, using a translated port, didn't work *inside* the container from SQL*Plus! When setting up connections, be careful not to lose track of which localhost is which!

Creating tnsnames.ora Configurations

As you might have guessed from the two previous sections, setting up a TNS connection requires applying the proper host, port, and service name to connection aliases. Adding an alias for a container database to a tnsnames.ora on the local machine uses the hostname and port mapped to the container. Listing 8-5 provides an example of entries in a tnsnames.ora file, defining a connection to the ORCLPDB1 service in my ORCL container. Remember, port 51521 on my host maps to the database listener's port 1521.

Listing 8-5. The tnsnames.ora entry for connecting from the host to the ORCLPDB1 service in a database inside a container. Using the port opened and mapped to the container directs traffic to the database listener

```
ORCLPDB1 =
  (DESCRIPTION =
    (ADDRESS = (PROTOCOL = TCP)(HOST = localhost)(PORT = 51521))
    (CONNECT_DATA =
      (SERVER = DEDICATED)
      (SERVICE_NAME = ORCLPDB1)
    )
  )
```

It looks very similar to the tnsnames.ora file in the container, located under $ORACLE_HOME/network/admin and shown in Listing 8-6. The only differences are the host and port. Remember, the database and software inside the container aren't affected by (or even aware of) the change taking place at the container-host network interface.

Listing 8-6. The tnsnames.ora entry for the ORCLPDB1 service inside the
database container doesn't encounter any port change because its traffic is
entirely internal to the container

```
ORCLPDB1=
  (DESCRIPTION =
    (ADDRESS = (PROTOCOL = TCP)(HOST = 0.0.0.0)(PORT = 1521))
    (CONNECT_DATA =
      (SERVER = DEDICATED)
      (SERVICE_NAME = ORCLPDB1)
    )
  )
```

Connect to Containers on Remote Hosts

These examples demonstrate connections between the container and client on the same
host. That's not always the case. I have a local lab environment dedicated to container
builds and operate additional containers on various cloud computing resources.
Accessing Oracle databases on remote hosts, whether another machine inside your
network or a virtual host somewhere in the cloud, is nearly identical to what you've seen.

The single change to the connection setup is the hostname. Replace localhost with
the name or IP address of the remote resource. For example, the hostname of my local
Docker lab is lab01. Connections to containers on the remote machine reference the
hostname, but the port remains the same. Provided my network allows connections over
that port, the remote host recognizes and routes traffic to the container.

That raises the additional consideration when connecting to remote Docker hosts.
Firewall rules aren't a concern in my home lab, where everything is inside my private
network. But connections to containers on the cloud require security rules allowing
traffic to the cloud network and firewall and routing rules on individual hosts.

163

Setting the Container Hostname

One final option available during docker run that makes using containers feel more normal is the --hostname flag.

Docker assigns unique alphanumeric strings for hostnames when creating containers, as seen in Listing 8-7. For noninteractive environments, that's not a problem. But random strings aren't very readable to humans working at the command line! The default prompt includes the hostname but doesn't offer anything meaningful. Configuring connections—between two databases, perhaps—that rely on name resolution is tedious. Who wants to type (or copy/paste) "f502c53c3c27" repeatedly?

Listing 8-7. Viewing hostname and host information in a container without setting the hostname

```
> docker exec -it ORCL bash
[oracle@f502c53c3c27 ~]$ hostname
f502c53c3c27

[oracle@f502c53c3c27 ~]$ cat /etc/hosts
127.0.0.1      localhost
::1      localhost ip6-localhost ip6-loopback
fe00::0      ip6-localnet
ff00::0      ip6-mcastprefix
ff02::1      ip6-allnodes
ff02::2      ip6-allrouters
172.17.0.2      f502c53c3c27
```

The --hostname option to docker run sets the hostname in the container. Listing 8-8 is an example of assigning a hostname to a container at creation, followed by verification within the new container using the same commands from Listing 8-7.

Listing 8-8. Setting and confirming the hostname in a container with the docker run --hostname flag

```
> docker run -d \
>      --name TEST \
>      --hostname TEST \
>      -p 51521:1521 \
```

```
>       oracle/database:19.3.0-ee
78f62ede3f889b3805d51428385b5d56826164c2517951019cf5f612c608b8be

> docker exec -it TEST bash
[oracle@TEST ~]$ hostname
TEST
[oracle@TEST ~]$ cat /etc/hosts
127.0.0.1     localhost
::1     localhost ip6-localhost ip6-loopback
fe00::0     ip6-localnet
ff00::0     ip6-mcastprefix
ff02::1     ip6-allnodes
ff02::2     ip6-allrouters
172.17.0.5     TEST
[oracle@TEST ~]$
```

Compare the output from the two containers. The second is easier to recognize with its meaningful name at the shell prompt. It also facilitates naming consistent with the standard practices in an environment. And, with DNS, intracontainer networking is direct and clear to human audiences. Alas, DNS in container networks is a topic for the next chapter!

Adding Ports to an Existing Container

When introducing port publication, I said the only time to open ports in a container was during creation. I also suggested a workaround, and while there's no magic for bypassing Docker's networking behavior, there's a way to achieve the result—with one caveat!

In Chapter 7, you discovered how Docker separates data from software and that data and configuration saved on a volume remain after removing the container. Data and configuration on a volume can be recycled—to clone databases—or used to recreate a database. With its /opt/oracle/oradata directory mapped to an existing volume, a new container doesn't know it's a new one. It just starts the existing database.

This same trick lets you add a port mapping to an existing container. Provided data was persisted to a volume, you can stop, remove, then recreate the container using the same values for database-specific settings (e.g., the ORACLE_SID and ORACLE_PDB) and the same volume mappings. Add the overlooked port mappings (or other configurations) to the new docker run command.

Summary

This chapter introduced the basics behind container networking and described how to use port publication to open communication between a host and its containers. You learned that ports can't be added after creating a container, but deleting and recreating a container can get around that oversight—provided its data was persisted to a volume!

Mapping resources between a host and container using the -p or --publish options follows the same pattern as assigning volumes with the -v or --volume, but it's a limited method. There are a finite number of ports, and not all are suitable destinations for translated traffic. Only use ports in the nonreserved or dynamic range, from 49152 to 65535, or risk conflicts with other services. To avoid using an already-assigned port, use the --expose and -P (or --publish-all) flags together to allocate network mappings.

Creating connections to databases running in containers is nearly identical to the process in non-container environments. The key difference is understanding which host and port to use and where. Processes running inside the container don't use the port mappings, while clients connecting from the host (or containers on remote hosts) will use the mapped port.

Finally, you learned how to set the hostname for a container and make the environment feel more normal and friendly. Setting hostnames is a prelude to the next chapter, where container networks and DNS features make orchestration and multiple database systems more fluid and natural.

Port publication is adequate for small systems, especially those running in localized environments like laptops or desktops. It doesn't make sense to complicate things by adding container networks. If your motivation for running Oracle databases in Linux containers is personal, having a few databases for experimentation, feel free to skip to Chapter 10. To learn more about container networking and how to build more robust and flexible networks or make containers appear as "normal" network resources (without remembering which container uses what port), you'll find answers in Chapter 9!

Container Networks

I have a confession: networking intimidates me. I spent years in environments with dedicated network administrators and didn't make time to learn much beyond the basics. It wasn't until I joined an operations team that I recognized the void in my skills. From what I've heard from other database administrators, I'm not alone.

I used port publishing to handle connections during my first few years working with Docker. Since I only needed local access to a few containers, it didn't make sense to go through the additional effort of creating dedicated networks. Plus, it's what everyone else was doing.

As my use and reliance on containers grew, I realized the burden and limitations port mapping created. It's a manual process that scales poorly and doesn't integrate with automation. I had to keep track of and assign open ports. If I let Docker assign ports, I needed to identify the mappings. And, if I forgot to set a port, I had to recreate the container! Network configurations aren't intuitive under port mapping, either. Connection strings and host identities vary based on where connections originate. Container networks eliminate these issues, simplifying access and usability, integrating containers with existing observation platforms, and reducing operational overhead.

This chapter isn't a deep dive into networking concepts. Instead, it concentrates on practical solutions to the networking issues faced when deploying Oracle database services in containers. Hopefully, it makes the subject less intimidating for others who share my anxiety about networking!

Container Networks

We've already seen how Docker isolates container resources, whether it's the ability to add users in a container that aren't present on the host or create private filesystems visible only to the container. But containers can't be completely cut off from the host. They still need to share host resources like CPU, memory, storage—and networking— delivered via *container networks*.

167

© Sean Scott 2023
S. Scott, *Oracle on Docker*, https://doi.org/10.1007/978-1-4842-9033-0_9

Container networks don't require much attention. They start automatically as part of the Docker engine startup. Each network has a default gateway and DNS capabilities, with DHCP services and IP assignments provided by the Docker daemon. And, operations like starting, stopping, creating, or removing containers don't impact networks.

The Docker daemon assigns container IP addresses using DHCP. Addresses are reassigned (and may change) whenever the host, container engine, or container network restarts. Treat container IP addresses as temporary and don't use them for networking configurations like `tnsnames.ora` files!

It's easy to take Docker networking for granted. Many container operations require a network, including connecting to a container command line or database and building images (which calls `yum` to retrieve OS updates over the host's Internet connection). Yet we didn't need to create or configure any networking because Docker added three default networks when installed: *bridge*, *host*, and *none*.

Docker Network Types

Container networks are *virtual* or *software-defined networks*. Rather than cables and physical cards, the rules and configurations define the network devices and routes. They still operate much like "normal" networks, but each type of container network addresses specific needs.

Bridge Networks

As the name suggests, bridge networks traverse the gaps between network devices. In container environments, the gap covered by a bridge network is between the host and the container network. Containers on the same bridge network can communicate *inside* the network while interacting with the host *across* the bridge. However, rules in the bridge driver prevent bridge networks from communicating with one another. While containers assigned to one bridge network can see and communicate with each other, they can't see or reach containers over other bridge networks. Bridge networks are limited to a single host or, more correctly, to the Docker daemon running on the host, but a single host may have multiple bridge networks.

Because bridge networking exposes containers to one another, it's most appropriate for labs and local environments hosting multiple interdependent services. Everything you've seen so far occurred over a bridge network like the one shown in Figure 9-1—specifically,

Docker's *default bridge network*. While the default bridge uses the same bridge driver as user-defined bridges, user-defined bridge networks have additional features and capabilities that make them more attractive in all but the most basic environments.

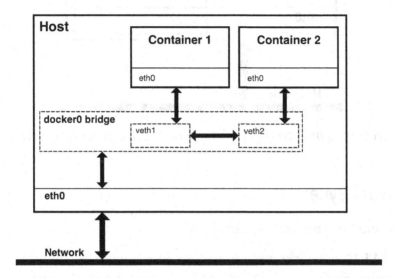

Figure 9-1. *Containers attached to bridge networks can see and communicate with other containers on the same network, while the "bridge" spans the gap between the container network and the host*

Host Networks

Host networks map container ports directly to the host. In effect, host networks make it seem like container services are running natively and not in a container. For an Oracle database container using a container host network, external clients reach the listener over the host's port 1521 instead of a mapped port.

One advantage of host networks is DNS transparency. Clients on the external network can resolve the container host and don't have to navigate any abstractions created by Docker. The two downsides are that host networking is only available on Linux, and a Docker host can't run multiple containers.

Container host networks like the one shown in Figure 9-2 are helpful for container hosts dedicated to a single service. They combine container benefits, like isolation and Infrastructure as Code, without complicating the network environment. When running Oracle databases, particularly where performance or capacity demands dedicated resources and infrastructure for individual databases, host networks reduce complexity and configuration overhead.

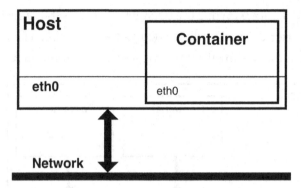

Figure 9-2. *Host networks connect containers directly to the host network interface*

Other Network Types

Docker offers additional network types, including

- **MACVLAN networks** make containers appear more like physical hosts by creating unique MAC addresses for each container on the network. Docker routes traffic to containers based on the MAC address. They're helpful when migrating legacy applications to containers on virtual machines (or physical hosts).

- **IPVLAN networks** offer fine-grained control over the IPv4 and IPv6 addresses assigned to containers. They typically require more attention and dedicated network design.

- **The "None" network** is just what it seems—no network. Connecting a container to the none network disables networking. It's most often used in conjunction with custom network drivers.

- **Overlay networks** join networks running over multiple Docker daemons into a single network, transparently linking services running on various hosts without intruding on existing (non-container) enterprise networks.

You're unlikely to encounter these specialty network types as you begin your Docker journey. The remainder of this chapter concentrates on bridge networking, the default bridge network and port mapping limitations, and creating and configuring user-defined bridge networks for multicontainer and multidatabase environments. To better appreciate these concepts, let's create a test environment consisting of two Oracle database containers.

Demonstrating Bridge Networking

The most common networking scenarios for Oracle databases are as follows:

- **Connect a client to a local database:** The client, in this case, is usually a command-line tool like SQL*Plus.

- **Connect a client to a database on a remote host:** The client may be SQL*Plus or a GUI development suite such as Oracle's SQL Developer or Quest Software's TOAD.

- **Create database links between two databases:** In practice, this is just a particular case of connecting to a remote host, where the local database is the database client.

- **Support for services, replication, and high availability:** This may appear to be just another local or remote client connection, but there's a twist. The previous examples initiate database connections via the database listener over a known port. Oracle GoldenGate, for instance, uses a different range of ports.

Databases hosted in Docker containers introduce an additional scenario: connecting clients on the host to a container. This seems to fall under the second example—a client connecting to a remote database—but with an added need to traverse the gap between the host and the container network.

An ideal networking solution won't require unique configurations or unreasonable effort. The same connection strings and tnsnames.ora files should work everywhere—in containers and on the container host. DNS should resolve containers by their hostname on the network. To explore and test these scenarios, create two Oracle database containers using the parameters listed in Table 9-1.

Table 9-1. *Properties assigned to the two database containers, ORCL1 and ORCL2*

	Container ORCL1	Container ORCL2
Container Name	DB1	DB2
Hostname	dbhost1	dbhost2
Database SID	ORA1	ORA2
PDB Name	PDB1	PDB2
Listener Port	1521	1521
Volume for oradata	/oradata/ORCL1	/oradata/ORCL2
Mapped Listener Port	51521	61521
SYSTEM Password	oracle123	oracle123

Listing 9-1 shows the docker run commands for creating the two containers. The ORACLE_SID and PDB name are set using environment variables, and the listener ports are mapped, as shown in the last chapter. Take note of the --hostname option. Docker adds an entry for the hostname to the container's /etc/hosts file during docker run. It defaults to the container name, but --hostname allows us to specify custom values.

Listing 9-1. Commands for creating the two Oracle database containers, ORCL1 and ORCL2

```
> docker run -d --name ORCL1 \
>        --hostname dbhost1 \
>        -e ORACLE_SID=ORA1 \
>        -e ORACLE_PDB=PDB1 \
>        -v /oradata/ORCL1:/opt/oracle/oradata \
>        -p 51521:1521 oracle/database:19.3.0-ee
3a15e84cd484b98f4c2437f4b0eabe10ebeb6c965dc992c09eb1d20d96b3589e

> docker run -d --name ORCL2 \
>        --hostname dbhost2 \
>        -e ORACLE_SID=ORA2 \
>        -e ORACLE_PDB=PDB2 \
```

```
>          -v /oradata/ORCL2:/opt/oracle/oradata \
>          -p 61521:1521 oracle/database:19.3.0-ee
e05023316788349978c96414e2c57bb489cd0d2d54d2168e2c2db2d5221af9d3
```

Connecting to these databases requires their hostname or IP address, the listener port, and a service name (or target database SID). If the databases described in Table 9-1 weren't running in containers, we could connect to them through SQL*Plus, using EZConnect connection syntax such as

```
$ORACLE_HOME/bin/sqlplus system/oracle123@//dbhost1:1521/ORA1
```

Any of the following connection strings[1] would work for dbhost1:

```
system/oracle123@//dbhost1:1521/ORA1
system/oracle123@//dbhost1/ORA1
system/oracle123@//dbhost1:1521/PDB1
system/oracle123@//dbhost1/PDB1
```

A similar set of connection strings would apply to dbhost2:

```
system/oracle123@//dbhost2:1521/ORA2
system/oracle123@//dbhost2/ORA2
system/oracle123@//dbhost2:1521/PDB2
system/oracle123@//dbhost2/PDB2
```

Once database creation completes, we can start exploring Docker's network environment.

Displaying Network Information

As you might expect, network management in Docker uses a set of docker network commands, summarized in Listing 9-2 using docker network --help. Reading through the options, notice Docker lets us create and remove networks, list and inspect a network, and connect containers to (and disconnect them from) a network.

---

[1] For those unfamiliar with EZConnect, it's a method for passing information normally supplied in a tnsnames.ora file directly to a database client. The connection string replaces the connection alias and uses the pattern <hostname>:<port>/<service name>. Including the port in EZConnect strings is optional if the target listener uses the default port, 1521.

Listing 9-2. Options for docker networks include commands to create, remove, list, and inspect networks and connect and disconnect containers to and from a network

```
> docker network --help

Usage:  docker network COMMAND

Manage networks

Commands:
  connect     Connect a container to a network
  create      Create a network
  disconnect  Disconnect a container from a network
  inspect     Display detailed information on one or more networks
  ls          List networks
  prune       Remove all unused networks
  rm          Remove one or more networks

Run 'docker network COMMAND --help' for more information on a command.
```

Docker Desktop systems run in virtual machines on Windows and Mac, where many of the host networking components and interfaces aren't easily visible from the host. The examples in this chapter are from an Oracle Enterprise Linux system running the Docker engine to simplify matters and better illustrate how Docker networking works (without the additional layer of abstraction introduced by the virtual machine).

List Networks

Show the networks on a system with docker network ls:

```
> docker network ls
NETWORK ID     NAME     DRIVER    SCOPE
0201c1b85336   bridge   bridge    local
8e74549be878   host     host      local
d0ce1f7bd49f   none     null      local
```

These three networks, *bridge*, *host*, and *none*, are the default networks created by Docker during installation. Starting the Docker engine on a host starts its container networks, too. There's no extra effort required to enable networking in Docker!

Inspect a Network

Let's look further into the `bridge`[2] network using `docker network inspect bridge`. The abridged output from my system, shown in Listing 9-3, includes entries for containers ORCL1 and ORCL2, including their IP addresses. Near the bottom, it shows that this is a default bridge network (`com.docker.network.bridge.default_bridge` is `true`) bound to the host on IP 0.0.0.0, with a network name of `docker0`.

Listing 9-3. Example output of docker network inspect bridge, showing details of the bridge network. Note the two containers created earlier, ORCL1 and ORCL2, are attached to this network

```
> docker network inspect bridge
[
    {
        "Name": "bridge",
        "Id": "0201c1b85336336a...",
        "Scope": "local",
        "Driver": "bridge",
        "IPAM": {
            "Driver": "default",
            "Config": [
                {
                    "Subnet": "172.17.0.0/16",
                    "Gateway": "172.17.0.1"
                }
            ]
        },
```

---

[2] Don't confuse the *bridge network* with the *bridge driver*. There is only one network with the name `bridge`. All bridge networks use the *bridge driver*.

```
    "Containers": {
        "3a15e84cd484b98f...": {
            "Name": "ORCL1",
            "IPv4Address": "172.17.0.2/16"
        },
        "e050233167883499...": {
            "Name": "ORCL2",
            "IPv4Address": "172.17.0.3/16"
        }
    },
    "Options": {
        "com.docker.network.bridge.default_bridge": "true",
        "com.docker.network.bridge.enable_icc": "true",
        "com.docker.network.bridge.enable_ip_masquerade": "true",
        "com.docker.network.bridge.host_binding_ipv4": "0.0.0.0",
        "com.docker.network.bridge.name": "docker0"
    },
  }
]
```

Inspect the Container's Network Entries

You just saw the output of docker network inspect reports the containers connected to
a network. We can also display network information of individual containers with docker
container inspect. Containers typically have more explicit content, and the JSON
output of inspecting a container can be rather lengthy. To filter and refine the output, use
the --format option of docker inspect to show only the JSON for the network settings,
then parse it with jq:

```
docker container inspect \
        --format '{{json .NetworkSettings}}' \
        <container name> | jq
```

Abridged networking information for container ORCL1 on my system appears in
Listing 9-4. I trimmed out some information to focus on what's relevant to us. Notice
that, in addition to showing the container's IP address, we can see the mapping between
container port 1521 and port 51521 on the host.

Listing 9-4. The abridged output of the network information from container ORCL1 is generated by the docker container inspect command

```
> docker container inspect \
>          --format '{{json .NetworkSettings}}' \
>          ORCL1 | jq

{
  "Bridge": "",
  "Ports": {
    "1521/tcp": [
      {
        "HostIp": "0.0.0.0",
        "HostPort": "51521"
      }
    ]
  },
  "EndpointID": "c3a9bbde24705f37516...",
  "Gateway": "172.17.0.1",
  "IPAddress": "172.17.0.2",
  "Networks": {
    "bridge": {
      "Aliases": null,
      "NetworkID": "0201c1b85336336a...",
      "EndpointID": "c3a9bbde24705f37...",
      "Gateway": "172.17.0.1",
      "IPAddress": "172.17.0.2"
    }
  }
}
```

Viewing Virtual Devices on the Container Network

Near the end of the docker network inspect bridge output in Listing 9-3, it reports network connections on an interface named docker0,[3] corresponding to a virtual (rather than a physical) host interface. The ifconfig command shows additional information about this interface, including a matching IP range:

```
> ifconfig -a docker0
docker0: flags=4163<UP,BROADCAST,RUNNING,MULTICAST>  mtu 1500
        inet 172.17.0.1  netmask 255.255.0.0  broadcast 172.17.255.255
        inet6 fe80::42:ebff:fe95:f6aa  prefixlen 64  scopeid 0x20<link>
        ether 02:42:eb:95:f6:aa  txqueuelen 0  (Ethernet)
        RX packets 158  bytes 8256 (8.2 KB)
        RX errors 0  dropped 0  overruns 0  frame 0
        TX packets 113  bytes 13510 (13.5 KB)
        TX errors 0  dropped 0 overruns 0  carrier 0  collisions 0
```

It may help to think of this as a network switch. Containers on the bridge network "plug in" to the switch on interfaces. List the bridge networks on a system with the Linux ip link show type bridge command:

```
> ip link show type bridge
4: docker0: <BROADCAST,MULTICAST,UP,LOWER_UP> mtu 1500 qdisc noqueue state
UP mode DEFAULT group default
    link/ether 02:42:eb:95:f6:aa brd ff:ff:ff:ff:ff:ff
```

Interfaces for each bridge are recorded in /sys/class/net/<BRIDGE NAME>/brif. Bridge docker0 has two interfaces listed:

```
> ls /sys/class/net/docker0/brif
veth7d17f7f   veth8c9057e
```

These virtual interfaces correspond to the two containers. The interfaces are also visible on the host through ifconfig:

---

[3] Remember, in Docker Desktop the container engine runs in a virtual machine. You'll only see the docker0 interface directly on Linux systems or within the Docker VM.

```
> ifconfig veth7d17f7f
veth7d17f7f: flags=4163<UP,BROADCAST,RUNNING,MULTICAST>  mtu 1500
        inet6 fe80::3cf4:90ff:fe19:17f5  prefixlen 64  scopeid 0x20<link>
        ether 3e:f4:90:19:17:f5  txqueuelen 0  (Ethernet)
        RX packets 104  bytes 6888 (6.8 KB)
        RX errors 0  dropped 0  overruns 0  frame 0
        TX packets 135  bytes 15226 (15.2 KB)
        TX errors 0  dropped 0 overruns 0  carrier 0  collisions 0

> ifconfig veth8c9057e
veth8c9057e: flags=4163<UP,BROADCAST,RUNNING,MULTICAST>  mtu 1500
        inet6 fe80::3845:f5ff:fed4:49c  prefixlen 64  scopeid 0x20<link>
        ether 3a:45:f5:d4:04:9c  txqueuelen 0  (Ethernet)
        RX packets 21  bytes 1394 (1.3 KB)
        RX errors 0  dropped 0  overruns 0  frame 0
        TX packets 47  bytes 3218 (3.2 KB)
        TX errors 0  dropped 0 overruns 0  carrier 0  collisions 0
```

This is the end of the "cable" plugged into the docker0 interface. Next, connect to the ORCL1 container:

```
> docker exec -it ORCL1 bash
```

Then, show the other end of the connection, attached to eth0 interface in the container, by running ifconfig on container ORCL1:

```
[oracle@dbhost1 ~]$ ifconfig eth0
eth0: flags=4163<UP,BROADCAST,RUNNING,MULTICAST>  mtu 1500
        inet 172.17.0.2  netmask 255.255.0.0  broadcast 172.17.255.255
        ether 02:42:ac:11:00:02  txqueuelen 0  (Ethernet)
        RX packets 134  bytes 15156 (14.8 KiB)
        RX errors 0  dropped 0  overruns 0  frame 0
        TX packets 104  bytes 6888 (6.7 KiB)
        TX errors 0  dropped 0 overruns 0  carrier 0  collisions 0
```

While connected to the container, display the contents of its /etc/hosts file, shown in Listing 9-5. The hostname provided to docker run via the --hostname option matches the IP address. Docker adds this entry during container creation. It also updates the file whenever the container starts, so even if the container's address changes, its /etc/hosts file includes the current IP. The hostname is usually the unique, randomly generated container name; specifying a hostname to the docker run command overrides that behavior.

Listing 9-5. The /etc/hosts file on the ORCL1 container includes an entry created by Docker for the hostname assigned during container creation

```
[oracle@dbhost1 ~]$ cat /etc/hosts
127.0.0.1      localhost
::1     localhost ip6-localhost ip6-loopback
fe00::0      ip6-localnet
ff00::0      ip6-mcastprefix
ff02::1      ip6-allnodes
ff02::2      ip6-allrouters
172.17.0.2      dbhost1
```

The Linux /etc/resolv.conf files on the containers, controlling DNS resolution, match the host:

```
[oracle@dbhost1 ~]$ cat /etc/resolv.conf
# This file is managed by man:systemd-resolved(8). Do not edit.
#
# This is a dynamic resolv.conf file for connecting local clients
directly to
# all known uplink DNS servers. This file lists all configured search
domains.
#
# Third-party programs must not access this file directly, but only
through the
# symlink at /etc/resolv.conf. To manage man:resolv.conf(5) in a
different way,
# replace this symlink by a static file or a different symlink.
#
# See man:systemd-resolved.service(8) for details about the supported
modes of
# operation for /etc/resolv.conf.
```

```
nameserver 192.168.1.1
search Home
```

They match because they're the same file:

```
> md5sum /etc/resolv.conf
c5dd1676e12d6ca9f7c6d03c5ca9b258  /etc/resolv.conf
```

```
> docker exec -it ORCL1 bash -c "md5sum /etc/resolv.conf"
c5dd1676e12d6ca9f7c6d03c5ca9b258  /etc/resolv.conf
```

Docker maps the host DNS configuration into the container as a layer in the container's overlay network, giving the container access to the same name resolution capabilities present on the host.

Figure 9-3 visualizes the network connections on the default bridge network and offers a starting point for testing network connections. We'll revisit the commands in this section to demonstrate the differences in each network configuration.

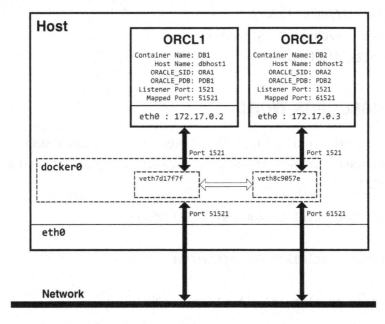

Figure 9-3. *Interfaces and endpoints of the two containers, ORCL1 and ORCL2, on the default bridge network*

Limitations of Default Bridge Networks

Default and user-defined bridge networks both use Docker's bridge network driver, and a default bridge network is a bridge network, right? Actually, no. The default bridge is a legacy feature of Docker, lacks capabilities found in user-defined bridges, and generally isn't considered suitable for production use. To see how they're different, connect to the ORCL1 container and test connections to the database using the connection strings shown earlier. As a reminder, the connection strings for dbhost1 are

```
system/oracle123@//dbhost1:1521/ORA1
system/oracle123@//dbhost1/ORA1
system/oracle123@//dbhost1:1521/PDB1
system/oracle123@//dbhost1/PDB1
```

For dbhost2

```
system/oracle123@//dbhost2:1521/ORA2
system/oracle123@//dbhost2/ORA2
system/oracle123@//dbhost2:1521/PDB2
system/oracle123@//dbhost2/PDB2
```

Local Connections Work

When logged in to container ORCL1, connections to the local databases work as expected, using the hostname we assigned to the container (dbhost1) and the default listener port 1521:

```
SQL> conn system/oracle123@//dbhost1:1521/ORA1
Connected.
SQL> conn system/oracle123@//dbhost1/ORA1
Connected.
SQL> conn system/oracle123@//dbhost1:1521/PDB1
Connected.
SQL> conn system/oracle123@//dbhost1/PDB1
Connected.
```

Local connections using the container ID work, too. So far, so good:

```
SQL> conn system/oracle123@//3a15e84cd484:1521/ORA1
Connected.
```

However, the container doesn't recognize the container name, ORCL1:

```
SQL> conn system/oracle123@//ORCL1:1521/ORA1
ERROR:
ORA-12154: TNS:could not resolve the connect identifier specified
```

Remote Connections Fail

Connections to the remote database on container ORCL2, however, do *not* work using either the default port or the mapped port:

```
SQL> conn system/oracle123@//dbhost2:1521/ORA2
ERROR:
ORA-12154: TNS:could not resolve the connect identifier specified

Warning: You are no longer connected to ORACLE.
SQL> conn system/oracle123@//dbhost2:61521/ORA2
ERROR:
ORA-12154: TNS:could not resolve the connect identifier specified
```

The reason? The container doesn't know any host called dbhost2. Remember that the /etc/hosts file on ORCL1 had only an entry for the local host, dbhost1. However, if I try connecting using the IP address of container ORCL2, it succeeds:

```
SQL> conn system/oracle123@//172.17.0.3:1521/ORA2
Connected.
```

Why? The default bridge network lacks DNS. Containers on the network are accessible to each other, but only by IP address, not a hostname. We could add entries to /etc/hosts for each host, but remember the IP addresses Docker assigns aren't guaranteed to work across restarts of the host or Docker resources. And, while Docker updates the /etc/hosts entry of the *local* host, it isn't aware of custom entries.

User-Defined Bridge Networks

Let's compare this behavior with a user-defined bridge network by creating a new network, using the `bridge` driver, attaching the two database containers, and testing connectivity.

Create the Network

Use the following command to create a new, user-defined bridge network named `database-bridge`:

```
docker network create database-bridge --attachable --driver bridge
```

The `--attachable` flag tells Docker we want the ability to manually attach containers to the network, while the `--driver` (or shorthand `-d`) option assigns the bridge driver. Once created, use the same `docker network ls` and `docker network inspect` commands to get information about the new network, as shown in Listing 9-6. The new network uses the same bridge driver as the default bridge, and Docker assigned a new, unique IP address range, 172.18.0.0/16. The network doesn't yet support any containers, and, compared to Listing 9-3, there is no host binding or bridge name.

Listing 9-6. The newly created database-bridge network operates on a unique IP address range but lacks the options present in the default bridge network

```
> docker network ls
NETWORK ID      NAME              DRIVER    SCOPE
0201c1b85336    bridge            bridge    local
9dfba096bf9a    database-bridge   bridge    local
8e74549be878    host              host      local
d0ce1f7bd49f    none              null      local

> docker network inspect database-bridge
[
    {
        "Name": "database-bridge",
        "Id": "9dfba096bf9a740e...",
        "Scope": "local",
        "Driver": "bridge",
```

```
    "IPAM": {
        "Driver": "default",
        "Options": {},
        "Config": [
            {
                "Subnet": "172.18.0.0/16",
                "Gateway": "172.18.0.1"
            }
        ]
    },
    "Internal": false,
    "Attachable": true,
    "Ingress": false,
    "ConfigFrom": {
        "Network": ""
    },
    "ConfigOnly": false,
    "Containers": {},
    "Options": {},
    "Labels": {}
    }
]
```

A new bridge also appears in the output of ip link show type bridge:

```
> ip link show type bridge
4: docker0: <BROADCAST,MULTICAST,UP,LOWER_UP> mtu 1500 qdisc noqueue state
UP mode DEFAULT group default
    link/ether 02:42:eb:95:f6:aa brd ff:ff:ff:ff:ff:ff
20: br-9dfba096bf9a: <BROADCAST,MULTICAST,UP,LOWER_UP> mtu 1500 qdisc
noqueue state UP mode DEFAULT group default
    link/ether 02:42:14:53:e0:c8 brd ff:ff:ff:ff:ff:ff
```

However, no interfaces are present for the new network in /sys/class/net/
br-9dfba096bf9a/brif:

```
> ls /sys/class/net/br-9dfba096bf9a/brif
```

Attach the Containers

There are no interfaces because nothing is yet attached to the network. Let's remedy that! Connect the containers using `docker network connect <network name> <container name>` and reinspect the new network as shown in Listing 9-7.

Listing 9-7. Connect containers ORCL1 and ORCL2 to the new database-bridge network and reinspect the output. The containers are in the network and have unique IP addresses within the 172.18.0.0 subnet

```
> docker network connect database-bridge ORCL1
> docker network connect database-bridge ORCL2
> docker network inspect database-bridge
[
    {
        "Name": "database-bridge",
        "Id": "9dfba096bf9a740e...",
        "Scope": "local",
        "Driver": "bridge",
        "IPAM": {
            "Driver": "default",
            "Options": {},
            "Config": [
                {
                    "Subnet": "172.18.0.0/16",
                    "Gateway": "172.18.0.1"
                }
            ]
        },
        "Internal": false,
        "Attachable": true,
        "Ingress": false,
        "ConfigFrom": {
            "Network": ""
        },
        "ConfigOnly": false,
```

```
    "Containers": {
        "3a15e84cd484b98f...": {
            "Name": "ORCL1",
            "EndpointID": "e4cb8fea4b119625...",
            "IPv4Address": "172.18.0.2/16"
        },
        "e050233167883499...": {
            "Name": "ORCL2",
            "EndpointID": "a6d9108c93c9b376...",
            "IPv4Address": "172.18.0.3/16"
        }
    },
    "Options": {},
    "Labels": {}
  }
]
```

In Listing 9-8, we see that attaching the containers to the `database-bridge` network updated their network configurations. Each received a new IP address on the new network and a new interface, eth1, and corresponding entries in /etc/hosts. These new IP addresses are *in addition* to those on the default bridge network, as evidenced by the separate host entries in /etc/hosts, one for each subnet.

Listing 9-8. Connecting the ORCL1 container to the network added a new network interface inside the container and updated its /etc/hosts file with the new IP address

```
[oracle@dbhost1 ~]$ ifconfig
eth0: flags=4163<UP,BROADCAST,RUNNING,MULTICAST>  mtu 1500
        inet 172.17.0.2  netmask 255.255.0.0  broadcast 172.17.255.255
        ether 02:42:ac:11:00:02  txqueuelen 0  (Ethernet)
        RX packets 135  bytes 15226 (14.8 KiB)
        RX errors 0  dropped 0  overruns 0  frame 0
        TX packets 104  bytes 6888 (6.7 KiB)
        TX errors 0  dropped 0 overruns 0  carrier 0  collisions 0
```

```
eth1: flags=4163<UP,BROADCAST,RUNNING,MULTICAST>   mtu 1500
        inet 172.18.0.2   netmask 255.255.0.0   broadcast 172.18.255.255
        ether 02:42:ac:12:00:02   txqueuelen 0   (Ethernet)
        RX packets 17   bytes 1462 (1.4 KiB)
        RX errors 0   dropped 0   overruns 0   frame 0
        TX packets 0   bytes 0 (0.0 B)
        TX errors 0   dropped 0 overruns 0   carrier 0   collisions 0

[oracle@dbhost1 ~]$ cat /etc/hosts
127.0.0.1       localhost
::1     localhost ip6-localhost ip6-loopback
fe00::0     ip6-localnet
ff00::0     ip6-mcastprefix
ff02::1     ip6-allnodes
ff02::2     ip6-allrouters
172.17.0.2      dbhost1
172.18.0.2      dbhost1
```

Connecting the containers to the database-bridge network created virtual interfaces on the host, corresponding to those in the containers, visible by listing the contents of /sys/class/net/br-9dfba096bf9a/brif:

```
> ls /sys/class/net/br-9dfba096bf9a/brif
veth9e1e709   vetheb94b3f
```

Running ifconfig against these newly created virtual interfaces produces the output in Listing 9-9.

Listing 9-9. After connecting the containers to the new bridge, Docker added virtual interfaces for each container on the Docker host

```
> ifconfig veth9e1e709
veth9e1e709: flags=4163<UP,BROADCAST,RUNNING,MULTICAST>   mtu 1500
        inet6 fe80::f412:9dff:fed8:b8c2   prefixlen 64   scopeid 0x20<link>
        ether f6:12:9d:d8:b8:c2   txqueuelen 0   (Ethernet)
        RX packets 0   bytes 0 (0.0 B)
        RX errors 0   dropped 0   overruns 0   frame 0
        TX packets 18   bytes 1532 (1.5 KB)
        TX errors 0   dropped 0 overruns 0   carrier 0   collisions 0
```

```
> ifconfig vetheb94b3f
vetheb94b3f: flags=4163<UP,BROADCAST,RUNNING,MULTICAST>  mtu 1500
        inet6 fe80::705e:8aff:fe63:8d14  prefixlen 64  scopeid 0x20<link>
        ether 72:5e:8a:63:8d:14  txqueuelen 0  (Ethernet)
        RX packets 0  bytes 0 (0.0 B)
        RX errors 0  dropped 0  overruns 0  frame 0
        TX packets 13  bytes 1006 (1.0 KB)
        TX errors 0  dropped 0 overruns 0  carrier 0  collisions 0
```

What About DNS?

Under the default bridge network, there was no DNS, and containers couldn't resolve the hostnames of other containers. Under the user-defined bridge, Docker provides internal DNS services, as shown by running nslookup.

```
[oracle@dbhost1 ~]$ nslookup dbhost1
Server:         127.0.0.11
Address:        127.0.0.11#53

Non-authoritative answer:
Name:    dbhost1
Address: 172.18.0.2

[oracle@dbhost1 ~]$ nslookup dbhost2
Server:         127.0.0.11
Address:        127.0.0.11#53

Non-authoritative answer:
Name:    dbhost2
Address: 172.18.0.3
```

The /etc/resolv.conf file reveals the DNS services provided by Docker:

```
[oracle@dbhost1 ~]$ cat /etc/resolv.conf
search Home
nameserver 127.0.0.11
options ndots:0
```

Compare that to the file's contents when the container was connected to only the default bridge network. With the addition of container DNS, both local and remote connections work as expected:

```
SQL> conn system/oracle123@//dbhost1:1521/ORA1
Connected.
SQL> conn system/oracle123@//dbhost1/ORA1
Connected.
SQL> select host_name from v$instance;

HOST_NAME
-----------------------------------------------------------------
dbhost1

SQL> conn system/oracle123@//dbhost2:1521/ORA2
Connected.
SQL> conn system/oracle123@//dbhost2/ORA2
Connected.
SQL> select host_name from v$instance;

HOST_NAME
-----------------------------------------------------------------
dbhost2
```

Remember, the default bridge recognized the hostname assigned with the --hostname option during container creation but not the container name. Under a user-defined bridge network, DNS also honors container names:

```
SQL> conn system/oracle123@//ORCL1:1521/ORA1
Connected.
SQL> conn system/oracle123@//ORCL2:1521/ORA2
Connected.
```

Finally, I can create database links between databases running in separate containers:

```
SQL> create database link DB2 connect to system identified by oracle123
using 'dbhost2:1521/ORA2';
```

```
Database link created.

SQL> select host_name from v$instance;

HOST_NAME
-----------------------------------------------------------------
dbhost1

SQL> select host_name from v$instance@DB2;

HOST_NAME
-----------------------------------------------------------------
dbhost2
```

The user-defined bridge network satisfies the objectives laid out at the beginning of the chapter:

- **Connect a client to a local database:** Connections from local clients behave as expected and recognize the whole gamut of hostnames: the custom hostname, the container name, and the container ID.

- **Connect a client to a database on a remote host:** Clients on containers can access remote databases by hostname over the traditional listener port.

- **Create database links between two databases:** The network supports the creation of database links between databases on separate containers.

- **Support for services, replication, and high availability:** Containers on the bridge network can access one another over any port.

Host Connections

Imagine how different surfing the Web would be if we had to remember and enter the IP address and port number of every site we visited! Thankfully, DNS translates human-friendly domain names into IP addresses in the background, while browsers connect to the default port 80 unless otherwise specified. At the beginning of the chapter, we set out to duplicate this experience for database connections, from container to container and host to container.

Under the user-defined bridge networks, connections between containers meet this goal and work as expected, using the default ports and standard connection syntax. Unfortunately, connections from host to container do not work this way with either default or user-defined bridge networks.

Problems with Port Mapping

Figure 9-4 gives some idea why. The default bridge network is virtual, defined in Docker, and insulates the container environment from the host. Port mappings defined during container startup traverse this firewall-like barrier between the host and containers. Unlike a regular firewall, though, there's no opportunity to add or change port mappings. More importantly, the interface exposing the mapped ports is the Docker host—not the containers or the container network.

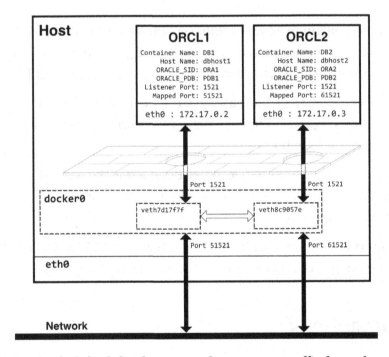

Figure 9-4. *Docker's default bridge network manages traffic from the containers, mapping them to ports on the host. Docker only allows connections between the host and containers using ports mapped during container creation*

The strings for connecting from the host to the database in container ORCL1 change to the following:

```
system/oracle123@//lab1:51521/ORA1
system/oracle123@//localhost:51521/ORA1
system/oracle123@//lab1:51521/PDB1
system/oracle123@//localhost:51521/PDB1
```

We need to update the connection strings for the database running in container ORCL2, also:

```
system/oracle123@//lab1:61521/ORA2
system/oracle123@//localhost:61521/ORA2
system/oracle123@//lab1:61521/PDB2
system/oracle123@//localhost:61521/PDB2
```

Port mapping is a manual process that scales poorly and doesn't integrate well with automation. I have to find and assign open ports, and if I let Docker do that for me, I still have to identify the ports assigned to each container. Building network configurations isn't intuitive under port mapping, either. Connection strings use `localhost` or the Docker host's hostname and a nondefault port instead of meaningful hostnames. Recognizing database connections doesn't follow standard patterns.

To reach the goals set at the beginning of the chapter for connecting to containers from host clients, we need two additional capabilities: the flexibility to add ports on the fly and something on the container host that maps container names into DNS.

Container DNS Resolution on Hosts

Fortunately, there are multiple methods of mapping Linux container names into DNS. My personal favorite is a simple Docker-based tool called `docker-hoster` (*https://github.com/dvddarias/docker-hoster*). It runs as a container and listens for events on the Docker daemon. As containers are added, removed, stopped, or stated, it captures the related network information and updates the `/etc/hosts` file on the Docker host. I use `docker-hoster` in my lab environments with the default, recommended setup:

```
docker run -d \
    -v /var/run/docker.sock:/tmp/docker.sock \
```

```
  -v /etc/hosts:/tmp/hosts \
  dvdarias/docker-hoster
```

After starting docker-hoster, the updated host file includes entries for the containers running on my system:

```
> cat /etc/hosts
127.0.0.1 localhost
127.0.1.1 lab01

#-----------Docker-Hoster-Domains----------
172.18.0.3    dbhost2    ORCL2    e05023316788
172.17.0.3    ORCL2    dbhost2
172.18.0.2    3a15e84cd484    ORCL1    dbhost1
172.17.0.2    ORCL1    dbhost1
172.17.0.4    docker-hoster    0d6f558aa6c0
#-----Do-not-add-hosts-after-this-line-----
```

With these entries present in the /etc/hosts file on my Docker host, I can access the container databases from the host using a database client like SQLcl (available for free from Oracle at *www.oracle.com/database/sqldeveloper/technologies/sqlcl/download*):

```
> sql system/oracle123@ORCL1:1521/ORA1

SQLcl: Release 22.2 Production on Mon Jul 18 14:32:40 2022
Copyright (c) 1982, 2022, Oracle.  All rights reserved.
Last Successful login time: Mon Jul 18 2022 14:32:41 +00:00

Connected to:
Oracle Database 19c Enterprise Edition Release 19.0.0.0.0 - Production
Version 19.3.0.0.0

SQL> select host_name from v$instance;

HOST_NAME
_____

dbhost1

SQL> conn system/oracle123@//dbhost2:1521/ORA2
Connected.
SQL> select host_name from v$instance;
```

HOST_NAME

_____

dbhost2

The containers now appear as if they were "real" database servers on the network!

You Don't Need Port Mapping

What might not jump out immediately in the preceding example is that the databases were accessible over the default listener port, 1521. These ports aren't mapped. The host recognized the containers as endpoints on the virtual interfaces assigned to the bridge networks and treated them as "ordinary" hosts communicating over a range of ports. The same technique works on the default bridge network, too, as proven by using the container IP address (remember, the default bridge network uses the 172.17.0.0/16 address range):

```
SQL> conn system/oracle123@//172.17.0.2:1521/ORA1
Connected.
SQL> conn system/oracle123@//172.17.0.3:1521/ORA2
Connected.
```

As long as there's a mechanism resolving container names to the host, there's no *need* to map ports. The containers are still accessible using the ports mapped to the Docker host over the default bridge network:

```
SQL> conn system/oracle123@//lab1:51521/ORA1
Connected.
SQL> conn system/oracle123@//lab1:61521/ORA2
Connected.
```

However, the *only* services visible over port mapping are those specified during container creation. And mapping ports to the host departs from the standard we established—having one connection string for each database that works anywhere in the environment.

You've seen how to create a custom bridge network with built-in DNS services and how to add DNS registration that works at the host. With these containers connected to the user-defined bridge, there's no reason to leave them attached to the default bridge!

Disconnect from the Default Bridge Network

Detaching the containers from the default bridge is a straightforward command: `docker network disconnect <network name> <container name>`. Disconnecting the containers (including `docker-hoster`) completes without fanfare:

```
> docker network disconnect bridge ORCL1
> docker network disconnect bridge ORCL2
> docker network disconnect docker-hoster
```

After the commands are complete, the bridge network configuration in Listing 9-10 shows no attached containers.

Listing 9-10. Abridged configuration details of the default bridge network after disconnecting the containers. Compare this with the original output in Listing 9-3

```
> docker network inspect bridge

[
    {
        "Name": "bridge",
        "Id": "0201c1b85336336a...",
        "Scope": "local",
        "Driver": "bridge",
        "IPAM": {
            "Driver": "default",
            "Options": null,
            "Config": [
                {
                    "Subnet": "172.17.0.0/16",
                    "Gateway": "172.17.0.1"
                }
            ]
        },
        "Internal": false,
        "Attachable": false,
        "Ingress": false,
        "ConfigFrom": {
```

```
            "Network": ""
        },
        "ConfigOnly": false,
        "Containers": {},
        "Options": {
            "com.docker.network.bridge.default_bridge": "true",
            "com.docker.network.bridge.enable_icc": "true",
            "com.docker.network.bridge.enable_ip_masquerade": "true",
            "com.docker.network.bridge.host_binding_ipv4": "0.0.0.0",
            "com.docker.network.bridge.name": "docker0",
            "com.docker.network.driver.mtu": "1500"
        },
        "Labels": {}
    }
]
```

Checking the virtual interfaces under /sys/class/net/docker0/brif confirms their removal:

```
> ls /sys/class/net/docker0/brif
```

The adapter still exists in the output from ifconfig because this is a default network where all newly created containers are assigned. Inside the containers, the original eth0 interface is gone, as is the entry in /etc/hosts associated with the 172.17.0.0/16 network segment:

```
[oracle@dbhost1 ~]$ ifconfig
eth1: flags=4163<UP,BROADCAST,RUNNING,MULTICAST>  mtu 1500
        inet 172.18.0.2  netmask 255.255.0.0  broadcast 172.18.255.255
        ether 02:42:ac:12:00:02  txqueuelen 0  (Ethernet)
        RX packets 298  bytes 57915 (56.5 KiB)
        RX errors 0  dropped 0  overruns 0  frame 0
        TX packets 221  bytes 55308 (54.0 KiB)
        TX errors 0  dropped 0 overruns 0  carrier 0  collisions 0

[oracle@dbhost1 ~]$ cat /etc/hosts
127.0.0.1      localhost
::1      localhost ip6-localhost ip6-loopback
```

fe00::0	ip6-localnet
ff00::0	ip6-mcastprefix
ff02::1	ip6-allnodes
ff02::2	ip6-allrouters
172.18.0.2	dbhost1

Docker handles these updates automatically whenever the network topology changes.

With the user-defined bridge network in place and the containers disconnected from the default bridge, Figure 9-5 represents the new network topology, with virtual interfaces on the bridge network spanning the host-container interface.

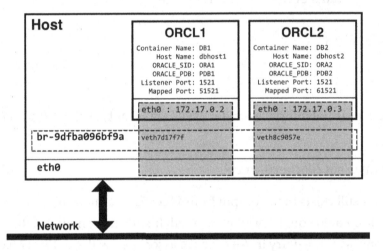

Figure 9-5. *User-defined bridge networks offer a more natural, integrated container networking environment without the limitations of port mapping*

Assign a Network During Container Creation

Hopefully, the benefits of user-defined bridge networks are clear, but connecting and disconnecting containers is a bit laborious. The docker run command includes an option for assigning networks when creating containers, allowing us to skip the extra effort spent "unplugging" from the default network.

The --network or --net option attaches containers to one or more existing networks.[4] The --network-alias flag assigns a network alias, recognized by Docker's DNS services, providing an additional method of identifying containers on networks. Listing 9-11 shows an updated version of the earlier commands to create two database containers, add network assignments and aliases, and remove the port mappings.

Listing 9-11. Updated docker run commands for the two database containers. The containers are assigned to the database-bridge created earlier, given a network alias, and no longer map ports to the host

```
> docker run -d --name ORCL1 \
>          --hostname dbhost1 \
>          -e ORACLE_SID=ORA1 \
>          -e ORACLE_PDB=PDB1 \
>          -v /oradata/ORCL1:/opt/oracle/oradata \
>          --network database-bridge \
>          --network-alias db-alias1 \
>          oracle/database:19.3.0-ee
d6e027dee0a65bc4dfccd7eb43bb6143e2a54803d3b6a699bb26dc645cc814e5

> docker run -d --name ORCL2 \
>          --hostname dbhost2 \
>          -e ORACLE_SID=ORA2 \
>          -e ORACLE_PDB=PDB2 \
>          -v /oradata/ORCL2:/opt/oracle/oradata \
>          --network database-bridge \
>          --network-alias db-alias2 \
>          oracle/database:19.3.0-ee
c3c1168cdb986f0a284a46eda67c41c1d4d7bfc3c8112db1920dd8be85b99889
```

Inside the containers, the network recognizes all of the following network identities:

- The container names: ORCL1, ORCL2

- Their assigned hostnames: dbhost1, dbhost2

---

[4] In multicontainer environments, overlapping networks allow administrators sophisticated, fine-grained access control. Containers that share a segment can interact, but cannot see the containers in networks they aren't attached to.

199

- The network aliases: db-alias1, db-alias2

- The container IDs and IP addresses

With the `docker-hoster` container (or similar provision) translating container names to host entries, the same names also work from the Docker host!

Summary

The preceding pages dove deep into the sometimes unpleasant, possibly intimidating, but necessary subject of networking in Linux container environments! Networks in Docker play an essential role by isolating and insulating containers from each other, the host, and the broader network landscape. There's no need to be an expert, but a solid foundation in container networking is a valuable skill for Oracle database administrators working in Docker environments.

Chapter 8 addressed connectivity through port mapping. In this chapter, we looked deeper at some of port mapping's limitations and introduced container networks as an alternative. Port mapping is a reasonable solution for smaller, localized implementations, but container networks are a better and more extensible alternative, mainly when working with multiple database containers.

We discussed differences between various network types, reviewed commands for reporting and managing network objects, and then dove into bridge networks' details. Next, we covered the relationship between bridge networks and virtual devices and how they support connectivity across interfaces. We examined distinctions between default and user-defined bridges—including limitations inherent in Docker's default bridge network. Finally, we discussed DNS in container networks and solutions for extending DNS to the host.

You now have a solid understanding and appreciation for containers and their capabilities. Over the last few chapters, you've learned how to manage storage and networking—arguably the most critical considerations for running databases. The next chapter combines concepts from the book's first half in a command reference, marrying lessons and recommendations into actionable recipes to begin and build your journey with Oracle on Docker!

CHAPTER 10

Container Creation Quick Reference

The first part of this book covered the essential elements of running Oracle databases in Linux containers and emphasized the importance of the docker run command. Anticipating how containers will create their databases, store data, and interact over the network prevents frustration and saves time revising or rebuilding containers later. The preceding chapters addressed these concepts individually, explaining the *whys* behind each recommendation.

I enjoy a summary covering how to do things when learning new technologies. This last chapter of Part 1 is just that—a quick reference, distilling everything covered thus far into a set of recipes and patterns for you to apply on your container journey.

This chapter comprises four parts: creating storage and networks, running containers, and miscellaneous commands for interacting with containers. While not required, storage and networking are prerequisites if you intend to persist data to the container host and take advantage of user-defined networking as described in Chapter 9. Once created, reference these resources during container creation.

Conventions

For clarity, more extended commands are split across multiple lines using the Linux continuation character, the backslash. Individual options are presented on separate lines, too, helping each to stand out:

```
docker run --name <CONTAINER NAME> \
       -e ORACLE_SID=<DATABASE SID> \
...
       <IMAGE_NAME>
```

© Sean Scott 2023
S. Scott, *Oracle on Docker*, https://doi.org/10.1007/978-1-4842-9033-0_10

Examples use the shorter flag when more than one is available, for instance, -e to set an environment variable rather than --env. Text between carets, < and >, identifies information to substitute according to your requirements.

Storage
Create Volumes

There are two ways to persist data to the container host:

- Map a directory on the host to a path in the container.

- Create a dedicated object called a Docker volume.

The former doesn't require anything special, but mounting a Docker volume requires that the volume is precreated. Directories used by bind-mounted volumes must exist before assigning them to containers.

To create a default volume, which will store data in Docker's virtual machine (/var/lib/docker):

```
docker volume create <VOLUME_NAME>
```

To create a bind-mounted volume with a user-defined location on the local filesystem:

```
docker volume create --opt type=none --opt o=bind \
    --opt device=<DIRECTORY_PATH> \
    <VOLUME_NAME>
```

Predefined Volumes in Oracle Database Containers

The ORADATA volume holds database configuration and datafiles under the /opt/oracle/oradata directory in Oracle's container images. Its high-level directory structure:

```
.
├── dbconfig
│   └── <ORACLE_SID>
├── fast_recovery_area
```

```
|       └── <ORACLE_SID>
|           └── archivelog
└── <ORACLE_SID>
    ├── controlfile
    ├── datafile
    └── onlinelog
```

The special dbconfig subdirectory houses configuration files for the database and network and where you'll find the database's init.ora and spfile, the password and oratab files, and networking configurations, including tnsnames.ora and listener.ora:

```
$ ls -l $ORACLE_BASE/oradata/dbconfig/$ORACLE_SID
total 24
-rw-r--r-- 1 oracle oinstall  234 Mar  6 22:04 listener.ora
-rw-r----- 1 oracle oinstall 2048 Mar  6 22:15 orapwORCLCDB
-rw-r--r-- 1 oracle oinstall  784 Mar  6 23:33 oratab
-rw-r----- 1 oracle oinstall 3584 Mar  6 23:33 spfileORCLCDB.ora
-rw-r--r-- 1 oracle oinstall   53 Mar  6 22:04 sqlnet.ora
-rw-r----- 1 oracle oinstall  211 Mar  6 23:33 tnsnames.ora
```

These files are soft-linked from their typical locations, meaning the ORADATA volume is a self-contained directory of everything the database needs.

Preparing Volumes for Oracle Databases

Volumes write data outside of the Docker environment and satisfy two very similar but distinct purposes:

- Saving data to local or attached storage

- Removing data from the container filesystem

The first example relates to protecting and persisting data and configurations. In production environments, it extends to choosing fast, durable storage that satisfies organizational objectives for performance and availability.

The second case, at first, may appear the same—put files someplace other than the container—but with a subtle difference. Here, the importance is managing volatile directories externally to the container. In Oracle databases, these are the log and audit directories. Leaving them in the container's filesystem places them at risk if there's ever a need to recreate the container, but it also contributes to growth in container layers.

Networking

Create User-Defined Bridge Networks

Certain functionality, including DNS, is absent from the default bridge network created by Docker on installation. User-defined bridge networks offer a more robust feature set. To create a bridge network:

```
docker network create <NETWORK_NAME> --attachable --driver bridge
```

Connect/Disconnect Containers to/from Networks

Containers may be attached to a network at any time in their lifecycle. Adding containers without port mappings to a network allows connections from the host using native ports. To add a container to a network:

```
docker network connect <NETWORK_NAME> <CONTAINER_NAME>
```

To disconnect from a network:

```
docker network disconnect <NETWORK_NAME> <CONTAINER_NAME>
```

Dedicated DNS

There are multiple solutions for adding DNS resolution to a container host, allowing clients on the host to reference containers by container ID, container name, assigned hostname, or network alias. dvdarias/docker-hoster is one such option. It reads Docker's event service and adds or removes containers to the host /etc/hosts file whenever they start or stop. To run it using the recommended defaults:

```
docker run -d \
      -v /var/run/docker.sock:/tmp/docker.sock \
      -v /etc/hosts:/tmp/hosts \
      dvdarias/docker-hoster
```

Containers

Basic Container Creation

The minimum command to create a database container:

```
docker run -d <IMAGE_NAME>
```

The -d flag runs the container as a background process.

The following command snippets illustrate the use of options for the docker run command.

Naming

Assigning names, hostnames, and network aliases to containers must occur during creation. Docker generates a random container name during creation if a name isn't specified.

Assign a Container Name

The container name is a human-friendly name referenced in container commands such as docker start, docker logs, or docker exec. Set the container name with the --name flag:

```
docker run -d \
      --name <CONTAINER_NAME> \
...
```

Assign a Hostname

The hostname is an optional identity separate from the container name. If not set, the hostname defaults to the container name:

```
docker run -d \
      --hostname <HOSTNAME> \
...
```

Define Environment Variables

The database creation and management scripts read variables from the container environment and use them to build and start the database. If not set manually, the container relies on its default settings. The most frequently used variables (with default values in brackets) are

- ORACLE_SID: The Oracle Database SID [ORCLCDB]

- ORACLE_PDB: The Oracle Database PDB name [ORCLPDB1]

- ORACLE_PWD: The Oracle Database SYS, SYSTEM, and PDB_ADMIN password [randomly generated during database creation]

- ENABLE_ARCHIVELOG: Enable archive logging [False]

To display all environment variables available in an image:

```
docker image inspect \
    --format '{{range .Config.Env}}{{printf "%s\n" .}}{{end}}' \
    <IMAGE_NAME> | sort
```

To set an individual variable, in this example ORACLE_SID, at the command line, use the -e option:

```
docker run -d \
    -e ORACLE_SID=ORCLDB \
...
```

Set multiple values using separate -e flags for each. Here, the ORACLE_SID and ORACLE_PDB are set in the container:

```
docker run -d \
    -e ORACLE_SID=ORCLDB \
    -e ORACLE_PDB=PDB1 \
...
```

The docker run command can read values from the host environment. Here, the ORACLE_SID is set using the value of $dbname defined in the local host environment:

```
docker run -d \
    -e ORACLE_SID=$dbname \
...
```

Docker can read values from a file, with each `VARIABLE=VALUE` pair on separate lines. Example contents of an environment file called `db.env`:

```
> cat db.env
ORACLE_SID=TEST
ORACLE_PDB=TESTPDB1
ORACLE_EDITION=EE
ENABLE_ARCHIVELOG=true
```

Reference the file in the `docker run` command with the `--env-file` option:

```
docker run -d \
      --env-file db.env \
...
```

Assign Storage

Persist data from the container database by mapping or mounting storage.

Bind-Mount a Directory with -v

Bind mounting maps a directory on the host to a path inside the container. Files in the container are written (and saved) to the container host's filesystem and persisted locally, even if the container is removed.

The `/opt/oracle/oradata` directory in Oracle database images includes all database configuration and datafiles. To map it to a directory on the host:

```
docker run -d \
      -v <HOST_DIRECTORY>:/opt/oracle/oradata
...
```

Bind-Mount a Directory with --mount

The syntax of `--mount` is more verbose and specific, and Docker recommends it over the `-v` option. The order of elements in `--mount` isn't important. To bind-mount a directory with `--mount`, use the `type=bind` option:

207

```
docker run -d \
        --mount type=bind,source=<HOST_DIRECTORY>,target=/opt/oracle/oradata
...
```

Remember to use unique directories for each container to avoid multiple databases writing to the same path and files!

Attach a Predefined Volume with -v

Docker Volumes are named objects managed by Docker. They must be precreated before being referenced in by docker run. To map the /opt/oracle/oradata directory in the container to an existing volume:

```
docker run -d \
        -v <VOLUME_NAME>:/opt/oracle/oradata
...
```

Attach a Predefined Volume with --mount

As in the example of using --mount to bind a directory, the order of elements is unimportant. To map a predefined volume to the /opt/oracle/oradata directory using --mount, use the type=volume option:

```
docker run -d \
        --mount type=volume,source=<VOLUME_NAME>,target=/opt/oracle/oradata
...
```

Entrypoints

Entrypoints are special directories in containers where scripts will search for and execute scripts during creation and startup. In Oracle container images, the entrypoints are

- **Entrypoint roots:** /docker-entrypoint-initdb.d or /opt/oracle/scripts

- **Startup scripts:** /opt/oracle/scripts/startup

- **Setup scripts:** /opt/oracle/scripts/setup

When mapping directories to an entrypoint root path, a `startup` and a `setup` directory must exist in the locally mapped directory. Otherwise, the management scripts won't find anything to run. To mount a single directory to the root entrypoint:

```
docker run -d \
    --mount type=bind,source=<ENTRYPOINT_DIR>,target=/docker-entrypoint-
    initdb.d \
...
```

To mount directories to the startup and setup entrypoints:

```
docker run -d \
    --mount type=bind,source=<STARTUP_DIR>,target=/opt/oracle/scripts/
    startup \
    --mount type=bind,source=<SETUP_DIR>,target=/opt/oracle/
    scripts/setup \
...
```

Networking

Map Ports to the Host

Port mapping routes network traffic from its native port on a container to a port on the host. It allows clients on the host (or host network) to access container resources. To map the Oracle listener on a container operating on port 1521:

```
docker run -d \
    -p <HOST_PORT>:1521 \
...
```

Map multiple ports with a separate declaration for each:

```
docker run -d \
    -p <HOST_PORT_1>:1521 \
    -p <HOST_PORT_2>:5500 \
...
```

Add to a Network

To attach a container to a specific network at startup:

```
docker run -d \
       --network <NETWORK_NAME> \
...
```

Containers may be added to (or removed from) networks at will and may even belong to multiple networks.

Complete Container Examples

The command in Listing 10-1 creates a simple container for an Oracle database and it

- Defines a custom container name

- Defines user-defined values for the database CDB and PDB names

- Maps the database listener to a port on the container host

- Bind-mounts the database's data directory to local storage for persistence

The resulting container delivers all the functionality needed to run a database in a local environment, such as a laptop or small lab, without creating volume or network objects.

Listing 10-1. An example for creating a named container with a custom container name, user-defined CDB, and PDB names, port mapping to the host, and database files and configuration persisted to a host directory

```
docker run -d \
       --name <CONTAINER_NAME> \
       -e ORACLE_SID=<ORACLE_SID> \
       -e ORACLE_PDB=<ORACLE_PDB> \
       -p <HOST_PORT>:1521 \
       --mount type=bind,source=<LOCAL_DIR>,target=/opt/oracle/oradata \
       <IMAGE_NAME>
```

The example in Listing 10-2 adds to the previous command, delivering additional features, including a Docker-managed volume bind-mounted to a local directory on the host and a user-defined bridge network that includes DNS. After creating the prerequisite objects, the docker run command

- Names the container

- Assigns a custom hostname

- Defines the CDB and PDB databases created in the container

- Mounts the predefined volume

- Attaches to the custom network

This configuration is well suited to intermediate and advanced deployments where databases interact with other container services (including other databases).

Listing 10-2. An example of building a more robust container environment is taking advantage of Docker's networking and volume management.

```
docker volume create --opt type=none --opt o=bind \
        --opt device=<DIRECTORY_PATH> \
        <VOLUME_NAME>

docker network create <NETWORK_NAME> --attachable --driver bridge

docker run -d \
        --name <CONTAINER_NAME> \
        --hostname <HOST_NAME> \
        -e ORACLE_SID=<ORACLE_SID> \
        -e ORACLE_PDB=<ORACLE_PDB> \
        --mount type=volume,source=<VOLUME_NAME>,target=/opt/oracle/
        oradata \
        --network <NETWORK_NAME> \
        <IMAGE_NAME>
```

Finally, the example of Listing 10-3 adds to the previous docker run command by adding a mapping for the container entrypoint. Docker will run any scripts it discovers under the startup subdirectory whenever the container starts. Scripts in the setup subdirectory run immediately after database creation in the container.

Listing 10-3. The docker run command from Listing 10-2, with the addition of an entrypoint definition

```
docker run -d \
      --name <CONTAINER_NAME> \
      --hostname <HOST_NAME> \
      -e ORACLE_SID=<ORACLE_SID> \
      -e ORACLE_PDB=<ORACLE_PDB> \
      --mount type=volume,source=<VOLUME_NAME>,target=/opt/oracle/
      oradata \
      --mount type=bind,source=<ENTRYPOINT_DIR>,target=/docker-entrypoint-
      initdb.d \
      --network <NETWORK_NAME> \
      <IMAGE_NAME>
```

Interact with Containers

Open a Shell

To access the command line inside the container, similar to ssh-ing to a remote host:

```
docker exec -it <CONTAINER_NAME> bash
```

The -it flags instruct Docker to open an interactive session. You can specify a different shell (or different command) by replacing bash with the shell or command name. Remember, commands that aren't part of the container's PATH variable require a full path.

Run SQL*Plus

To run SQL*Plus directly in a container:

```
docker exec -it <CONTAINER_NAME> sqlplus / as sysdba
```

Run a Script

To remotely run scripts in the background of a container, omit the -it flags and pass the path and script name *as it exists in the container:*

```
docker exec <CONTAINER_NAME> <PATH_TO_SCRIPT>/<SCRIPT_NAME>
```

The script must be executable by the container's default user (the oracle user for the containers we're working with).

Connect As Root

To connect to a container as a user other than the default (including the root user), pass the username along with the -u flag:

```
docker exec -it -u <USER> <CONTAINER_NAME> bash
```

Manage Passwords

To set (or reset) the privileged database passwords of a container database, use docker exec to run the /opt/oracle/setPassword.sh script in the container, providing the new password as an argument:

```
docker exec <CONTAINER_NAME> /opt/oracle/setPassword.sh <PASSWORD>
```

Here, I changed the password in container ORCL1 to "oracle123":

```
> docker exec ORCL1 /opt/oracle/setPassword.sh oracle123
The Oracle base remains unchanged with value /opt/oracle

SQL*Plus: Release 19.0.0.0.0 - Production on Tue Mar 29 00:44:36 2022
Version 19.3.0.0.0

Copyright (c) 1982, 2019, Oracle.  All rights reserved.

Connected to:
Oracle Database 19c Enterprise Edition Release 19.0.0.0.0 - Production
Version 19.3.0.0.0

SQL>
```

```
User altered.

SQL>
User altered.

SQL>
Session altered.

SQL>
User altered.

SQL> Disconnected from Oracle Database 19c Enterprise Edition Release
19.0.0.0.0 - Production
Version 19.3.0.0.0
```

Docker Deployment Examples

Over the past few pages, I've offered snippets of code, but I want to show you how
my typical Docker workflow looks, using real examples run from a Linux or WSL
command line.

New Environment Setup

If I'm working in a new container environment, my first step is adding the directories
and users necessary for running Oracle in Docker. On Linux systems, I separate storage
into two partitions, one for databases and another for Docker-related files:

```
sudo mkdir /oradata /docker
sudo chown $(id -un):$(id -gn) /docker
```

The second command changes the owner and group of the /docker directory to my
local user so I can add files later without invoking sudo.

The /oradata mount point serves as the root directory for database volumes
and mounts. To avoid issues with bind mounts on Linux, I create an oracle user and
oinstall group, with ID values matching those in the Oracle preinstallation RPMs, then
set the ownership on the /oradata directory:

```
sudo groupadd -g 54321 oinstall
```

```
sudo useradd -u 54321 -g oinstall
sudo chown oracle:oinstall /oradata
```

By default, Docker saves its data in the /var/lib/docker directory. Linux systems, particularly those running in cloud services, often have block storage separate from the boot volume that offers faster or larger partitions for container operations. If so, I relocate /var/lib/docker to a new partition. Here, I'm moving it under the /docker partition:

```
systemctl stop docker.service
systemctl stop docker.socket
sed -i 's|ExecStart=/usr/bin/dockerd|ExecStart=/usr/bin/dockerd -g /
docker|g' /lib/systemd/system/docker.service
rsync -aqxP /var/lib/docker/ /docker/.docker 2>/dev/null
systemctl daemon-reload
systemctl start --no-block docker.service
```

Add the Oracle Repository

New systems need a copy of Oracle's Docker repository. Assuming git is installed, I can clone the repo into the /docker path:

```
git clone https://github.com/oracle/docker-images /docker
```

After copying the appropriate installation media to the version directories under /docker/OracleDatabase/SingleInstance/dockerfiles/, I can begin building the images:

```
cd /docker/OracleDatabase/SingleInstance/dockerfiles/
./buildContainerImage.sh -v 19.3.0 -e
./buildContainerImage.sh -v 21.3.0 -e
```

Networking

Next, I turn my attention to networking, adding a new bridge network, which I usually name oracle-db:

```
docker network create oracle-db --attachable --driver bridge
```

More formal environments may require multiple networks for improved isolation. If so, I will revisit this step.

If I anticipate a need for DNS, I start a `docker-hoster` container, too:

```
docker run -d \
        --name oracle-db-dns \
        -v /var/run/docker.sock:/tmp/docker.sock \
        -v /etc/hosts:/tmp/hosts \
        dvdarias/docker-hoster
```

Running Containers

The steps I follow when creating containers depend on how I plan to use them. It generally falls into two categories: "disposable" databases I don't intend to keep very long and production or production-like databases.

Disposable Environments

I persist the /opt/oracle/oradata volume for *every* database container but rarely do much more for disposable databases due to their short lifespans. In the example in Listing 10-4, I set environment variables for the container, database, and PDB name. The script uses these variables, adding a directory and bind-mounting it to a volume, then creates an Oracle 19c database container. I'm also mounting a local directory, /oradata/ scripts, into a new mount point on the container, called /scripts. This is a common, shared directory of—you guessed it—scripts, tools, and utilities I may want available in the container as I work.

Listing 10-4. Example code showing steps for creating resources and running a "disposable" Oracle 19c database container

```
CONTAINER_NAME=test
ORACLE_SID=ORCLCDB
ORACLE_PDB=ORCLPDB1

mkdir -p /oradata/${CONTAINER_NAME}

docker volume create --opt type=none --opt o=bind \
        --opt device=/oradata/${CONTAINER_NAME} \
        ${CONTAINER_NAME}_data
```

```
docker run -d \
      --name ${CONTAINER_NAME} \
      -e ORACLE_SID=${ORACLE_SID} \
      -e ORACLE_PDB={ORACLE_PDB} \
      --volume ${CONTAINER_NAME}_data:/opt/oracle/oradata \
      --volume /oradata/scripts:/scripts \
      --network oracle-db \
      oracle/database:19.3.0-ee
```

Persistent Environments

Critical databases require more discipline and resources, including additional volumes for diagnostic and audit directories. Listing 10-5 is an example of a script for automating the steps to create directories, assign volumes, and run containers.

Listing 10-5. A script for automating the creation of multiple directories and bind-mounted volumes for a database's audit, data, and diagnostic directories

```
CONTAINER_NAME=prod
ORACLE_SID=ORCLCDB
ORACLE_PDB=ORCLPDB1

 for dir in audit data diag
  do mkdir -p /oradata/${CONTAINER_NAME}/${dir}
     docker volume create --opt type=none --opt o=bind \
           --opt device=/oradata/${CONTAINER_NAME}/${dir} \
           ${CONTAINER_NAME}_${dir}
done

mkdir -p /oradata/${CONTAINER_NAME}_entry/{setup,startup}

docker run -d \
      --name ${CONTAINER_NAME} \
      -e ORACLE_SID=${ORACLE_SID} \
      -e ORACLE_PDB={ORACLE_PDB} \
      --volume ${CONTAINER_NAME}_data:/opt/oracle/oradata \
      --volume ${CONTAINER_NAME}_diag:/opt/oracle/diag \
      --volume ${CONTAINER_NAME}_audit:/opt/oracle/admin \
```

```
--volume /oradata/${CONTAINER_NAME}_entry:/opt/oracle/scripts \
--volume /oradata/scripts:/scripts \
--network oracle-db \
oracle/database:19.3.0-ee
```

Notice I create dedicated entrypoint directories for each container. This is where I place any scripts used to modify the container's setup and startup operations. Having dedicated directories allows more control, creating links to global copies or writing custom scripts as needed.

Summary

This chapter is a quick reference of the most common commands and options you'll use when creating and running containers and closes the first part of the book covering containers. We covered container fundamentals, focusing on how they apply to Oracle databases. You should now feel comfortable writing and using docker run commands; stopping, starting, and managing containers; and getting information from Docker about images and containers.

A key takeaway of this first part relates to persistence, covered in Chapter 7. Understanding the benefits of mapping data from volatile directories in containers to storage on the local host is essential. Containers use layered (or overlay) filesystems to achieve speed and save space. Layered filesystems are efficient when files are stable but perform poorly as the number of changes increases. Mapping directories that experience many changes (particularly those containing database files) to storage outside the container improves performance and persists data independently of the container's lifecycle.

In the case of Oracle databases, everything needed to clone or recreate a database exists under the /opt/oracle/oradata directory. Saving this directory path to the container host lets us clone or recreate a database in seconds!

We've touched upon a few peculiarities of containers—like the absence of text editors—and accepted or worked around them as products of their underlying images. In the next section, our focus moves from running containers to modifying those images to suit our needs better. That begins with an exploration of image builds and several scripts that control image and database creation.

PART II

Building and Customizing Images

You're now well versed at running containers, and in this second part, our attention turns to building and customizing images. We begin by demonstrating modifications to the existing Oracle container repository introduced in Chapter 4, delve into the art of writing and troubleshooting Dockerfiles, then conclude with a discussion of saving images to repositories.

CHAPTER 11

Customizing Images

Something I love about working with Oracle (and databases in general) is the variety. Each day brings something new, and problems often have multiple solutions. Every shop has its way of doing things, and solutions vary from customer to customer based on industry practices, security, and conventions.

Docker (and other automation tools) complement and help enforce these standards. Container images are infrastructure templates. Rather than building things by hand and introducing the potential for human error, container images offer a guaranteed starting point, preconfigured to meet specific requirements.

But templates are rarely one size fits all, and neither are container images. In the images we've worked with, Oracle decided how to configure the environment and what to include. Chapter 3 raised this issue when we discovered the default Ubuntu image lacks a vi editor. Containers don't need editors when run at scale, but they may be a requirement in a test or lab system, and satisfying that need requires a different template. We could add an editor manually, but we'd be defeating the whole idea of automation in general and containers in particular: having a ready-to-run image with everything we need already installed.

When it comes to building Oracle database images to meet specific needs, there are two options. The first is writing *Dockerfiles*, the recipes Docker uses to build images, as described in Chapters 12 and 13. The second technique, covered in this chapter, extends existing scripts to tailor the generated templates.

Remember, the containers we're working with run Oracle Enterprise Linux. All the commands in the container environment, whether running a container or building an image, must be appropriate to the container's operating system. For Linux users running different distribution flavors, bear in mind that commands used on the host may differ from those needed in the container. For example, Ubuntu users update packages on their systems with apt-get but use yum in Oracle database containers.

S. Scott, *Oracle on Docker*, https://doi.org/10.1007/978-1-4842-9033-0_11

Script Modifications

Except for the Dockerfile and two response files, the files reviewed in this chapter are all bash shell scripts. The intent here isn't to delve deeply into the scripts themselves but to point out how and where to update them to accomplish various modifications to the resulting images. And the good news is you don't need to be a scripting expert to understand these changes!

The files we'll work with in this chapter are part of the Docker repository, introduced in Chapter 4. Recall that after copying the repository to your system, you navigated down a (rather lengthy) path to build your first image: docker-images/OracleDatabase/ SingleInstance/dockerfiles. Beneath that directory were several subdirectories, one for each database version:

```
drwxr-xr-x    8 seanscott   staff    256 May 27 20:51 11.2.0.2
drwxr-xr-x   18 seanscott   staff    576 May 27 20:51 12.1.0.2
drwxr-xr-x   16 seanscott   staff    512 May 27 20:51 12.2.0.1
drwxr-xr-x   16 seanscott   staff    512 May 27 20:51 18.3.0
drwxr-xr-x    8 seanscott   staff    256 May 27 20:51 18.4.0
drwxr-xr-x   19 seanscott   staff    608 May 27 21:00 19.3.0
drwxr-xr-x   21 seanscott   staff    672 May 27 21:00 21.3.0
-rwxr-xr-x    1 seanscott   staff   7091 May 27 20:51 buildContainerImage.sh
```

These version-specific subdirectories all include several scripts that perform the general setup and configuration operations under four categories:

- Operating system installation and configuration

- Oracle database software installation

- Database creation

- Container startup, including starting the Oracle listener and database

The examples in this chapter are based on the 19c scripts but apply to any version. You'll navigate to the subdirectory matching the database version you want to work with, where you'll find the files have the same names and purposes. Since these files are on your local system, you can perform the changes using your favorite text editor.

It's a good idea to create a backup of each file before making any changes. Still, if something breaks, remember you can always redownload or copy the files from the original GitHub repository.

OS Install and Configuration

Containers running in production environments are designed to be as minimal as possible, for many reasons, with space savings and security near the top. The container images used as baselines for more complex or specialized applications (including Oracle databases) typically leave out anything that isn't essential. It's faster and easier to add what's needed than remember to remove what isn't, and safer, too. Attackers can't exploit software vulnerabilities in programs and packages that aren't present in a container!

One type of functionality commonly excluded from images is editors. All necessary files are preinstalled in production deployments and the environment preconfigured. There's no need to edit anything manually, and the default database images reflect that thinking.

On the other hand, if you're using containers as an interactive or experimental platform, having editors and tools for navigating the environment makes sense. The same holds for containers used in security or penetration testing, evaluating new features, and validating patches or procedures.

setupLinuxEnv.sh

In Linux, packages deliver these capabilities and features through a *package manager*. Different "flavors" of Linux use different package managers. Oracle Enterprise Linux 7 uses a package manager called yum, which stands for *Yellowdog Updater, Modified*.

Navigate to your preferred version subdirectory under docker-images/ OracleDatabase/SingleInstance/dockerfiles in your repository, and you'll find a file called setupLinuxEnv.sh. Open that file in your favorite editor and look for a line beginning yum -y install. The line in the 19.3.0 version is

```
yum -y install oracle-database-preinstall-19c openssl && \
```

For those unfamiliar with Linux or yum, the meanings of elements on this line are as follows:

- yum: Invokes yum.

- -y: This flag is a shorthand confirmation, telling yum to proceed with whatever operations without user input. It allows scripted or automated commands to complete without human interaction.

- install: There are several options available to yum, and, as you might suspect, install tells the package manager to install something.

- oracle-database-preinstall-19c and openssl: These are the packages yum will install. The first is the Oracle preinstallation package (itself a collection of packages) containing everything necessary to install and run an Oracle. Each database version has its own package, so the version you see may be different. openssl is a cryptographic package. (The 12cR1 script also installs tar.)

- && and \: The double ampersand (&&) is a logical operation instructing Linux to execute the following command if the current command completes successfully. The backslash (\) is a continuation character, telling Linux that this isn't the end of the command and to continue reading on the following line for more.

Note that a single yum command can install multiple packages, listing each individually after the install operation. yum (and other package managers) resolves (most) dependencies in a given list of packages. The order of packages doesn't matter. We can add packages to the existing yum command—packages like editors!

The packages I typically install that improve my interactive experience in Oracle container images:

- oracle-epel-release-el7: EPEL, or *Extra Packages for Enterprise Linux,* is a collection of development packages providing additional features and functionality.

- bash-completion: A set of helper functions for autocompleting Linux commands.

- git: Adds libraries necessary for interacting with git-based repositories.

- `less`: A file viewer, similar to `more`, for reading and searching text files on Linux systems.

- `strace`: A debugging and diagnostic tool for inspecting signals and system calls. `strace` is invaluable for investigating potential problems in the database kernel.

- `tree`: Displays directory structures visually as a hierarchal "tree" of entries with parent-child relationships.

- `vi`: My editor of choice!

- `which`: A helpful tool for displaying the locations of executables in the user's `PATH`.

To update the `yum install` command to include additional packages, add them anywhere between the `install` keyword and the double ampersand, `&&`, that marks the end of the `yum` command. For example, to add `less`, `strace`, `tree`, and `vi`, change the command to

```
yum -y install oracle-database-preinstall-19c openssl less strace tree vi
&& \
```

After building a new image using the updated script, all containers run from the new image will include the added commands.

Dockerfile

There's one potential modification for improving or customizing interaction in containers. This change, in the default Dockerfile, creates a `.bashrc` file. This file runs every time an interactive `bash` session starts and can be used to set the shell prompt, environment variables, and aliases and even execute commands.

The following two chapters address Dockerfiles in depth, but not everyone needs the additional control available from custom images. This tip has broader applications, so I include it here.

Open the `Dockerfile` in your repository and navigate to the end of the file. In the 19c and 21c versions, you'll find a line that reads

```
# Add a bashrc file to capitalize ORACLE_SID in the environment
RUN echo 'ORACLE_SID=${ORACLE_SID:-ORCLCDB}; export ORACLE_SID=${ORACLE_
SID^^}' > .bashrc
```

If your version doesn't have this line, you can add one just before the line that begins `HEALTHCHECK`.

To understand this command, let's break down its parts:

- `RUN`: The `RUN` command in the Dockerfile tells the build process to run one or more commands. Don't confuse it with `docker run`! The former is a step in the image build process, while the latter is for creating a new container. Following `RUN` are commands Docker uses to construct the image.

- `echo 'ORACLE_SID=` through `${ORACLE_SID^^}'`: This is the command Docker runs in the image. `echo` displays output to stdout or *standard output*, usually the terminal. The text it prints is everything between the single quotes (`'`).

- `> .bashrc`: The single right caret (`>`) is an *output redirection* that sends the output of the `echo` statements to a file. A single caret overwrites the file contents; two carets (`>>`) append the output to the end of the file. The file receiving the result is `.bashrc`.

I want to call attention to the use of single quotes in the `echo` command. Single quotes treat their contents literally, without interpreting or substituting anything in the quoted string. If double quotes bounded the string, `bash` would replace `$ORACLE_SID` using its value in the environment. Compare the different results produced by the same command, using single vs. double quotes:

```
echo 'ORACLE_SID=${ORACLE_SID:-ORCLCDB}; export ORACLE_SID=${ORACLE_SID^^}'
ORACLE_SID=${ORACLE_SID:-ORCLCDB}; export ORACLE_SID=${ORACLE_SID^^}
```

```
echo "ORACLE_SID=${ORACLE_SID:-ORCLCDB}; export ORACLE_SID=${ORACLE_SID^^}"
ORACLE_SID=ORCLCDB; export ORACLE_SID=
```

The substitution is empty in the second example, using double quotes, because $ORACLE_SID isn't set. This command anticipates an environment where the $ORACLE_SID is defined but runs during the image build *before setting the variable*!

This RUN command creates a new .bashrc file in the oracle user's home directory and runs each time the oracle user logs in. The first part sets the ORACLE_SID to whatever value is in the environment. If the docker run command that started the container included an -e flag and value for ORACLE_SID, that is assigned. If there's no value, the bash manipulation, :-ORCLCDB, gives a default value of ORACLECDB:

```
ORACLE_SID=${ORACLE_SID:-ORCLCDB}
```

The next part converts the ORACLE_SID to upper case, using the ^^ manipulation, and exports it to the environment:

```
export ORACLE_SID=${ORACLE_SID^^}
```

We can build on the existing RUN command in the 19c and 21c Dockerfiles (or add a similar line to the Dockerfiles in other versions) that write entries to a .bashrc file. This pattern facilitates other changes to the container environment, too. Two examples are modifying the shell prompt and creating a login.sql file for SQL*Plus.

Modify the Default Shell Prompt

The special PS1 variable controls the appearance of the shell prompt, with a library of special characters for displaying (among other things) the date, current directory, and even setting colors. The following syntax sets the prompt to show the user (\u), the ORACLE_SID, and the current directory (\w), followed by a hash prompt on a new line (\n#):

```
export PS1="[\u - ${ORACLE_SID}] \w\n# "
```

To add this to the existing RUN command:

```
RUN echo 'ORACLE_SID=${ORACLE_SID:-ORCLCDB}; export ORACLE_SID=${ORACLE_
SID^^}; export PS1="[\u - ${ORACLE_SID}] \w\n# "' > .bashrc
```

The brackets in the PS1 variable are special characters that must be inside quotes.

Add a login.sql File

Oracle reads two files whenever starting SQL*Plus: the glogin.sql *global login* file under $ORACLE_HOME/sqlplus/admin and an optional login.sql *login* file present in the $ORACLE_PATH. These files can contain any SQL or SQL*Plus statements or commands to run when SQL*Plus sessions start. The global login file runs for everyone, but individual users can assign custom login files and set the path in their local environment.

To understand why you might want a login file, open SQL*Plus and run the following statement:

```
select * from v$database;
```

The table has one line, with output scattered among repeated headings. It's ugly and difficult to read. The underlying cause is Oracle's default setting of pagesize, which controls how many lines of text to put on each page:

```
SQL> show pages
pagesize 14
```

To see the output presented more digestibly, change the pagesize to a larger value, 9999:

```
set pages 9999
```

If you want to see things formatted differently, you could run this set command manually *every time you log in*. Or, add it to a login.sql file and let Oracle do it for you. To incorporate the latter automated solution into a Docker image, we need to set the $ORACLE_PATH variable in the image's .bashrc file and create a new login.sql file in the $ORACLE_PATH directory.

This is a somewhat more complex set of instructions. We could add multiple RUN lines to the Dockerfile, but (for reasons covered in Chapter 12), keeping the number of RUN commands to a minimum is desirable. Instead, I'll take advantage of the double ampersand (&&) and backslash (\) we saw before to string several commands together across multiple lines, all as part of a single RUN instruction:

```
RUN echo 'ORACLE_SID=${ORACLE_SID:-ORCLCDB}; export ORACLE_SID=${ORACLE_
SID^^}' > .bashrc && \
    echo 'export ${ORACLE_PATH}=/home/oracle' >> .bashrc && \
    echo 'set pages 9999' > /home/oracle/login.sql
```

Notice that the redirection on the second line uses two carets to append text to the `.bashrc` file rather than overwriting it.

Avoid changing the `glogin.sql` file! It applies to all SQL*Plus activity, including any automated or background processes. Running SQL or changing the environment can create odd or devastating effects on your database!

Hopefully, these examples spark your imagination and offer a vehicle for you to extend and enhance your containers!

Database Installation

After readying the operating system for Oracle, automated database installation begins. There isn't much in the software installation procedure itself; it's a fairly generic process controlled by the `installDBBinaries.sh` script. The exciting part is how the installation script works with the `db_inst.rsp` response file.

installDBBinaries.sh

As mentioned earlier, we generally try to make containers as small as possible, and the database installation is no exception. There's a section near the end of the 19c and 21c scripts dedicated to that purpose:

```
if $SLIMMING; then
    # Remove not needed components
    # APEX
    rm -rf "$ORACLE_HOME"/apex && \
    # ORDS
    rm -rf "$ORACLE_HOME"/ords && \
    # SQL Developer
    rm -rf "$ORACLE_HOME"/sqldeveloper && \
    # UCP connection pool
    rm -rf "$ORACLE_HOME"/ucp && \
    # All installer files
    rm -rf "$ORACLE_HOME"/lib/*.zip && \
```

```
    # OUI backup
    rm -rf "$ORACLE_HOME"/inventory/backup/* && \
    # Network tools help
    rm -rf "$ORACLE_HOME"/network/tools/help && \
    # Database upgrade assistant
    rm -rf "$ORACLE_HOME"/assistants/dbua && \
    # Database migration assistant
    rm -rf "$ORACLE_HOME"/dmu && \
    # Remove pilot workflow installer
    rm -rf "$ORACLE_HOME"/install/pilot && \
    # Support tools
    rm -rf "$ORACLE_HOME"/suptools && \
    # Temp location
    rm -rf /tmp/* && \
    # Database files directory
    rm -rf "$INSTALL_DIR"/database
fi
```

At the time of writing, these statements aren't wrapped in an if statement for versions before 19c, but similar logic may be added for consistency.

This if statement checks the value of a build argument, SLIMMING, removing several directories from the database home after installation. To prevent the script from removing these directories, set the SLIMMING variable to false. One way of accomplishing this is editing the Dockerfile and changing true in the following line to false:

```
ARG SLIMMING=true
```

There's currently no option in the buildContainerImage.sh script to influence the build and not remove these directories. Again, that functionality may be added later.

The real reason I highlighted this part of the script relates to 19c upgrades from earlier versions of Oracle. A powerful use of Docker is planning and preparing for database upgrades. Before upgrading older versions of Oracle to 19c, you'll need to remove older APEX installations. The scripts for removing APEX are located under $ORACLE_HOME/apex.

But look at what the installDBBinaries.sh scripts do when it comes to APEX, for each version:

```
rm -rf "$ORACLE_HOME"/apex
```

How can you remove APEX if the directory with the script for removing APEX is missing?

An alternative to changing the value of SLIMMING in the Dockerfile is commenting out individual lines with a hash (#) character:

```
#rm -rf "$ORACLE_HOME"/apex
```

The takeaway is to remember that the database installation script "slims down" the database home by default. If your plans for Docker include anything in one of the removed directories, save yourself some headaches and update the installDBBinaries. sh script appropriately!

db_inst.rsp

I mentioned before that the installDBBinaries.sh script uses a second file, the db_inst.rsp response file. For those that haven't worked with them in the past, response files store the answers to all the questions typically answered in the GUI-based installation process. These include the ORACLE_BASE and ORACLE_HOME to the "*Do you want to receive security updates from Oracle*" question near the end. Without response files, we couldn't perform unattended installations in Docker (or other automation platforms like Vagrant, Ansible, or Terraform, for that matter).

Oracle provides default response files for each database version, prepopulated with every available option. Most entries are commented out with hashes (#) and include some descriptive or informational text. Take this entry from a 19c response file, for instance, that identifies the purpose and possible options of the oracle.install.option parameter:

```
#-----------------------------------
# Specify the installation option.
# It can be one of the following:
#    - INSTALL_DB_SWONLY
#    - INSTALL_DB_AND_CONFIG
#    - UPGRADE_DB
#-----------------------------------
oracle.install.option=INSTALL_DB_SWONLY
```

The db_inst.rsp file is the response file Docker uses to install the database. Working again with the 19c version of the repository, I've selected only the "uncommented" lines that the installer reads during the installation. These are the "answers" to each of the "questions" a database installation needs:

```
oracle.install.responseFileVersion=/oracle/install/rspfmt_dbinstall_
response_schema_v19.0.0
oracle.install.option=INSTALL_DB_SWONLY
UNIX_GROUP_NAME=dba
INVENTORY_LOCATION=###ORACLE_BASE###/oraInventory
ORACLE_HOME=###ORACLE_HOME###
ORACLE_BASE=###ORACLE_BASE###
oracle.install.db.InstallEdition=###ORACLE_EDITION###
oracle.install.db.OSDBA_GROUP=dba
oracle.install.db.OSOPER_GROUP=dba
oracle.install.db.OSBACKUPDBA_GROUP=dba
oracle.install.db.OSDGDBA_GROUP=dba
oracle.install.db.OSKMDBA_GROUP=dba
oracle.install.db.OSRACDBA_GROUP=dba
SECURITY_UPDATES_VIA_MYORACLESUPPORT=false
DECLINE_SECURITY_UPDATES=true
```

A few of these lines—the ones with ### surrounding part of the "answer"—might stand out. What do you suppose ###ORACLE_HOME### and ###ORACLE_BASE### mean here? They're placeholders that the installDBBinaries.sh script replaces with real values with this group of commands:

```
# Replace place holders
# --------------------
sed -i -e "s|###ORACLE_EDITION###|$EDITION|g" "$INSTALL_DIR"/"$INSTALL_
RSP" && \
sed -i -e "s|###ORACLE_BASE###|$ORACLE_BASE|g" "$INSTALL_DIR"/"$INSTALL_
RSP" && \
sed -i -e "s|###ORACLE_HOME###|$ORACLE_HOME|g" "$INSTALL_
DIR"/"$INSTALL_RSP"
```

The sed command in Linux stands for *stream editor*, a powerful (and sometimes cryptic) tool for programmatically modifying text files. The three commands in the installation script perform a find-and-replace operation against the response file, identified here as "$INSTALL_DIR"/$INSTALL_RSP". It substitutes values from the environment for the placeholders. (Keep this bit of code in mind for the next section on database creation, where it plays a much more valuable role in customizing the database.)

The default response files produce generic database installations. If your needs go beyond those in the default responses, make those changes in the db_inst.rsp file.

Database Creation

As with database installation, the database creation script has a partner response file. What's important to remember is these files, createDB.sh and dbca.rsp.tmpl, are added to the image *during the image build* but *called* during docker run. You'll need to rebuild the image before new containers recognize changes to these scripts.

Just as the db_inst.rsp contains the answers needed to complete a database installation, the dbca.rsp.tmpl file includes the answers asked during database creation. You may even recognize some entries from the last time you ran the Database Configuration Assistant (DBCA) GUI! And, like the installation response file, the file contains placeholders identified by three hashes (###). Once again, from the 19c directory, the noncommented entries are

```
responseFileVersion=/oracle/assistants/rspfmt_dbca_response_schema_v19.0.0
gdbName=###ORACLE_SID###
sid=###ORACLE_SID###
createAsContainerDatabase=true
numberOfPDBs=1
pdbName=###ORACLE_PDB###
pdbAdminPassword=###ORACLE_PWD###
templateName=General_Purpose.dbc
sysPassword=###ORACLE_PWD###
systemPassword=###ORACLE_PWD###
emConfiguration=DBEXPRESS
emExpressPort=5500
```

```
dbsnmpPassword=###ORACLE_PWD###
characterSet=###ORACLE_CHARACTERSET###
nationalCharacterSet=AL16UTF16
initParams=audit_trail=none,audit_sys_operations=false
automaticMemoryManagement=FALSE
totalMemory=2048
```

The database creation script, `createDB.sh`, has similar `sed` commands:

```
# Replace place holders in response file
cp "$ORACLE_BASE"/"$CONFIG_RSP" "$ORACLE_BASE"/dbca.rsp
# Reverting umask to original value
umask 022
sed -i -e "s|###ORACLE_SID###|$ORACLE_SID|g" "$ORACLE_BASE"/dbca.rsp
sed -i -e "s|###ORACLE_PDB###|$ORACLE_PDB|g" "$ORACLE_BASE"/dbca.rsp
```

Add a Non-CDB Option

The software install response file doesn't offer many interesting options, but the DBCA response file has more exciting possibilities. Take, for instance

```
createAsContainerDatabase=true
```

Maybe you'd prefer a 19c database that *isn't* a container database. You could change that value to `false`, but remember this file is written into the image. Once you change the container database option from `true` to `false`, *every database* created from *this image* will necessarily be a non-container database, reversing the original problem. If you need both, you could maintain separate images for each or create one that has both! How?

Use this technique to introduce variable-driven control over nearly any option you'd care to add to the database creation process.

First, update the response file template to read

```
createAsContainerDatabase=###CREATE_CDB###
```

Then, add a default value for a new environment variable that matches the placeholder, CREATE_CDB, and a sed command to perform the substitution. I chose to add the code just before the first sed command in the existing script:

```
[ "$CREATE_CDB" == "false" ] || CREATE_CDB=true
sed -i -e "s|###CREATE_CDB###|$CREATE_CDB|g" "$ORACLE_BASE"/dbca.rsp
```

The first line checks to see if the value of CREATE_CDB is false. The two pipes (||) are a logical expression that instructs bash to execute the following command when the statement is false. In plain English, it says, "If CREATE_CDB is false, leave it that way; otherwise, set it to true." The sed expression on the following line performs the substitution.

Where, then, does the CREATE_CDB value in the condition come from? It will be present in the container environment, and we can pass a value in a docker run command with the -e flag:

```
docker run -d \
    -e CREATE_CDB=false
...
    <IMAGE_NAME>
```

Any value passed to CREATE_CDB that isn't false (including no value at all) defaults to true, and the script creates a CDB and PDB. The container only creates a non-CDB database when CREATE_CDB is explicitly set to false.

There's one more change we'll need to make. The 19c database creation script includes CDB- and PDB-specific commands that produce errors in databases built as non-CDB. To adapt these commands to a non-CDB environment, use the same logic earlier. Near the end of the script, you'll find a sqlplus command block:

```
sqlplus / as sysdba << EOF
    ALTER SYSTEM SET control_files='$ORACLE_BASE/oradata/$ORACLE_SID/
    control01.ctl' scope=spfile;
    ALTER SYSTEM SET local_listener='';
    ALTER PLUGGABLE DATABASE $ORACLE_PDB SAVE STATE;
    EXEC DBMS_XDB_CONFIG.SETGLOBALPORTENABLED (TRUE);

    ALTER SESSION SET "_oracle_script" = true;
    CREATE USER OPS\$oracle IDENTIFIED EXTERNALLY;
```

```
    GRANT CREATE SESSION TO OPS\$oracle;
    GRANT SELECT ON sys.v_\$pdbs TO OPS\$oracle;
    GRANT SELECT ON sys.v_\$database TO OPS\$oracle;
    ALTER USER OPS\$oracle SET container_data=all for sys.v_\$pdbs
    container = current;

    exit;
EOF
```

We need to remove three CDB- and PDB-specific commands for non-CDB databases:

```
ALTER PLUGGABLE DATABASE $ORACLE_PDB SAVE STATE;
GRANT SELECT ON sys.v_\$pdbs TO OPS\$oracle;
ALTER USER OPS\$oracle SET container_data=all for sys.v_\$pdbs container =
current;
```

The following code checks the same CREATE_CDB environment variable and assigns these commands to three variables, PDB_CMD1, PDB_CMD2, and PDB_CMD3:

```
[ "$CREATE_CDB" == "false" ] || PDB_CMD1="ALTER PLUGGABLE DATABASE $ORACLE_
PDB SAVE STATE;"
[ "$CREATE_CDB" == "false" ] || PDB_CMD2='GRANT SELECT ON sys.v_$pdbs TO
OPS$oracle;'
[ "$CREATE_CDB" == "false" ] || PDB_CMD3='ALTER USER OPS$oracle SET
container_data=all for sys.v_$pdbs container = current;'
```

Pay attention to the quotes! The first variable uses double quotes, so bash substitutes the value of $ORACLE_PDB into the command. The second and third use single quotes, preventing bash from interpreting the dollar signs ($) as part of an environment variable. The original commands prefix the dollar signs with the backslash (\) to escape the dollar sign because they're part of a "*here document*." The *here document* passes everything between the << EOF, after the sqlplus login, and the closing tag, EOF, as if typed directly into SQL*Plus.

Now, substitute these variables into the original code:

```
sqlplus / as sysdba << EOF
    ALTER SYSTEM SET control_files='$ORACLE_BASE/oradata/$ORACLE_SID/
    contro01.ctl' scope=spfile;
```

```
ALTER SYSTEM SET local_listener='';
$PDB_CMD1
EXEC DBMS_XDB_CONFIG.SETGLOBALPORTENABLED (TRUE);

ALTER SESSION SET "_oracle_script" = true;
CREATE USER OPS\$oracle IDENTIFIED EXTERNALLY;
GRANT CREATE SESSION TO OPS\$oracle;
$PDB_CMD2
GRANT SELECT ON sys.v_\$database TO OPS\$oracle;
$PDB_CMD3

exit;
EOF
```

When creating a CDB, the variables equate to the original commands, where they're interpreted in the here document and passed to SQL*Plus. For non-CDB databases, they'll be undefined, creating blank lines in the script!

There's one more change to make in the database *health check*. Docker uses health checks to report the state of the container. If we omit this step, any container running a non-CDB database will report an "*unhealthy*" status. The scripts that run the database rely on the same checks to identify whether database creation completed properly. Left as they are, we'll see errors in the database logs, an unhealthy state in docker ps output, and potentially break functionality that runs only in a "healthy" database.

The checkDBStatus.sh script performs the database and container health check. We'll use the same method to modify the following section, located near the top of the file:

```
checkPDBOpen() {
    # Obtain OPEN_MODE for PDB using SQLPlus
    PDB_OPEN_MODE=$(sqlplus -s / << EOF
set heading off;
set pagesize 0;
SELECT DISTINCT open_mode FROM v\$pdbs;
exit;
EOF
```

The script assumes it's working with a CDB. For a non-CDB database, change the reference from pdbs to database:

```
[ "$CREATE_CDB" == "false" ] && PDB_CMD=database || PDB_CMD=pdbs
```

The logic check is like those used before, with the addition of a *logical and* represented by two ampersands (&&). This means "If CREATE_CDB is false, set PDB_CMD to database; otherwise, set it to pdbs."

Finally, substitute the variable into the SELECT DISTINCT line in the checkDBHealth.sh script:

```
SELECT DISTINCT open_mode FROM v\$$PDB_CMD;
```

Pay attention to the sequence with the backslash and two dollar signs (\$$). The backslash "escapes" the first dollar sign but allows substitution of $PDB_CMD. The health check runs its SELECT against v$database or v$pdbs, depending on the value of CREATE_PDB.

Congratulations! You've extended a database image to create CDB and non-CDB databases, run appropriate post-creation commands, and call the proper health check command simply by passing a variable to the docker run command!

Adapting database creation scripts to accommodate CDB and non-CDB databases is a complex change since it touches on multiple moving parts: the response file, substituting a placeholder and conditionally updating SQL statements in createDB.sh, and changing the database health check. Not every change is this involved. By adapting all or part of this technique, you'll be able to incorporate additional flexibility into images.

Start and Run the Database

The final scripts to examine manage the behavior of containers and databases when containers start. Recalling the "start" event during docker start and docker run is essential. Thinking back to Chapter 7, cloning databases is possible because the container doesn't know whether it's starting for the first time. The startup script looks to see if specific files are present and, if so, *assumes* it's not a new container and proceeds to start the database. Otherwise, it creates a new database from scratch.

The same script, `runOracle.sh`, handles both scenarios and offers multiple opportunities to introduce features. It sets the defaults for several environment variables and calls the `createDB.sh` script, invokes entrypoint scripts, and starts the database and listener by calling `startDB.sh`. It also controls database and listener shutdown when the container receives a shutdown signal from `docker stop`.

Summary

In this chapter, you learned how Docker uses scripts to build images and discovered ways of updating existing scripts in Oracle's repository to change and add functionality to images and containers. You saw where the configuration of container operating systems occurs. You can add additional packages to container images and modify the Dockerfile to customize the environment and write files to images. We also covered steps performed during database installation and how response files complement Oracle software installation and database creation.

We explored techniques for adding new features to database containers and how to drive their use through environment variables. You should also have a deeper appreciation for the inner workings of containers and recognize which scripts are called during startup. You should also have a general idea of the role health checks play in reporting database and container status, internally and externally.

For many, the concepts covered in this chapter are adequate for tailoring containers to suit your needs better. If you're using Docker exclusively for noncritical work, it's unlikely you'll need to write custom Dockerfiles. If so, feel free to skip ahead to Chapter 14.

However, if you intend to use containers for more specific or critical applications or simply want to understand more about Docker's inner workings, continue with the following three chapters, beginning with Chapter 12.

Dockerfile Syntax

One of my favorite activities is cooking, and like any creative endeavor, the best results come when you understand how to use the tools of the craft. It helps to know the rules, which are ironclad (don't add water to hot oil) and which have flexibility (how much garlic is "too much!"). Others may enjoy the result, but only the chef appreciates the process!

I see many parallels between cooking and coding and find creative outlets in both. There are accepted, "right" ways to do certain things, but for the most part, each allows practitioners liberty to stamp their style into the result. Sometimes, I review code and come across a block I don't immediately understand. After working through it, I realize it's functionally identical to a technique I've used for years, just a completely different approach. Two authors with different backgrounds, experiences, influences, and habits still produce the same result. I often adopt those methods into my library of "cool ways to do stuff."

Keep that thought in mind across the next few chapters on Dockerfiles. This isn't an authoritative or definitive guide but an introduction to the rules and tools you'll need to concoct image recipes—Dockerfiles—used by Docker's build process to construct images. At its core, that's what a Dockerfile is:

- **Ingredients:** The files and objects needed by the image. In Docker, this is known as the *build context*.

- **Preparation:** The order and method for combining elements. A recipe can have one step or many. For instance, the first step in baking a cake combines dry ingredients like flour, sugar, and baking soda; the second mixes the eggs and milk. In the third, the wet ingredients from step two are added to the dry ingredients from step one. The steps in a Dockerfile are called *stages*, and a *multistage* build works along the same lines as the cake recipe. Early stages make

© Sean Scott 2023
S. Scott, *Oracle on Docker*, https://doi.org/10.1007/978-1-4842-9033-0_12

intermediate preparations that combine in a later stage, producing a completed product.

- **Cooking:** How to build and deliver the image. This is *metadata*. In a recipe, it's measurements, temperature, and baking time. In Docker, the metadata sets the environment, defines runtime commands called when containers start, and health checks that report status.

Databases have unique needs with different treatments than ordinary container images, and the following few chapters are more sharply focused on addressing techniques and considerations for building good database images. Let's set aside definitions of "good" database images for now and focus on how Dockerfiles work!

The good news is that there aren't many commands to learn in the Dockerfile instruction set! The elements are relatively straightforward, and Dockerfiles read from top to bottom, with each line a separate instruction that tells the *build process* how to construct a new image. They boil down to

- What image to start from

- How to modify the starting image by adding environment variables, copying files, and running commands

- Finally, how the finished product should behave when run as a container

This chapter assumes some familiarity with Linux and writing bash shell scripts.

The Role of Layers in the Build Process

Behind the scenes, the build process is a series of scripted docker run–like operations that start a container (using an existing image), do something to modify the container, and save the result as a new image. In builds, Docker doesn't lump multiple changes into a single bucket. Every step is its own image. Docker layers the individual images together to make a final image.

The layers in Docker images are like those in the overlay filesystems we looked at in Chapter 7. Remember that a layer overlays a base layer with changes. Remember our layered filesystem example, looking down at a game of Tic-Tac-Toe?

Containers have a single intermediate layer that stores the cumulative changes made over a container's lifetime. Everything is lumped together because there's little chance that individual changes are reusable. Docker handles images differently, though. Where containers have a single upper layer for all changes, each step in an image build adds its own "glass shelf," as in Figure 12-1, adding depth to the stack of layers.

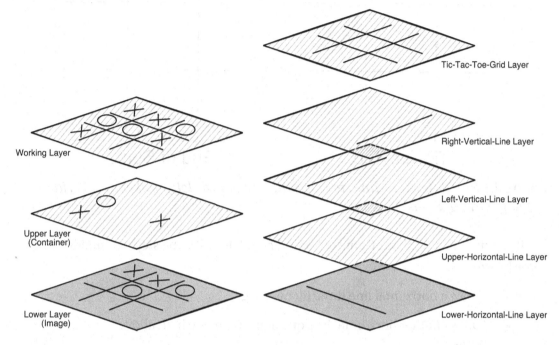

Figure 12-1. *Containers (left) capture all changes into a single upper layer. The container view is a merger of the upper and lower layers, projected into the working layer. Images (right) add new layers for every operation. The final image is a union of many layers*

The reason behind this multilayer approach is reusability. Think of the steps involved in "building" a Tic-Tac-Toe board—you draw the same four lines every time. It's a predictable, repeatable process. But drawing lines is fundamental to building the grids used by other games. Figure 12-2 shows a Tic-Tac-Toe game beside a *"La Grille de Sommes[1]"* (Grid of Sums), introduced in France's *Le Monde* newspaper in 2013.

---

[1] In a Grid of Sums, you select a cell and enter a number equal to the sum of its neighbors. If the adjacent cells have no values, enter "1." The objective is to reach the highest possible total in the final cell. See www.dr-mikes-math-games-for-kids.com/le-monde-grid-puzzle.html for examples and more information.

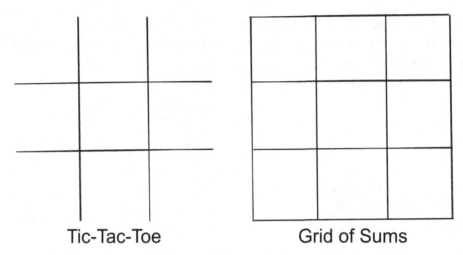

Tic-Tac-Toe   Grid of Sums

Figure 12-2. *Adding four lines to a Tic-Tac-Toe board (left) makes a 3x3 grid for playing "Grid of Sums"*

If you didn't know about Game of Sums, I could describe the steps for building the game board:

- "Draw a horizontal line three inches long."

- "Draw another horizontal line of equal length one inch above the first."

- "Draw a three-inch vertical line, intersecting the horizontal lines one inch from their left end."

- Etc.

Or, I could simply ask you to "Draw a Tic-Tac-Toe board and add a border around the outside."

You cached those steps into memory as layers when you learned how to build a Tic-Tac-Toe board. Those layers are reusable foundations you can use for constructing new and potentially more complex games, and it's far more efficient to reference the set of known operations—draw a Tic-Tac-Toe board—than describe the procedure.

Docker builds images the same way. Each layer in an image is reusable and available to other builds, from "lower horizontal line" through "Tic-Tac-Toe board." As we build database images, you'll see how efficient this is. If I need two images for Oracle Database 19c, one with the 19.10 Release Update and another with the 19.11 Release Update, *everything* up to applying the patch is identical, as in Figure 12-3: configure the operating system and environment; add prerequisites; install the Oracle 19c software. I then have a 19.3.0 database I can patch to the desired level.

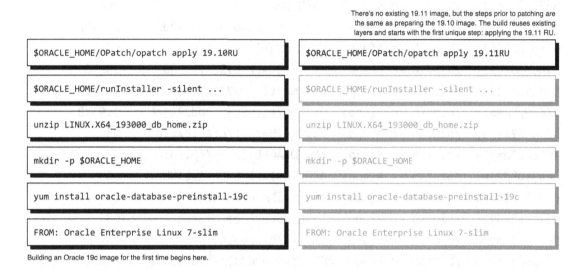

Building an Oracle 19c image for the first time begins here.

Figure 12-3. *Creating images for Oracle 19c databases patched with the 19.10 and 19.11 Release Updates follows the same initial steps. Docker doesn't repeat the work performed in existing layers. Instead, it starts with the latest or uppermost recyclable layer*

Listing 12-1 shows the simplified output from running docker image history for an Oracle 19c database image to see how this looks in a Docker image. docker image history displays the composite layers that form a final image and the commands that created them.

Listing 12-1. The first command displays the history of an Oracle 19c database image. Read the output from bottom to top to see the commands used to create each layer of the final image and how it evolved from a starting point to its final form. The second command lists information on the final database and Oracle Enterprise Linux 7-slim images, including their unique identifiers and sizes

```
> docker image history -H oracle/database:19.3.0-ee
IMAGE           CREATED BY                                    SIZE
f53962475832    /bin/sh -c #(nop)  CMD ["/bin/sh" "-c" "exec…  0B
dceea9dcf380    /bin/sh -c #(nop)  HEALTHCHECK &{["CMD-SHELL…  0B
```

```
e6a7408b308b  /bin/sh -c #(nop) WORKDIR /home/oracle          0B
f94cd312d82e  /bin/sh -c #(nop)  USER oracle                  0B
1664ac9ff6d4  /bin/sh -c $ORACLE_BASE/oraInventory/orainst…   21.8MB
6688786dc411  /bin/sh -c #(nop)  USER root                    0B
b6fb885c6988  /bin/sh -c #(nop) COPY --chown=oracle:dbadir…   6.19GB
0dfd2be6867c  /bin/sh -c #(nop)  USER oracle                  0B
64bee30fc72f  /bin/sh -c chmod ug+x $INSTALL_DIR/*.sh &&  …   184MB
53ce8dbf2fe1  /bin/sh -c #(nop) COPY multi:db377117e0d23af…   36.8kB
74619cb4eafe  /bin/sh -c #(nop) COPY multi:08c35eebd2349e6…   1.96kB
bd4c7a72aa97  /bin/sh -c #(nop)  ENV PATH=/opt/oracle/prod…   0B
167ee23df373  /bin/sh -c #(nop)  ENV ORACLE_BASE=/opt/orac…   0B
0e43108d92e1  /bin/sh -c #(nop)  ARG INSTALL_FILE_1=LINUX.…   0B
0de06b15c6b1  /bin/sh -c #(nop)  ARG SLIMMING=true            0B
d1215483892c  /bin/sh -c #(nop)  LABEL provider=Oracle iss…   0B
9ec0d85eaed0  /bin/sh -c #(nop)  CMD ["/bin/bash"]            0B
<missing>     /bin/sh -c #(nop) ADD file:b0df42f2bb614be48…   133MB

> docker images
REPOSITORY         TAG            IMAGE ID        SIZE
oracle/database    19.3.0-ee      f53962475832    6.53GB
oraclelinux        7-slim         9ec0d85eaed0    133MB
```

The last line is the starting image. Each line above it is a layer, or "glass shelf," that introduced a modification. By reading the output from the bottom up, you see how the final image evolved through a series of operations, from a starting image (the ADD file: entry at the bottom) through completion. Each image layer has a unique ID in the first column and a size in the last.

While we haven't yet covered the different Dockerfile commands, look at the size column. The layers that *aren't* zero bytes have something in common. Most ADD or COPY operations do just that—add or copy something into the mix. The output is truncated for the remaining two commands, but were the lines printed in their entirety, you'd see they're running scripts or commands. These nonzero-byte layers are like the glass shelves with something on them. The layer's size matches the amount of change contained on each shelf.

What about the zero-byte layers? These are metadata instructions Docker uses to run the image. They don't occupy space in the image. In keeping with the cooking theme, image metadata is the information needed to prepare and finish a recipe. Things like oven temperature and baking time aren't physical ingredients in a cake, yet they're still critical to the process. In the Dockerfile, the USER root and USER oracle instructions fill this role, telling Docker to run one or more subsequent commands as a particular user. If you're familiar with Oracle database installations, you might even recognize a familiar pattern here:

```
1664ac9ff6d4   /bin/sh -c $ORACLE_BASE/oraInventory/orainst…   21.8MB
6688786dc411   /bin/sh -c #(nop)  USER root                     0B
```

Again, reading from the bottom up, Docker sets the user to root and runs something in $ORACLE_BASE/oraInventory/orasinst.... The full command on that line is

```
$ORACLE_BASE/oraInventory/orainstRoot.sh && $ORACLE_HOME/root.sh
```

That's Docker running Oracle's post-installation root scripts! Changing the user is a metadata operation. Running the post-installation root scripts created 21.8MB in changes to the layers below.

Layers are powerful because they're reusable. We don't completely rewrite documentation just to add a minor change, nor do we rebuild images containing identical steps. Suppose I changed the Dockerfile used to build the database image shown earlier. In that case, Docker understands that everything *up to my edit* is the same and *reuses existing image layers* instead of reexecuting the steps. Given the layer appearing here:

```
b6fb885c6988   /bin/sh -c #(nop) COPY --chown=oracle:dbadir…   6.19GB
```

The last column shows the layer uses 6.19GB of disk space. Docker can recycle that layer (and everything before it) in new images that have changes *after* that step. In that case, the 6.19GB layer isn't duplicated—all images *share the same copy*!

FROM

You've learned that building an image runs a container, makes changes, then saves the result as a new image. The first step—running a container—requires an image, and the FROM command tells Docker the image's name. The format is straightforward: FROM <image name>:

```
FROM oraclelinux:7-slim
```

Building an image requires an image. Where did the *first* image come from? Isn't it a chicken and the egg paradox? Not really! A special image, called `scratch`, creates an empty filesystem. The advantage of using existing images is they're pre-built, tested, reusable, and save us the time and effort of starting from "scratch" (literally)!

Notice the sizes of the first layer of the database image (the entry recorded with an image ID of `<missing>`) and the Oracle Enterprise Linux 7-slim image in Listing 12-1 are both 133MB. Docker added the image (`ADD file:b0df42f2bb614be48…`) in the first step as the foundation for the following modifications.

Build Stages

There's an additional capability of FROM that preserves the result of steps to use locally, later in the same build. It's a foundation of *multistage builds*. Each *stage* of a multistage build is a collection of commands—parts of a single step in a recipe. While the alias appears in the FROM command marking the beginning of the stage, it references the result after all operations in the stage are complete. To create an alias, add the AS keyword after the image referenced in FROM:

```
FROM oraclelinux:7-slim AS base
```

It's functionally identical to a recipe that reads

Step 1. Combine flour, sugar, baking soda, and salt in a bowl. Set aside.

The alias is the name of the stage, and it's referenced in subsequent FROM commands using the alias:

```
FROM base
```

The equivalent in a recipe is

Step 3. Retrieve the bowl of dry ingredients from Step 1 and…

In complex builds, calls to *stages* can have their own aliases, imparting a very modular feel to the build process:

```
FROM base AS builder
```

Stages are local and temporary, and build processes aren't aware of stages created in other Dockerfiles.[2]

`base` and `builder` are common aliases for stages in a Dockerfile. `base` usually represents a foundation result used repeatedly throughout a build. For example, a `base` image for an Oracle database often starts with an OS image (`oraclelinux:7-slim`) and adds standard environment variables, the `oracle` user, and prerequisite packages.

`builder` is typically an intermediate or temporary stage for creating or manipulating content for later use. You'll see examples of this in the two following chapters.

Configure Environments: ARG and ENV

After initiating the build process with a starting image, it's time to start customizing things! One of the most common next steps is setting environment variables. On a regular Linux host, the `.login`, `.bash_login`, `.bashrc`, or similar script sets the environment at login.

The image in the `FROM` command doesn't have the information we need. It needs to be added. The `ENV`, or *environment*, command is the most direct and simple way of setting environment variables. It assigns a value to a variable following the same pattern as exporting a variable to the local environment in Linux:

```
ENV ORACLE_HOME=/opt/oracle/product/19c/dbhome_1
```

Simple, right?

---

[2] Docker does cache build information internally and, depending on its configuration, may still take advantage of cached layers to improve performance. However, stage names only exist locally in the build process and aren't available to other builds or subsequent executions of the same build.

Extending Images

There's just one problem with the preceding command. It sets the ORACLE_HOME to a static, hard-coded value. Ideally, images should have some flexibility. Users that want to build an image with Oracle installed under a different directory structure must edit the ENV command in the Dockerfile and change the assignment of ORACLE_HOME to their preferred location.

The ARG, or *argument*, command offers an alternative to assigning static values with ENV. The format of the two commands is the same:

```
ARG ORACLE_HOME=/opt/oracle/product/19c/dbhome_1
```

We still need to configure the environment with a value for ORACLE_HOME, but instead of a hard-coded value, we'll assign it using the value of the argument, expressed as a shell variable ($ORACLE_HOME):

```
ENV ORACLE_HOME=$ORACLE_HOME
```

At first, this seems to accomplish the same thing and creates more work! There's still a static value, and now two commands instead of one:

```
ARG ORACLE_HOME=/opt/oracle/product/19c/dbhome_1
ENV ORACLE_HOME=$ORACLE_HOME
```

What makes this better?

Recall we can override the default values for environment variables using the -e option of the docker run command. It makes database images far more flexible than being locked into predefined settings. The docker build command has a similar feature, --build-arg, for overriding arguments set in the Dockerfile. (We'll delve into docker build in Chapter 14.)

There's some confusion when it comes to ARG and ENV. Briefly:

- ARG sets default values for a variable. Arguments are only visible to the build process and only within the stage where they're defined. They aren't written into the image nor persist into subsequent build stages. During the build process, the --build-arg option can override the defaults.

- ENV assigns values to variables and preserves them in the image. Since they're part of the image, environment variables set in one stage carry over into later stages. Environment variables can't be changed during a build.

Any variables that don't require flexibility can be defined with ENV. Anything that might need adjustment during the build should use both ARG and ENV.

Assigning an empty value to ARG initializes a variable and makes it available as a build argument:

```
ARG INSTALL_OPTIONS=
ENV INSTALL_OPTIONS=$INSTALL_OPTIONS
```

Here, ARG initializes a variable, INSTALL_OPTIONS, and sets it to an empty value. ENV assigns the value of the argument to a variable in the environment. It remains empty in the image unless the build gives it a value.

We can create new variables in containers on the fly, using the docker run -e flag, but that same functionality doesn't exist for building images. The --build-arg option can only reference an argument present in the Dockerfile.

The relationship between ARG and ENV needn't be one to one. Take the following example that uses arguments for database version and ORACLE_BASE and constructs an ORACLE_HOME path:

```
ARG DB_VERSION=19c
ARG ORACLE_BASE=/opt/oracle
ENV ORACLE_HOME=$ORACLE_BASE/product/$DB_VERSION/dbhome_1
ENV ORACLE_BASE=$ORACLE_BASE
```

Argument and Environment Scope During Builds

I mentioned earlier that variables set with ARG are only visible to the build process, but those set with ENV are passed to the image. We can use the scope of arguments to disguise certain aspects of the build process.

Connect to an Oracle database container and run env | sort to print a sorted list of environment variables, as seen in Listing 12-2. It shows entries we expect to see on an Oracle database host and some residue from the build process.

Listing 12-2. Default environment variables set in an Oracle database container

```
bash-4.2$ env | sort
ARCHIVELOG_DIR_NAME=archive_logs
CHECKPOINT_FILE_EXTN=.created
CHECK_DB_FILE=checkDBStatus.sh
CHECK_SPACE_FILE=checkSpace.sh
CLASSPATH=/opt/oracle/product/19c/dbhome_1/jlib:/opt/oracle/product/19c/
dbhome_1/rdbms/jlib
CLONE_DB=false
CONFIG_RSP=dbca.rsp.tmpl
CREATE_DB_FILE=createDB.sh
CREATE_OBSERVER_FILE=createObserver.sh
DG_OBSERVER_NAME=
DG_OBSERVER_ONLY=false
ENABLE_ARCHIVELOG=false
HOME=/home/oracle
HOSTNAME=59ae22d8ed19
INSTALL_DB_BINARIES_FILE=installDBBinaries.sh
INSTALL_DIR=/opt/install
INSTALL_FILE_1=LINUX.X64_193000_db_home.zip
INSTALL_RSP=db_inst.rsp
LD_LIBRARY_PATH=/opt/oracle/product/19c/dbhome_1/lib:/usr/lib
ORACLE_BASE=/opt/oracle
ORACLE_HOME=/opt/oracle/product/19c/dbhome_1
ORACLE_SID=ORCLCDB
PATH=/opt/oracle/product/19c/dbhome_1/bin:/opt/oracle/product/19c/dbhome_1/
OPatch/:/usr/sbin:/usr/local/sbin:/usr/local/bin:/usr/sbin:/usr/bin:/
sbin:/bin
PRIMARY_DB_CONN_STR=
PWD=/home/oracle
PWD_FILE=setPassword.sh
RELINK_BINARY_FILE=relinkOracleBinary.sh
RUN_FILE=runOracle.sh
SETUP_LINUX_FILE=setupLinuxEnv.sh
SHLVL=1
```

```
SLIMMING=true
STANDBY_DB=false
START_FILE=startDB.sh
TERM=xterm
USER_SCRIPTS_FILE=runUserScripts.sh
WALLET_DIR=
_=/usr/bin/env
```

Some of these environment variables don't need to be here, including those that begin with INSTALL. These variables all point to files and directories used in the Dockerfile during the Oracle database software installation step. The artifacts they point to aren't present in the final image—they're removed (or, more accurately, not included) in the final image used by docker run:

```
bash-4.2$ ls -l $INSTALL_DIR
ls: cannot access /opt/install: No such file or directory
bash-4.2$ find / -name $INSTALL_DB_BINARIES_FILE 2>/dev/null
bash-4.2$ find / -name $INSTALL_FILE_1 2>/dev/null
bash-4.2$ find / -name $INSTALL_RSP 2>/dev/null
bash-4.2$
```

For those unfamiliar with the 2>/dev/null syntax: It sends errors into the void! The number 2 is shorthand for stderr, the error messages we'd generally see printed to the terminal. The caret, >, redirects these errors to the Linux null device file, /dev/null. This trick prevents "permission denied" errors for directories the oracle user can't read from cluttering the output.

The database software installation scripts need this information. The container doesn't. Strictly speaking, they don't need to persist in the container environment. Don't get me wrong—I greatly respect the authors and contributors that maintain Oracle's container repository, and their work over the years is remarkable and insightful. I'm not saying it's wrong for these variables to be in the final image, merely because my coding style and preferences differ. But, their presence helps illustrate how to leverage differences in ARG and ENV!

Passing these values as arguments instead of adding them to the environment would define them to the build process. They'd be visible to the software installation scripts called during the build but absent from the final image. My arguments in favor of this approach are as follows:

- It produces a "cleaner," less cluttered environment.

- It makes it less apparent the database is running in a Linux container.

- It limits information an attacker could use to gain information about methods used to build the image.

Again, there's no right or wrong here, just different ways of doing things.

Another option for passing variables to scripts without setting them in the environment is to define them as part of a command string. The RUN instruction, covered later in this chapter, can include a locally scoped variable definition as part of its command:

```
RUN INSTALL_DIR=/opt/install && \
    INSTALL_DB_BINARIES_FILE=installDBBinaries.sh && \
    $INSTALL_DIR/$INSTALL_DB_BINARIES_FILE
```

The variables here are set only in the scope of the RUN command that needs them.

Build Dockerfile Templates with Arguments

The FROM command must be the first command in a Dockerfile. It makes sense—it's challenging to do anything without a starting image! The single exception that proves the rule is the ARG command.

A Dockerfile can have arguments as the first instructions and use those arguments in a FROM command. It's helpful for writing Dockerfile templates that add flexibility to builds. For instance, all the database images we've worked with so far use Oracle Enterprise Linux 7-slim as the base image. That image name is hard-coded into the FROM statement. But what if we wanted to use a different version? Rewriting the Dockerfile and changing the image is one option. Another is using an argument-based image:

```
ARG IMAGE_TAG=7-slim
FROM oraclelinux:$IMAGE_TAG
```

A Dockerfile written this way is more flexible and potentially future-proof.

Assign Multiple Variables

Another difference between ARG and ENV is that arguments must be set individually, but a single ENV command can set multiple variables:

```
ARG VAR1=VALUE1
ARG VAR2=VALUE2
ARG VAR3=VALUE3
ENV VAR1=VALUE1 \
    VAR2=VALUE2 \
    VAR3=VALUE3
```

The backslash (\) is a continuation character that tells Linux there's more to the command on the following line. The preceding ENV command could also be written as

```
ENV VAR1=VALUE1 VAR2=VALUE2 VAR3=VALUE3
```

The advantage of the first method is clarity. Each variable could also be defined in separate ENV commands, but since every instruction in a Dockerfile creates a new layer, combining commands into as few lines as necessary reduces overhead.

Variables and Secrets

Don't use variables to pass secrets to images or containers! As you can see, environment variables set during the build persist into the final image and are inherited by containers! Instead, use Docker secrets discussed in the section on RUN later in the chapter.

LABEL

Labels are optional instructions for setting image metadata. It's considered good practice to add labels to images, particularly for injecting usage information users might find helpful for running your images.

Like ENV, labels are key-value pairs, and a single LABEL instruction can set multiple labels. The value of a label should be enclosed in double quotes. Any arguments or environment variables set during the build and included in a label are reflected in the image metadata. Consider the partial contents of a Dockerfile with some arguments, environment variables, and labels:

```
ARG ORACLE_BASE=/opt/oracle

ENV ORACLE_BASE=$ORACLE_BASE \
    ORACLE_HOME=$ORACLE_HOME \
    PATH=$PATH:$ORACLE_HOME/bin

LABEL "oracle_home"="$ORACLE_HOME" \
      "oracle_base"="$ORACLE_BASE" \
      "description"="This is a database image"
```

The metadata of the final image contains three labels (assuming the argument for ORACLE_BASE isn't overridden during the build):

```
"Labels": {
    "description" = "This is a database image"
    "oracle_base"="/opt/oracle"
    "oracle_home"="/opt/oracle/product/19c/dbhome_1"
}
```

Labels are unstructured, and there are no strict rules covering what should and shouldn't be labeled. They often capture image properties such as volumes, ports, and contact information. In this case, the convention for label names is to separate elements with dots, such as function.name. There are good examples in the Oracle Dockerfile. It sets the following labels:

```
LABEL "provider"="Oracle"                                        \
      "issues"="https://github.com/oracle/docker-images/issues" \
      "volume.data"="/opt/oracle/oradata"                        \
      "volume.setup.location1"="/opt/oracle/scripts/setup"       \
      "volume.setup.location2"="/docker-entrypoint-initdb.d/setup" \
      "volume.startup.location1"="/opt/oracle/scripts/startup"   \
      "volume.startup.location2"="/docker-entrypoint-initdb.d/startup" \
      "port.listener"="1521"                                     \
      "port.oemexpress"="5500"
```

To view an image's label metadata, run the inspect command and review the Labels section:

```
"Labels": {
    "issues": "https://github.com/oracle/docker-images/issues",
    "port.listener": "1521",
    "port.oemexpress": "5500",
    "provider": "Oracle",
    "volume.data": "/opt/oracle/oradata",
    "volume.setup.location1": "/opt/oracle/scripts/setup",
    "volume.setup.location2": "/docker-entrypoint-initdb.d/setup",
    "volume.startup.location1": "/opt/oracle/scripts/startup",
    "volume.startup.location2": "/docker-entrypoint-initdb.d/startup"
}
```

To limit and format the output of docker inspect to only display labels:

```
docker inspect \
    --format='{{range $p,$i:=.Config.Labels}}{{printf "%s = %s\n" $p $i}}
    {{end}}' \
    <IMAGE NAME>
```

The result:

```
issues = https://github.com/oracle/docker-images/issues
port.listener = 1521
port.oemexpress = 5500
provider = Oracle
volume.data = /opt/oracle/oradata
volume.setup.location1 = /opt/oracle/scripts/setup
volume.setup.location2 = /docker-entrypoint-initdb.d/setup
volume.startup.location1 = /opt/oracle/scripts/startup
volume.startup.location2 = /docker-entrypoint-initdb.d/startup
```

USER

In the section on layers, you saw that the USER instruction sets the login user for running commands. Docker runs commands as the root user by default, but it's a good practice to set the user in your Dockerfile explicitly.

Stages in Dockerfiles aren't limited to a single user. It's perfectly acceptable to set a user, run a command, set a new user, run another command, and so on. You see that in Listing 12-1, where the user changes from oracle to root and back to oracle. When you consider what's happening during an Oracle database software installation, it parallels the manual steps:

- As the oracle user, prepare the environment, copy and unzip the installation files, and run the installation.

- As the root user, run the post-installation root scripts.

- As the oracle user, finalize the installation.

The USER command is a "cooking instruction" affecting the commands that follow. It sets the active user (and with it the group) ID, and the rules are no different than you'd experience were you directly logged into a system. The active user must have the proper permissions on files and directories to successfully copy or execute files. The results inherit permissions just as they do in a typical environment.

COPY

The COPY instruction adds ingredients into images, copying source files from the local system to a destination inside the image. It follows the same general rules as the Linux cp command, including the ordering syntax of source followed by destination and how it interprets wildcards and regular expressions.

The Dockerfile in Oracle's container repository includes some examples of COPY in practice:[3]

```
COPY $SETUP_LINUX_FILE $CHECK_SPACE_FILE $INSTALL_DIR/
```

---

[3] Remember that the file names and directory shown here are set as variables in the container environment.

A single COPY instruction can add multiple source files to a single directory, as seen here, where the $SETUP_LINUX_FILE and $CHECK_SPACE_FILE are copied to the $INSTALL_DIR directory. The last argument is the destination, while everything before is interpreted as a source.

Setting Ownership

Files copied into images are owned by the current user set in the stage. The ownership must change if they need to be modified or executed later by a different user. We can accomplish that in two steps—copy the files, then change the ownership—but COPY has a facility to do both at once: the --chown flag. With --chown=<USER>:<GROUP>, the user (and optionally group) ownership is set within the COPY command itself:

```
COPY --chown=oracle:dba $INSTALL_FILE_1 $INSTALL_RSP $INSTALL_DB_BINARIES_
FILE $INSTALL_DIR/
```

This example from the Oracle container repository copies three files, the database installation zip file ($INSTALL_FILE_1) and the software installation and response files ($INSTALL_DB_BINARIES_FILE and $INSTALL_RSP, discussed in Chapter 11), to the installation directory path and sets their ownership to the oracle user and dba group. The oracle user then has the necessary rights to update and run the files later in the build.

Context in the Build Process

Look back on these examples of COPY commands and notice that they reference files using a *relative path*. An *absolute path* is fully qualified against the filesystem root, like /etc/oratab. Absolute paths begin with a slash, while relative paths reference locations on a filesystem based on the current working directory. If my current working directory is /etc, the relative path to the oratab file is just oratab. Absolute paths are precise—there's no question about what file or directory we're talking about. Relative paths are, well, relative. They require some sort of *context*.

In Docker, this *build context* is the directory where the build runs. If the Dockerfile is our recipe, the context is the kitchen and COPY the instructions for finding each ingredient. I set the context—navigating to the kitchen—and assemble all the ingredients before beginning. (If you've ever prepared a meal in someone else's kitchen, think of the COPY command as asking where they keep the salt!)

Context isn't only crucial for the success of a build. It also affects the speed and size of the build process. How? Listing 12-3 shows a fictitious directory tree, where I consolidated database installation files into one subdirectory, db_files. The scripts used to construct an image are in a second subdirectory, scripts.

Listing 12-3. An alternative, fictitious directory structure consolidating installation media and management scripts into their directories

```
> tree .
.
├── db_files
│   ├── linuxamd64_12102_database_1of2.zip
│   ├── linuxamd64_12102_database_2of2.zip
│   ├── linuxamd64_12102_database_se2_1of2.zip
│   ├── linuxamd64_12102_database_se2_2of2.zip
│   ├── linuxx64_12201_database.zip
│   ├── LINUX.X64_180000_db_home.zip
│   ├── LINUX.X64_193000_db_home.zip
│   └── LINUX.X64_213000_db_home.zip
└── scripts
    ├── checkDBStatus.sh
    ├── checkSpace.sh
    ├── createDB.sh
    ├── dbca.rsp.tmpl
    ├── db_inst.rsp
    ├── installDBBinaries.sh
    ├── runOracle.sh
    ├── runUserScripts.sh
    ├── setPassword.sh
    ├── setupLinuxEnv.sh
    └── startDB.sh
```

When starting a build from this directory, Docker performs an inventory of the context—the directory where the build is running *and all its subdirectories.* It's cataloging *all* the available ingredients, whether they're used in the recipe or not. The database installation media under the db_files directory are roughly 3GB to 4GB per version. Docker reads *all of these files*, or just shy of 19GB, into its context. It's unnecessarily time-consuming and wastes memory and storage in the Docker engine.

Think back to Chapter 4. You copied the database installation files into a version-specific directory. Keeping the files for each version separate, in their own directories, reduces build context. Each directory is its own kitchen, containing only the tools and ingredients necessary for preparing a single database version.

Context can affect image size, too. COPY accepts directories as a source and works with wildcards and regular expressions. But be careful! Working from the same directory structure in Listing 12-3, the following commands are equally bad for build context, but the second inflates the image size:

```
COPY db_files/LINUX.X64_193000_db_home.zip /opt/install
COPY db_files/LINUX* /opt/install
```

In each case, the context includes the whole 19GB db_files directory, but

- The first command only copies a single file, LINUX.X64_193000_db_home.zip, into the image.

- The second command uses a wildcard to copy all files beginning with LINUX into the /opt/install directory, adding 7.2GB to the image!

Wildcard-based and full directory copy operations are convenient but may introduce confidential information into images. I can copy the full scripts directory:

```
COPY scripts /home/oracle
```

This copies the contents of the scripts directory (relative to the directory where the build runs) into the image's /home/oracle directory. If keys, certificates, or other sensitive information exist in the scripts directory, they're now part of the image! Anyone with access to the image (or the containers that use the image) can see and read that information! Keep the scripts and files needed for Docker builds in separate, dedicated directories. Not only will it shorten build time and save resources, but it also reduces the likelihood of sharing private information.[4]

---

[4]If you need to pass sensitive information to a build, use Docker secrets. Secrets securely mount directories and files for consumption by a build, including files otherwise beyond build context. Secret information is unavailable outside the step where the secret is mounted into the image.

Copy from Images and Build Stages

Docker takes a very modular approach to building infrastructure. From layers in containers and images to images themselves, there's a tendency toward reusability, extending to the COPY instruction. Besides files on the local host, the source of a COPY instruction can be files and directories in existing images—including the aliased images created by build stages.

To copy from existing images, use the --from=<IMAGE NAME> option as in this example from an Oracle Dockerfile:

```
COPY --chown=oracle:dba --from=builder $ORACLE_BASE $ORACLE_BASE
```

Revisiting the cake recipe:

Step 3. Retrieve the bowl of dry ingredients from Step 1 and fold in the wet ingredients from Step 2.

In the preceding command, the entire $ORACLE_BASE directory is copied from an image called builder—part of a multistage build—to the $ORACLE_BASE directory in the target image, with directory ownership set to oracle:dba. On the surface, this might appear wasteful or redundant. The builder stage is part of the same build, and we can rightly assume the $ORACLE_BASE directory already exists. Copying it from one place to another isn't changing anything in the directory, so why make an effort?

We'll cover this further in the following two chapters, but briefly, the reason behind this is (again) image size and layers. The stage, builder, where the $ORACLE_BASE is created, includes installation media and scripts that aren't needed in the final database image. Remember earlier where we looked for the files and directories listed as environment variables beginning INSTALL? Those are all created in the builder stage, in directories outside the ORACLE_BASE. The stage creates the ORACLE_BASE directory, which includes the database software and inventory.[5]

The other steps involved in the software installation are creating and modifying files elsewhere in the image. In a "normal" environment, we'd simply delete the files we no longer needed. But in overlay filesystems, deleting files doesn't delete them. It just adds an opaque layer to hide what's below. The original file is still there. It still takes up space.

To get around this, we copy files into the builder stage and perform the installation, then copy only what we need—the ORACLE_BASE—into a new, pristine image!

---

[5] While the oraInventory directory normally exists outside the ORACLE_BASE, Oracle's Docker builds add the inventory here.

Copying from existing images has other applications for Oracle databases, including patching and database upgrades.

Patching

Oracle's quarterly database patches are *cumulative*. Patches for a new version are valid for any prior edition. If I'm patching a 19c database with the 19.15 Release Update (RU) patch, all the following paths *should* result in the same outcome:

- Base database version 19.3; apply 19.15 RU

- Base database version 19.3; apply 19.14 RU; apply 19.15 RU

- Base database version 19.3; apply 19.7 RU; apply 19.14 RU; apply 19.15 RU

- Base database version 19.3; apply 19.7 RU; apply 19.10 RU; rollback to 19.7 RU; apply 19.14 RU; apply 19.15 RU

While they *should* all work the same, I'll wager the first is least likely to encounter problems and reflects the construct in Figure 12-3. It's one patch. Chances are good it's a well-tested, if not the *most tested,* path. The others introduce complexity and, with it, uncertainty. How many times do you suppose Oracle tested the last scenario? What's the likelihood that others have taken the same steps, discovered issues, and reported them to Oracle? Now think of the different database features, options, and configurations unique to your environment that might complicate testing and validation. Multiply this by every possible Release Update. Wouldn't you rather upgrade from 19.3 every time?

These scenarios all have one thing in common: they begin with a base version. One Docker image—a *reference* or *gold* image—built with a 19.3 database home supports any 19c patch using the simplest, easiest, and presumably safest path:

```
COPY --chown=oracle:dba --from=oracle/database:19.3.0-ee $ORACLE_BASE
$ORACLE_BASE
COPY --chown=oracle:dba <patch file> /opt/install
```

The only difference is the patch ID. The process and `opatch` command are the same. One automated process that takes the patch ID as a parameter handles any patch. The final images, one for each Release Update, are reference images in their own right.[6]

Database Upgrades

Database upgrades require two database homes: one for the source and another for the target. You could write a Dockerfile to install source and target database homes from scratch or copy the already-configured homes from existing database images. For an upgrade from 12.2.0.1 to 19.3.0:

```
ENV ORACLE_19C_HOME=$ORACLE_BASE/product/19c/dbhome_1
COPY --chown=oracle:dba --from=oracle/database:12.2.0.1-ee $ORACLE_
BASE      $ORACLE_BASE
COPY --chown=oracle:dba --from=oracle/database:19.3.0-ee    $ORACLE_19C_HOME
$ORACLE_19C_HOME
```

Pay attention to the files being copied and the values of environment variables! The first `COPY` adds the entire source database installation at the `$ORACLE_BASE`, which includes the database inventory—the second copies only the contents of the new 19c database home to a new target location. Using `ORACLE_BASE` overwrites files and directories under the 12c structure with the same name, and `ORACLE_HOME` replaces the 12c database home.[7]

RUN

The `RUN` instruction is where the real work of building images takes place. I'm concentrating on its applications for building database images: running commands, executing scripts, and calling secrets.

---

[6] This is one way of patching databases in Docker. Some others

- Build a Dockerfile that uses the base database version in the beginning `FROM` instruction.
- Use one Dockerfile recipe and dynamically read patches from a directory.

[7] This is a high-level example of the usefulness of copying from existing images. Preparing an upgrade-ready image requires additional steps. The image that receives the two database homes must be prepared with the Oracle 19c prerequisites, and the target database home needs to be registered in the database inventory.

Running Commands and Scripts

RUN calls scripts and shell commands just as you would at an ordinary command prompt. And as with many instructions covered so far, RUN can include multiple commands and span more than one line, using two ampersands, &&, as a logical connection between each instruction and the backslash, \, to continue a line. Reaching once more into Oracle's 19c Dockerfile, the following snippet copies files into the image, makes all the *.sh scripts in the $INSTALL_DIR executable, and runs two scripts:

```
COPY $SETUP_LINUX_FILE $CHECK_SPACE_FILE $INSTALL_DIR/


RUN chmod ug+x $INSTALL_DIR/*.sh && \
    $INSTALL_DIR/$CHECK_SPACE_FILE && \
    $INSTALL_DIR/$SETUP_LINUX_FILE
```

Stringing commands together in a single RUN consolidates them into one layer, producing smaller, more efficient images.

Commands or Scripts?

We looked at the setupLinuxEnv.sh file in Chapter 11. The commands in Listing 12-4 are part of that script and prepare the operating system for an Oracle installation.

Listing 12-4. The commands executed by the setupLinuxEnv.sh script for a 19.3.0 database

```
mkdir -p "$ORACLE_BASE"/scripts/setup && \
mkdir "$ORACLE_BASE"/scripts/startup && \
mkdir -p "$ORACLE_BASE"/scripts/extensions/setup && \
mkdir "$ORACLE_BASE"/scripts/extensions/startup && \
ln -s "$ORACLE_BASE"/scripts /docker-entrypoint-initdb.d && \
mkdir "$ORACLE_BASE"/oradata && \
mkdir -p "$ORACLE_HOME" && \
chmod ug+x "$ORACLE_BASE"/*.sh && \
yum -y install oracle-database-preinstall-19c openssl && \
rm -rf /var/cache/yum && \
ln -s "$ORACLE_BASE"/"$PWD_FILE" /home/oracle/ && \
```

```
echo oracle:oracle | chpasswd && \
chown -R oracle:dba "$ORACLE_BASE"
```

These could be part of the Dockerfile RUN command:

```
RUN chmod ug+x $INSTALL_DIR/*.sh && \
    $INSTALL_DIR/$CHECK_SPACE_FILE && \
    mkdir -p "$ORACLE_BASE"/scripts/setup && \
    mkdir "$ORACLE_BASE"/scripts/startup && \
    mkdir -p "$ORACLE_BASE"/scripts/extensions/setup && \
    mkdir "$ORACLE_BASE"/scripts/extensions/startup && \
    ln -s "$ORACLE_BASE"/scripts /docker-entrypoint-initdb.d && \
    mkdir "$ORACLE_BASE"/oradata && \
    mkdir -p "$ORACLE_HOME" && \
    chmod ug+x "$ORACLE_BASE"/*.sh && \
    yum -y install oracle-database-preinstall-19c openssl && \
    rm -rf /var/cache/yum && \
    ln -s "$ORACLE_BASE"/"$PWD_FILE" /home/oracle/ && \
    echo oracle:oracle | chpasswd && \
    chown -R oracle:dba "$ORACLE_BASE"
```

Which is better? There are arguments in favor of both. It boils down to coding style, needs, and what's easiest for you and your team to test and manage.

EXPOSE and VOLUME

Use the EXPOSE instruction to define the specific ports (and protocols) available by default when the image runs as a container. Chapter 8 discussed that the network ports *exposed* by an image could be mapped to ports on the host. Ports that aren't explicitly exposed in an image can be added during docker run through the --expose flag. Adding containers to networks, covered in Chapter 9, is often a better option than port mapping.

The VOLUME instruction sets the directories inside a container that are available as *volumes* when running the image.

These instructions don't provide functionality that isn't already available through docker run and, as such, seem to have fallen out of favor.

WORKDIR

WORKDIR, for Working Directory, sets the default directory used by specific following instructions, including CMD. For our purposes, it's part of the environment setup for users logging in to database containers:

```
USER oracle
WORKDIR /home/oracle
```

Unless otherwise defined, users log in as the oracle user with their session beginning in /home/oracle.

CMD

The CMD, or *command* instruction, is the default command Docker runs whenever a container starts. For Oracle's database containers, it's the runOracle.sh script. You may recall from Chapter 11 that this script contains the logic Docker uses to start a database if one exists. Otherwise, create a new database from values set in or passed to the environment through the docker run command.

HEALTHCHECK

The HEALTHCHECK is the set of rules Docker uses for reporting whether running containers are healthy. Sometimes, a basic command is all that's needed to check status. A more conditional set of rules is often necessary for a database, and the health check is a script. For Oracle's database images, it's the checkDBStatus.sh script.

HEALTHCHECK requires a command (or script) that generates an exit code of 0, resulting in a healthy status, or 1 to show the container as unhealthy. The frequency and other check characteristics are controlled through optional flags:

- --interval=<check interval>: The number of seconds between each health check. The default is 30 seconds, and the first health check runs interval seconds after startup or once the startup period (below) ends.

- --timeout=<timeout>: How many seconds Docker waits for the check to complete before reporting failure. The default is 30 seconds.

- `--start-period=<startup timeout>`: How long Docker waits before attempting the first health check. During the start period, Docker reports the container as "starting." The default is zero, meaning containers show "starting" during the initial interval.

Remember the different actions it performs when selecting startup timeouts for database containers and viewing status. Starting an existing database takes a few seconds, while creating a database may take several minutes, and environments that alert on unhealthy containers must settle on a reasonable balance. A long startup time that accommodates new database creation won't immediately recognize existing databases that didn't start successfully. A short startup time catches failed database startups but incorrectly reports containers creating new databases as unhealthy.

Summary

Understanding Dockerfiles is the key to building images tailored to your own needs. The knowledge you've gained elevates your image "cooking" skills from microwaving prepackaged frozen entrees to preparing delicious, healthy meals! This was a lot of information to digest, and you did a great job with this cooking lesson! The essential concepts we covered in this chapter that will help you understand and write Dockerfiles were layers, extensibility, and context.

Image layers, like the layers in a container's overlay filesystem, are the additions and modifications projected, one atop another, to produce a result. Each instruction in a Dockerfile creates a layer and can potentially be shared with other similar images. Reusing layers reduces Docker's footprint on a host and improves overall speed and efficiency. Copying images from remote repositories will skip layers already on a host instead of recopying the existing data.

Extensibility is more art than science since it involves anticipating the things you might want to do in the future, then integrating that flexibility into your Dockerfiles. The argument instruction introduces that adaptability into builds. Use it to set defaults while offering the option to change aspects of images as they're built.

Context has implications for performance, resource use, and security. It's essential to recognize which directories and files are part of the build context to avoid adding unnecessary content to images or accidentally exposing sensitive information. Use caution and avoid overly broad COPY commands that could include extraneous files!

The Dockerfile is much more than a set of assembly instructions. It's also the metadata Docker uses to manage containers. Metadata appears in images as zero-byte layers that tell Docker what user to invoke, the commands or scripts to run on startup, and the rules to use for reporting the health and status of containers.

In the next chapter, we'll look at examples of Dockerfiles and offer some opportunities and solutions to consider when adapting or developing Dockerfiles for Oracle databases. If writing custom Dockerfiles from scratch is more than you need, skip to Chapter 14, covering the commands and options available in `docker build`.

## CHAPTER 13

Oracle Dockerfile Recipes

When I was 13 years old, I saw a movie called *Breaking Away*, a coming-of-age story about four friends trying to find their place in the world after high school. The main character is a young man who's so enamored with bike racing that he pretends to be an Italian cyclist. The following day, by chance, I attended a local bike race. That one-two punch was all it took, and that same afternoon I headed to the local bike shop and announced to anyone who'd listen that I was going to be a bike racer! I was a wide-eyed, impressionable teenager and soaked up advice and opinions from local cycling club members, regulars at bike shops, and articles and photos in magazines. One shop in town had a beautiful Italian Colnago. It was black, with gold accents and gold-plated Campagnolo components. It was the epitome of Italian cycling equipment, displayed on the wall behind the register like a piece of art!

I made friends with a gentleman at the shop,[1] and he became my mentor in the sport. He turned my attention away from my dream bike—and for that matter, any Colnago—and recommended a less-elegant Campania instead. It had an ugly gray paint job and seemed twice the weight of anything else. In its defense, it sported an Italian name, and a decal pronounced it was "Professional" in gold script, somewhat softening its less-than-eye-catching appearance alongside the bike of my dreams!

What was truly important: the Campania turned out to be a near-indestructible workhorse, forgiving of a clumsy beginner like me, and affordable for a high school kid with a part-time job. (The same couldn't be said of any Colnago the shop sold—gold plated or not!) That bike served me well and survived the mishaps and crashes that were part of my learning curve. It was the right bike for me at the time. It got me through the beginner stage of the sport, and when the time came to replace it, I'd learned enough to know, beautiful as they are, a Colnago wasn't right for me.

Think of a hobby or activity you enjoy and recall how you started. Chances are you were unsure where to begin or what equipment you needed. During those early days

---

[1] Thank you Bob from Two Wheel Transit Authority, wherever you are!

© Sean Scott 2023
S. Scott, *Oracle on Docker*, https://doi.org/10.1007/978-1-4842-9033-0_13

of learning the ropes, you might have done research or joined a club to get advice on what to buy and how to hone your skills. You probably didn't buy the most expensive equipment, starting instead with something more basic. Spending time improving your skills with introductory gear prepares you for the next step and helps justify investing in something better (and likely more expensive).

The Oracle GitHub repository is great for breaking into the world of Linux containers. It's full of ready-made formulas that remove the risk and cost of exploring container platforms. There's no better introduction for anyone curious about using containers as a platform for Oracle technology. Indeed, it's where I got my start with Docker, and it carried me through my first few years. Without it, you wouldn't be reading this book! It's an introductory resource, though, and there comes the point where you'll need something more appropriate and tailored to your needs and plans—particularly if you intend to use containers as a production platform for Oracle databases.

This chapter opens by highlighting limitations you're likely to encounter with ready-made, multipurpose images available in public repositories. We'll introduce additional Dockerfile features that broaden the possibilities for repository design and discuss the pros and cons of dedicated vs. all-in-one directory structures. Then, after demonstrating techniques for adding extensibility to Dockerfiles and building templates, I'll offer patterns for solving challenges you'll encounter when designing and authoring your own Dockerfile libraries. Readers should be comfortable with shell scripting and familiar with basic Dockerfile instructions and concepts. Think of this as a guide to selecting a "second bike" after putting in some miles, getting comfortable in the saddle, learning how containers work, and determining where you want to go next!

Multipurpose Image Limitations

Back in the days when I worked in a physical office with an on-site data center, I carried a multitool (basically a Swiss Army Knife) on my belt. It had pliers, Phillips and Flathead screwdrivers, a wire stripper, and a few blades. When I needed to work on something in the data center, most of the tools I needed were conveniently located on my hip. The quality of the tools was perfectly adequate for quick work—replacing a hard drive or network card, securing a server in a rack, or prying loose a stubborn, ill-fitting part. Would I use a multitool knife for chopping vegetables? No.

Ready-made, multipurpose images fill a similar need. They're reliable and convenient and provide an easy on-ramp into the world of containers. But while they're adaptable and fit wide-ranging needs, you'll eventually encounter situations that require more precise tools. In some cases, you'll be able to leverage existing scripts, adapting or rewriting them to add features or modify functionality. We identified the scripts responsible for implementing basic functionality in Chapter 11. Minor modifications to these scripts address limitations and oddities in multipurpose image builds.

Fixed Directory Paths

Containers typically provide services to clients. They're endpoints that accept input and produce results. For our container databases, the values of the ORACLE_HOME and ORACLE_BASE directories inside containers aren't important if the results are correct. It's no different than traditional environments. Clients connecting to databases on physical hosts or virtual machines don't care about the implementation details.

These paths are essential for consistency and monitoring, though. If you're introducing containers as analogs for simulating or testing existing systems, scripts and procedures are only portable across systems when the directory structures match. The same applies to monitoring systems and utilities. Standard configurations shared across environments simplify management and maintenance.

Users have two choices for adapting existing Dockerfiles and scripts, depending on the need for flexibility. The first is simply changing hard-coded values to match standards by editing the ENV assignments in Dockerfiles. The path is still hard-coded. It's just set to the same value used elsewhere.

The second option leverages arguments, introducing a default value but adding the option to override the default during the build:

```
# Set a default value for the ORACLE_BASE:
ARG ORACLE_BASE=/u01/opt/oracle

# Assign the ORACLE_BASE to environment variables in the image:
ENV ORACLE_BASE=$ORACLE_BASE
ENV ORACLE_HOME=$ORACLE_BASE/product/19c/dbhome_1
```

This is more appropriate for users working across multiple environments and a foundation for more adaptable image construction.

Contradictions

I confess that one of my pet peeves in Oracle images is having the Oracle Inventory
Directory installed under ORACLE_BASE. Oracle's *OFA*, or *Optimal Flexible Architecture*,
places the inventory outside ORACLE_BASE to support multiple installations. In a *Real
Application Clusters*, or *RAC,* system, an OFA-compliant directory structure might look
like this:

```
# Oracle Inventory
/u01/app/oraInventory

# Database BASE and HOME:
/u01/app/oracle
/u01/app/oracle/product/$DB_VERSION/dbhome_1

# Grid Infrastructure BASE and HOME:
/u01/app/grid
/u01/app/$GRID_VERSION/grid
```

The separate, dedicated directories allow distinct ownership and permissions
necessary to support role separations, all managed from a single inventory directory.

There's a reasonable explanation for doing it differently in containers. Look at one of
Oracle's Dockerfiles, and near the end, you'll see the following block:

```
USER oracle
COPY --chown=oracle:dba --from=builder $ORACLE_BASE $ORACLE_BASE

USER root
RUN $ORACLE_BASE/oraInventory/orainstRoot.sh && \
    $ORACLE_HOME/root.sh
```

The COPY command copies the whole ORACLE_BASE directory structure from a
prior stage, referenced by the --from=builder argument, into the final image. The
following instructions run the post-installation root scripts in the final image, setting the
permissions on the inventory directory and registering the ORACLE_HOME.

If the inventory directory is under the ORACLE_BASE, a single command copies
everything—the inventory, the ORACLE_BASE, and the ORACLE_HOME. Since every
command creates a separate layer in the image, consolidating the inventory under
the ORACLE_BASE reduces the number of layers (and potentially, the final image size).

Running docker history against the image shows the single layer created by this copy. I've used the format command to print just the "CREATED BY" field, showing only the command used to create the layer for clarity:

```
> docker image history --no-trunc --format "table {{.CreatedBy}}" oracle/
database:19.3.0-ee
CREATED BY
...
/bin/sh -c $ORACLE_BASE/oraInventory/orainstRoot.sh &&      $ORACLE_
HOME/root.sh
/bin/sh -c #(nop)  USER root
/bin/sh -c #(nop) COPY --chown=oracle:dbadir:7f7ee78c2762cb56f03228b45ce0c
0301ea5fd88c4ac14dd98d74eb5621054e4 in /opt/oracle
/bin/sh -c #(nop)  USER oracle
...
```

This is another situation where, from the end user's perspective, the inventory location in the container doesn't matter. It doesn't make a difference to clients—the endpoint is a database that does database things. It does matter for

- Real Application Clusters or Global Service Manager installations
- Systems with multiple ORACLE_BASE directories
- Environments with role separation
- Remaining consistent with existing infrastructure
- Preventing installer errors

In the last case, if the inventory location is under the ORACLE_BASE, the Oracle installation may return the following warnings (along with a nonzero exit code):

```
Attention: INS-32056: The specified Oracle Base contains the existing
Central Inventory location.
Recommendation: Oracle recommends that the Central Inventory location is
outside the Oracle Base directory. Specify a different location for the
Oracle Base.
```

or

```
[WARNING] [INS-32056] The specified Oracle Base contains the existing
Central Inventory location: /opt/oracle/oraInventory.
ACTION: Oracle recommends that the Central Inventory location is
outside the Oracle Base directory. Specify a different location for the
Oracle Base.
```

In a *perfect* world, automation should fail on errors and warnings, flag the conditions for review, or include conditional exception handlers to ignore them. Suppose the warning isn't caught or treated as a potential failure. In that case, there's no way to differentiate an expected, "safe to ignore" warning from others that could affect the reliability or accuracy of images.

There are multiple ways to get around this issue. In my scripts, I create an argument and environment variable for the ORACLE_INVENTORY and add a second COPY instruction to the Dockerfile for the inventory directory:

```
ARG ORACLE_INVENTORY=/u01/app/oraInventory
ENV ORACLE_INVENTORY=$ORACLE_INVENTORY
```

We'll also need to add a new COPY instruction to handle the inventory:

```
USER oracle
COPY --chown=oracle:dba --from=builder $ORACLE_BASE $ORACLE_BASE
COPY --chown=oracle:dba --from=builder $ORACLE_INVENTORY $ORACLE_INVENTORY
```

Then, update the RUN command that executes the post-installation root scripts by changing the reference to ORACLE_BASE to the new ORACLE_INVENTORY variable:

```
USER root
RUN $ORACLE_INVENTORY/oraInventory/orainstRoot.sh && \
    $ORACLE_HOME/root.sh
```

That addresses the steps in the Dockerfile. We also need to push the new directory location to the database installation. The database installation response file, db_inst.rsp, sets the inventory path via the INVENTORY_LOCATION entry. Change the following line from

```
INVENTORY_LOCATION=###ORACLE_BASE###/oraInventory
```

to

```
INVENTORY_LOCATION=###ORACLE_INVENTORY###/oraInventory
```

The last step is adding a line to the `installDBBinaries.sh` script to substitute the placeholder with the inventory location from the environment. Modify the section of code that replaces the placeholders to read:

```
# Replace place holders
# ---------------------
sed -i -e "s|###ORACLE_EDITION###|$EDITION|g" "$INSTALL_DIR"/"$INSTALL_
RSP" && \
sed -i -e "s|###ORACLE_BASE###|$ORACLE_BASE|g" "$INSTALL_DIR"/"$INSTALL_
RSP" && \
sed -i -e "s|###ORACLE_HOME###|$ORACLE_HOME|g" "$INSTALL_DIR"/"$INSTALL_
RSP" && \
sed -i -e "s|###ORACLE_INVENTORY###|$ORACLE_INVENTORY|g" "$INSTALL_
DIR"/"$INSTALL_RSP"
```

There's some work involved in updating the inventory. Still, it's a worthwhile (and sometimes necessary) step for adding versatility to images, maintaining consistency with existing conventions, or remaining compliant with standards and recommended practices. It also removes a disparity between containers and "traditional" environments that objectors raise as arguments against containers!

Extended Multitenancy Options

Oracle introduced the multitenant database option in version 12c. Multitenant architecture becomes mandatory with version 21c and beyond. Oracle container images create multitenant databases consisting of the container database, or CDB, and a single pluggable database, or PDB. Users can set the names of the container and pluggable databases by passing environment variables to the `docker run` command. However, there's no option to create a non-container database or automatically add multiple pluggable databases during the initial database setup.

Create Non-CDB Databases

Oracle may prefer we create and use container databases in versions 12c through 19c. Still, non-CDB installations dominate real-world installations and will likely remain in the majority for the next several years. It makes sense then that we should be able to choose the architecture created in containers. Chapter 11 presented the steps for passing an option to docker run for selecting between container or non-container architectures. Briefly, it involves

- Updating the dbca.rsp.tmpl template, replacing the hard-coded value given to createAsContainerDatabase with a placeholder. When a new container starts, it calls the createDB.sh script, referencing the *Database Configuration Assistant*, or *DBCA*, template for database creation. The placeholder introduces the option of changing the database creation method by substituting an environment variable.

- Adding a sed find/replace command to conditionally substitute either true or false, based on an optional environment variable, into the DBCA template.

- Modifying the database health check, in checkDBStatus.sh, to read the value of open mode from either v$pdbs (for container databases) or v$database (for non-container) databases.

- Conditionally removing commands specific to pluggable databases from the database creation script.

This pattern, in whole or part, can be adapted to add similar functionality during database creation and startup.

Create Multiple Pluggable Databases

Pluggable databases can increase database infrastructure's usefulness, capacity, and lifespan by consolidating multiple stand-alone databases into pluggable databases, or PDBs, on a single host. Like schemas, PDBs offer another means of segmenting or separating data, and it's not unusual to see container databases housing two or more PDBs. It makes sense to reflect this practice into database images, adding the ability to create multiple PDBs during initial container creation. There are two avenues to achieve this. The first changes the DBCA template and reads variables from the environment. The second leverages the Docker entrypoint directory and runs a script after the database setup completes.

The first method works similarly to creating a non-CDB database, inserting a placeholder to the Database Creation Assistant template, and adding a `sed` command to conditionally substitute the placeholder with a value derived from the environment. The key in the DBCA template is `numberOfPDBs`, set by default to one:

```
numberOfPDBs=1
```

Replace this with a placeholder:

```
numberOfPDBs=###PDB_COUNT###
```

Add a `sed` command to the **createDB.sh** script to change the placeholder. Keep in mind the need to validate the incoming variable is a positive number, provide a default value, and perhaps set a practical upper limit for the number of pluggable databases:

```
if ! [[ $PDB_COUNT =~ '^[0-9]+$' ]]                # PDB_COUNT must be
                                                   a number
then PDB_COUNT=1
elif [ "$PDB_COUNT" -ge 1 -a "$PDB_COUNT" -le 5 ]  # PDB_COUNT must be
                                                   between 1 and 5
then PDB_COUNT=$PDB_COUNT
else PDB_COUNT=1                                    # Set all other cases to
                                                   the default
fi
sed -i -e "s|###PDB_COUNT###|$PDB_COUNT|g" "$ORACLE_BASE"/dbca.rsp
```

You could control the creation of CDB vs. non-CDB databases through the same variable by checking whether `PDB_COUNT` is zero. If so, create a non-CDB database.

When the `numberOfPDBs` variable is greater than one, the Database Configuration Assistant creates the container database and first pluggable database, then creates the additional pluggable databases. When `numberOfPDBs` is greater than one, Oracle uses the value of `pdbName` in the response file as the prefix and appends the PDB's index. It derives the value of `pdbName` in the template from `ORACLE_PDB` in the environment. Be aware of this behavior to avoid unexpected pluggable database names! Remember, the default value of `ORACLE_PDB` is `ORCLPDB1`, and for a PDB count of one, Oracle creates a single PDB called `ORCLPDB1`. But, if the PDB count is two, Oracle uses the PDB name as a base value, and the PDB names will be `ORCLPDB11` and `ORCLPDB12`!

Use the Setup Entrypoint

We introduced Docker's *entrypoint directories* in Chapter 7. If you need a quick refresher, the entrypoint is a special path in Docker, usually `/docker-entrypoint-initdb.d`, for mounting a local host directory. Container startup scripts may look here for scripts and run them. I say they *may* look here because it's up to the author—it's not an automatic feature, and if the startup script doesn't recognize the directory (or looks elsewhere), Docker treats the files mounted at the entrypoint as, well, files!

Oracle's container repository recognizes entrypoints at the standard location, `/docker-entrypoint-initdb.d`, and `/opt/oracle/scripts`. It expects two subdirectories—`setup` and `startup`—searching them for scripts with either a `.sh` or `.sql` suffix. Automation built into the container checks for files in the `setup` directory and runs them once only after the initial database creation completes.[2] The files in the `startup` directory run every time the container starts—including after the initial database setup.

Here are a few tips and cautions when using entrypoints in database containers.

Files in entrypoint directories are processed in alphanumeric order, regardless of the file type. Name files in the `setup` and `scripts` directory with numeric prefixes to guarantee their execution order:

`01_add_pdb.sh`

`02_add_users.sql`

`03_update_passwords.sql`

Shell scripts, with the `.sh` suffix, are executed as the container's default user, `oracle`. SQL scripts are passed to SQL*Plus and run as the SYSDBA user.

Remember to set the container in the script for SQL commands intended for pluggable databases.

---

[2] A new container referencing an oradata volume containing an existing database (a trick for rapid database cloning) won't run setup actions. The script logic looks to see whether a database is present and, if not, executes code to call the Database Configuration Assistant and any post-installation setup scripts. It will, however, still perform the startup actions.

Files mounted in the `startup` directory run every time a container starts.
They're not part of the image. Changes to these files on the local host (or in other
containers) reflect into all containers sharing the host directory, potentially leading
to unexpected behavior and failures when containers restart. Remember this when
using a shared directory for multiple containers and when changing files!

The setup entrypoint lets us invoke the Database Configuration Assistant with the
-createPluggabledatabase option and add pluggable databases via a script like the one
shown in Listing 13-1.

Listing 13-1. A setup script for creating an additional pluggable database, adding
a TNS entry, and setting the pluggable database state. Save the file to a directory
and mount it to a volume at either /dockerfile-entrypoint-initdb.d/setup or
/opt/oracle/scripts/setup

```
#!/bin/bash
# Create an additional pluggable database.

$ORACLE_HOME/bin/dbca -silent -createPluggableDatabase -pdbName PDB2
-sourceDB $ORACLE_SID -createAsClone true -createPDBFrom DEFAULT
-pdbAdminPassword "oracle123" || exit 1

cat << EOF >> $ORACLE_HOME/network/admin/tnsnames.ora

PDB2 =
  (DESCRIPTION =
    (ADDRESS = (PROTOCOL = TCP)(HOST = 0.0.0.0)(PORT = 1521))
    (CONNECT_DATA =
      (SERVER = DEDICATED)
      (SERVICE_NAME = PDB2)
    )
  )
EOF

$ORACLE_HOME/bin/sqlplus / as sysdba << EOF
alter pluggable database PDB2 save state;
EOF
```

I named this file 01_add_pdb.sh and ran a new container called SETUP to demonstrate the call to the script:

```
docker run -d --name SETUP \
            -e ORACLE_SID=ORCLPDB \
            -e ORACLE_PDB=PDB1 \
            -v ~/setup:/opt/oracle/scripts/setup \
            oracle/database:19.3.0-ee
```

Docker calls the usual database creation scripts. When DBCA completes, the script reads the contents of the setup directory and runs files with a .sh or .sql suffix. It finds and runs the 01_add_pdb.sh script in the setup location. The tail output in Listing 13-2 shows the tail end of the docker logs output where the custom user script ran and created the pluggable database.

Listing 13-2. Output from docker logs showing custom user script execution during container creation. The 01_add_pdb.sh script creates a pluggable database, named PDB2. When it completes, it returns control to the createDB.sh script, which in turn reports the database is ready for users

```
Executing user defined scripts
/opt/oracle/runUserScripts.sh: running /opt/oracle/scripts/setup/01_
add_pdb.sh
Prepare for db operation
13% complete
Creating Pluggable Database
15% complete
19% complete
23% complete
31% complete
53% complete
Completing Pluggable Database Creation
60% complete
Executing Post Configuration Actions
100% complete
Pluggable database "PDB2" plugged successfully.
```

Look at the log file "/opt/oracle/cfgtoollogs/dbca/CDB/PDB2/CDB.log" for further details.

SQL*Plus: Release 19.0.0.0.0 - Production on Wed Jan 17 17:55:13 2022
Version 19.3.0.0.0

Copyright (c) 1982, 2019, Oracle. All rights reserved.

Connected to:
Oracle Database 19c Enterprise Edition Release 19.0.0.0.0 - Production
Version 19.3.0.0.0

SQL>
Pluggable database altered.

SQL> Disconnected from Oracle Database 19c Enterprise Edition Release
19.0.0.0.0 - Production
Version 19.3.0.0.0

DONE: Executing user defined scripts

The Oracle base remains unchanged with value /opt/oracle
#########################
DATABASE IS READY TO USE!
#########################

The example in Listing 13-1 creates a single pluggable database using a fixed name and password. It works for a limited, specific case. What if we wanted to create multiple pluggable databases or needed a more flexible solution to add PDBs based on a runtime condition?

Let's extend the original script as seen in Listing 13-3. Instead of a static value for the PDB name, the script checks to see whether a new environment variable, PDB_LIST, is set. The variable represents a comma-delimited list of one or more pluggable database names to add once database creation finishes. It loops over each list element and performs the same steps as the original version—create a new PDB, add a TNS entry, and set the PDB state—but does so dynamically.

Listing 13-3. This modified script dynamically adds pluggable databases, looping over a comma-delimited list of PDB names passed to the container in an environment variable

```bash
#!/bin/bash
# Create additional pluggable databases.

  if [ -n "$PDB_LIST" ] # A PDB list is defined
then

# Capture the existing IFS (Internal Field Separator)
OLDIFS=$IFS

# Set IFS to a comma before looping:
IFS=,

# Loop over PDBs in the list:
 for pdb_name in $PDB_LIST
  do

# Return IFS to its original value while inside the loop:
IFS=$OLDIFS

# Create the PDB:
$ORACLE_HOME/bin/dbca -silent -createPluggableDatabase -pdbName $pdb_name
-sourceDB $ORACLE_SID -createAsClone true -createPDBFrom DEFAULT
-autoGeneratePasswords || exit 1

# Add a TNS entry:
cat << EOF >> $ORACLE_HOME/network/admin/tnsnames.ora

$pdb_name =
  (DESCRIPTION =
    (ADDRESS = (PROTOCOL = TCP)(HOST = 0.0.0.0)(PORT = 1521))
    (CONNECT_DATA =
      (SERVER = DEDICATED)
      (SERVICE_NAME = $pdb_name)
    )
  )
EOF
```

```
# Open the PDB, save its state:
sqlplus / as sysdba << EOF
alter pluggable database $pdb_name save state;
EOF

# Set IFS back to a comma before returning to the next loop step:
IFS=,

done

# Set IFS back to its original value:
IFS=$OLDIFS

fi
```

After dropping the original SETUP container, I rerun the command, this time defining the PDB_LIST variable to "TEST,DEV":

```
docker run -d --name SETUP \
          -e ORACLE_SID=ORCLPDB \
          -e ORACLE_PDB=PDB1 \
          -e PDB_LIST="TEST,DEV" \
          -v ~/setup:/opt/oracle/scripts/setup \
          oracle/database:19.3.0-ee
```

The createDB.sh script checks the setup entrypoint and finds the 01_add_pdb. sh script, just as before. The script checks whether the PDB_LIST variable is set. If not, it returns control to the createDB.sh script. The variable is present in this example, though, and the loop processes the list elements, creating the TEST and DEV pluggable databases and TNS entries, and saves the PDB states. Listing 13-4 shows the output from docker logs for the new container, using the updated PDB script.

Listing 13-4. The tail end of the docker logs output in a container running the updated version of the 01_add_pdb.sh script, showing the creation of two pluggable databases, TEST and DEV

```
Executing user defined scripts
/opt/oracle/runUserScripts.sh: running /opt/oracle/scripts/setup/01_
add_pdb.sh
Prepare for db operation
13% complete
Creating Pluggable Database
15% complete
19% complete
23% complete
31% complete
53% complete
Completing Pluggable Database Creation
60% complete
Executing Post Configuration Actions
100% complete
Pluggable database "TEST" plugged successfully.
Look at the log file "/opt/oracle/cfgtoollogs/dbca/CDB/TEST/CDB.log" for
further details.

SQL*Plus: Release 19.0.0.0.0 - Production on Wed Jan 17 20:16:39 2022
Version 19.3.0.0.0

Copyright (c) 1982, 2019, Oracle.  All rights reserved.

Connected to:
Oracle Database 19c Enterprise Edition Release 19.0.0.0.0 - Production
Version 19.3.0.0.0

SQL>
Pluggable database altered.

SQL> Disconnected from Oracle Database 19c Enterprise Edition Release
19.0.0.0.0 - Production
Version 19.3.0.0.0
```

Prepare for db operation
13% complete
Creating Pluggable Database
15% complete
19% complete
23% complete
31% complete
53% complete
Completing Pluggable Database Creation
60% complete
Executing Post Configuration Actions
100% complete
Pluggable database "DEV" plugged successfully.
Look at the log file "/opt/oracle/cfgtoollogs/dbca/CDB/DEV/CDB.log" for
further details.

SQL*Plus: Release 19.0.0.0.0 - Production on Wed Jan 17 20:20:34 2022
Version 19.3.0.0.0

Copyright (c) 1982, 2019, Oracle. All rights reserved.

Connected to:
Oracle Database 19c Enterprise Edition Release 19.0.0.0.0 - Production
Version 19.3.0.0.0

SQL>
Pluggable database altered.

SQL> Disconnected from Oracle Database 19c Enterprise Edition Release
19.0.0.0.0 - Production
Version 19.3.0.0.0

DONE: Executing user defined scripts

The Oracle base remains unchanged with value /opt/oracle
#########################
DATABASE IS READY TO USE!
#########################

One thing to notice in the modified script is the presence of
-autoGeneratePasswords rather than a fixed password in the dbca command. It has to
do with the sequence of events for creating a database in a new container:

- The container starts and executes runOracle.sh.

- runOracle.sh checks for an existing database and finds none. It
  calls createDB.sh and passes the value of ORACLE_PWD to the script.
  ORACLE_PWD isn't exported or present in the environment unless it's
  set explicitly as part of the docker run command or a Podman secret
  is passed.[3]

- createDB.sh creates the database. For the password, it first checks
  whether an Oracle Wallet is present and, if so, uses the wallet value.
  If not, the value of ORACLE_PWD passed from runOracle.sh isn't
  empty; it uses that. Otherwise, it instructs the Database Configuration
  Assistant to generate a password.

- When it finishes, createDB.sh returns control to runOracle.sh.

- runOracle.sh next calls runUserScripts.sh but does not pass the
  value of ORACLE_PWD.

- runUserScripts.sh discovers the 01_add_pdb.sh script and runs it.

Because of the way Linux shells work, the ORACLE_PWD variable isn't guaranteed
to have a value beyond the runOracle.sh and createDB.sh scripts. If it doesn't,
-pdbAdminPassword "$ORACLE_PWD" produces an error. In the interest of simplicity and
brevity, I let PDB creation autogenerate the PDB password. Adding similar logic to that
found in createDB.sh, checking for a wallet and the presence of a Podman secret would
further improve the script.

Create a Read-Only Database Home

Oracle Database 18c added an option to create *read-only database homes*, removing
configuration files from the Oracle database software directory. In older versions of
Oracle, the ORACLE_HOME is a mix of software and configuration. The ORACLE_HOME/

---

[3] Podman secrets are mechanisms for sharing confidential information to containers, similar to
build secrets.

dbs directory is the default location for password files and the parameter files used during database startup. The ORACLE_HOME/network/admin directory holds network configurations, including the listener.ora, sqlnet.ora, and tnsnames.ora files. When database homes support multiple instances, these database-specific files aren't well separated and are vulnerable to being confused or overwritten by actions from another database. This shortcoming is evident in how Docker moves and copies configuration files out of the database home to a special directory under /opt/oracle/oradata/dbconfig. It's key to cloning databases from an ordinary directory backup, as covered in Chapter 5.

With the addition of the read-only homes came the need to track information about the home. Oracle records this in a special file called the orabasetab. It's patterned on the /etc/oratab file and located at $ORACLE_HOME/install/orabasetab. In a legacy, read-write home, the contents of the file look like this:

```
#orabasetab file is used to track Oracle Home associated with Oracle Base
/opt/oracle/product/19c/dbhome_1:/opt/oracle:OraDB19Home1:N:
```

Individual fields, separated by colons, reflect different properties of the home. In order:

1. The ORACLE_HOME directory, /opt/oracle/product/19c/dbhome_1.

2. The ORACLE_BASE used by the home, /opt/oracle.

3. The unique Oracle Home Name, assigned during installation, OraDB19Home1.

4. The read-only status of the home is indicated by Y or N.

The fourth field in this file, set to N, means this home is not read-only, and its configuration files are in the "normal" places. The database and network configuration files in a read-only home move from the ORACLE_HOME to new locations under the ORACLE_BASE. Two new environment variables, the ORACLE_BASE_CONFIG and ORACLE_BASE_HOME, track these directories, and they default to

```
ORACLE_BASE_CONFIG=$ORACLE_BASE
ORACLE_BASE_HOME=$ORACLE_BASE/homes/<HOME NAME>
```

The HOME NAME in the $ORACLE_BASE_HOME is the third field in the orabasetab. Based on the preceding example, substituting the values from the orabasetab reveals the base locations for configuration files if this was a read-only home:

```
ORACLE_BASE_CONFIG=/opt/oracle
ORACLE_BASE_HOME=/opt/oracle/homes/OraDB19Home1
```

Everything that used to exist under $ORACLE_HOME/dbs—parameter, server parameter, and password files—moves to $ORACLE_BASE_CONFIG/dbs. What was previously stored in $ORACLE_HOME/network/admin—the TNS, SQL*Net, and listener files—relocates to $ORACLE_BASE_HOME/network/admin.

The ORACLE_BASE_CONFIG and ORACLE_BASE_HOME environment variables are optional, and Oracle provides two new binaries for reporting their locations:

- orabaseconfig, for ORACLE_BASE_CONFIG

- orabasehome, for ORACLE_BASE_HOME

They derive the correct locations by checking the fourth, read-only home field in the orabasetab. Through these two environment variables, we can divine the right path to database configurations in a database home, no matter the type of home. It's important to know these directories in any database but essential in a container environment because they contain configuration files that must relocate to the volume mounted to /opt/oracle/oradata to retain containers' full function and capability. Remember that this volume holds the complete contents of a database—including its configuration—and we begin to realize that modifying the container image to include a Read-Only Home option involves

- Performing actions to convert the database software directory to a Read-Only Home

- Setting the proper directory paths for configuration files

- Updating scripts to use the correct destinations when referencing configurations

Convert a Database Home to Read-Only

A single command, $ORACLE_HOME/bin/roohctl -enable (for Read-Only Oracle Home Control), converts pre-21c database homes to read-only.[4] It's executed after installing the database software but before creating a database.[5] There are two opportunities for running the command in the Docker lifecycle:

- During image creation, following the database software installation steps

- When starting a new database container, before creating the database

Converting the ORACLE_HOME to read-only during image creation forces every container run from the image to use a read-only home. Leaving this option until runtime offers more flexibility for our containers and is the solution pursued here.

As you've probably guessed, we'll control whether to convert the home by checking a runtime environment variable. I'm using ROOH:

```
# Enable read-only Oracle Home:
  if [ "${ROOH^^}" = "ENABLE" ]
then $ORACLE_HOME/bin/roohctl -enable
fi
```

This reads the value of ROOH from the environment and converts it to uppercase using bash variable expansion—the ^^ characters. When the result matches ENABLE, the script converts the home to read-only. Place this command in the createDB.sh script, near the beginning of the file and before any operations that run the Database Configuration Assistant. (I added it just before the check for INIT_SGA_SIZE and INIT_PGA_SIZE.)

Resolve Configuration Directories

We'll use the two new binaries Oracle added for reporting configuration directories: orabaseconfig and orabasehome. In a read-write home, they default to the ORACLE_ HOME, but in read-only homes respond with their new placement under ORACLE_ BASE. Regardless of the type of home—read-only or read-write—we use these commands

---

[4] There's no option to disable a read-only home.

[5] Among the tasks performed by DBCA are creating and populating configuration files. Whether the ORACLE_HOME is read-only or read-write affects the location of those files.

to assign the proper values for ORACLE_BASE_CONFIG and ORACLE_BASE_HOME in scripts. Since we'll perform this action repeatedly, I chose to create a function:

```
function setOracleBaseDirs {
  export ORACLE_BASE_CONFIG="$($ORACLE_HOME/bin/orabaseconfig)"
  export ORACLE_BASE_HOME="$($ORACLE_HOME/bin/orabasehome)"
}
```

The function should appear at the top of the createDB.sh and runOracle.sh scripts, above any other function that calls setOracleBaseDirs to populate the configuration directories.

Update Scripts

The existing repository only anticipates a read-write home and relies on the "old" default—ORACLE_HOME—for all its configuration files. We need to change them to use the new references:

- $ORACLE_HOME/dbs becomes $ORACLE_BASE_CONFIG/dbs.

- $ORACLE_HOME/network/admin becomes $ORACLE_BASE_HOME/network/admin.

In createDB.sh, these appear in two functions, setupNetworkConfig and setupTnsnames. Listing 13-5 shows the modifications I made, calling the setOracleBaseDirs at the start of each function and using the new variables.

Listing 13-5. The setOracleBase function assigns appropriate values to variables. It's used in the two networking setup functions, and references to ORACLE_HOME/network/admin change to ORACLE_BASE_HOME/network/admin to accommodate read-only homes

```
############## Set the ORACLE_BASE_CONFIG and ORACLE_BASE_HOME variables
##############
function setOracleBaseDirs {
  export ORACLE_BASE_CONFIG="$($ORACLE_HOME/bin/orabaseconfig)"
  export ORACLE_BASE_HOME="$($ORACLE_HOME/bin/orabasehome)"
}
```

```
############## Setting up network related config files (sqlnet.ora,
listener.ora) ##############
function setupNetworkConfig {
  setOracleBaseDirs
  mkdir -p "$ORACLE_BASE_HOME"/network/admin

  # sqlnet.ora
  echo "NAMES.DIRECTORY_PATH= (TNSNAMES, EZCONNECT, HOSTNAME)" > "$ORACLE_
  BASE_HOME"/network/admin/sqlnet.ora

  # listener.ora
  echo "LISTENER =
(DESCRIPTION_LIST =
  (DESCRIPTION =
    (ADDRESS = (PROTOCOL = IPC)(KEY = EXTPROC1))
    (ADDRESS = (PROTOCOL = TCP)(HOST = 0.0.0.0)(PORT = 1521))
  )
)

DEDICATED_THROUGH_BROKER_LISTENER=ON
DIAG_ADR_ENABLED = off
" > "$ORACLE_BASE_HOME"/network/admin/listener.ora

}

###################### Setting up tnsnames.ora #########################
function setupTnsnames {
  setOracleBaseDirs
  mkdir -p "$ORACLE_BASE_HOME"/network/admin

  # tnsnames.ora
  echo "$ORACLE_SID=localhost:1521/$ORACLE_SID" > "$ORACLE_BASE_HOME"/
  network/admin/tnsnames.ora
  echo "$ORACLE_PDB=
(DESCRIPTION =
  (ADDRESS = (PROTOCOL = TCP)(HOST = 0.0.0.0)(PORT = 1521))
  (CONNECT_DATA =
    (SERVER = DEDICATED)
```

```
    (SERVICE_NAME = $ORACLE_PDB)
  )
)" >> "$ORACLE_BASE_HOME"/network/admin/tnsnames.ora

}
```

I made similar changes to runOracle.sh in Listing 13-6, adding the new function and updating references to ORACLE_HOME/dbs and ORACLE_HOME/network/admin in the three helper functions, moveFiles, symLinkFiles, and undoSymLinkFiles.

Listing 13-6. Updates to the runOracle.sh script for handling the variable directory paths in read-only and read-write homes

```
############## Set the ORACLE_BASE_CONFIG and ORACLE_BASE_HOME variables
##############
function setOracleBaseDirs {
  export ORACLE_BASE_CONFIG="$($ORACLE_HOME/bin/orabaseconfig)"
  export ORACLE_BASE_HOME="$($ORACLE_HOME/bin/orabasehome)"
}
########### Move DB files ############
function moveFiles {
  setOracleBaseDirs
  if [ ! -d "$ORACLE_BASE"/oradata/dbconfig/"$ORACLE_SID" ]; then
    mkdir -p "$ORACLE_BASE"/oradata/dbconfig/"$ORACLE_SID"/
  fi;

  mv "$ORACLE_BASE_CONFIG"/dbs/spfile"$ORACLE_SID".ora "$ORACLE_BASE"/
  oradata/dbconfig/"$ORACLE_SID"/
  mv "$ORACLE_BASE_CONFIG"/dbs/orapw"$ORACLE_SID" "$ORACLE_BASE"/oradata/
  dbconfig/"$ORACLE_SID"/
  mv "$ORACLE_BASE_HOME"/network/admin/sqlnet.ora "$ORACLE_BASE"/oradata/
  dbconfig/"$ORACLE_SID"/
  mv "$ORACLE_BASE_HOME"/network/admin/listener.ora "$ORACLE_BASE"/
  oradata/dbconfig/"$ORACLE_SID"/
  mv "$ORACLE_BASE_HOME"/network/admin/tnsnames.ora "$ORACLE_BASE"/
  oradata/dbconfig/"$ORACLE_SID"/
```

```
  mv "$ORACLE_HOME"/install/.docker_* "$ORACLE_BASE"/oradata/
  dbconfig/"$ORACLE_SID"/

  # oracle user does not have permissions in /etc, hence cp and not mv
  cp /etc/oratab "$ORACLE_BASE"/oradata/dbconfig/"$ORACLE_SID"/

  symLinkFiles;
}

########### Symbolic link DB files ############
function symLinkFiles {
  setOracleBaseDirs
  if [ ! -L "$ORACLE_BASE_CONFIG"/dbs/spfile"$ORACLE_SID".ora ]; then
    ln -s "$ORACLE_BASE"/oradata/dbconfig/"$ORACLE_SID"/spfile"$ORACLE_
    SID".ora "$ORACLE_BASE_CONFIG"/dbs/spfile"$ORACLE_SID".ora
  fi;
  if [ ! -L "$ORACLE_BASE_CONFIG"/dbs/orapw"$ORACLE_SID" ]; then
    ln -s "$ORACLE_BASE"/oradata/dbconfig/"$ORACLE_SID"/orapw"$ORACLE_
    SID" "$ORACLE_BASE_CONFIG"/dbs/orapw"$ORACLE_SID"
  fi;
  if [ ! -L "$ORACLE_BASE_HOME"/network/admin/sqlnet.ora ]; then
    ln -s "$ORACLE_BASE"/oradata/dbconfig/"$ORACLE_SID"/sqlnet.ora
    "$ORACLE_BASE_HOME"/network/admin/sqlnet.ora
  fi;
  if [ ! -L "$ORACLE_BASE_HOME"/network/admin/listener.ora ]; then
    ln -s "$ORACLE_BASE"/oradata/dbconfig/"$ORACLE_SID"/listener.ora
    "$ORACLE_BASE_HOME"/network/admin/listener.ora
  fi;
  if [ ! -L "$ORACLE_BASE_HOME"/network/admin/tnsnames.ora ]; then
    ln -s "$ORACLE_BASE"/oradata/dbconfig/"$ORACLE_SID"/tnsnames.ora
    "$ORACLE_BASE_HOME"/network/admin/tnsnames.ora
  fi;

  # oracle user does not have permissions in /etc, hence cp and not ln
  cp "$ORACLE_BASE"/oradata/dbconfig/"$ORACLE_SID"/oratab /etc/oratab
}
```

```
########## Undoing the symbolic links ############
function undoSymLinkFiles {
  setOracleBaseDirs
  if [ -L "$ORACLE_BASE_CONFIG"/dbs/spfile"$ORACLE_SID".ora ]; then
    rm "$ORACLE_BASE_CONFIG"/dbs/spfile"$ORACLE_SID".ora
  fi;
  if [ -L "$ORACLE_BASE_CONFIG"/dbs/orapw"$ORACLE_SID" ]; then
    rm "$ORACLE_BASE_CONFIG"/dbs/orapw"$ORACLE_SID"
  fi;
  if [ -L "$ORACLE_BASE_HOME"/network/admin/sqlnet.ora ]; then
    rm "$ORACLE_BASE_HOME"/network/admin/sqlnet.ora
  fi;
  if [ -L "$ORACLE_BASE_HOME"/network/admin/listener.ora ]; then
    rm "$ORACLE_BASE_HOME"/network/admin/listener.ora
  fi;
  if [ -L "$ORACLE_BASE_HOME"/network/admin/tnsnames.ora ]; then
    rm "$ORACLE_BASE_HOME"/network/admin/tnsnames.ora
  fi;
}
```

Run Containers with Read-Only Homes

The preceding script changes are only present in the repository. We'll have to rebuild or recreate the image before the modified scripts are available to new containers. Navigate to the docker-images/OracleDatabase/SingleInstance/dockerfiles directory and run the buildContainerImage.sh script to recreate the image with the new script versions:

```
./buildContainerImage.sh -v 19.3.0 -e
```

When the build completes, run a new container and add the ROOH=ENABLE environment variable to create a read-only home in the container:

```
docker run -d --name ROOH \
          -e ROOH=ENABLE \
          oracle/database:19.3.0-ee
```

Then, report the output by tailing the container log with docker logs -f ROOH. The first output from the log shows the creation of the read-only home and its assets:

Enabling Read-Only Oracle home.
Update orabasetab file to enable Read-Only Oracle home.
Orabasetab file has been updated successfully.
Create bootstrap directories for Read-Only Oracle home.
Bootstrap directories have been created successfully.
Bootstrap files have been processed successfully.
Read-Only Oracle home has been enabled successfully.
Check the log file /opt/oracle/cfgtoollogs/roohctl/roohctl-220821PM123432.
log for more details.

That's followed by the familiar listener startup message, but with a twist! It references the listener.ora in its new location, /opt/oracle/homes/OraDB19Home1/network/admin, under the ORACLE_BASE_HOME:

LSNRCTL for Linux: Version 19.0.0.0.0 - Production on 21-AUG-2022 12:34:33
Copyright (c) 1991, 2019, Oracle. All rights reserved.
Starting /opt/oracle/product/19c/dbhome_1/bin/tnslsnr: please wait...

TNSLSNR for Linux: Version 19.0.0.0.0 - Production
System parameter file is /opt/oracle/homes/OraDB19Home1/network/admin/
listener.ora
Log messages written to /opt/oracle/diag/tnslsnr/d06ab6991050/listener/
alert/log.xml
Listening on: (DESCRIPTION=(ADDRESS=(PROTOCOL=ipc)(KEY=EXTPROC1)))
Listening on: (DESCRIPTION=(ADDRESS=(PROTOCOL=tcp)(HOST=0.0.0.0)
(PORT=1521)))

Connecting to (DESCRIPTION=(ADDRESS=(PROTOCOL=IPC)(KEY=EXTPROC1)))
STATUS of the LISTENER

Alias   LISTENER
Version   TNSLSNR for Linux: Version 19.0.0.0.0 -
Production
Start Date   21-AUG-2022 12:34:46
Uptime   0 days 0 hr. 0 min. 13 sec
Trace Level   off
Security   ON: Local OS Authentication
SNMP   OFF

```
Listener Parameter File    /opt/oracle/homes/OraDB19Home1/network/admin/
listener.ora
Listener Log File          /opt/oracle/diag/tnslsnr/d06ab6991050/listener/
alert/log.xml
Listening Endpoints Summary...
  (DESCRIPTION=(ADDRESS=(PROTOCOL=ipc)(KEY=EXTPROC1)))
  (DESCRIPTION=(ADDRESS=(PROTOCOL=tcp)(HOST=0.0.0.0)(PORT=1521)))
The listener supports no services
The command completed successfully
```

Log in to the container and review the contents of $ORACLE_HOME/install/
orabasetab. The fourth field, indicating whether or not the home is read-only, is Y in the
new container:

```
#orabasetab file is used to track Oracle Home associated with Oracle Base
/opt/oracle/product/19c/dbhome_1:/opt/oracle:OraDB19Home1:Y:
```

In the container's $ORACLE_BASE directory, you'll see two new directories, dbs and
homes. Once database creation finishes, the runOracle.sh script moves the configuration
files to /opt/oracle/oradata/dbconfig and adds links:

```
bash-4.2$ ls -l $ORACLE_BASE/dbs
total 12
-rw-rw---- 1 oracle oinstall 1544 Jan 21 15:57 hc_ORCLCDB.dat
-rw-r----- 1 oracle oinstall   43 Jan 21 15:56 initORCLCDB.ora
-rw-r----- 1 oracle oinstall   24 Jan 21 14:43 lkORCLCDB
lrwxrwxrwx 1 oracle oinstall   49 Jan 21 15:58 orapwORCLCDB -> /opt/oracle/
oradata/dbconfig/ORCLCDB/orapwORCLCDB
lrwxrwxrwx 1 oracle oinstall   54 Jan 21 15:58 spfileORCLCDB.ora -> /opt/
oracle/oradata/dbconfig/ORCLCDB/spfileORCLCDB.ora
bash-4.2$ ls -l $ORACLE_BASE/homes/OraDB19Home1/network/admin
total 0
lrwxrwxrwx 1 oracle oinstall 49 Jan 21 15:58 listener.ora -> /opt/oracle/
oradata/dbconfig/ORCLCDB/listener.ora
lrwxrwxrwx 1 oracle oinstall 47 Jan 21 15:58 sqlnet.ora -> /opt/oracle/
oradata/dbconfig/ORCLCDB/sqlnet.ora
lrwxrwxrwx 1 oracle oinstall 49 Jan 21 15:58 tnsnames.ora -> /opt/oracle/
oradata/dbconfig/ORCLCDB/tnsnames.ora
```

```
bash-4.2$ ls -l /opt/oracle/oradata/dbconfig/ORCLCDB/
total 24
-rw-r--r-- 1 oracle oinstall  234 Jan 21 14:38 listener.ora
-rw-r----- 1 oracle oinstall 2048 Jan 21 14:47 orapwORCLCDB
-rw-r--r-- 1 oracle oinstall  780 Jan 21 15:58 oratab
-rw-r----- 1 oracle oinstall 3584 Jan 21 16:17 spfileORCLCDB.ora
-rw-r--r-- 1 oracle oinstall   54 Jan 21 14:38 sqlnet.ora
-rw-r----- 1 oracle oinstall  197 Jan 21 15:58 tnsnames.ora
```

If I create a container without setting the ROOH value, these files appear in their expected locations:

```
bash-4.2$ ls -l $ORACLE_HOME/dbs
total 12
-rw-rw---- 1 oracle oinstall 1544 Jan 21 17:42 hc_ORCLCDB.dat
-rw-r--r-- 1 oracle dba      3079 May 14  2015 init.ora
-rw-r----- 1 oracle oinstall   24 Jan 21 16:23 lkORCLCDB
lrwxrwxrwx 1 oracle oinstall   49 Jan 21 17:43 orapwORCLCDB -> /opt/oracle/
oradata/dbconfig/ORCLCDB/orapwORCLCDB
lrwxrwxrwx 1 oracle oinstall   54 Jan 21 17:43 spfileORCLCDB.ora -> /opt/
oracle/oradata/dbconfig/ORCLCDB/spfileORCLCDB.ora
bash-4.2$ ls -l $ORACLE_HOME/network/admin
total 8
lrwxrwxrwx 1 oracle oinstall   49 Jan 21 17:43 listener.ora -> /opt/oracle/
oradata/dbconfig/ORCLCDB/listener.ora
drwxr-xr-x 2 oracle dba      4096 Apr 17  2019 samples
-rw-r--r-- 1 oracle dba      1536 Feb 14  2018 shrept.lst
lrwxrwxrwx 1 oracle oinstall   47 Jan 21 17:43 sqlnet.ora -> /opt/oracle/
oradata/dbconfig/ORCLCDB/sqlnet.ora
lrwxrwxrwx 1 oracle oinstall   49 Jan 21 17:43 tnsnames.ora -> /opt/oracle/
oradata/dbconfig/ORCLCDB/tnsnames.ora
bash-4.2$ ls -l /opt/oracle/oradata/dbconfig/ORCLCDB
total 24
-rw-r--r-- 1 oracle oinstall  234 Jan 21 16:19 listener.ora
-rw-r----- 1 oracle oinstall 2048 Jan 21 16:28 orapwORCLCDB
-rw-r--r-- 1 oracle oinstall  780 Jan 21 17:43 oratab
```

```
-rw-r----- 1 oracle oinstall 3584 Jan 21 17:46 spfileORCLCDB.ora
-rw-r--r-- 1 oracle oinstall   54 Jan 21 16:19 sqlnet.ora
-rw-r----- 1 oracle oinstall  197 Jan 21 17:43 tnsnames.ora
```

Scripting Image Customization

I run a mix of images intended for different environments. My interactive images include tools I use for viewing and editing files, performing tests, and collecting diagnostic information. They also set the environment to be familiar and user-friendly, with my favorite command-line prompt, aliases and shortcuts that simplify navigation, and a login.sql file to customize my SQL*Plus experience. My production images follow container principles and aim for minimal footprint, reduced attack surface, and eliminating unnecessary packages and libraries. I could manage separate repositories dedicated to different purposes, but that would mean managing two sets of code, increasing work spent testing and validating changes, and introducing more opportunities for human error. With build arguments, a single repository can support both image categories.

Multiple options exist for managing image content, including

- **Scripts with conditional operations:** Useful when options are limited, well defined, and won't change significantly over time.

- **Appending or substituting values:** Best for dynamic inputs that aren't well defined in advance.

- **Conditionally copying files:** Suitable for relatively static modifications that are extensive, complex, or environment specific.

The following recipes suggest applications of these techniques to produce customized images from a single repository.

Conditional Operations

Supporting multiple outcomes with less code reduces maintenance overhead. Adding conditions to scripts is one strategy toward that end and works best when deciding among a limited set of options with clear-cut actions. The source of the condition could be an argument passed to the docker build command or discovered from the environment.

The public repository we've worked with throughout this book has separate directories for each database version: 11.2.0.2, 12.1.0.2, 12.2.0.1, 18.3.0, 18.4.0, 19.3.0, and 21.3.0. Within each of these directories are the same scripts. Some are identical, others contain minor differences in formatting and style, and a few introduce version-specific functionality. For instance, if I run the `diff` command to show the differences between the 19c and 21c versions of `installDBBinaries.sh`, I see

```
> diff 19.3.0/installDBBinaries.sh 21.3.0/installDBBinaries.sh
24c24
< if [ "$EDITION" != "EE" -a "$EDITION" != "SE2" ]; then
---
> if [ "$EDITION" != "EE" ] && [ "$EDITION" != "SE2" ]; then
```

They're identical but for a minor difference in an `if` statement. Elsewhere are differences reflecting code improvements, like this check in the `runOracle.sh` scripts:

```
<     mv "$ORACLE_HOME"/install/.docker_* "$ORACLE_BASE"/oradata/
      dbconfig/"$ORACLE_SID"/
---
>     if [ -a "$ORACLE_HOME"/install/.docker_* ]; then
>         mv "$ORACLE_HOME"/install/.docker_* "$ORACLE_BASE"/oradata/
          dbconfig/"$ORACLE_SID"/
>     fi;
```

The 19c version tries to move files matching `$ORACLE_HOME/install/.docker_*`. It will return an error if no files match the pattern. The 21c version wraps the move command in an `if` statement, checking whether matching files are present before attempting to move them. The 21c versions include actions specific to Oracle 21c Express Edition, but the scripts are mostly the same. Is it practical to combine the 19c and 21c repositories into a single, common directory, then pass a version to the build?

There are good reasons to separate versions into individual directories. In the previous chapter, when discussing *build context*, you learned that Docker reads all the files beneath the build path. Combining 19c and 21c in a single Dockerfile means storing the database installation media for both versions in the same directory. They're large files, and having both in the same directory increases context size and processing time.

The downside of separate directories is maintenance. The file differences are mostly minor, but every improvement made in the 21c version hasn't graduated to others. As the count of supported versions grows, so does the need to track and test fixes and improvements to an ever-widening code base.

The context issues can be solved with build features covered in Chapter 14. With that problem out of the way, it's more reasonable to consider passing the version to the Dockerfile through a build argument. The version then controls unique aspects of the build process, notably:

- Applying the correct preinstallation RPM packages in setupLinuxEnv.sh

- Performing additional checks needed for enabling Express Edition in 21c

- Tagging images with the correct database version and edition

Make no mistake: converting existing scripts to handle multiple versions is an involved task that varies according to your objectives and a single example of why you might embed conditional checks in setup scripts. Therefore, listing specific changes is not practical, but we can explore techniques that illustrate the practice. The Linux case statement, for instance, presents a very convenient method for determining the correct set of packages by version:

```
case $DB_VERSION in
        11*)   RPM_LIST="oracle-rdbms-server-11gR2-preinstall unzip" ;;
        12.1*) RPM_LIST="oracle-rdbms-server-12cR1-preinstall tar" ;;
        12.2*) RPM_LIST="oracle-database-server-12cR2-preinstall" ;;
        18*)   RPM_LIST="oracle-database-preinstall-18c" ;;
        19*)   RPM_LIST="oracle-database-preinstall-19c" ;;
        21*)   RPM_LIST="oracle-database-preinstall-21c" ;;
        *)     exit 1 ;;
  esac
```

Then, pass the $RPM_LIST variable to the yum install command:[6]

```
yum -y install "$RPM_LIST" openssl
```

---

[6] The openssl package is common to every version and could easily be part of RPM_LIST. Doing so is repetitive. Sometimes, less is more!

I want to emphasize that neither approach is "right" or "wrong." Coding is an art, and teams choose the methods best suited to their style, background, and purpose. In my practice, I prefer a single set of scripts for every version, but for Oracle's container images, I concede that separate directories are better. The code base introduces new users to containers, and having a directory for each version is easier to understand. As you grow more comfortable with containers and expand your image library, consolidating versioned builds beneath a unified directory structure may present a better alternative. Additional examples of this method (and perhaps inspiration) are available on my GitHub: https://github.com/oraclesean/docker-oracle.

Appending Values in Dockerfiles

The yum install command in the preceding section leads to a second opportunity for modifying images, this time related to the nature of the intended environment. Production images should be lean and free of unnecessary packages that might add to image size or introduce vulnerabilities. Images used for experimentation have different requirements, including editors and diagnostic tools, and these will vary by need and personal taste. I prefer vi; others like emacs. You may want tree or strace included. The point here isn't *what* packages need installation; it's the variable nature of the list, and the challenge to solve is how best to include them.

One approach is logging in to running containers as the root user:

```
docker exec -it -u root <CONTAINER NAME> bash
```

Then yum install packages:

```
# yum -y install vi less tree which
```

The disadvantages of this approach are as follows:

- Its manual nature. I have to perform these steps in every container.

- It's a prerequisite to activities requiring the extra packages and one that's easily forgotten until you realize something's not there.

- The installation changes files in the container's overlay filesystem, adding to the container's size.

For unique additions, it makes sense to take this route. It isn't practical to spend several minutes building a custom image with "that package you need this one time" simply because you don't want to add a few megabytes to a container or run an extra command, particularly if that container won't be around very long.

When those tools appear regularly in images, it makes more sense to integrate them into the image itself through a build argument.

Unlike the environment variables used in docker run, we can't "make up" build arguments on the fly. They must be defined through an ARG instruction in the Dockerfile. However, they don't require a value. Let's create a new argument in the Dockerfile to accept a list of optional packages to install in an image:

```
ARG RPM_SUPPLEMENT=""
```

It should appear with the other arguments passed to the first build stage. It's the one that runs the $INSTALL_DIR/$SETUP_LINUX_FILE step. There's no need to add it to the environment with an associated ENV command. Arguments are available within the context of the stage and, if not needed in later steps, don't have to be promoted to the container's environment.

Next, in the setupLinuxEnv.sh script, update the yum install command to include the new argument:

```
yum -y install oracle-database-preinstall-19c openssl $RPM_SUPPLEMENT
```

If we pass nothing to the build argument, the Linux setup script runs and appends an empty string to the end of the yum command. But, if we give the build argument a list of packages:[7]

```
docker build ...
        --build-arg RPM_SUPPLEMENT="vi less tree which"
...
```

The yum command sees the custom argument in the variable and installs the additional packages.

---

[7] Builds are covered in Chapter 14.

Conditional File Copy

The modifications presented in the first part of this section addressed a case where scripts use arguments for if-then or case-based decision-making. The scripts must necessarily embed the logic for evaluating and acting on conditions. The example in that section considered consolidating scripts for two or more versions into a single directory structure. Many of the helper files in the repository are identical or similar enough to be interchangeable across versions, and it makes sense to combine them. But others—including the database installation script—include unique steps for specific conditions. As Oracle introduces new versions, a "one ring to rule them all" style approach for database installation may not be practical. Accommodating differences in Express, Standard, and Enterprise Editions for every version, from 11g to 21c and beyond, is a complex task. Testing updates against every combination would quickly grow out of hand.

There's a security aspect to think about as well. Look at the files present in the `$ORACLE_BASE` directory of an Oracle database container:

```
/opt/oracle/runOracle.sh
/opt/oracle/createObserver.sh
/opt/oracle/relinkOracleBinary.sh
/opt/oracle/setPassword.sh
/opt/oracle/checkDBStatus.sh
/opt/oracle/runUserScripts.sh
/opt/oracle/configTcps.sh
/opt/oracle/createDB.sh
/opt/oracle/dbca.rsp.tmpl
/opt/oracle/startDB.sh
```

Logic embedded in scripts reveals how things work under different conditions and might expose ways attackers can exploit your database infrastructure. Someone with access to one image or an unsecured or "unimportant" container can infer configurations and even reverse engineer other containers in your environment.

Perhaps there's a happy medium—one set of shared files that apply to any version and dedicated files without conditional logic that's overly complex or revealing. To imagine how that might work, let's look at the top section of a 19c Dockerfile, focusing on the arguments and environment settings in Listing 13-7. I've narrowed it down by removing some of the specialized environment variables that aren't important to this exercise.

Listing 13-7. A portion of an Oracle 19c Dockerfile showing argument and environment instructions. The environment settings focus on those related to files and directories

```
# Argument to control removal of components not needed after db software
installation
ARG SLIMMING=true
ARG INSTALL_FILE_1="LINUX.X64_193000_db_home.zip"

# Environment variables required for this build (do NOT change)
# -------------------------------------------------------------
ENV ORACLE_BASE=/opt/oracle \
    ORACLE_HOME=/opt/oracle/product/19c/dbhome_1 \
    INSTALL_DIR=/opt/install \
    INSTALL_FILE_1=$INSTALL_FILE_1 \
    INSTALL_RSP="db_inst.rsp" \
    CONFIG_RSP="dbca.rsp.tmpl" \
    PWD_FILE="setPassword.sh" \
    RUN_FILE="runOracle.sh" \
    START_FILE="startDB.sh" \
    CREATE_DB_FILE="createDB.sh" \
    SETUP_LINUX_FILE="setupLinuxEnv.sh" \
    INSTALL_DB_BINARIES_FILE="installDBBinaries.sh" \
    # Directory for keeping Oracle Wallet
    WALLET_DIR=""
```

For argument's sake, let's say that the runOracle.sh and createDB.sh scripts are different enough across database versions that combining their logic isn't practical or desirable. The response files aren't interchangeable, either. In Listing 13-8, I added an argument for the database version and incorporated it into the existing environment.

Listing 13-8. A modified Dockerfile that accepts a database version in an argument and inserts it into the names of select scripts and templates defined in the environment

```
# Argument to control removal of components not needed after db software
installation
ARG SLIMMING=true
ARG INSTALL_FILE_1="LINUX.X64_193000_db_home.zip"
ARG DB_VERSION=19.3.0

# Environment variables required for this build (do NOT change)
# ----------------------------------------------------------------
ENV ORACLE_BASE=/opt/oracle \
    ORACLE_HOME=/opt/oracle/product/19c/dbhome_1 \
    INSTALL_DIR=/opt/install \
    INSTALL_FILE_1=$INSTALL_FILE_1 \
    INSTALL_RSP="db_inst.${DB_VERSION}.rsp" \
    CONFIG_RSP="dbca.rsp.${DB_VERSION}.tmpl" \
    PWD_FILE="setPassword.sh" \
    RUN_FILE="runOracle.${DB_VERSION}.sh" \
    START_FILE="startDB.sh" \
    CREATE_DB_FILE="createDB.${DB_VERSION}.sh" \
    SETUP_LINUX_FILE="setupLinuxEnv.sh" \
    INSTALL_DB_BINARIES_FILE="installDBBinaries.sh" \
    # Directory for keeping Oracle Wallet
    WALLET_DIR=""
```

The Dockerfile supports multiple versions without adding complex logic to the scripts themselves. Files common to all versions are shared. Dedicated scripts are substituted where necessary. This same technique helps address environmental differences, too. The .bashrc file used to set up the look and feel of production systems may be quite different from the one I'd use in an experimental container. The 19c and 21c Dockerfiles add entries to the container's .bashrc files:

```
RUN echo 'ORACLE_SID=${ORACLE_SID:-ORCLCDB}; export ORACLE_SID=${ORACLE_
SID^^}' > .bashrc
```

We could extend that command to include customizations to the prompt:

```
export PS1="[\u - \${ORACLE_SID}] \w\n# "
```

Now we're getting into rough territory, though. Attempting to reproduce this string with echo:

```
# Without quotes: backslash before the dollar sign and trailing whitespace
are lost.
echo export PS1="[\u - \${ORACLE_SID}] \w\n# "
export PS1=[\u - ${ORACLE_SID}] \w\n#

# With double quotes, escaping embedded quotes: backslash is lost.
echo "export PS1=\"[\u - \${ORACLE_SID}] \w\n# \""
export PS1="[\u - ${ORACLE_SID}] \w\n# "

# Double-escaped the backslash: works!
echo "export PS1=\"[\u - \\\${ORACLE_SID}] \w\n# \""
export PS1="[\u - \${ORACLE_SID}] \w\n# "

# Single quotes prevent bash from evaluating the string: works!
echo 'export PS1="[\u - \${ORACLE_SID}] \w\n# "'
export PS1="[\u - \${ORACLE_SID}] \w\n# "
```

The bash shell has sensitivities and quirks that aren't always obvious. Figuring out how to make it print strings containing special characters can be frustrating! An alternative is writing dedicated files for each environment in advance, then copying them into the image. A no-nonsense production file, bashrc.prod:

```
ORACLE_SID=${ORACLE_SID:-ORCLCDB}
export ORACLE_SID=${ORACLE_SID^^}
```

And a file for test, bashrc.test, that sets the ORACLE_SID and adds settings for the prompt and other environment variables:

```
ORACLE_SID=${ORACLE_SID:-ORCLCDB}
export ORACLE_SID=${ORACLE_SID^^}

export PS1="[\u - \${ORACLE_SID}] \w\n# "
export ORACLE_BASE_CONFIG="$($ORACLE_HOME/bin/orabaseconfig 2>/dev/null ||
echo $ORACLE_HOME)"
```

```
export ORACLE_BASE_HOME="$($ORACLE_HOME/bin/orabasehome 2>/dev/null || echo
$ORACLE_HOME)"
export TNS_ADMIN=$ORACLE_BASE_HOME/network/admin
export ORACLE_PATH=/home/oracle
```

In the following snippet from the 19c Dockerfile, I modified the final build stage to accept an argument and replaced the RUN command with a COPY for inserting the correct file into the image:

```
##############################################
# --------------------------------------------
# Start new layer for database runtime
# --------------------------------------------
##############################################

FROM base

ARG ENV=prod

USER oracle
COPY --chown=oracle:dba --from=builder $ORACLE_BASE $ORACLE_BASE

USER root
RUN $ORACLE_BASE/oraInventory/orainstRoot.sh && \
    $ORACLE_HOME/root.sh

USER oracle
WORKDIR /home/oracle

# Add an environment-specific bashrc file to the image
COPY bashrc.$ENV /home/oracle/.bashrc
```

Whether working with scripts or configuration files, it may be easier (and potentially less error-prone and frustrating) to work with files containing the exact code or text needed in the image!

Summary

As you gain experience working with ready-made container images, you'll discover things you like and things you'd like to change. It's part of the learning curve, and robust, forgiving tools help build the confidence and skills to take the next step. Whether it's a first racing bike or a new technology, time in the saddle creates muscle memory and familiarity. Once using the tools becomes second nature, your mind can fully concentrate on developing a clearer vision of what you want to do and, with it, understand how your tools may limit your progress.

The four friends in *Breaking Away* struggle against the expectations of parents and society as they search for their own unique identities. While they can't change who they are or where they're from, they realize their origins don't define their future direction. The same holds for the image repositories we've worked with throughout this book. They're foundations that shape our understanding of running databases in containers but don't prevent us from dreaming big and charting our own course.

This chapter introduced recipes to help you take those next steps with containers. They tackle issues you're likely to face as you work with database images, but they're also adaptable to other needs. That's the beauty of recipes—whether in cooking or coding, it's a blend of art and science. There's rarely a single answer to a question, yet the methods or patterns for solving one problem often apply to others. I hope the examples in this chapter inspire you to imagine solutions for the challenges you encounter on your Docker journey! The next chapter looks deeper into how Docker builds images with an eye toward writing efficient and effective Dockerfiles.

CHAPTER 14

Building Images

There are certain mysteries in life I don't need (or even want) to understand. Avoiding the knowledge preserves a bit of wonder for the world around me. Sewing machines are one of those things. I can sew by hand, albeit without much talent, but I've never figured out how a machine can duplicate that effort. Even with easy access to the Internet, where I could surely find a YouTube video that reveals the entire process in slow motion with stitch-by-stitch expert narration, I've resisted learning the underlying principles of sewing machines. How a machine pokes a needle partway through the fabric and then secures each stitch from below is beyond me. I know better, but the best explanation I can imagine involves tiny gremlins that live inside the machine, furiously looping bobbin thread through each stitch. I'm content not knowing—it nourishes a fascination and appreciation of everyday things and reminds me there are wonderfully intelligent and inventive people all around! Or that magic truly exists!

There are conveniences I simply take for granted. Mulling over the technology surrounding me, I understand my laptop uses DHCP to get a network address. I don't know the details, but it seems like something I could figure out if I needed to, and it doesn't hold the same mystery as a sewing machine. It makes joining a network easy and removes the guesswork of finding an available IP address on hotel WiFi.

Automation and scripts fall into a similar bucket. They make it faster and easier to perform everyday tasks and allow us "forget" the details. (To be completely honest, sometimes I look at the code and wonder how I was either so naive or so inspired!) Codifying knowledge converts it into tools we can share with others and use as the building blocks of bigger, better things. In Chapter 4, the `buildContainerImage.sh` script did just that. You gave it a database version and edition and constructed and ran a `docker build` command for you in the background.

Gaining greater control over image creation means getting hands-on with the build process. Even if your plans don't include writing custom Dockerfiles, understanding elements of the build command provides a greater appreciation of what takes place

© Sean Scott 2023
S. Scott, *Oracle on Docker*, https://doi.org/10.1007/978-1-4842-9033-0_14

behind the curtains and makes sense of the magic! And I promise that building images doesn't approach the mystery of sewing machines nor involves armies of gremlins laboring inside your computer!

Build Command Syntax

docker build may be the most straightforward command in the Docker lexicon. In its most minimal form, this is valid:

```
docker build .
```

That doesn't seem like much! How could something this simple do anything? It all has to do with context!

Context

Building images requires a *Dockerfile*—the instructions or recipe—and a *build context,* the files, assets, or ingredients. Context is everything at or below the directory where the build runs. Oracle database builds include the software installation media, scripts for managing the build (preparing the operating system and installing a database), and scripts used by the container runtime (creating a database, starting a database, reporting health, and so on).

In the preceding build command, the dot represents the context. The dot, or period, is a shorthand character in Linux that points to the current directory.[1] Docker builds the image using whatever files it finds there. Builds need a Dockerfile, too, and if not explicitly defined, Docker looks for a file named "Dockerfile" among the context.

To get a better idea for context, I created a simple Dockerfile in a new directory, shown in Listing 14-1. It begins with the alpine image, a minimalist Linux distribution popular for containers. The Dockerfile runs a COPY instruction. The first argument, the asterisk wildcard, copies all files from the build context—the local directory—into the target destination, the container's root directory (represented by the slash).

---

[1] A relative path simply means "relative to the current position in the directory tree" and isn't very different than giving someone directions for reaching a destination from your current location. Absolute paths are anchored at a reference point. On Linux systems, it's the root directory, /. Relative paths start with a dot; absolute paths begin with a slash.

Listing 14-1. A simple Dockerfile for demonstrating context

```
FROM alpine
COPY * /
CMD ls -l /
```

The final CMD instruction runs when executing the image and lists the contents of the container's root directory. Listing 14-2 includes the output produced by running the simple command earlier.

Listing 14-2. The output generated when running docker build for the Dockerfile is shown in Listing 14-1

```
> docker build .
Sending build context to Docker daemon  2.048kB
Step 1/3 : FROM alpine
latest: Pulling from library/alpine
213ec9aee27d: Pull complete
Digest: sha256:bc41182d7ef5ffc53a40b044e725193bc10142a1243f395ee852a
8d9730fc2ad
Status: Downloaded newer image for alpine:latest
 ---> 9c6f07244728
Step 2/3 : COPY * /
 ---> 1d5ae09bcac7
Step 3/3 : CMD ls -l /
 ---> Running in 7aab4d9ea957
Removing intermediate container 7aab4d9ea957
 ---> 8cf63acc1f17
Successfully built 8cf63acc1f17
```

Take a look at the output:

- "*Sending build context to Docker daemon*," read all the files in the context—the local directory—and sent them to the Docker daemon. Only then did it begin reading the Dockerfile and performing work.

- The first step of the Dockerfile instructed Docker to pull the alpine image. It added this to a newly created layer, 9c6f07244728. (Each layer is prefixed by three dashes and a right caret: --->.)

- The second step copied files into another new layer, 1d5ae09bcac7.

- The third step ran the ls -l / command in an intermediate container, 7aab4d9ea957.

- After removing the intermediate container, Docker created a final layer, 8cf63acc1f17.

Running docker images reports the newly created image, as well as the alpine image, pulled in by the FROM instruction:

```
> docker images
REPOSITORY       TAG        IMAGE ID       CREATED          SIZE
<none>           <none>     8cf63acc1f17   21 seconds ago   5.54MB
alpine           latest     9c6f07244728   2 weeks ago      5.54MB
oracle/database  19.3.0-ee  1b588736c8c1   2 months ago     6.67GB
```

The image ID of the new container matches that shown in the image listing. Notice the image doesn't have a repository or tag. Commands for managing or reporting image information, or running the image as a container, must use the ID (for now). Let's pass the image ID to the docker history command to view the image's layers:

```
> docker history 8cf63acc1f17
IMAGE           CREATED          CREATED BY                                      SIZE
   COMMENT
8cf63acc1f17    2 minutes ago    /bin/sh -c #(nop)  CMD ["/bin/sh" "-c" "ls -...
   0B
1d5ae09bcac7    2 minutes ago    /bin/sh -c #(nop) COPY file:a45abb589c97bd2f...
   34B
9c6f07244728    2 weeks ago      /bin/sh -c #(nop)  CMD ["/bin/sh"]
   0B
<missing>       2 weeks ago      /bin/sh -c #(nop) ADD file:2a949686d9886ac7c...
   5.54MB
```

History output reads from newest at the top to oldest at the bottom. Notice the ID values of each layer correspond to those in the docker build output. One of these, layer 1d5ae09bcac7, has a size of 34 bytes. That's the same size as the Dockerfile in this directory:

```
> ls -l
total 8
-rw-r--r--   1 seanscott  staff     34 Aug 25 10:57 Dockerfile
```

This layer contains one file, the Dockerfile added to the "base" alpine image by the COPY command!

The final layer, 8cf63acc1f17, is zero bytes. This is a metadata layer. It's not part of the image, at least not in a way that a user inside the container can see. It's used by Docker when invoking the image through docker run. We can see that by running the image:

```
> docker run 8cf63acc1f17
total 60
-rw-r--r--    1 root      root          34 Aug 25 16:57 Dockerfile
drwxr-xr-x    2 root      root        4096 Aug  9 08:47 bin
drwxr-xr-x    5 root      root         360 Aug 25 17:54 dev
drwxr-xr-x    1 root      root        4096 Aug 25 17:54 etc
drwxr-xr-x    2 root      root        4096 Aug  9 08:47 home
drwxr-xr-x    7 root      root        4096 Aug  9 08:47 lib
drwxr-xr-x    5 root      root        4096 Aug  9 08:47 media
drwxr-xr-x    2 root      root        4096 Aug  9 08:47 mnt
drwxr-xr-x    2 root      root        4096 Aug  9 08:47 opt
dr-xr-xr-x  332 root      root           0 Aug 25 17:54 proc
drwx------    2 root      root        4096 Aug  9 08:47 root
drwxr-xr-x    2 root      root        4096 Aug  9 08:47 run
drwxr-xr-x    2 root      root        4096 Aug  9 08:47 sbin
drwxr-xr-x    2 root      root        4096 Aug  9 08:47 srv
dr-xr-xr-x   13 root      root           0 Aug 25 17:54 sys
drwxrwxrwt    2 root      root        4096 Aug  9 08:47 tmp
drwxr-xr-x    7 root      root        4096 Aug  9 08:47 usr
drwxr-xr-x   12 root      root        4096 Aug  9 08:47 var
>
```

Remember that containers perform functions or services somewhat like an executable program. The CMD instruction defines the action. Everything else in the container—the libraries, packages, binaries, and scripts—is only there to support its runtime, or executable, function. It explains why image footprints are typically limited compared to the filesystem and OS on a VM or physical host. The operation fixed in the image's CMD instruction confines the container's scope. In this case, the CMD runs a command, ls -l /. With that task complete, it exits and returns control to the host command prompt.

Listing 14-2 included these lines:

```
Step 3/3 : CMD ls -l /
 ---> Running in 7aab4d9ea957
Removing intermediate container 7aab4d9ea957
```

Docker didn't read or save the result of this operation. The "intermediate container" is where Docker checked the command syntax.

A reminder about layers: Running ls -l / in this container isn't showing the filesystem of the container in a customary way. Instead, it shows the merged contents of two layers: the filesystem in the base alpine image, in layer 9c6f07244728, and the filesystem in the layer created by the COPY command, 1d5ae09bcac7. Separating these into layers allows Docker to reuse the same alpine layer in multiple containers without using additional space!

The build context in this example was the current directory where the build ran. It needn't be the *current* directory. Docker expects a path.[2] Substituting a directory path for the dot controls where builds run and what files are included in the context. In the preceding command, the dot represents a path to the build context and can be written more generally as

```
docker build <PATH>
```

Docker looks for a file called Dockerfile in the <PATH> and uses everything at or below the <PATH> as its context. To illustrate how this works, I navigated up one level in my directory tree and reran docker build, this time passing the relative directory path, ./demo, as the context for the build:

```
> cd ..

> docker build ./demo
Sending build context to Docker daemon  2.048kB
```

---

[2] Docker also accepts context using text files and URLs of remote repositories and tarballs. You're unlikely to encounter these when building larger images, including databases. URL-based builds transfer their context over a network. It's not a practical or efficient method when the context includes larger files like those used to install Oracle.

```
Step 1/3 : FROM alpine
 ---> 9c6f07244728
Step 2/3 : COPY * /
 ---> Using cache
 ---> 1d5ae09bcac7
Step 3/3 : CMD ls -l /
 ---> Using cache
 ---> 8cf63acc1f17
Successfully built 8cf63acc1f17
```

Notice anything interesting about this result? It didn't pull the `alpine` image and skipped the intermediate container, yet it reports the identical layer IDs as the original build! The "using cache" messages indicate that after passing its context to the daemon, Docker recognized no changes were necessary, and the layers were already in its build cache!

The `COPY` and `ADD` operations in the Dockerfile don't read files or directories directly from the host. They read them from the *context* built at the outset of the build process. It's a subtle but essential distinction.

Select a Dockerfile

We've seen that Docker looks for a file named Dockerfile in its context, the directory where it's running. We can override that behavior by specifying a Dockerfile outside the build context using the `-f` flag:

```
docker build -f <FILE_NAME> <PATH>
```

`docker build` expects but isn't limited to using files named `Dockerfile`. It's the default, but Docker accepts different file names in the `-f` option.

I'll build on the preceding example, moving the Dockerfile out of the `demo` directory and copying my `/etc/passwd` file into the `demo` directory. This gives Docker something to consume into its context and copy into the image:

```
> mv demo/Dockerfile .

> cp /etc/passwd ./demo

> ls -l ./demo
-rw-r--r--  1 seanscott  staff  7868 Aug 25 13:30 passwd
```

```
> ls -l
-rw-r--r--  1 seanscott  staff     34 Aug 25 10:57 Dockerfile
drwxr-xr-x  3 seanscott  staff     96 Aug 25 13:31 demo
```

The new target directory for the build is demo, under my current directory. Docker needs the build path, and because there's no Dockerfile in the demo directory, my build command needs the location of the Dockerfile via the -f option:

```
docker build -f ./Dockerfile ./demo
```

Notice a few differences in the output:

```
> docker build -f ./Dockerfile ./demo
Sending build context to Docker daemon  10.27kB
Step 1/3 : FROM alpine
 ---> 9c6f07244728
Step 2/3 : COPY * /
 ---> 37b005627fc0
Step 3/3 : CMD ls -l /
 ---> Running in 8188378b8894
Removing intermediate container 8188378b8894
 ---> 70b49717401f
Successfully built 70b49717401f
```

First, more information was sent to the Docker daemon, thanks to the file I added to the demo directory. The base image didn't change, though, and Docker reports the same image ID, meaning it reused the contents of its cache. However, the remaining layers are all new. The contents of the demo directory are different, which changed the files copied into the image. And while the command run in the CMD instruction is identical in both images, they aren't shared because the underlying layers are different.

Running the new image produces similar, but not identical, output, reflecting changes to the build context. It's the same filesystem from the alpine image layer in both images (and containers). Adding a file to the demo directory changed the files the COPY command added to the layer created in Step 2:

```
> docker run 70b49717401f
total 64
drwxr-xr-x     2 root      root           4096 Aug  9 08:47 bin
drwxr-xr-x     5 root      root            340 Aug 25 23:16 dev
drwxr-xr-x     1 root      root           4096 Aug 25 23:16 etc
drwxr-xr-x     2 root      root           4096 Aug  9 08:47 home
drwxr-xr-x     7 root      root           4096 Aug  9 08:47 lib
drwxr-xr-x     5 root      root           4096 Aug  9 08:47 media
drwxr-xr-x     2 root      root           4096 Aug  9 08:47 mnt
drwxr-xr-x     2 root      root           4096 Aug  9 08:47 opt
-rw-r--r--     1 root      root           7868 Aug 25 19:30 passwd
dr-xr-xr-x   345 root      root              0 Aug 25 23:16 proc
drwx------     2 root      root           4096 Aug  9 08:47 root
drwxr-xr-x     2 root      root           4096 Aug  9 08:47 run
drwxr-xr-x     2 root      root           4096 Aug  9 08:47 sbin
drwxr-xr-x     2 root      root           4096 Aug  9 08:47 srv
dr-xr-xr-x    13 root      root              0 Aug 25 23:16 sys
drwxrwxrwt     2 root      root           4096 Aug  9 08:47 tmp
drwxr-xr-x     7 root      root           4096 Aug  9 08:47 usr
drwxr-xr-x    12 root      root           4096 Aug  9 08:47 var
```

No Symbolic Links or Shortcuts Allowed in the Context

In Chapter 4, you added the Oracle database installation media into a version-specific directory like $HOME/docker-images/OracleDatabase/SingleInstance/dockerfiles/19.3.0. When you ran the buildContainerImage.sh script, Docker processed the files in that directory to develop its context. Docker *didn't* read files in the neighboring directories. They're outside the build path and not useful to the build anyway—Oracle doesn't need 21c installation media for a 19c image, and vice versa. The assets aren't shared, and organizing files into separate directories makes sense.

That's true when versions are entirely different, but things get vague when dealing with minor releases. The 19.15 and 19.16 Release Updates (RU) use the same fundamental assets—installation media and OPatch—but not the patches themselves. Splitting them into versioned directories means duplicating some, but not all, of the files:

```
19c
├─── 19.15
│    ├─── LINUX.X64_193000_db_home.zip
│    ├─── p6880880_190000_Linux-x86-64.zip
│    └─── patch-for-1915-RU.zip
└─── 19.16
     ├─── LINUX.X64_193000_db_home.zip
     ├─── p6880880_190000_Linux-x86-64.zip
     └─── patch-for-1916-RU.zip
```

Each release adds more duplication, uses more space, and may even mismatch files. In the preceding directory structure, the OPatch files, beginning p6880880, have the same *name*, but that doesn't guarantee they're the *same file* or the latest version. Both directories should, ideally, use the same centrally managed file.

Could we add a link or shortcut to Docker's context and avoid duplicating the LINUX. X64_193000_db_home.zip file in two places? To test this, I added a link to the image context we've been working with and reran the same build:

```
> ln -s /etc/passwd demo/linked_file

> ls -l ./demo
total 16
lrwxr-xr-x  1 seanscott  staff     11 Aug 25 17:28 linked_file -> /
etc/passwd
-rw-r--r--  1 seanscott  staff  7868 Aug 25 13:30 passwd

> docker build -f ./Dockerfile ./demo
Sending build context to Docker daemon   10.8kB
Step 1/3 : FROM alpine
 ---> 9c6f07244728
Step 2/3 : COPY * /
COPY failed: file not found in build context or excluded by .dockerignore:
stat linked_file: file does not exist
```

Unfortunately, Docker only recognizes physical files in its context. Since linked_ file wasn't physically present in Docker's build directory, it wasn't added to the context. The COPY command understood the file existed in the directory and tried to copy it but failed when it wasn't found in its context.

Docker doesn't follow symbolic links to files stored elsewhere on the filesystem[3] to maintain consistency. When context—the media and scripts needed to produce an image—is self-contained, builds are guaranteed to generate identical results across hosts. Linking to files or directories outside the context potentially breaks that assurance. In the preceding example, not only is the file unique, it could be under a different path on another machine or may not exist at all!

That doesn't fix the problem we sought to solve—reducing file duplication. But the error message in the failed build alludes to something called .dockerignore, which, it turns out, can help us reach that goal!

Ignore Files

Before sending information to the daemon, Docker looks for a .dockerignore file in its context directory. The .dockerignore file informs the build of any files or directories to exclude and prevents builds from sending unnecessary or potentially sensitive content to the daemon. Ignored files aren't available to COPY or ADD operations because, while they may be on the filesystem, they're not in the build context sent to the Docker engine in the earliest part of the build.

.dockerignore files match files and directories by name or pattern. Numerous resources offer details pattern matching, and, rather than duplicating that information, I'll cover just the basic options:

- Lines that begin with the hash (#) denote comments and are ignored.

- The asterisk (*) matches one or more characters in a file or directory name.

- Two consecutive asterisks (**) match any number of directories in the file's path.

- A question mark (?) matches a single character.

- The exclamation point (!) creates an exception.

---

[3] Nothing prevents shortcuts or links in the context, provided they're not referenced by COPY or ADD instructions in the Dockerfile.

The paths in ignore files are evaluated relative to the *root directory of the context—* even if the path in the ignore file begins with a slash, apparently referencing an absolute path. Some examples:

```
# A comment

# Ignore the Dockerfile in the root directory of the build context:
Dockerfile

# Ignore all files in a directory called test:
test/*

# Ignore files in any directory that begins "patch", followed by a single
character:
patch?/*

# Ignore files in any directory with a suffix of ".key"
**/*.key

# Ignore files with a ".zip" suffix in any directory immediately below the
root directory:
*/*.zip

# Override the prior exclusion for files named "LINUX.X64_193000_db_
home.zip":
!*/LINUX.X64_193000_db_home.zip
```

Bear in mind that Docker reads ignore files sequentially. The last condition takes precedence. In the following example, the first rule ignores all files in the software directory. The second makes an exception for the LINUX.X64_193000_db_home.zip file. The third then ignores any file in any directory that ends in .zip, excluding LINUX.X64_193000_db_home.zip:

```
# Ignore files in the "software" directory:
software/*

# Include the "software/LINUX.X64_193000_db_home.zip" file:
!software/LINUX.X64_193000_db_home.zip

# Ignore files in any directory that end in ".zip"
**/*.zip
```

Switching the order of these rules, placing the exception for LINUX.X64_193000_db_home.zip last, allows its inclusion in the context:

```
# Ignore files in the "software" directory:
software/*
```

```
# Ignore files in any directory that end in ".zip"
**/*.zip
```

```
# Include the "software/LINUX.X64_193000_db_home.zip" file:
!software/LINUX.X64_193000_db_home.zip
```

Filtering, especially with wildcards, based on the current or expected directory contents doesn't guarantee an outcome. Rather than allowing files based on patterns, consider a least-privilege model that excludes everything and makes exceptions *only* for specific files that *should* be part of the build. The first pattern in this example excludes everything. The following lines add exceptions for file1 and file2:

```
*
!file1
!file2
```

Everything else in the build directory is omitted and unavailable to ADD or COPY commands—even those using wildcards!

There's no separate option, similar to the -f flag for naming Dockerfiles, for identifying ignore files. Docker looks for ignore files called .dockerfile in the same directory as the Dockerfile itself:

```
docker build -f Dockerfile_test .
```

Tagging Images

The build command run in the preceding sections created images, but they leave something to be desired for naming. docker images reports the image ID, but there's no human-friendly name:

```
> docker images
REPOSITORY         TAG           IMAGE ID        CREATED         SIZE
<none>             <none>        8cf63acc1f17    21 seconds ago  5.54MB
alpine             latest        9c6f07244728    2 weeks ago     5.54MB
```

This should feel normal by now—Docker seems reluctant to give things helpful or meaningful names—but in fairness, I didn't tell it how, or even whether, to name the image. Fortunately, we have remedies, naming images after the fact or during the build process, even assigning multiple names to a single image!

Repositories, Image Names, Tags, and Tagging   It's easy to confuse these terms. Image names consist of an (optional) repository namespace, an image name or repository, and an optional tag. The repository namespace, if present, is separated from the image name by a slash. The tag, if present, is separated from the image name by a colon:

`[<NAMESPACE>/]<IMAGE_NAME>[:<TAG>]`

Looking at the `oracle/database:19.3.0-ee` image used throughout the book, `oracle` is the namespace; `database` is the image name; `19.3.0-ee` is the tag, often used to distinguish different versions of an image.

The output of `docker images` combines the namespace and image name under the `REPOSITORY` column.

The terms "*image name*" and "*tag*" are frequently used interchangeably to reference the combined repository namespace, image name, and tag.

Repository, *image name*, and *tag* are nouns that identify the *source*, *name*, and *version* of images. *Tagging* is the action of *naming images*.

Add Tags to Images

Let's name this image using the docker tag command. docker tag takes two arguments—an image ID or name and a new tag. My image doesn't (yet) have a name. I need to reference it by its ID:

```
> docker tag 8cf63acc1f17 alpine-demo

> docker images
REPOSITORY        TAG       IMAGE ID       CREATED          SIZE
alpine-demo       latest    8cf63acc1f17   24 minutes ago   5.54MB
alpine            latest    9c6f07244728   2 weeks ago      5.54MB
```

After tagging the image, it appears in docker images with the new name, listed under the REPOSITORY column, and a TAG of latest. It replaced the original, unnamed entry in the image list.

I can create an additional tag for this image, this time referencing it by its new name, alpine-demo:

```
> docker tag alpine-demo alpine-new
```

```
> docker images
REPOSITORY         TAG          IMAGE ID        CREATED           SIZE
alpine-new         latest       8cf63acc1f17    26 minutes ago    5.54MB
alpine-demo        latest       8cf63acc1f17    26 minutes ago    5.54MB
alpine             latest       9c6f07244728    2 weeks ago       5.54MB
```

It added a second entry for the image with the same image ID value. Docker didn't create a new image. Tags are aliases that make it easier for humans to identify, classify, and work with images.

It may be more appropriate to give this image a *tag* that identifies its purpose or version rather than a new name. I'll tag it again, this time with the alpine name and a tag of demo:

```
> docker tag alpine-demo alpine:demo
```

```
> docker images
REPOSITORY         TAG          IMAGE ID        CREATED           SIZE
alpine-new         latest       8cf63acc1f17    27 minutes ago    5.54MB
alpine             demo         8cf63acc1f17    27 minutes ago    5.54MB
alpine-demo        latest       8cf63acc1f17    27 minutes ago    5.54MB
alpine             latest       9c6f07244728    2 weeks ago       5.54MB
```

This is rather messy—three aliases for the same image! Let's use docker rmi and clean up the duplicate images, alpine-demo, and alpine-new:

```
> docker rmi alpine-demo
Untagged: alpine-demo:latest
```

```
> docker rmi alpine-new
Untagged: alpine-new:latest
```

Notice the response from Docker. It *untagged* the images but didn't delete them. `docker images` shows a single entry for this image, using the `alpine:demo` name/tag combination:

```
> docker images
REPOSITORY        TAG        IMAGE ID       CREATED          SIZE
alpine            demo       8cf63acc1f17   29 minutes ago   5.54MB
alpine     .      latest     9c6f07244728   2 weeks ago      5.54MB
```

With only one alias remaining for this image, running `docker rmi alpine:demo` completely removes the image from the system:[4]

```
> docker rmi alpine:demo
Untagged: alpine:demo
Deleted: sha256:8cf63acc1f17c28d78ce7efac26f19f428847e895db81182ec1063e41b4246b4
Deleted: sha256:1d5ae09bcac7b79cb3dea2209118be4199b2cc91050968aca0037d
aea0a4728c
```

Tag Images During Builds

The `tag` command provides a means of naming existing images and adding aliases. It's far easier to assign names and tags during the build itself. `docker build`'s `-t` option does just that:

```
docker build ...
        -t [<NAMESPACE>/]<IMAGE_NAME>[:<TAG>]
...
```

We've seen this pattern in the images used throughout this book:

```
oracle/database:19.3.0-ee
oraclelinux:7-slim
```

---

[4] You won't be able to remove images used by any containers without adding the `-f` option to `docker rmi` or first deleting its container(s) with `docker rm`.

And in the output of the docker images command:

```
REPOSITORY        TAG        IMAGE ID       CREATED        SIZE
oracle/database   19.3.0-ee  1b588736c8c1   2 months ago   6.67GB
oraclelinux       7-slim     9ec0d85eaed0   4 months ago   133MB
```

To read an image name

- The part before the last slash[5] is the repository namespace, `oracle`. The Oracle Linux image isn't associated with a namespace.

- The image names are `database` and `oraclelinux`.

- Tags, preceded by a colon, typically represent version information that differentiates otherwise similar images, like `19.3.0-ee` and `7-slim`.

I lean heavily on tags and consistent image naming to organize and make sense of my images. As you begin building images, take a moment to consider the patterns that will work best for you or your team!

You can assign multiple tags to a single `build`:

```
docker build ...
       -t oracledb:19.15-ee \
       -t my_namespace/oracledb:19.15-ee \
...
```

This saves time in environments with local and remote repositories. The image in this example has two aliases: `oracledb:19.15-ee` and `my_namespace/oracledb:19.15-ee`. The second references a remote repository, and once the build completes, the finished image is already tagged and available to upload or *push* to the destination. Chapter 16 discusses this in detail.

---

[5] Repositories may have multiple parts to their path, like this example from a repository in the Oracle Cloud: *phx.ocir.io/ax3qrddf103e/oracle/database:19.13.1-ee*. The image name is *database*. Everything before that is the repository path.

Arguments

The section on arguments in Chapter 12 covered their implementation in Dockerfiles. As a reminder, arguments initiate variables and (optionally) set their default values:

```
ARG ORACLE_HOME=/opt/oracle/product/19c/dbhome_1
ENV ORACLE_HOME=$ORACLE_HOME
```

Use the `--build-arg` option to pass custom values to arguments during a build:

```
docker build ...
       --build-arg ORACLE_HOME=/u01/oracle/product/19.3.0/dbhome_1
       ...
```

The build process overrides the value of the `ORACLE_HOME` argument in the Dockerfile, which in turn assigns the environment value in the image.

In Chapter 12, you learned that `ARG` is the only Dockerfile command that can precede a `FROM` statement. The argument is only available to the `FROM` statement that follows and allows manipulation of the base image used by the build:

```
ARG IMAGE_NAME=oraclelinux:7-slim
FROM $IMAGE_NAME
...
```

Using `--build-arg` alters the base image used by the Dockerfile in the preceding example:

```
docker build ...
       --build-arg IMAGE_NAME=oraclelinux:7
...
```

Define multiple arguments with an individual `--build-arg` for each.

Housekeeping

Every step in a Dockerfile runs a container based on an image generated in a previous step or referenced in a `FROM` statement. It makes sense—images are immutable, after all—and the commands in Dockerfiles are essentially scripts that run a series of images as containers, make some changes, and save the result. It's visible when looking back at Listing 14-2. Notice the build process creates two intermediate containers before completing the image.

There's a saying, "To find the easiest way of doing something, ask a lazy person." In that sense, Docker is *extremely* lazy, doing everything in its power to limit the work it has to do! In the build process, that means caching layers and saving intermediate containers, just in case it *might* need them later!

I didn't realize this when I began exploring Docker and building images. As a hands-on learner who likes to experiment, I did my fair share of trial and error, making minor changes to Dockerfiles and examining the results.

Every change, every experiment, and every mistake along the way resulted in new intermediate containers that Docker helpfully cached away, just in case I needed them later.

Until one day, Docker just... stopped. My build cache grew to several gigs, consuming all the space in Docker's virtual machine! Fortunately, there are reactive and proactive solutions to this situation.

Pruning

The reactive fix is purging Docker's build cache. We can view space used in the build cache, along with other objects like images, containers, and volumes, with docker system df:

```
> docker system df
TYPE            TOTAL       ACTIVE      SIZE        RECLAIMABLE
Images          12          10          21.89GB     11.13MB (0%)
Containers      12          7           24.87GB     434.1MB (1%)
Local Volumes   6           4           853.6MB     1.53kB (0%)
Build Cache     19          0           48.38MB     48.38MB
```

You notice I have 19 objects in my build cache, using just over 48MB. Docker identified all of that space as reclaimable. Purge the space with docker builder prune:

```
> docker builder prune
WARNING! This will remove all dangling build cache. Are you sure you want
to continue? [y/N]
```

Docker asks for confirmation and reports the cache it removed from the system:

```
> docker builder prune
WARNING! This will remove all dangling build cache. Are you sure you want
to continue? [y/N] y
Deleted build cache objects:
h5x3svswlc8ju3p6kpfp3kfxq
zq3ddt7nkeurbb7dw9wh87yfv
vhxgyd4wznuu43d8petp2byqo
7xesrmsi56gium8iir4e3wdey
krhuiazatl6wovkvljxnicdyr
s6p7a4olr4ioaj8rjo0klbehr
vxc9v14ogunwqi2see58xmj35
fm2kxjek8n93c91sczhp4ld3z
wodldqvqsfgtd40s8ulo3nkb2
b1ua49rpznnz4t1wk4c16zzqr
ssz3lpns9rxxp2agb2011kvwl

Total reclaimed space: 48.38MB
```

Once completed, rerun `docker system df` and verify it reclaimed the space:

```
> docker system df
TYPE            TOTAL       ACTIVE      SIZE        RECLAIMABLE
Images          12          10          21.89GB     11.13MB (0%)
Containers      12          7           24.87GB     434.1MB (1%)
Local Volumes   6           4           853.6MB     1.53kB (0%)
Build Cache     8           0           0B          0B
```

Another command, `docker system prune`, takes a more severe approach by removing build cache, unused networks, stopped containers, and dangling images:

```
> docker system prune
WARNING! This will remove:
  - all stopped containers
  - all networks not used by at least one container
  - all dangling images
  - all dangling build cache

Are you sure you want to continue? [y/N] n
```

This is the same as running four separate commands:

```
docker container prune
docker network prune
docker image prune
docker builder prune
```

Use it with caution![6] Pruning Docker objects is irreversible!

Cache Management

If you'd rather avoid the mystery and unpleasantness of "things not working," apply an ounce of prevention to your builds and remove or bypass cache altogether with the build's cache management options: `--rm`, `--force-rm`, and `--no-cache`.

- `--rm=true` removes intermediate containers (the ones created in steps 1 and 2 in Listing 14-2) after a build succeeds. This is the default. Setting this to false may improve build performance if you frequently build images with the same or similar hierarchy, where only the final few steps are different. Allowing Docker to keep intermediate images increases the chance that subsequent, similar builds will find matching layers and bypass some work.

- `--force-rm=true` deletes intermediate containers whether or not the build succeeds. Forcing removal, even for failed images, limits troubleshooting options (as you'll see in Chapter 15).

- `--no-cache=true` prevents Docker from using (or creating) cache. Besides saving space on your system, the `--no-cache=true` option has a less obvious benefit—forcing Docker to pull the latest base image. The `--no-cache=true` option effectively causes Docker to build every image from scratch.

Including cache management in builds, alongside checks to monitor space consumption, helps keep the system healthy and trim. These settings apply fine-grained control to caching in individual build activities. For testing and troubleshooting,

---

[6] If you're absolutely sure that you want to prune a resource and prefer to skip Docker's nagging "*Are you sure?*" dialog, add the `-f` or `--force` flag.

`--rm=false` preserves build artifacts that can aid in diagnosing failures. The `--force-rm=true` or `--no-cache=true` options suit unique images that are unlikely to share content. And preventing caching altogether through `--no-cache=true` guarantees images are reading the latest versions of assets.

The downside of `--no-cache=true` is the risk of change to base images that can break a build. For instance, using `FROM centos`, without any version or tag, really means `centos:latest`.[7] The "latest" version of CentOS is a moving target, over time changing from `centos:6` to `centos:7` to `centos:8`, with stops at minor releases along the way. An image that worked when the "latest" was CentOS 7 may break by moving to CentOS 8— and this illustrates why it's always a good idea to identify specific versions for the assets you source![8]

Note   The `buildContainerImage.sh` script provided by Oracle manages cache with hard-coded values of `--force-rm=true` and `--no-cache=true`.

BuildKit

BuildKit is an advanced image builder that adds security features, better cache efficiency, and speed to existing build activities. It's been part of Docker since version 18.06. It supports builds of Linux-based container images on Windows, Mac, and Linux systems.

BuildKit is an improvement over the legacy build engine and the default builder on newer Docker releases. Verify whether it's the default in Docker Desktop environments, as in Figure 14-1, by navigating to the settings pane and confirming the following line is present:

```
"features": { "buildkit": true }
```

---

[7] I'm using CentOS as an example here because the official images publish a "latest" tag. The official Oracle Linux images don't typically provide a "latest" tag that leads to this confusion.

[8] It's easy to imagine base images are static and overlook them as the cause behind errors or changing behavior in images. Fixing the version of source images referenced in the Dockerfile's FROM clause makes troubleshooting image development easier and eliminating them as variables in the equation.

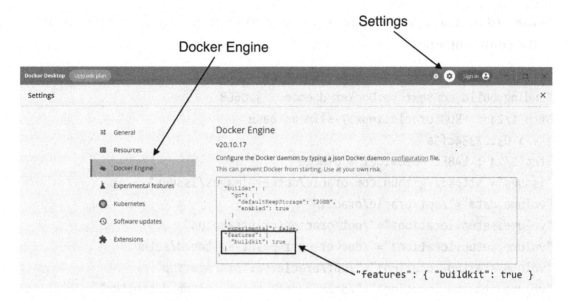

Figure 14-1. *In Docker Desktop, navigate to the Settings pane and look under the Docker Engine section for the BuildKit feature entry*

If BuildKit isn't enabled and you'd like to try it out, add the BuildKit flag, `DOCKER_BUILDKIT=1`, to the beginning of any build command:

```
DOCKER_BUILDKIT=1 docker build ...
```

Notice there's nothing between the environment setting and the `docker build` command itself in this example, and this syntax enables BuildKit only for the build in question. You can also export the value in the environment:

```
export DOCKER_BUILDKIT=1
```

Alternately, disable BuildKit by setting the `DOCKER_BUILDKIT` variable to zero.

Progress

The most noticeable difference between BuildKit and the legacy engine is the output. The default output from the legacy engine in Listing 14-3 is a continuous log of activity.

Listing 14-3. The legacy engine generates a continuous, lengthy output stream at the command line

```
Building image 'oracle/database:19.3.0-ee' ...
Sending build context to Docker daemon    3.06GB
Step 1/24 : FROM oraclelinux:7-slim as base
 ---> 03c22334cf5a
Step 2/24 : LABEL "provider"="Oracle"
"issues"="https://github.com/oracle/docker-images/issues"
"volume.data"="/opt/oracle/oradata"
"volume.setup.location1"="/opt/oracle/scripts/setup"
"volume.setup.location2"="/docker-entrypoint-initdb.d/setup"
"volume.startup.location1"="/opt/oracle/scripts/startup"
"volume.startup.location2"="/docker-entrypoint-initdb.d/startup"
"port.listener"="1521"
"port.oemexpress"="5500"
 ---> Running in 82a69d6a2ffc
Removing intermediate container 82a69d6a2ffc
 ---> d3e64e2a7cad
```

The output from BuildKit, in Listing 14-4, is more compact.

Listing 14-4. BuildKit produces more compact output during a build

```
Building image 'oracle/database:19.3.0-ee' ...
[+] Building 63.7s (7/14)
 => [internal] load build definition from Dockerfile              2.5s
 => => transferring dockerfile: 5.11kB                            0.2s
 => [internal] load .dockerignore                                4.0s
 => => transferring context: 2B                                  0.1s
 => [internal] load metadata for docker.io/library/oraclelinux:7-slim   0.0s
 => CACHED [base 1/4] FROM docker.io/library/oraclelinux:7-slim    0.0s
 => [internal] load build context                                13.5s
 => => transferring context: 3.06GB                              11.2s
 => [base 2/4] COPY setupLinuxEnv.sh checkSpace.sh /opt/install/   29.1s
```

The --progress option of docker build controls the output format.
Set --progress=plain to produce output as seen in Listing 14-3 or --progress=tty to
see results like those in Listing 14-4.

I prefer the TTY-style output of BuildKit for several reasons. First, the Oracle
database build is lengthy, and running --progress=plain sends several thousand lines
to the terminal. But it's more than just brief. Progress in the TTY method, seen in
Listing 14-5, is more granular and informative.

Listing 14-5. The complete output from building an Oracle Database 19c image
with BuildKit

```
Building image 'oracle/database:19.3.0-ee' ...
[+] Building 1045.0s (15/15) FINISHED
 => [internal] load build definition from Dockerfile      2.5s
 => => transferring dockerfile: 5.11kB                    0.2s
 => [internal] load .dockerignore                         4.0s
 => => transferring context: 2B                           0.1s
 => [internal] load metadata for docker.io/library/or     0.0s
 => CACHED [base 1/4] FROM docker.io/library/oracleli     0.0s
 => [internal] load build context                         13.5s
 => => transferring context: 3.06GB                       11.2s
 => [base 2/4] COPY setupLinuxEnv.sh checkSpace.sh /o     29.1s
 => [base 3/4] COPY runOracle.sh startDB.sh createDB.      4.2s
 => [base 4/4] RUN echo "INSTALL_DIR = /opt/install"     393.8s
 => [builder 1/2] COPY --chown=oracle:dba LINUX.X64_1     43.8s
 => [builder 2/2] RUN chmod ug+x /opt/install/*.sh &&    329.0s
 => [stage-2 1/4] COPY --chown=oracle:dba --from=buil    157.2s
 => [stage-2 2/4] RUN /opt/oracle/oraInventory/orains      9.3s
 => [stage-2 3/4] WORKDIR /home/oracle                     4.4s
 => [stage-2 4/4] RUN echo 'ORACLE_SID=${ORACLE_SID:-      2.9s
 => exporting to image                                    28.0s
 => => exporting layers                                   27.9s
 => => writing image sha256:b0be5db0705d826560d064522      0.0s
 => => naming to docker.io/oracle/database:19.3.0-ee       0.0s
```

Several things are worth noticing in the result:

- The second line shows the elapsed time, the current step, and its status.

- BuildKit counts steps in the Dockerfile differently and breaks them down by stage. The plain output in Listing 14-3 shows a total step count of 24. The TTY output reports progress separately within the base, builder, and stage-2 stages. While the step is running, the timing at the right updates continuously, showing its progress. When complete, it displays elapsed time for the action.

- While steps are active, the TTY output scrolls activity in a windowed section at the bottom of the screen.

The timings and labels for stage and step make it clear where builds spend their time. It's a bit like an AWR report for a Docker build! If I wanted to speed up this build, I'd look at step 4 in the *base* stage, step 2 in the *builder* stage, and perhaps step 1 of *stage-2*.[9]

Ignore Files

We discussed separating context earlier, exploring a directory structure for building similar images:

```
19c
├── 19.15
│   ├── Dockerfile
│   ├── LINUX.X64_193000_db_home.zip
│   ├── p6880880_190000_Linux-x86-64.zip
│   └── patch-for-1915-RU.zip
└── 19.16
    ├── Dockerfile
    ├── LINUX.X64_193000_db_home.zip
    ├── p6880880_190000_Linux-x86-64.zip
    └── patch-for-1916-RU.zip
```

---

[9] In step 1 of stage-2, Docker copies directories from the image created in the builder stage. As an OS operation, I can't easily improve it short of moving to faster storage. However, I could look at the size and contents copied in this step and either limit what's being copied or reduce the size at the source, created in earlier stages.

The first two files in each subdirectory are identical. Docker doesn't allow links or aliases in the build context, and it appeared there was no good solution that prevented duplicating the files other than putting them all in one directory:

```
19c
├── Dockerfile
├── LINUX.X64_193000_db_home.zip
├── p6880880_190000_Linux-x86-64.zip
├── patch-for-1915-RU.zip
└── patch-for-1916-RU.zip
```

Now we have a single copy of the software media and OPatch files, but left wondering which version the Dockerfile belongs to! Fortunately, you learned earlier that we could specify custom Dockerfiles with the -f option, meaning we can write different Dockerfile recipes for each database version:

```
19c
├── Dockerfile.19.15
├── Dockerfile.19.16
├── LINUX.X64_193000_db_home.zip
├── p6880880_190000_Linux-x86-64.zip
├── patch-for-1915-RU.zip
└── patch-for-1916-RU.zip
```

Then, build either version by calling the appropriate Dockerfile:

```
docker build -f Dockerfile.19.15 .
docker build -f Dockerfile.19.16 .
```

This eliminates duplicate files, but now both patch files are in context. When building a database patched with the 19.15 version, docker build reads *both* the 19.15 *and* 19.16 patches. That might not matter if there are just a few small patches, but in reality, we're more likely to encounter growing numbers of patches added during Oracle's quarterly updates.

An ignore file could solve this, telling the build to ignore all but the desired patch:

```
# Ignore all files:
*
```

```
# Add an exception for LINUX.X64_193000_db_home.zip:
!LINUX.X64_193000_db_home.zip

# Add an exception for p6880880_190000_Linux-x86-64.zip p:
!p6880880_190000_Linux-x86-64.zip

# Add an exception for the 19.15 patch:
!patch-for-1915-RU.zip
```

The ignore file limits Docker's context to the three files used for building a version 19.15 database. However, it breaks builds for version 19.16! docker build has no facility for referencing a custom ignore file, only the default, .dockerignore.

BuildKit solves this. Rather than introducing a switch for picking an ignore file, it adds support for custom ignore files with names derived from custom Dockerfiles.

Typically, the build looks for a file named .dockerignore in the same directory as the Dockerfile. When BuildKit features are enabled, it first looks for an ignore file with the same name as the Dockerfile, suffixed by ".dockerignore." If it doesn't find a custom ignore file, it searches next for a file with the default name.

Now, each Dockerfile version can have its own ignore file:

```
19c
├── Dockerfile.19.15
├── Dockerfile.19.15.dockerignore
├── Dockerfile.19.16
├── Dockerfile.19.16.dockerignore
├── LINUX.X64_193000_db_home.zip
├── p6880880_190000_Linux-x86-64.zip
├── patch-for-1915-RU.zip
└── patch-for-1916-RU.zip
```

Custom ignore files, tied to version-specific Dockerfiles, address the build context problem created by consolidating duplicate or common files into a single directory!

BuildKit Syntax

Certain BuildKit features must be enabled at the top of the Dockerfile as a comment identifying the frontend builder version. For instance:

```
# syntax=docker/dockerfile:1.4
```

Syntax directives enable new build features and bug fixes without requiring an update of the Docker daemon and allow users to test experimental features. These typically enable advanced components. If BuildKit isn't enabled, the syntax directive behind the comment is simply ignored.

Summary

Images, and the automation they contain, might seem mysterious or even magical at first. After pulling back the curtain, it's clear that there's nothing unusual or special going on, just shell scripts and ordinary Linux commands!

You can build images and assign names with your new understanding of Docker's build syntax. You've seen the similarities between build arguments in images and environment variables in containers and learned how to extend Dockerfiles by dynamically adding functionality and flexibility with build arguments.

We discussed features for gaining control over the build cache and tools for viewing and managing the artifacts left behind during builds. As your container use grows, I promise the purge commands we covered will prove their worth!

One of the challenges I've encountered while building database images is managing the source files—the database installation media and patches needed for each version. Preventing duplicates and tracking file versions is easier with files centrally located in a single, dedicated inventory. Saving space by condensing everything into one location comes with a cost, and every file contributes to the potential build context. Employing named Dockerfiles, alongside custom ignore files enabled through BuildKit, avoids any need to sacrifice context against control.

With this knowledge, building images should feel less intimidating, and I hope you'll consider stitching together a few of your own! Like anything, there's a learning curve, but don't let that stop you! While you're sure to encounter some bumps along the way, I've shared some of the troubleshooting and debugging techniques I've found helpful when working with images and containers in the next chapter!

CHAPTER 15

Debugging and Troubleshooting

"New" and "different" are often intimidating and scary. We're forced to learn or invent new approaches to familiar or comfortable tasks and perhaps even alter our perceptions and understanding. Tried and true is stable, even secure.

Yet everything we do, especially in IT, was once new and different. I started on Oracle 7, long before the days of RMAN, Real Application Clusters, or Data Guard. The cloud? Not a thing. Exadata was still a dream. Today, I take them for granted as part of my day-to-day work with Oracle, but I had to learn my way around each technology at some point.

Docker is no different. When I started working with containers, I didn't fully grasp the relationship between images and containers or realize that builds were a series of "run an image in a container, do something, save the result as an image, repeat" operations. Understanding that made it easier to see how and where to troubleshoot the process.

I read an article recently by a new developer who said the second worst part of their job was not understanding why code didn't work. (The worst? Not understanding why their code *did* work!) This chapter discusses approaches and recipes to help navigate the new and different world of containers! I'll cover ways of extracting information from failing images and containers that lead to understanding what happened, why it happened, and how to fix it!

Most of this isn't new in its own right—echoing variables from scripts goes back decades, at least. But how these methods are applied and work in containers isn't always obvious or intuitive.

© Sean Scott 2023
S. Scott, *Oracle on Docker*, https://doi.org/10.1007/978-1-4842-9033-0_15

View and Manipulate Output

If you've built an Oracle Database using the buildContainerImage.sh script, you've probably seen output like that in Listings 15-1 and 15-2 displayed on your screen.

Listing 15-1. A portion of the output generated while building an Oracle database image. Note the ID values identified with "--->," the step tracking, and the list of commands executed in each step

```
 ---> f33a827c1bc8
Step 6/24 : ENV PATH=$ORACLE_HOME/bin:$ORACLE_HOME/OPatch/:/
usr/sbin:$PATH     LD_LIBRARY_PATH=$ORACLE_HOME/lib:/usr/
lib     CLASSPATH=$ORACLE_HOME/jlib:$ORACLE_HOME/rdbms/jlib
 ---> Running in d64a3700b791
Removing intermediate container d64a3700b791
 ---> bb272db209e2
Step 7/24 : COPY $SETUP_LINUX_FILE $CHECK_SPACE_FILE $INSTALL_DIR/
 ---> 18dc49d4a53b
Step 8/24 : COPY $RUN_FILE $START_FILE $CREATE_DB_FILE $CREATE_OBSERVER_
FILE $CONFIG_RSP $PWD_FILE $CHECK_DB_FILE $USER_SCRIPTS_FILE $RELINK_
BINARY_FILE $CONFIG_TCPS_FILE $ORACLE_BASE/
 ---> 183467ad6373
Step 9/24 : RUN chmod ug+x $INSTALL_DIR/*.sh &&     sync &&     $INSTALL_
DIR/$CHECK_SPACE_FILE &&     $INSTALL_DIR/$SETUP_LINUX_FILE &&     rm -rf
$INSTALL_DIR
 ---> Running in 5367f8d86861
```

Listing 15-2. Part of an image build for an Oracle 19c database, showing part of the database software installation step

```
Launching Oracle Database Setup Wizard...

[WARNING] [INS-32055] The Central Inventory is located in the Oracle base.
   ACTION: Oracle recommends placing this Central Inventory in a location
   outside the Oracle base directory.
[WARNING] [INS-13014] Target environment does not meet some optional
requirements.
```

CAUSE: Some of the optional prerequisites are not met. See logs for details. installActions2022-09-24_10-13-19PM.log
ACTION: Identify the list of failed prerequisite checks from the log: in stallActions2022-09-24_10-13-19PM.log. Then either from the log file or from installation manual find the appropriate configuration to meet the prerequisites and fix it manually.

The response file for this session can be found at:
 /opt/oracle/product/19c/dbhome_1/install/response/
db_2022-09-24_10-13-19PM.rsp

You can find the log of this install session at:
 /tmp/InstallActions2022-09-24_10-13-19PM/installActions2022-09-24_10-
13-19PM.log

As a root user, execute the following script(s):
    1. /opt/oracle/oraInventory/orainstRoot.sh
    2. /opt/oracle/product/19c/dbhome_1/root.sh

Execute /opt/oracle/oraInventory/orainstRoot.sh on the following nodes:
[331db970408a]
Execute /opt/oracle/product/19c/dbhome_1/root.sh on the following nodes:
[331db970408a]
Removing intermediate container 331db970408a

This *progress output* from the build should be the first place to look for clues in identifying the cause of failures. There's nothing special about this output, and it's no different than what you'd see by manually executing the commands. That allows us to employ techniques similar to those we'd use in a "normal" system.

If the log output doesn't show anything obvious, the next step is adding output to report the information and details needed to diagnose the situation.

Echo Information

Step 9, shown in Listing 15-1, runs a series of commands:

```
RUN chmod ug+x $INSTALL_DIR/*.sh &&       sync &&       $INSTALL_DIR/$CHECK_
SPACE_FILE &&       $INSTALL_DIR/$SETUP_LINUX_FILE &&       rm -rf $INSTALL_DIR
```

These correspond to a RUN block in the Dockerfile:

```
RUN chmod ug+x $INSTALL_DIR/*.sh && \
    sync && \
    $INSTALL_DIR/$INSTALL_DB_BINARIES_FILE $DB_EDITION
```

If one or more variables from this block were set incorrectly, I'd have no way of knowing by looking at the output. Everything references environment variables. But, I can add commands to this block of code and display the variable settings in the build output:

```
RUN echo "INSTALL_DIR = $INSTALL_DIR" && \
    echo "INSTALL_DB_BINARIES_FILE = $INSTALL_DB_BINARIES_FILE" && \
    echo "DB_EDITION = $DB_EDITION" && \
    chmod ug+x $INSTALL_DIR/*.sh && \
    sync && \
    $INSTALL_DIR/$INSTALL_DB_BINARIES_FILE $DB_EDITION
```

When I rerun the build, I'll see the values printed to the build output:

```
Step 9/24 : RUN echo "INSTALL_DIR = $INSTALL_DIR" && echo "INSTALL_DB_
BINARIES_FILE = $INSTALL_DB_BINARIES_FILE" && echo "DB_EDITION = $DB_
EDITION" && chmod ug+x $INSTALL_DIR/*.sh && sync && $INSTALL_DIR/$CHECK_
SPACE_FILE && $INSTALL_DIR/$SETUP_LINUX_FILE && rm -rf $INSTALL_DIR
 ---> Running in e5331bac34fc
INSTALL_DIR = /opt/install
INSTALL_DB_BINARIES_FILE = installDBBinaries.sh
DB_EDITION =
```

Be aware that the position of diagnostic checks may affect results. In this example, I echoed the values as part of an existing step in the Dockerfile. Had I added them to a separate RUN block, either before or after, they would run in their own container. The values might not reflect their settings during the step in question.

Echoing values isn't limited to the Dockerfile. The scripts Docker uses to complete each build task interact with the process output, as in Listing 15-2, and the same techniques apply.

Add a Debug Option

Calling bash scripts with `bash -x` enables debugging output that prints the commands and arguments executed within the script. If you experienced problems during step 9 in the last example and wanted to see details of everything the database binary installation did, you could modify the Dockerfile to

```
RUN chmod ug+x $INSTALL_DIR/*.sh && \
    sync && \
    bash -x $INSTALL_DIR/$INSTALL_DB_BINARIES_FILE $DB_EDITION
```

Adding `bash -x` before the script execution on the last line adds visibility into the script's actions without changing the result. The downside comes in the effort required to add and remove debugging commands in the Dockerfile. But, with the help of our friend, ARG, that's not a problem!

Add a new, empty argument called DEBUG at the top of the Dockerfile:

```
ARG DEBUG=
```

Then prefix each script executed in the Dockerfile with $DEBUG:

```
RUN chmod ug+x $INSTALL_DIR/*.sh && \
    sync && \
    $DEBUG $INSTALL_DIR/$INSTALL_DB_BINARIES_FILE $DB_EDITION
```

Any regular call to `docker build` harmlessly substitutes the empty DEBUG argument before the script execution. However, passing a value to the argument turns on debugging:

```
docker build ...
        --build-arg DEBUG="bash -x" \
...
```

This trick has an additional application for debugging containers, too. Remember that containers perform services defined by scripts, and with our database containers, the root of these activities is `runOracle.sh`. As you discovered in Chapter 6, `runOracle.sh` calls other scripts to perform functions like starting and creating databases. Modifying these calls with a similar $DEBUG variable adds runtime debugging to containers, as in Listing 15-3.

Listing 15-3. Adding a $DEBUG option to the individual script executions, such as this call to the database startup script, enables runtime debugging in containers through an environment variable

```
# Start database
$DEBUG "$ORACLE_BASE"/"$START_FILE";
```

In this case, the DEBUG variable isn't an argument interpreted during the build. It's part of the script copied into the image. The DEBUG variable is visible in the container and, left undefined, is empty. As before, it adds nothing to the script nor alters the container's behavior or function. Defining a value for the environment variable as part of the docker run command activates debugging:

```
docker run ...
        -e DEBUG="bash -x" \
...
```

Do not implement built-in debugging like this in production images—it's command injection, plain and simple—but including it in development images has saved me countless hours. There's no need to update the Dockerfile or scripts or to rebuild images with debugging included if it's already there!

View Container Logs

When containers fail, it's generally during the startup phase, caused by errors in automation scripts. For databases, the events most likely to fail are database creation in new containers and database startup on existing ones. Error messages are nearly always visible in the container logs.

To check the logs from a container, run

```
docker logs <CONTAINER NAME>
```

This dumps the entire content of the log to the command line, and it may be easier to read by piping the command output into a file reader like less or more, also adding search capabilities:

```
docker logs <CONTAINER NAME> | less
```

The logs are available in Docker whether the container is running or not, and since most errors occur shortly after startup, there's a good chance you'll spot trouble in the opening lines!

Override Container Startup

Just because an image builds successfully doesn't mean it works. When containers fail or misbehave, the root cause is in the image. Fixing those problems ultimately means rebuilding the image after integrating the necessary fixes. How and where you identify, develop, and test those fixes matters. If you can't try and test things in a container, your only course is updating the Dockerfile and its automation, then rebuilding the image. That's a potentially time-consuming cycle.

It may feel like you've hit a dead end when containers fail on startup. Is there any option if you can't log in and the container won't run? Absolutely!

The following techniques alter container behavior during startup. They're not methods for diagnosing problems with the build process per se, but they can help get failing images up and running long enough to discover what's broken!

Through most of this book, I've shown you how to run containers using the -d flag, creating them as detached processes in the background:

```
docker run -d ...
```

You might think of this as running a database service or daemon in the background—the container starts and prepares to service client requests. What runs—and, in turn, provides the service—is defined by the CMD instruction in the Dockerfile.

docker run reads the image metadata and kicks off that command in the container. If the command fails, the container typically stops because it couldn't perform the actions necessary to sustain its service. As a user, you'll usually only see the container name reported at the command prompt after it starts, with no indication it's failed. It isn't until something attempts to *consume* the container's services that you begin to see something isn't right!

If the container status displayed by docker ps -a reports a nonzero exit code, it's unlikely to respond favorably to docker start, either. Running containers as detached processes invokes the startup command, but you can bypass this behavior by passing a different command—like a shell—to the container in interactive mode:

```
docker run -it oracle/database:19.3.0-ee bash
```

This looks like connecting to a container with docker exec, using the image name instead of the container name. Giving the container something different to do short-circuits the startup process. Even after several minutes, no database processes are running in the container:

```
> docker run -it oracle/database:19.3.0-ee bash
bash-4.2$ ps -ef | grep oracle
oracle         1       0  0 21:07 pts/0     00:00:00 bash
oracle       132       1  0 21:12 pts/0     00:00:00 ps -ef
oracle       133       1  0 21:12 pts/0     00:00:00 grep oracle
```

Checking the container logs in a separate session shows only the commands I ran at the command prompt!

```
> docker logs -f adoring_colden
bash-4.2$ ps -ef | grep oracle
oracle         1       0  0 21:07 pts/0     00:00:00 bash
oracle       132       1  0 21:12 pts/0     00:00:00 ps -ef
oracle       133       1  0 21:12 pts/0     00:00:00 grep oracle
```

With a running container, I'm positioned to query the environment, run scripts, and even step through the failing startup commands.

The container in this example is tied to my session, and when I exit, the container stops. However, the commands usually called at startup are replaced by bash. Every future docker start follows suit, starting bash in the container. From this point, I can stop and start the container, and while it doesn't *do* what's expected, I can duplicate the failure by running the "normal" startup command!

Intermediate Containers

Every step in a build consists of running a container, doing some work, then saving the container as an image to use in a subsequent step. A single image may have dozens of steps, each building upon the last and contributing to the outcome. It also means multiple layers can contribute to a problem, making it less intuitive to find what's broken.

Some problems are best addressed by building an image partially, up to the point of failure, then running it as a container and stepping through the automation scripts manually. Every intermediate image generated during a build is a target for work defined in the Dockerfile.

If Docker can run these images, so can we—the only trick is identifying the right image to run! With visibility of the system state and logs at each point and an inventory of commands to run, we can apply and test changes manually in the intermediate containers under the same conditions Docker experiences during a build.

Build to a Target

One avenue for reaching this "partial" state is trimming the Dockerfile down by commenting or removing lines. There's a more straightforward, built-in option for multistage builds: the --target option. Targeting a named stage in a Dockerfile halts the build on completion of the stage:

```
docker build ...
      --target stage-name \
...
```

In the following Dockerfile, I removed everything but the FROM statements, highlighting its three stages: base, builder, and a final, unnamed stage:

```
FROM oraclelinux:7-slim as base
<snip>

FROM base AS builder
<snip>

FROM base
<snip>
```

With --target, I can tell Docker to build through the builder stage, stopping before performing the final stage:

```
docker build \
      --target builder \
      -t builder-stage \
      -f Dockerfile .
```

Tagging the image with a new name, `builder-stage`, identifies the image. After the build completes, run the image interactively, starting a bash shell:

```
docker run -it builder-stage bash
```

The image is incomplete without a startup command, so we need an approach similar to that used to override the default operations in a container, namely, giving the container a command to run. Here, I ran the container with the `-it` flags, which started an interactive session and opened a bash shell.

Run Cached Layers

I can apply a similar approach to layers in Docker's build cache—assuming they're still there! The `buildContainerImage.sh` script builds images using the `--force-rm=true` and `--no-cache=true` options. The `--force-rm=true` switch removes intermediate images, even if the build fails, so intermediate images aren't available until the option is changed in the script:[1]

```
"${CONTAINER_RUNTIME}" build --force-rm=false --no-cache=false \
      "${BUILD_OPTS[@]}" "${PROXY_SETTINGS[@]}" --build-arg DB_
      EDITION=${EDITION} \
      -t "${IMAGE_NAME}" -f "${DOCKERFILE}" . || {
  echo ""
  echo "ERROR: Oracle Database container image was NOT successfully
  created."
  echo "ERROR: Check the output and correct any reported problems with the
  build operation."
  exit 1
}
```

Comment the `prune` instruction appearing just after the build command, too:

```
# Remove dangling images (intermitten images with tag <none>)
#yes | "${CONTAINER_RUNTIME}" image prune > /dev/null
```

---

[1] Don't delete these flags and leave build as the last thing on the line. The Docker CLI expects something to follow build, before the backslash continuation character. With nothing there, the build will fail with unable to prepare context: path " " not found.

With these changes in place, progress reported from the build, shown in Listing 15-4, appears slightly different from that seen earlier, under Listing 15-1. The "*Removing intermediate container*" messages are gone, replaced by "*Using cache.*"

Listing 15-4. A portion of the build output after disabling cache management in the buildContainerImage.sh script

```
Step 6/24 : ENV PATH=$ORACLE_HOME/bin:$ORACLE_HOME/OPatch/:/
usr/sbin:$PATH      LD_LIBRARY_PATH=$ORACLE_HOME/lib:/usr/
lib      CLASSPATH=$ORACLE_HOME/jlib:$ORACLE_HOME/rdbms/jlib
 ---> Using cache
 ---> 2d1f2466fe4f
Step 7/24 : COPY $SETUP_LINUX_FILE $CHECK_SPACE_FILE $INSTALL_DIR/
 ---> Using cache
 ---> 2e6a13841ca5
Step 8/24 : COPY $RUN_FILE $START_FILE $CREATE_DB_FILE $CREATE_OBSERVER_
FILE $CONFIG_RSP $PWD_FILE $CHECK_DB_FILE $USER_SCRIPTS_FILE $RELINK_
BINARY_FILE $CONFIG_TCPS_FILE $ORACLE_BASE/
 ---> Using cache
 ---> bd581e634499
Step 9/24 : RUN echo "INSTALL_DIR = $INSTALL_DIR" &&      echo "INSTALL_DB_
BINARIES_FILE = $INSTALL_DB_BINARIES_FILE" &&      echo "DB_EDITION = $DB_
EDITION" &&      chmod ug+x $INSTALL_DIR/*.sh &&      sync &&      $INSTALL_
DIR/$CHECK_SPACE_FILE &&      $INSTALL_DIR/$SETUP_LINUX_FILE &&      rm -rf
$INSTALL_DIR
 ---> Running in 3ea3d1739ebb
```

The ID values of each image processed in the build are visible in the output. Under BuildKit and builds using --progress=tty, the image IDs aren't printed. In these cases, or if the original build output isn't available, the intermediate images are still available in the image's history:

```
> docker history oracle/database:19.3.0-ee
IMAGE           CREATED         CREATED BY                         SIZE
      COMMENT
bdbb8b83217b    3 minutes ago   /bin/sh -c #(nop)  CMD ["/bin/sh" "-c"
"exec...    0B
```

```
fa9ccf999db3    3 minutes ago     /bin/sh -c #(nop)  HEALTHCHECK &{["CMD-
SHELL...    0B
a6382dfde8a3    3 minutes ago     /bin/sh -c echo 'ORACLE_SID=${ORACLE_SID:-
OR...    69B
8b9a86303988    3 minutes ago     /bin/sh -c #(nop) WORKDIR /home/
oracle          0B
2a63bb2ba0e2    3 minutes ago     /bin/sh -c #(nop)  USER
oracle                   0B
3dc4a02582f5    3 minutes ago     /bin/sh -c $ORACLE_BASE/oraInventory/
orainst...    21.8MB
b8ad822c9f7b    3 minutes ago     /bin/sh -c #(nop)  USER
root                    0B
a51c124a4630    4 minutes ago     /bin/sh -c #(nop) COPY
--chown=oracle:dbadir...    6.19GB
80165c9dd6e6    6 minutes ago     /bin/sh -c #(nop)  USER
oracle                  0B
7df11e1c33c2    13 minutes ago    /bin/sh -c echo "INSTALL_DIR = $INSTALL_
DIR"...    332MB
bd581e634499    5 weeks ago       /bin/sh -c #(nop) COPY
multi:267aa3de5580180...    43kB
2e6a13841ca5    5 weeks ago       /bin/sh -c #(nop) COPY
multi:08c35eebd2349e6...    1.96kB
2d1f2466fe4f    5 weeks ago       /bin/sh -c #(nop)  ENV PATH=/opt/oracle/
prod...    0B
6f7b027f7ba1    5 weeks ago       /bin/sh -c #(nop)  ENV ORACLE_BASE=/opt/
orac...    0B
bfa620b5677f    5 weeks ago       /bin/sh -c #(nop)  ARG INSTALL_
FILE_1=LINUX....    0B
6fbdf293ec56    5 weeks ago       /bin/sh -c #(nop)  ARG
SLIMMING=true             0B
e930d325050c    5 weeks ago       /bin/sh -c #(nop)  LABEL provider=Oracle
iss...    0B
03c22334cf5a    2 years ago       /bin/sh -c #(nop)  CMD ["/bin/
bash"]              0B
```

```
<missing>      2 years ago        /bin/sh -c #(nop) ADD
file:0846801b1ef59a751...    131MB
<missing>      2 years ago        /bin/sh -c #(nop)  LABEL org.
opencontainers....   0B
```

The output of docker image history shows the latest operations first and identifies the images where each command ran. Now, examine a step by running the associated image and supplying a command, like bash, to execute:

```
docker run --name test -it 3dc4a02582f5 bash
```

You can also run intermediate images in the background, using the -d flag:

```
docker run --name test -d 3dc4a02582f5 bash
```

When running intermediate images, it's critical to remember the image won't have a built-in instruction. Without supplying something for the container to do, like open a shell, it exits immediately!

After starting intermediate images as containers, they behave just like the "regular" images we've worked with throughout the book. The same commands used to manage and connect still work. For the two examples earlier, you can open a bash terminal using docker exec:

```
docker exec -it test bash
```

There's usually no need to add environment variables, assign a network, or map ports while troubleshooting processes in intermediate images. However, you might consider mapping a bound volume.

Access Container Files

Let's assume you've written a Dockerfile and used it to build an image. When you ran the image, something went wrong. You followed some of the recommendations in this chapter, allowing you to start a container and change some scripts. How do you access the changed files from the container?

You could copy and paste the file contents from the container's shell into a file on the local host. I can't count how many times I've done this, and it's a perfectly reasonable solution up to a point.

For larger files where copy and paste aren't practical, use Docker's copy utility, `docker cp`. It takes two arguments, copying from the first (source) to the second (destination). Identify the location in the container by prefixing the container name, followed by a colon:

```
docker cp my_container:/source_path/filename /destination_path/
```

This copies `/source_path/filename` from container "my_container" to `/destination_path` on the host.

Unfortunately, `docker cp` won't process wildcards:

```
> docker cp ORCL:/home/oracle/* $HOME/
Error: No such container:path: ORCL:/home/oracle/*
```

Nor does it copy directory contents. Copying a few files is viable, but dozens could get tedious!

Managing multiple files during troubleshooting is best addressed with attached volumes. I suggest mapping a bind volume to a nonexistent mount point in the container and associating it to a directory on the local host:

```
docker run -it \
        -v $HOME:/debug \
        3dc4a02582f5 bash
```

This has uses for sharing files *into* the container, too. Most database administrators have a collection of diagnostic scripts they're comfortable using. You'll do yourself a favor by anticipating the need and making them available in the container environment!

Summary

When I was younger, I discovered a love of mathematics and logic. I remember stumbling on a book of logic puzzles at my library, *Aha! Insight*, by *Scientific American* columnist Martin Gardner. Every problem seemed to fall one piece short of having enough information to solve the paradox. Often, though, it turned out he gave too much data by including a red herring—some "fact" or random number—that I'd stew over until realizing (sometimes only after skimming the answers in the back) it was a distraction! Most of the puzzles had simple, elegant solutions that led to "Aha! Insight!" moments!

I see the same patterns in troubleshooting and debugging code. All too often, a simple answer hides among meaningless information that confuses and clutters the scene. The trick is understanding how to extract data from systems and where to focus the search for solutions.

The most obvious starting point is logs. In image builds, Docker relays script output and messages to the console, and in this chapter, you learned strategies for adding supplemental debugging information to existing output. Perhaps my favorite method, adding DEBUG arguments before script calls, has saved me hours. Just remember that it's a potential attack vector and not something to use in production code!

You also discovered ways of circumventing container startup failures by bypassing initialization and starting them at a shell prompt. Then, you can step through the automation code and (hopefully) find and fix whatever's interfering with the container's operations. The same technique, applied to intermediate images, is valuable for identifying hiccups in builds.

With these approaches added to your toolkit, you're fully prepared to confidently build and troubleshoot container images and reach your "Aha! Insight!" moment as quickly and painlessly as possible!

## CHAPTER 16

Docker Hub and Image Repositories

Docker is an Infrastructure as Code tool, or IaC. Dockerfiles are the code, a set of instructions that direct Docker through the steps of creating (or recreating) images. Since Docker is platform agnostic, the same Dockerfile generates identical images on Windows, Mac, and Linux, on private machines, or in the cloud!

There's a caveat, though. You've seen how the arguments in Dockerfiles add flexibility and variety to builds. I maintain a repository with a single Dockerfile capable of building versions of Oracle from 11g through 21c and applying one or more patches to the final image. On its own, a Dockerfile is merely a template, and just as a Word template provides a foundation for new documents, the thought and content poured into each file makes it unique. And so it is with Dockerfiles. The supporting scripts and resources make a difference in the outcome.

Database images depend heavily on third-party content—the database installation files and patches. It makes little sense for database administrators to tell developers, "Download files from Oracle, put them in the right directories, and build your image with this Dockerfile according to some instructions." It's faster than filling individual requests for database images but lacks guarantees that everyone's working with the same image.

Image repositories address this precise need. Authors run a build and produce an asset—the image—which they then "push" to a central image repository. Anyone with access to the repository can "pull" specific images, ready to use according to need. Without realizing it, you've been using a repository called *Docker Hub* for the exercises in this book when calling `docker run ... alpine` or writing and building Dockerfiles with `FROM` clauses referencing existing image content like Oracle Linux.

The primary focus of this chapter is Docker Hub, but other vendors offer similar container registries for personal and enterprise use. Individuals and organizations can turn to container registry services from cloud vendors, like *Oracle Cloud Infrastructure*, or OCI, to manage and host their content.

© Sean Scott 2023
S. Scott, *Oracle on Docker*, https://doi.org/10.1007/978-1-4842-9033-0_16

Docker Hub

I mentioned you've been using Docker Hub this whole time. Even without signing in or registering an account, the nearly ten million images stored in Docker Hub are available to users! Navigate to *https://hub.docker.com*, seen in Figure 16-1, and click the "Explore" link in the upper right.

Figure 16-1. *Click the "Explore" link from the Docker Hub home page to browse repository images*

The registry explorer, shown in Figure 16-2, lists all public images and includes filtering functions on the left-hand side for narrowing the scope of the content. Notice that the "Trusted Content" section has options for Docker Official Images, Verified Publishers, and Sponsored OSS.

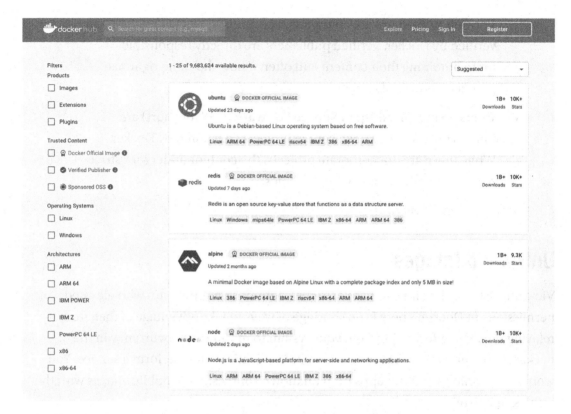

Figure 16-2. *The main screen from Docker Hub's image repository search. Note the filter options at the left, particularly those for selecting only "Trusted Content"*

Trusted Content

Docker Hub is a bit of a free for all! Registered users can upload and share most anything, including malicious content! Bad actors will take advantage of any opportunity to compromise unsuspecting users. Docker marks content as "Trusted" to assure those image authors are reputable and their images free of malware. There are levels of "trust":

- **Docker Official Images** are standard solutions that make developing and deploying software easier. They're typically the most popular images, scanned for vulnerabilities, maintained by trusted organizations actively engaged in open source software development, and vetted by the large community of users that consume the content.

- **Verified Publishers** are commercial partners in Docker's ecosystem verified by Docker. Verified publishers are directly responsible for maintaining their content and often follow the same rigorous practices as official images.[1]

- **Docker Sponsored Open Source Software** (OSS for short) are images published by open source projects sponsored by Docker. While these are not corporate projects, the content undergoes strict review for malware and vulnerabilities.

And then, there's everything else.

Untrusted Images

View untrusted public images with extreme caution. Containers run with elevated permissions in Docker. There is no shortage of ways to take advantage of that, from relaying sensitive information from your system to mining cryptocurrency in the background. Remember that images are like applications that perform a service. You wouldn't download and run apps from unknown sources. Treat public images with the same skepticism!

That's not to say every image is intentionally malicious! Docker partners with several third parties, including Snyk (*www.snyk.io*), that offer scanning services (and even remediation). Scanned images display a summary of any identified vulnerabilities. Figure 16-3 shows an example of vulnerabilities identified by scanning an Oracle 11.2.0.4 database image. Figure 16-4 displays a detailed list of each problem and its associated Common Vulnerability and Exposure, or CVE note.

---

[1] Docker Hub once included verified images for Oracle database products. Oracle stopped updating the content and instead maintains images in the Oracle Container Registry.

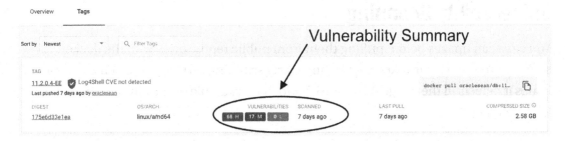

Figure 16-3. *Image summary (from a private repository) for an Oracle 11.2.0.4 Enterprise Edition image. Scanning is an optional feature authors can request when uploading images to Docker Hub. Here, the image shows when it was last scanned and a summary of the high, medium, and low severity vulnerabilities present in the image*

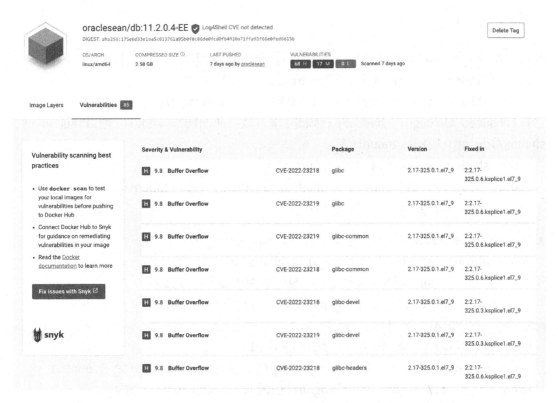

Figure 16-4. *The Snyk scan result for an Oracle 11.2.0.4 Enterprise Edition image. It shows a detailed list of the vulnerability and severity score, the CVE note detailing the problem, the source package and version, and the package version that fixed the issue*

361

Vulnerability Scanning

You can scan images before pulling them from public repositories with the docker scan command. This invokes Snyk's third-party scanning service and produces a list of issues it detects in the image. Listing 16-1 shows an example of running a scan on the Ubuntu image.

Listing 16-1. Abbreviated output from a Snyk scan of an Ubuntu image, showing low and medium severity vulnerabilities

```
> docker scan ubuntu
Docker Scan relies upon access to Snyk, a third party provider, do you
consent to proceed using Snyk? (y/N)
y

Testing ubuntu...

X Low severity vulnerability found in shadow/passwd
  Description: Time-of-check Time-of-use (TOCTOU)
  Info: https://snyk.io/vuln/SNYK-UBUNTU2204-SHADOW-2801886
  Introduced through: shadow/passwd@1:4.8.1-2ubuntu2, adduser@3.118ubuntu5,
shadow/login@1:4.8.1-2ubuntu2
  From: shadow/passwd@1:4.8.1-2ubuntu2
  From: adduser@3.118ubuntu5 > shadow/passwd@1:4.8.1-2ubuntu2
  From: shadow/login@1:4.8.1-2ubuntu2

X Low severity vulnerability found in gmp/libgmp10
  Description: Integer Overflow or Wraparound
  Info: https://snyk.io/vuln/SNYK-UBUNTU2204-GMP-2775169
  Introduced through: gmp/libgmp10@2:6.2.1+dfsg-3ubuntu1,
coreutils@8.32-4.1ubuntu1, apt@2.4.7
  From: gmp/libgmp10@2:6.2.1+dfsg-3ubuntu1
  From: coreutils@8.32-4.1ubuntu1 > gmp/libgmp10@2:6.2.1+dfsg-3ubuntu1
  From: apt@2.4.7 > gnutls28/libgnutls30@3.7.3-4ubuntu1.1 > gmp/
libgmp10@2:6.2.1+dfsg-3ubuntu1
  and 1 more...
```

```
X Medium severity vulnerability found in zlib/zlib1g
  Description: Out-of-bounds Write
  Info: https://snyk.io/vuln/SNYK-UBUNTU2204-ZLIB-2975633
  Introduced through: meta-common-packages@meta
  From: meta-common-packages@meta > zlib/zlib1g@1:1.2.11.dfsg-2ubuntu9

X Medium severity vulnerability found in perl/perl-base
  Description: Improper Verification of Cryptographic Signature
  Info: https://snyk.io/vuln/SNYK-UBUNTU2204-PERL-2789081
  Introduced through: meta-common-packages@meta
  From: meta-common-packages@meta > perl/perl-base@5.34.0-3ubuntu1


Package manager:    deb
Project name:       docker-image|ubuntu
Docker image:       ubuntu
Platform:           linux/amd64
Base image:         ubuntu:22.04


Tested 102 dependencies for known vulnerabilities, found 12
vulnerabilities.

According to our scan, you are currently using the most secure version of
the selected base image

For more free scans that keep your images secure, sign up to Snyk at
https://dockr.ly/3ePqVcp
```

For untrusted public images, avoid unknown or anonymous contributors, do your research, and take advantage of free scanning services!

Licensing

One more thing to consider before downloading public images from Docker Hub: licensing. Oracle prohibits users from distributing its database content, and anyone downloading Oracle software must agree to their licensing agreement. Anyone distributing images containing Oracle database software through a public repository is probably violating that license. Downloading such an image may place you at risk, too.

Docker Hub Accounts

Docker Hub makes a wealth of free content available to users without requiring registration or login. Creating an account entitles you to additional services across four plans: Personal, Pro, Team, and Business. I've highlighted the significant feature differences between the Personal and Pro accounts, which are most suited for individuals wanting the advantages of Docker Hub:

- **A Personal subscription** is free and includes the use of Docker Desktop and an unlimited number of public repositories and one private repository. It also includes 200 monthly local vulnerability scans with Snyk. This is probably everything most people need—unless you intend to maintain multiple private repositories of Oracle database images!

- **The Pro subscription** is $7 a month or $60 annually.[2] It includes everything offered in the Personal tier, plus unlimited private repositories; automated tests and builds; integration with GitHub, Bitbucket, and Slack; and commercial support. (I subscribe to the Pro tier to take advantage of the unlimited private repositories.)

After creating an account and logging in to the Docker Hub, create a repository by clicking the "Repository" menu item at the upper right, followed by the "Create repository" button at the far right, as in Figure 16-5.

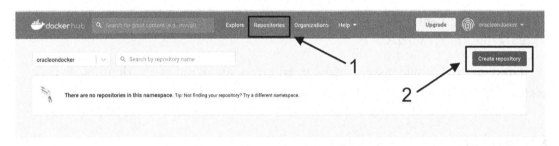

Figure 16-5. *Create a new repository in Docker Hub. Click the "Repository" item in the menu (1), then the "Create repository" button (2)*

This takes you to the screen in Figure 16-6, where you give the new repository a name, select whether the content is public or private, and finally create the repository. This example is from a Personal subscription, and I've made a private repository named "database."

---

[2] Features and pricing as of September 2022. For full details, see www.docker.com/pricing.

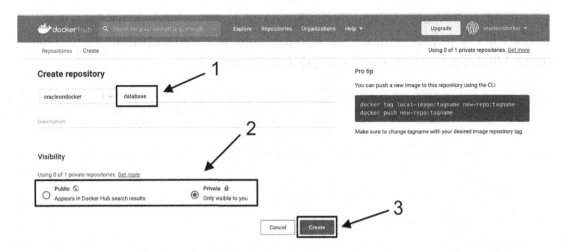

Figure 16-6. *To create a repository, give it a name (1), select either Public or Private visibility (2), and click the "Create" button (3)*

After creating the repository, you're taken to the repository details screen in Figure 16-7. Here, you can add descriptive information and manage the content.

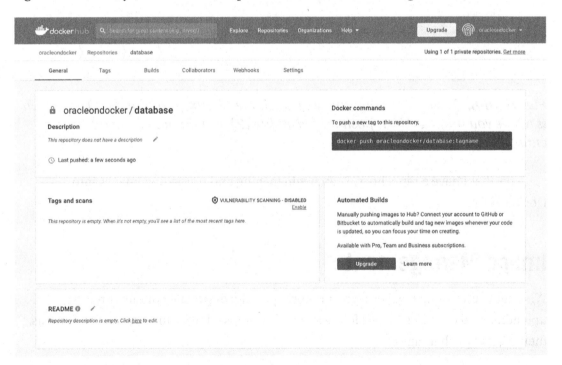

Figure 16-7. *The detail screen for a newly created repository in Docker Hub*

Click the repository's "Settings" tab, shown in Figure 16-8, and you have access to enable vulnerability scanning (available in paid subscriptions) and the option to change the visibility of the repo from public to private, and vice versa.

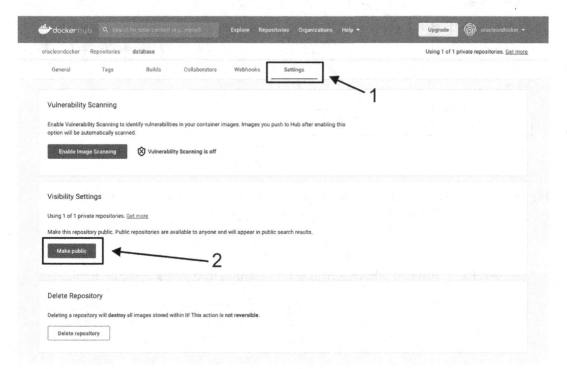

Figure 16-8. *Manage the repository through the "Settings" option (1). This screen is where you manage the repository's visibility (2) and, in paid subscriptions, enable image scanning*

Now that I have a repository, I can begin tagging and uploading images into Docker Hub!

Image Management

Whether you're using Docker Hub or different public or private container registry, uploading and curating images follows the same steps—log in and provide credentials, then tag and push images.

Registry Login

Log in to access your registry from the command line or Docker Desktop. Here, I'm logging in to my newly created account with the username and password I created earlier, using the docker login command:

```
> docker login
Login with your Docker ID to push and pull images from Docker Hub. If you
don't have
a Docker ID, head over to https://hub.docker.com to create one.
Username: oracleondocker
Password:
Login Succeeded

Logging in with your password grants your terminal complete access to your
account.
For better security, log in with a limited-privilege personal access
token. Learn
more at https://docs.docker.com/go/access-tokens/
```

Once you've logged in to a registry, Docker preserves your credentials for future use, and there's no persistent state that requires repeated login.[3] However, if you're into an account and wish to remove the stored credentials, use docker logout:

```
> docker logout
Removing login credentials for https://index.docker.io/v1/
```

Once logged in, I can tag and push images.

Tag an Image

Chapter 14 covered the components of tags and how to use docker tag for assigning a namespace, image or repository name, and a tag to an image. Now that we've created a registry account, the purpose of the namespace should be more apparent—it's the name of the registry account.

---

[3] Logging in to a registry doesn't preclude access to public Docker Hub images, and the public images on Docker Hub are always available.

When listing images on my system, I see an image built from Oracle's GitHub repository, tagged oracle/database:19.3.0-ee, followed by four more database images belonging to my namespace, oraclesean, saved to a repository called db:

```
> docker images
REPOSITORY          TAG           IMAGE ID        CREATED        SIZE
oracle/database     19.3.0-ee     bdbb8b83217b    3 days ago     6.68GB
oraclesean/db       11.2.0.4-EE   c1015174e910    6 months ago   6.72GB
oraclesean/db       12.1-EE       1db44c287b80    6 months ago   6.9GB
oraclesean/db       19.13.1-EE    27fdf297483b    5 months ago   7.81GB
oraclesean/db       21.5-EE       656c63dad153    5 months ago   8.69GB
```

In the examples from the previous section, I created a new user and repository in Docker Hub, with a username of oracleondocker and a private repository named database. I'd like to push a copy of one of these images to my new account, but I first need to tag it.[4]

I can share the oraclesean/db:11.2.0.4-EE image with either of the following commands, referencing the image by an existing tag or its image ID value:

```
docker tag oraclesean/db:11.2.0.4-EE oracleondocker/database:11.2.0.4-EE
docker tag c1015174e910 oracleondocker/database:11.2.0.4-EE
```

When I list images from my system once again, I see the new tag appearing on the second line:

```
> docker tag oraclesean/db:11.2.0.4-EE oracleondocker/database:11.2.0.4-EE

> docker images
REPOSITORY                TAG           IMAGE ID        CREATED        SIZE
oracle/database           19.3.0-ee     bdbb8b83217b    3 days ago     6.68GB
oracleondocker/database   11.2.0.4-EE   c1015174e910    6 months ago   6.72GB
oraclesean/db             11.2.0.4-EE   c1015174e910    6 months ago   6.72GB
oraclesean/db             12.1-EE       1db44c287b80    6 months ago   6.9GB
oraclesean/db             19.13.1-EE    27fdf297483b    5 months ago   7.81GB
oraclesean/db             21.5-EE       656c63dad153    5 months ago   8.69GB
```

The Image ID is the same for both images. Only the tag is different.

---

[4] Remember that tagging doesn't make a new copy of an image. It's merely creating an alias.

Push an Image

Tagging an image doesn't physically add it to the repository. If I navigate to Docker Hub and search the repository, it's still empty. I need to upload, or *push*, the image:

```
docker push oracleondocker/database:11.2.0.4-EE
```

Pushing implies a remote registry, and I can't use an image ID for this operation—I have to specify the tag. The tag tells Docker I want to upload a tagged image, 11.2.0.4-EE, to my oracleondocker namespace and place it in the database repository. Docker reports the upload progress:

```
> docker push oracleondocker/database:11.2.0.4-EE
The push refers to repository [docker.io/oracleondocker/database]
5f70bf18a086: Pushed
d67ad3eaa615: Pushing [=>                                     ]   40.07MB/1.094GB
fb92f0f7e7a1: Pushed
8741e0584bcd: Pushing [>                                      ]   32.31MB/4.875GB
b9cd4d53c8a0: Pushed
0c7211f52f51: Pushed
59e93d414d42: Pushed
4fa651f55709: Pushing [>                                      ]   2.146MB/619.3MB
4d82e938e5ad: Pushed
d7d3f0b240dc: Mounted from library/oraclelinux
```

Notice it's pushing multiple items—as you might have guessed, these are the image layers. When various images share layers, Docker saves time and bandwidth during upload (push) and download (pull) actions by skipping any layers already present on the system!

The completed push command reports the image's digest, a hash that uniquely identifies the image:

```
> docker push oracleondocker/database:11.2.0.4-EE
The push refers to repository [docker.io/oracleondocker/database]
5f70bf18a086: Pushed
d67ad3eaa615: Pushed
fb92f0f7e7a1: Pushed
8741e0584bcd: Pushed
```

369

```
b9cd4d53c8a0: Pushed
0c7211f52f51: Pushed
59e93d414d42: Pushed
4fa651f55709: Pushed
4d82e938e5ad: Pushed
d7d3f0b240dc: Mounted from library/oraclelinux
11.2.0.4-EE: digest: sha256:e94665072e69fa398181a9d852d193beee5ca3fedfe65c2
6c8684762b90c710f size: 2417
```

Once the image is pushed to the registry, it's visible in Docker Hub's console, as in Figure 16-9.

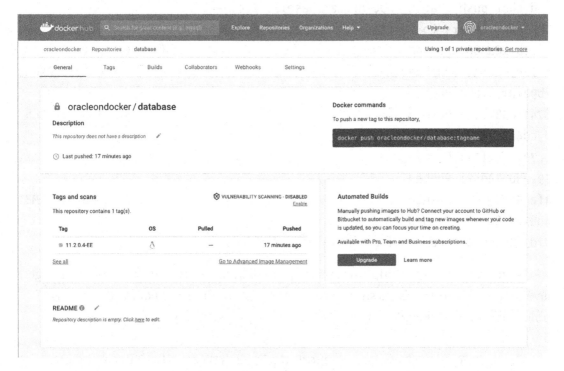

Figure 16-9. *After successfully pushing the image to my new account, the tag is visible in the online Docker Hub console*

If I rebuilt this image, either locally or in a different repository, the new version isn't propagated to or replace the image in `oracleondocker/database:11.2.0.4-EE`. The hash (and image ID) metadata provides a unique identity for the image, useful for tracking the version of images stored and shared across multiple locations.

CLI Registry Search

The Docker command-line interface, or CLI, includes a feature for searching repositories and images in a registry:

```
docker search <KEYWORD>
```

I find the CLI search capability is limited. It shows 25 results by default, extendable to 100, and doesn't include an ability to list tags. So, it may not be helpful unless you know the tag you want (or you're satisfied with the "latest" version).

Listing 16-2 shows the top results when searching for `oracle` in Docker Hub. You'll notice the output is sorted by Stars, indicating the number of people who've marked the repository as a favorite. There's also an "Official" column, which, as you might expect, indicates this is an Official repository.

Listing 16-2. The truncated output from searching Docker Hub for repositories including the keyword "oracle"

```
> docker search oracle
NAME                DESCRIPTION                         STARS   OFFICIAL   AUTOMATED
oraclelinux         Official Docker builds of Oracle Linux.   928      [OK]
oracleinanutshell/oracle-xe-11g                         237
gvenzl/oracle-xe  Oracle Database XE (21c, 18c, 11g) for every... 115
```

There are options for refining search results:

- **is-official=true:** Set to *true* shows only official repositories.

- **is-automated=true:** Shows only automated image builds. Automated builds are a paid subscription feature that builds images from source code, automatically pushing them to Docker Hub.

- **stars=n:** Limit results to repositories with at least *n* stars, where *n* is an integer value.

Pair these options with the -f or --filter flag. For example, to search Docker Hub for Official images with the oracle keyword:

```
> docker search -f is-official=true oracle
NAME            DESCRIPTION                           STARS     OFFICIAL    AUTOMATED
oraclelinux    Official Docker builds of Oracle Linux.     928        [OK]
```

Perform a search of images with at least 100 stars:

```
> docker search -f stars=100 oracle
NAME            DESCRIPTION                           STARS     OFFICIAL    AUTOMATED
oraclelinux    Official Docker builds of Oracle Linux.     928        [OK]
oracleinanutshell/oracle-xe-11g                                    237
gvenzl/oracle-xe   Oracle Database XE (21c, 18c, 11g) for every... 115
```

Apply multiple search criteria using a separate -f flag for each. Here, I searched for Official repositories with at least 100 stars:

```
> docker search -f stars=100 -f is-official=true oracle
NAME            DESCRIPTION                           STARS     OFFICIAL    AUTOMATED
oraclelinux    Official Docker builds of Oracle Linux.     928        [OK]
```

Pulling Images

Throughout this book, we've *pulled* images like alpine, ubuntu, and oraclelinux without using a namespace (the part before the / in the push command earlier). These were all Official images in Docker Hub and existed under the "root" of the registry. They're not part of a namespace owned by an individual or organization.

However, when I say we pulled these images, we didn't do so explicitly. Issuing docker run for an image not already present on the system performs a docker pull in the background. Maybe you've noticed:

```
> docker run alpine
Unable to find image 'alpine:latest' locally
latest: Pulling from library/alpine
213ec9aee27d: Pull complete
Digest: sha256:bc41182d7ef5ffc53a40b044e725193bc10142a1243f395ee852a
8d9730fc2ad
Status: Downloaded newer image for alpine:latest
```

Pulling or running images from public repositories requires the same fully qualified registry format as the docker push example earlier—a namespace, a registry or image name, and a tag (if present). In Figure 16-10, I browsed through the Docker Hub and located a Verified Publisher image for bitnami/mariadb.

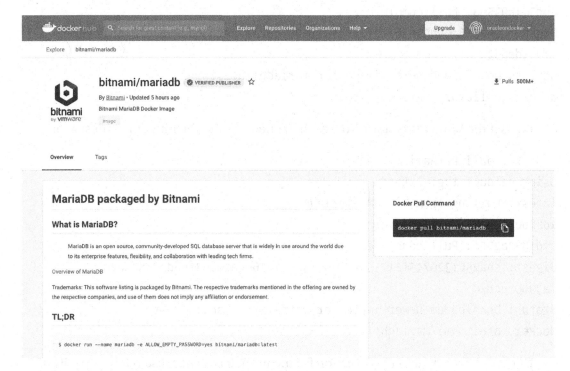

Figure 16-10. *The main repository page for Bitnami's MariaDB distribution*

MariaDB is a popular MySQL fork, and it stands to reason there's an official image available, too. If I docker pull mariadb without any namespace, I get something:

```
> docker pull mariadb
Using default tag: latest
latest: Pulling from library/mariadb
2b55860d4c66: Pull complete
4bf944e49ffa: Pull complete
020ff2b6bb0b: Pull complete
977397ae9bc6: Pull complete
b361cf449d40: Pull complete
21d261950157: Pull complete
```

```
296a47dd9435: Pull complete
bbe841bf5cfe: Pull complete
758db05dd921: Pull complete
9c2c0a21c9e6: Pull complete
4bc311b9359a: Pull complete
Digest: sha256:05b53c3f7ebf1884f37fe9efd02da0b7faa0d03e86d724863f359
1f963de632c
Status: Downloaded newer image for mariadb:latest
docker.io/library/mariadb:latest
```

But is it the Bitnami version? No. For that, I need to add the Bitnami namespace:

```
> docker pull bitnami/mariadb
Using default tag: latest
latest: Pulling from bitnami/mariadb
1d8866550bdd: Pull complete
cfd1823a275f: Pull complete
Digest: sha256:320745f11755f950a6ffa80a7e16dca108b3fe6df76873e2ec22
fa3900fecb20
Status: Downloaded newer image for bitnami/mariadb:latest
docker.io/bitnami/mariadb:latest
```

Docker retrieved the "latest" version for me in each case because I didn't specify a tag. If I go to the Tags section of the Bitnami image in Figure 16-11, I see a variety of tags. To get something other than "latest," I have to use its tag, here 10.5.17:

```
> docker pull bitnami/mariadb:10.5.17
10.5.17: Pulling from bitnami/mariadb
1d8866550bdd: Already exists
0f5b0c3c18cf: Pull complete
Digest: sha256:ec6bb285c67d5b66a6ee1fca667e9d73906d767b02cc5dbb2bff
1159d97e7fbe
Status: Downloaded newer image for bitnami/mariadb:10.5.17
docker.io/bitnami/mariadb:10.5.17
```

Notice Docker didn't download the first layer in the image, 1d8866550bdd. It's identical to the first layer of the "latest" image and indicates it's most likely the underlying foundation of many of Bitnami's MariaDB images. Version-specific content is confined to the second layer.

There's something else worth noticing in the two MariaDB images. The Bitnami image is just two layers, while the official image is eleven. This reflects differences in how they're built. The Official, trusted MariaDB image exposes every step in the build process as layers. The Bitnami image reduces the layer content to improve security. Pull these images on your own and run the following docker history commands (the --no-trunc flag prevents Docker from truncating the output in the original Dockerfile):

```
docker image history --no-trunc bitnami/mariadb
docker image history --no-trunc mariadb
```

Compare the output and look for information like default passwords and configurations an attacker might leverage against the system. The lesson? Just because images are Official or Trusted doesn't necessarily mean they're appropriate for production environments!

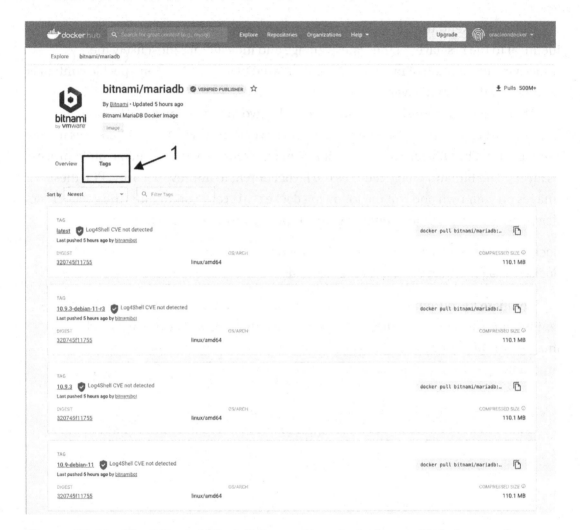

Figure 16-11. *The Bitnami MariaDB repository includes multiple images for different versions, each identified by its tag*

If I run docker images on my system, I see the three images are all different:

```
REPOSITORY        TAG         IMAGE ID       CREATED       SIZE
bitnami/mariadb   10.5.17     0470be367c25   9 hours ago   341MB
bitnami/mariadb   latest      ca73fbad9ff3   5 hours ago   344MB
mariadb           latest      11aee66fdc31   6 days ago    384MB
```

By referencing the MariaDB images in Bitnami's namespace and using tags for discrete versions, I obtained slightly different versions of MariaDB.

Pulling private images follows the same pattern, with the additional requirement that the user is logged in to the correct namespace (or has a security token granting access to the repository).

Oracle Container Registry

Oracle once kept official database images on Docker Hub but removed them for the licensing concerns I noted before. Anybody could download the content without accepting Oracle's licensing agreement.

Oracle database images are still available, however, in the *Oracle Container Registry*, at `https://container-registry.oracle.com`. Before accessing its images, you must first log in using your My Oracle Support credentials and accept the Standard Terms and Restrictions. The good news is once you accept the terms, the registry recognizes the status and allows future access to your account without further "nagging!"

Before pulling images from Oracle's registry, log in from a terminal session, using the registry address, `container-registry.oracle.com`:

```
> docker login container-registry.oracle.com
Authenticating with existing credentials...
```

```
Login Succeeded
```

Once logged in, you'll have access to the registry and can search and pull images, just as you saw with Docker Hub. Unfortunately, the CLI's search capabilities are touchy. After logging in to the container registry, if I search for Official images matching "oracle," the results don't appear any different than before:

```
> docker search -f is-official=true oracle
INDEX           NAME            DESCRIPTION
STARS           OFFICIAL        AUTOMATED
docker.io       oraclelinux     Official Docker builds of Oracle
Linux.    928              [OK]
```

However, if I change the search string to the container registry's namespace, I get the results I expected. In this example, I narrowed the search to the database registry within the namespace, `container-registry.oracle.com/database`:

```
> docker search -f is-official=true container-registry.oracle.com/database
INDEX      NAME        DESCRIPTION                     STARS    OFFICIAL    AUTOMATED
oracle.com database/enterprise Oracle Database Enterprise Edition  0 [OK]
oracle.com database/express   Oracle Database Express Edition     0 [OK]
oracle.com database/gsm       Oracle Global Service Manager       0 [OK]
oracle.com database/instantclient Oracle Instant Client           0 [OK]
oracle.com database/observability-exporter   Oracle Database Observability
                   Exporter (Metr...                              0 [OK]
oracle.com database/operator  This image is part of and for use with
                              the O...                             0 [OK]
oracle.com database/ords      Oracle REST Data Services (ORDS) with
                              Applic...                            0 [OK]
oracle.com database/otmm      Oracle Transaction Manager for
                              Microservice                         0 [OK]
oracle.com database/rac       Oracle Real Application Clusters     0 [OK]
oracle.com database/sqlcl     Oracle SQLDeveloper Command Line
                              (SQLcl)                              0 [OK]
oracle.com database/standard  Oracle Database Standard Edition  2  0 [OK]
```

The output reveals options for Standard and Enterprise Edition database images but offers no details of how they're tagged. For that, it's best to return to the Container Registry page in Figure 16-12.

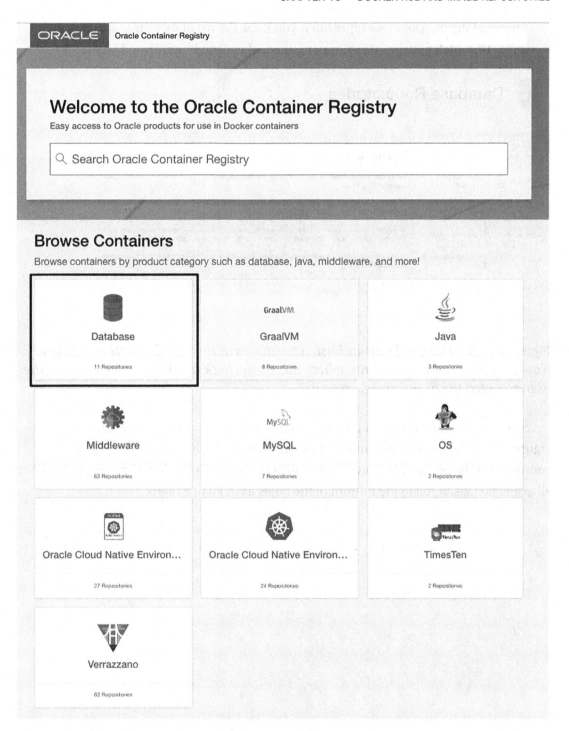

Figure 16-12.   *The Oracle Container Registry home page shows the available repositories. The Database repository at the top left is highlighted*

After clicking the Database repository, you'll see the list of its subrepositories in Figure 16-13, which matches the output of the docker search performed before.

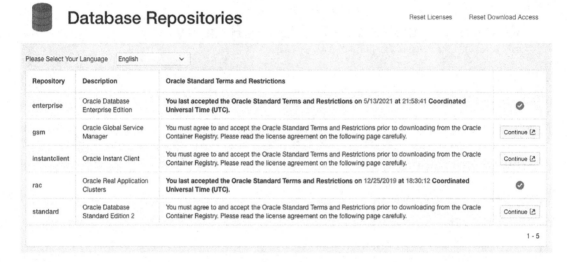

Figure 16-13. *The first five database repositories in the Oracle Container Registry. Note the far right-hand column, where the green check marks indicate whether the user accepted the licensing agreements*

Selecting the "enterprise" repository takes me to the repository page seen in Figure 16-14. Here, you'll find information on using the image and a docker pull command at the far right. However, this is the command for the *latest* image tag. To see all available tags, scroll to the bottom of the page, as in Figure 16-15.

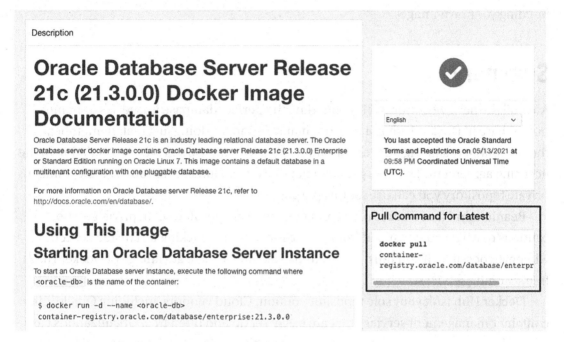

Figure 16-14. *The Enterprise Edition repository page includes instructions for using the image, plus a docker pull command, highlighted at the right, for downloading the latest version of the image*

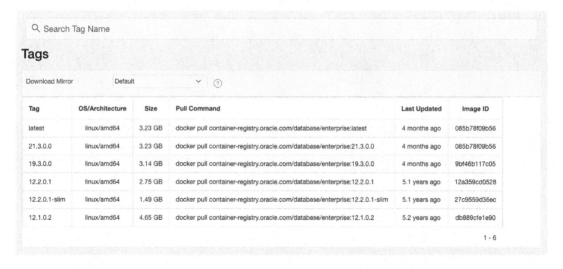

Figure 16-15. *At the bottom of each repository page is a summary of all available tags, each listing image information, and the appropriate docker pull command*

The images in the Oracle Container Registry are ready-made solutions for running Oracle databases in Docker. While convenient, they lack the customizations afforded by building your own images.

Summary

After all the hard work poured into building the perfect database image, it's a shame not to share it! Docker Hub is a free, popular solution for doing just that. Remember, though, publicly sharing images containing Oracle database software is a violation of the licensing agreement. The free, personal tier of Docker Hub allows you to create a single, private repository you can use for this purpose.

Bear in mind that Docker runs containers with an elevated set of privileges. Be cautious of what you download from public repositories, sticking to Trusted content whenever possible. If you must use an untrusted image, take advantage of Docker Hub's free scanning services.

Docker Hub isn't your sole repository option. Cloud vendors, including Oracle, offer container management services that are easily set up and often free. Organizations can deploy homegrown repositories that integrate with existing development workflows.

CHAPTER 17

Conclusion

In the first part of this book, you discovered how containers work and how to run an Oracle database in Docker. You learned methods for persisting vital database content—the datafiles and configuration—outside the confines of the container. You're also fluent in container networking concepts and can connect client applications running on a host, like SQL Developer, to databases in containers. You can also leverage container networks to communicate among databases running containers.

The second part covered images and the recipes for building them: Dockerfiles. You discovered how to customize the stock images provided in Oracle's container repository and gained insights into techniques for extending Dockerfiles to suit your needs. Of course, not every image runs smoothly at first! Fortunately, we covered several methods and approaches for troubleshooting images and containers. Once everything runs smoothly, you learned how to add and manage images in repositories.

My introduction to running Oracle databases in containers wasn't positive. I was convinced it was a fool's errand and destined for miserable failure. In the years since, I've seen the power and potential of containers firsthand. They're an integral, indispensable part of my daily work. In this book, I've attempted to capture my appreciation of the technology behind Linux containers and share with you the things I wish I'd known earlier in my Docker experience. I sincerely hope you find it helpful and that it inspires you to begin or further your journey with Docker!

© Sean Scott 2023
S. Scott, *Oracle on Docker*, https://doi.org/10.1007/978-1-4842-9033-0_17

PART III

Appendixes

APPENDIX A

Installing Docker Desktop

Install Docker Desktop

Docker Desktop is available as a free download from `www.docker.com`. Linux users can install Docker Desktop or Docker Engine, a native environment for running Docker containers.

Windows 10 and 11

Behind the scenes, Docker Desktop on Windows runs Linux in a Hyper-V virtual machine. Earlier versions of Docker Desktop were notorious for conflicts between Hyper-V and VirtualBox, and performance often left something to be desired.

Windows Subsystem for Linux version 2, or *WSL 2*,[1] available on Windows 10, marked a significant improvement for Docker Desktop on Windows. Docker Desktop under WSL 2 boasts improved system resource management, better performance, and more robust integration with the host operating system.

WSL provides a fully functional Linux experience inside the Windows operating system. The command examples used throughout this book work identically in the WSL environment, as in Linux or Mac systems.

---

[1] WSL (or Windows Subsystem for Linux 1) is a Linux interpretation or translation layer sitting between the Linux shell and the Windows OS. In WSL 2, the Linux kernel runs natively within a virtual machine and offers tighter integration and wider compatibility with Linux tools— including Docker!

© Sean Scott 2023
S. Scott, *Oracle on Docker*, https://doi.org/10.1007/978-1-4842-9033-0_18

Set Up Windows Subsystem for Linux

Set up the Windows Subsystem for Linux according to Microsoft's instructions at *https://docs.microsoft.com/en-us/windows/wsl/install*. On my system (Windows 10), I opened a PowerShell session as an administrator, then ran `wsl --install`, as in Figure A-1. This performs a default installation of WSL and installs Ubuntu Linux. After the command completes, reboot the machine.

```
Administrator: Windows PowerShell                                                          —    ☐    ✕
Windows PowerShell
Copyright (C) Microsoft Corporation. All rights reserved.

Try the new cross-platform PowerShell https://aka.ms/pscore6

PS C:\Windows\system32> wsl --install
```

Figure A-1. *Install WSL 2 from a PowerShell session running as an administrator*

By default, WSL downloads Ubuntu Linux and requires a restart, as shown in Figure A-2. Reboot the machine to finish setting up WSL and begin the Linux installation.

```
Administrator: Windows PowerShell                                                          —    ☐    ✕
Windows PowerShell
Copyright (C) Microsoft Corporation. All rights reserved.

Try the new cross-platform PowerShell https://aka.ms/pscore6

PS C:\Windows\system32> wsl --install
Installing: Virtual Machine Platform
Virtual Machine Platform has been installed.
Installing: Windows Subsystem for Linux
Windows Subsystem for Linux has been installed.
Downloading: WSL Kernel
Installing: WSL Kernel
WSL Kernel has been installed.
Downloading: Ubuntu
The requested operation is successful. Changes will not be effective until the system is rebooted.
PS C:\Windows\system32> ▪
```

Figure A-2. *After WSL finishes installing, reboot the machine*

Configure and Update Linux

After the machine reboots, WSL installs the Linux distribution. This takes a few minutes. When the installation completes, you'll need to create a Linux user, as seen in Figure A-3. I used docker as the user on my system.

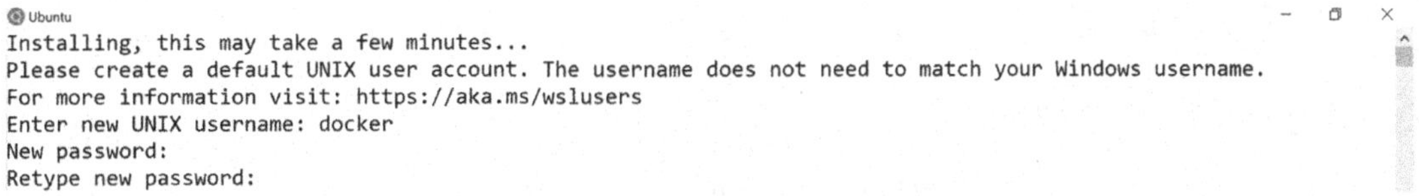

```
Ubuntu                                                                              –  □  ×
Installing, this may take a few minutes...
Please create a default UNIX user account. The username does not need to match your Windows username.
For more information visit: https://aka.ms/wslusers
Enter new UNIX username: docker
New password:
Retype new password:
```

Figure A-3. *After installation finishes, create a user to use in the Linux subsystem*

Be sure to update your Linux distribution. For Ubuntu systems, run the following command in the terminal window:

```
sudo apt update && sudo apt upgrade
```

Now is also an excellent time to install Windows Terminal from the Windows Store. For details on installing Windows Terminal, see the section "Terminal Environments."

Install Docker Desktop

When WSL setup completes, refer to Docker's installation guide at *https://docs. microsoft.com/en-us/windows/wsl/install-manual* and follow the latest instructions, completing all prerequisites, then download and install Docker Desktop from *www. docker.com.*

Double-click the installation files to open the installation wizard. Be sure the box for "*Use WSL 2 instead of Hyper-V (recommended)*" is marked, as in Figure A-4.

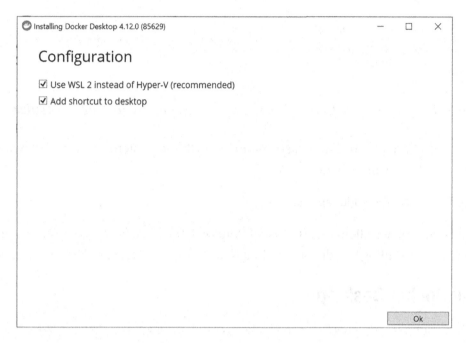

Figure A-4. *In the Docker Desktop install wizard, mark the option to "Use WSL 2 instead of Hyper-V"*

Navigate to the Start menu and select Docker Desktop from the list of applications. After accepting the license agreement, Docker Desktop starts and opens a brief tutorial.

Configure Docker Desktop

Click the gear icon at the upper right to access the Settings menu to access the General settings shown in Figure A-5. Ensure the "Use the WSL 2 based engine" box is checked.

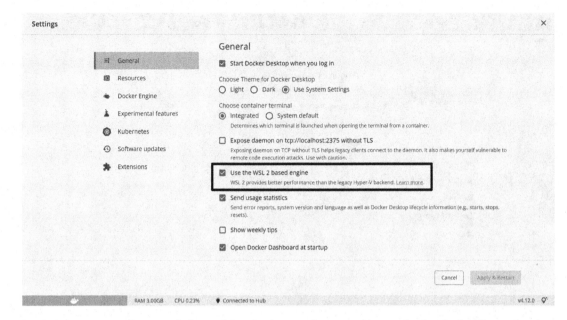

Figure A-5. *Under Docker Desktop's General settings panel, check the "Use the WSL 2 based engine" option*

Next, click the Resources option and select WSL Integration. Confirm that "Enable integration with my default WSL distro" is enabled as in Figure A-6. Set the slider "on" for the distributions you'll use with Docker that appear under the "Enable integration with additional distros" section. If the "Apply & Restart" button at the lower right is highlighted, click it to commit your changes.

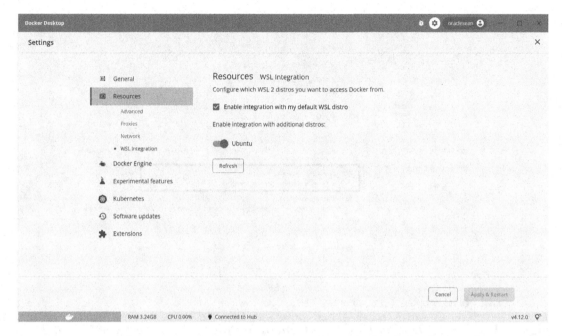

Figure A-6. *Confirm WSL integration is turned on for the default distribution, and it's enabled for any other distributions that need Docker Desktop integration*

Set WSL Resources

The default resources assigned to Docker Desktop under WSL are usually adequate. If you experience issues and need to adjust CPU, memory, or other settings, they're configurable through the *.wslconfig* file in the user's home directory (typically `C:\Users\<User Name>\.wslconfig`).

Before editing or adding the `.wslconfig` file, stop WSL from a terminal session as an administrator:

```
wsl --shutdown
```

Then edit the file:

```
notepad "$env:USERPROFILE/.wslconfig"
```

Listing A-1 shows an example of a `.wslconfig` file to limit the memory and processor available to WSL. For complete information on options available in the `.wslconfig` file, see *https://docs.microsoft.com/en-us/windows/wsl/wsl-config*.

Listing A-1. An example of a `.wslconfig` file for limiting CPU and memory consumption for Windows Subsystem for Linux

```
[wsl2]
processors=4 # Limit of 4 processors for WSL.
memory=8GB   # Limit WSL to 8GB memory.
```

Mac (Intel)

Before installing Docker Desktop for Mac, review and complete the prerequisites at *https://docs.docker.com/desktop/install/mac-install/*, then download Docker Desktop from `www.docker.com`. Navigate to the download directory and double-click the *Docker.dmg* file to open the installer seen in Figure A-7. Drag the *Docker.app* file to the *Applications* folder.

Figure A-7. *Drag and drop the Docker.app file to the Applications folder*

When the file copy completes, navigate to the *Applications* folder, scroll to the *Docker.app* application, and double-click to start Docker Desktop. Accept the licensing terms and continue to Docker Desktop's main screen.

Configure Resources

Click the gear icon in the upper right, or press the Command and comma keys together (⌘ + ,) to access Docker Desktop's settings and preferences. The default values in the General preferences pane shown in Figure A-8 are appropriate.

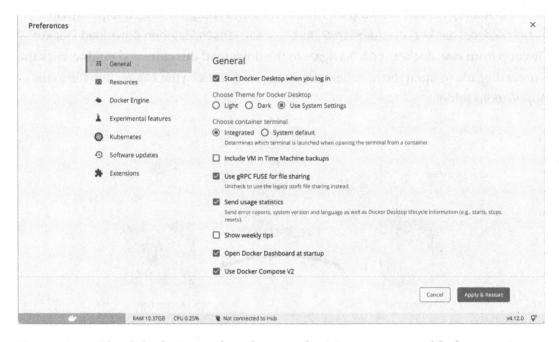

Figure A-8. *The default General preferences for Mac are acceptable for running Oracle containers*

Next, click the *Resources* tab in the left-side menu and select *Advanced* as in Figure A-9. To run Oracle database containers, allocate a minimum of 4GB of memory. Oracle is a memory-intensive application, and the more memory you can assign, the better it performs. The same is true for CPUs. 10–20GB is a reasonable starting point for disk space. You can harmlessly increase disk space for Docker Desktop later if you need to. Shrinking disk space, however, removes all images, containers, and volumes.

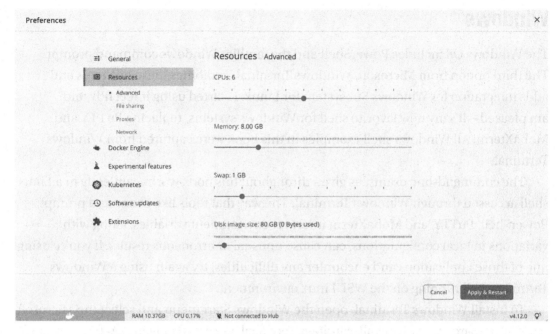

Figure A-9. *Configure resources for the Docker environment*

Mac (Apple Silicon)

As of this writing, architecture differences prevent Oracle database images from running in Docker on Apple Silicon machines. The community is actively working to address this issue, with promising progress.

Docker Desktop and Docker Engine for Linux

See Docker's website for information on installing Docker Desktop and Docker Engine for different flavors of Linux. Instructions for Docker Desktop are located at *https:// docs.docker.com/desktop/install/linux-install*, while directions for Docker Engine are found at *https://docs.docker.com/engine/install*.

Terminal Environments

Most interaction with Docker occurs at the command line or shell. You'll need a *terminal program* to access the command line on your host, and there are plenty to choose from on each operating system.

Windows

The Windows OS includes PowerShell and the familiar Windows command prompt. The third option from Microsoft, Windows Terminal, combines these two tools and adds integration for Windows Subsystem for Linux. I started using it recently and am pleased—it's my new favorite shell for Windows systems, replacing PuTTY and MobaXterm! All Windows shell examples in this book were captured from Windows Terminal.

The command-line examples given throughout this book work seamlessly in a Linux shell accessed through Windows Terminal. The way that tools like command prompt, PowerShell, PuTTY, and MobaXterm interpret environment variables, along with variations in local configurations, can cause unusual or erroneous results. If you're using one of those applications and encounter any difficulties, try again using a Windows Terminal shell running on the WSL Linux environment.

To install Windows Terminal, open the Windows Start menu and select the Microsoft Store app. Search for and install Windows Terminal, as shown in Figure A-10.

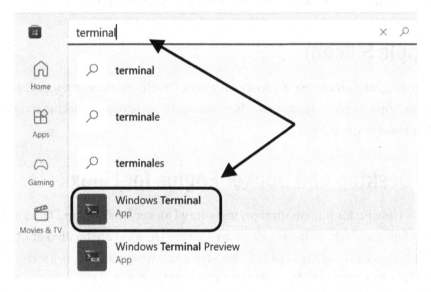

Figure A-10. *Search for "terminal" in the Windows Store and install the Windows Terminal application*

This adds Windows Terminal to the system. Go to the Start menu and open the new Terminal application. The Terminal session in Figure A-11 shows the options for opening new tabs. Clicking the "plus" icon to the right of the tab will open a new default session.

Clicking the down arrow opens a dialog with options for opening a command prompt, a PowerShell session, a Linux (Ubuntu) session, or an Azure Cloud Shell.

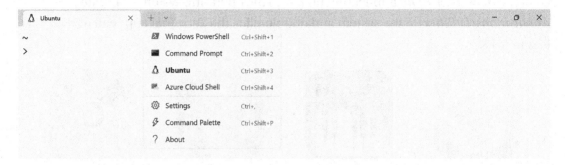

Figure A-11. *Windows Terminal supports multiple shell types and automatically integrates with any virtual environments running under the Windows Subsystem for Linux*

The Ubuntu option is thanks to Windows Terminal integration with the Windows Subsystem for Linux. It detects the virtual environments running in WSL and includes shell options for each. Figure A-12 illustrates examples of the different shell environments: Ubuntu Linux, a command prompt, and PowerShell.

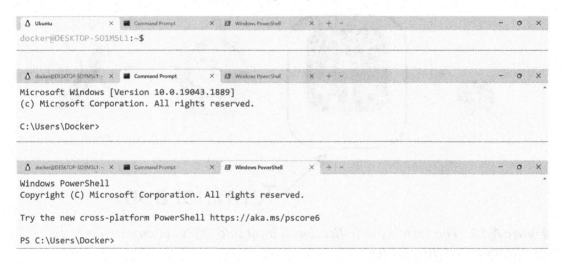

Figure A-12. *Examples of an Ubuntu Linux shell (top), a Windows command prompt (middle), and a PowerShell session (bottom) running as tabs in Windows Terminal*

Mac Terminal

OS-X includes a *Terminal* application built into the operating system. Navigate to /
Applications/Utilities on the system and double-click the Terminal app seen in
Figure A-13.

Figure A-13.   *The Terminal application is built into OS-X systems in the /
Applications/Utilities folder*

Terminal is a native Linux shell. Installing Docker Desktop adds the docker
command to the user's shell path, and all Docker features are available at the
command line.

Docker Desktop Features

Users can inspect and manage containers, images, and volumes from Docker Desktop and create new volumes and containers.

Container Management

The container menu lists all containers on the system and includes controls for starting, stopping, pausing, and deleting containers. Users can also navigate to individual containers and access logs, inspect the environment and container statistics, and access a command line inside the container.

Container Terminal

Docker recently updated Docker Desktop, adding an integrated command shell. You can access the CLI for any running container on the host from within Docker Desktop, with identical results on any operating system.

To use the integrated shell, first, ensure it's enabled. Open Docker Desktop's settings menu by clicking the gear icon, seen in Figure A-14, at the upper-right corner of the screen. Then, ensure the "Integrated" option under "Choose container terminal" is marked.

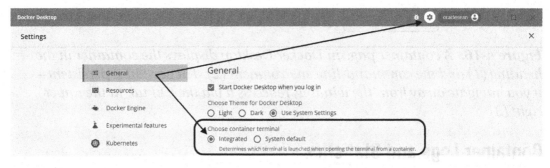

Figure A-14. *Select the gear icon in the upper-right corner of Docker Desktop to access the Settings page. Then, select "Integrated" as the container terminal in the General options pane*

From Docker Desktop, choose "Containers" from the left menu to see a list of containers running on the system. Select a container; then click the three vertical dots on the far right to access the "Show container actions" options. From the drop-down box that appears, select "Open in terminal" as in Figure A-15.

Figure A-15. *To access a container's shell, select the Container menu (1), click the three dots to access the "Show container actions" drop-down (2), and select the "Open in terminal" option*

This opens a /bin/sh terminal session (not /bin/bash) on the container, as in Figure A-16. The terminal window is fully functional, with copy/paste and scroll capabilities. It's also persistent—if you navigate away from the CLI session, it remains active in the background. Reaccess it through the *CLI tab* in the upper right of the container page.

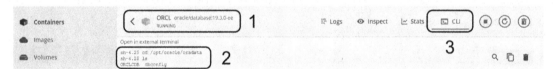

Figure A-16. *A container page in Docker Desktop displays the container in the heading (1) and the command-line environment (2). The session is persistent—if you navigate away from the window, reaccess it via the CLI tab at the upper right (3)*

Container Logs and Statistics

View container logs from the *Logs tab* in the container view, seen in Figure A-17.

Figure A-17. *The Logs tab shows the container's log output*

Container Statistics

The Stats tab in Figure A-18 displays the container's current CPU, memory, I/O, and network usage.

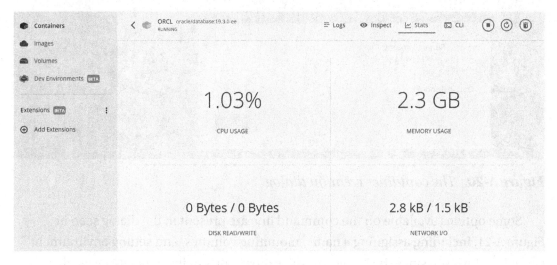

Figure A-18. *Resource consumption of a container from the Stats tab*

Image Management

The Images page in Docker Desktop lists images on the system and provides an interactive service for creating a new container from an image.

To create a new container from an image, hover over the image, revealing the "*RUN*" option in Figure A-19. Click the *RUN* button, which starts the container creation dialog.

Figure A-19. *Hover over an image to access the option to create a new container*

This opens the dialog in Figure A-20. Expand the "Optional settings" by clicking the arrow to the right.

Figure A-20. *The container creation dialog*

Some options available on the command line are present in the dialog seen in Figure A-21, including assigning a name, mounting volumes, and setting environment variables. However, since the image doesn't expose ports in its metadata, users don't have the option of mapping a port.

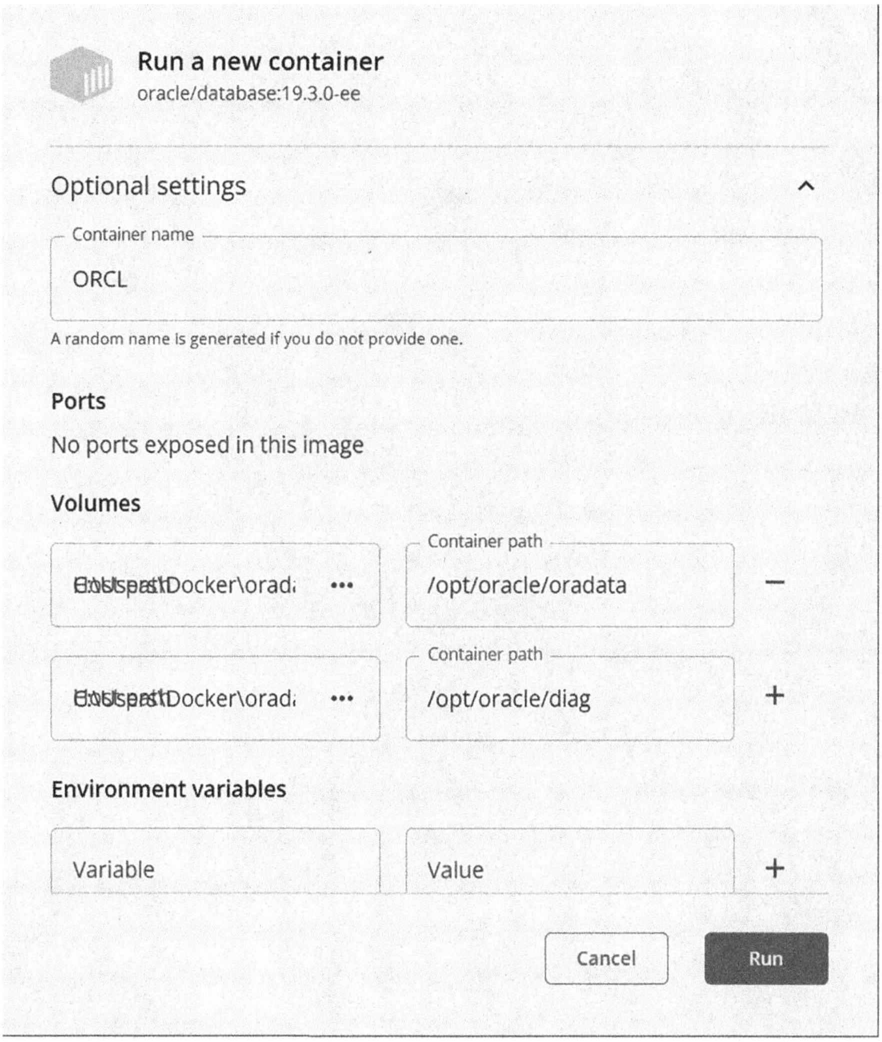

Run a new container
oracle/database:19.3.0-ee

Optional settings ^

Container name

ORCL

A random name is generated if you do not provide one.

Ports

No ports exposed in this image

Volumes

| ExtUsersDocker\orad: ••• | Container path /opt/oracle/oradata | — |

| ExtUsersDocker\orad: ••• | Container path /opt/oracle/diag | + |

Environment variables

| Variable | Value | + |

Cancel   **Run**

Figure A-21. The "Run a new container" dialog includes only basic container creation options

Volume Management

Volume management in Docker Desktop is limited. Users can list volumes (but not bind mounts) on a system but can only create internally stored volumes.

Aliases and Functions

Aliases and functions simplify and accelerate command-line tasks. By adding them to your shell login profile, they're loaded into your environment every time you log in. The following are some I've adopted over the years to make working with Docker faster and easier.

Aliases

Aliases are shortcuts for long or complex commands. They can even pull values from the environment! Even if you're not familiar with aliases, you've probably used them without realizing it—many Linux installations include default aliases.

To see the aliases defined in your session, simply type alias at the command prompt:

```
$ alias
alias egrep='egrep --color=auto'
alias fgrep='fgrep --color=auto'
alias grep='grep --color=auto'
alias l.='ls -d .* --color=auto'
alias ll='ls -l --color=auto'
alias ls='ls --color=auto'
alias vi='vim'
alias which='alias | /usr/bin/which --tty-only --read-alias --show-dot
--show-tilde'
```

These are aliases included in bash on Oracle Linux 7.9.

I use aliases extensively to apply --format options to Docker commands, reordering and customizing their output, sometimes called "*pretty printing*."

© Sean Scott 2023
S. Scott, *Oracle on Docker*, https://doi.org/10.1007/978-1-4842-9033-0_19

Report Containers

This was the first Docker alias I created. Initially, I used it to make the output of docker ps -a more compact and readable during presentations and live demos:

```
alias dps='docker ps -a --format "table {{.Names}}\t{{.Image}}\t{{.
Ports}}\t{{.Status}}"'
```

The default output of docker ps includes columns I wasn't interested in and made the result too wide for some displays. This alias reorders the fields, placing the human-friendly name of each container at the left, and omits fields I don't usually need:

```
> dps
NAMES      IMAGE                         PORTS      STATUS
ORA19C     oracle/database:19.3.0-ee                Up 13 days (healthy)
ORCL       oracle/database:19.3.0-ee                Up 2 weeks (healthy)
```

Extended Container Information

docker ps shows port assignments but doesn't display mounts or container size. I need this information now and then, but not frequently enough for the -s=true part to stick in my memory!

```
alias dpm='docker ps -a -s=true --no-trunc=true --format "table
{{.Names}}\t{{.Image}}\t{{.Ports}}\t{{.Size}}\t{{.Mounts}}\t{{.Status}}"'
```

This command may take a few moments to run as it has to collect the size of all containers:

```
> dpm
NAMES      IMAGE            PORTS      SIZE                 MOUNTS      STATUS
ORA19C     oracle/database:19.3.0-ee  5.04GB (virtual 11.7GB)  Up 13 days
                                                                  (healthy)
ORCL       oracle/database:19.3.0-ee  5.35GB (virtual 12GB)  Up 2 weeks
                                                                  (healthy)
```

Sorted List of Images

The default sorting for docker images is by created date. If you'd rather see them sorted by image name, try this:

```
alias images="docker images | awk 'NR<2{print \$0; next}{print \$0 |
\"sort\"}'"
```

It passes the output of docker images through awk to preserve the header rows (NR<2{ print \$0; next } prints rows with a row number, RN, less than 2), then sorts the remaining output.

List Dangling Volumes

"Dangling" volumes—those not referenced by any containers—are potentially unused, consuming space on the host. To find them, check the dangling flag of docker volume:

```
alias dangvol='docker volume ls -f dangling=true'
```

List Dangling Images

Like volumes, unused or "dangling" images may take up space in a system. Find them with

```
alias dangimg='docker images -f dangling=true'
```

Functions

Functions, like aliases, make it easier to call repetitive or lengthy commands. Aliases support fixed or passive actions, but functions are more powerful. They're shell scripts in their own right, can accept and process input variables, and perform more extensive or sophisticated tasks.

Start a Container Shell

Without question, the action I perform most in Docker is connecting to a container. Rather than typing the full command each time:

```
docker exec -it <container name> bash
```

I created this function. It takes the container name as input and substitutes it into docker exec to start a shell session:

```
dbash(){
  docker exec -it $1 bash
}
```

Inspect Function

The docker inspect command reports metadata information for Docker objects— containers, images, volumes, etc.—in JSON format. I typically run docker inspect to see one section of its total output, which can be lengthy for images and containers.

Like other Docker CLI commands, docker inspect accepts the --format option, with additional syntax for filtering out individual metadata sections. Of course, it means you need to know how Docker identifies the section you want and remember the expression for formatting the result.

I don't use either often enough to commit the syntax to memory, so I created a function to do it for me!

I'm including this snippet to demonstrate the capabilities of functions and hopefully spark your imagination. It's something you can adapt to fit your needs:

```
di() {
  case $1 in
    env)   docker inspect --format '{{range .Config.Env}} {{printf "%s\n"
    .}} {{end}}' $2 | sort ;;
    ip)    docker inspect --format '{{range.NetworkSettings.Networks}}
    {{.IPAddress}} {{end}}' $2 ;;
    ports) docker inspect --format '{{range $p,$i := .NetworkSettings.
    Ports}} {{$p}} -> {{(index $i 0).HostPort}} {{end}}' $2 ;;
```

```
    mount) docker inspect --format '{{.Name}} {{.Options.o}}:{{.Options.
    device}}' $2 ;;
    *) ;;
  esac
}
```

Call it with

```
di <inspection type> <object name>
```

The case statement processes the first value, the type of inspection to perform, and calls docker inspect against the object, applying the appropriate template to the output.

The inspection types included here are as follows:

- **env:** Reports a container's environment variables

- **ip:** Shows the IP address of a container

- **ports:** Lists all ports mapped to a container

- **mount:** Displays a volume's mount option and device name or directory

- ***:** Exits when there's no matching type

Be sure to revisit your functions often! As you use Docker and learn more about its capabilities, you'll encounter new opportunities to add or build your function library, and this last case is a great example!

Index

A

ADD instruction, *see* Dockerfiles
Aliases, 405
    extended container information, 406
    report containers, 406
    sorting, 407
Ansible, 231
Application software, 7
ARG Instruction, *see* Dockerfiles
Attack surface, 90
Automated processes, 3
Automatic Shared Memory
    Management, 77
Automation, 3, 11, 12, 16, 26, 89, 110, 221,
    276, 280, 311, 349

B

.bash_login file, 249
.bashrc file, 225, 227, 228, 249, 307
Bridge networks, 168–173, 175, 178,
    181–185, 189–192, 195–198,
    204, 211
Build cache, 136, 140, 329, 330
    reporting size, 329
buildContainerImage.sh, 63, 64, 230, 296,
    311, 342, 350, 351
    buildDockerImage.sh, 63
Build context, 63, 241, 259, 312
    ignore Files, 321 (*see also* Dockerfiles)
    and image size, 261, 301
    links and shortcuts not allowed, 63, 319

Building images, 30, 48, 63
    build cache, 244, 317 (*see also* Cache
        management)
    layers, 247
    troubleshooting, 343 (*see also*
        Dockerfiles)
BuildKit, 332
    enable, disable, 333
    feature entry, 333
    ignore files, 336–338
        (*see also* Dockerfiles)
        limiting context, 338
    progress, 333, 335
    syntax, 338
Business continuity, 6

C

Cache management, 331, 332
    build cache, pruning, 140, 329
    reporting size, 136
checkDBStatus.sh, 237, 267, 278
    non-CDB option, adding, 237
CMD Instruction, *see* Dockerfiles
Common Vulnerability and Exposure
    (CVE), 360
Configuration management, 4, 11, 12
Container advantages, 5, 8, 20, 49
    autonomy, 5, 12, 100
    confidence, 12
    consistency, 11
    cost, 12, 16

411